Language Experiences in Communication

Houghton Mifflin Company   Boston

Atlanta   Dallas   Geneva, Illinois   Hopewell, New Jersey   Palo Alto   London

Language Experiences in Communication

Roach Van Allen / *University of Arizona*

Photo Credits

Cover photograph Ingbert Grüttner.   Courtesy Wightwood School for Childhood *Chapter 1* Photo Trends *Chapter 2* Cary Wolinsky, Stock, Boston *Chapter 3* Urban, Stock, Boston *Chapter 4* Ingbert Grüttner *Chapter 5* Ingbert Grüttner *Chapter 6* Ingbert Grüttner *Chapter 7* Ingbert Grüttner *Chapter 8* Ingbert Grüttner *Chapter 9* Ingbert Grüttner *Chapter 10* Ingbert Grüttner *Chapter 11* Ingbert Grüttner *Chapter 12* Ingbert Grüttner *Chapter 13* Ingbert Grüttner *Chapter 14* Sandra Joseph / Houston Independent School District *Chapter 15* Ingbert Grüttner *Chapter 16* Frank Siteman, Stock, Boston *Chapter 17* Ingbert Grüttner *Chapter 18* Cary Wolinsky, Stock, Boston *Chapter 19* Frank Siteman, Stock, Boston *Chapter 20* NP Reporter H. Charles Bergy, Editor: Courtesy North Penn School District, Oak Park Elementary School *Chapter 21* Courtesy Encyclopaedia Britannica Educational Corp. *Chapter 22* Ingbert Grüttner *Chapter 23* Ingbert Grüttner *Chapter 24* Ingbert Grüttner
Title page photographs John Running / Stock, Boston   Rick Smolan / Stock, Boston   John Running / Stock, Boston

TEXT CREDITS

Pages 61–65   From Roach Van Allen, Richard Venezky, and Harry T. Hahn, *Language Experiences in Reading, Level I*, Encyclopaedia Britannica Educational Corp., 1974.

Pages 222–224   From Roach Van Allen and Claryce Allen, *Language Experiences in Early Childhood*, Encyclopaedia Britannica Educational Corp., 1969.

Page 247   From Roach Van Allen and Claryce Allen, *Language Experiences in Reading, Level III*, Encyclopaedia Britannica Educational Corp., 1967.

Library of Congress Catalog Card Number: 75-31011

ISBN: 0-395-18624-2

Preface

The basic ideas and fundamental concepts underlying *Language Experiences in Communication* are rooted in antiquity. They are not *new* ideas on the current scene of reading instruction. What is *new* is the curriculum rationale that embraces the natural language of learners as a basic ingredient throughout the elementary school experience. This curriculum rationale is explained in Part One, and its major components are elaborated in Parts Two, Three, and Four.

An early statement of the curriculum rationale, which forms the outline for twenty of the chapters of this book, was formulated as a part of the San Diego County Reading Research Project. This project was sponsored by the Department of Education, San Diego County, California, from 1958 through 1965. The first use of the term *language experience approach* grew out of a research question of the project. "Of all the language experiences available for study in the elementary school years, which ones have the greatest contribution to make to reading?" While researchers pursued the question to the point of developing curriculum materials for in-service education, the label *language experience approach* came into their language.

The term was understood by those involved in the early research efforts to mean that certain language experiences related to reading could be used over and over in a curriculum design that moved the experiences to increasingly mature levels. Twenty of the language experiences selected for study survived the rigorous research efforts. These are the ones identified as contributing most to reading:

1. Sharing experiences—telling or illustrating something on a purely personal basis
2. Discussing experiences—interacting with what other people say and write
3. Listening to stories—hearing what others have to say and relating it to one's own experiences
4. Telling stories—organizing one's thinking so that it can be shared in a clear and interesting manner
5. Dictating—choosing from all that might be said the most important part for someone else to write and read
6. Developing relationships between speaking, writing, and reading—conceptualizing reading as speech that has been written
7. Making and reading books—organizing one's ideas into a form that others can use; also using ideas that others have shared through books
8. Developing awareness of common vocabulary—recognizing that

language contains many common words and patterns of expression

9. Expanding vocabulary—expanding one's vocabulary chiefly through listening and speaking
10. Writing independently—writing one's ideas and presenting them in a form for others to read
11. Improving style and form—profiting from listening to and reading well-written materials
12. Using a variety of resources—recognizing and using many resources in expanding vocabulary, improving oral and written expression, and sharing ideas
13. Reading whole books—reading books for information, recreation, and improvement of reading skills on an individualized basis
14. Reading a variety of symbols such as clock, calendar, radio and television dials, and thermometer—reading in the total environment
15. Studying words—finding the correct pronunciation and meaning of words and spelling the words in writing activities
16. Improving comprehension—through oral and written activities gaining skill in following directions, in understanding words in the context of sentences and paragraphs, in reproducing the thought in a passage, in reading for detail, and in reading for general significance
17. Outlining—using various methods of briefly stating ideas in the order in which they were written or spoken
18. Summarizing—getting the main impression, the outstanding idea, or the details of what has been read or heard
19. Integrating and assimilating ideas—using reading and listening for specific, personal purposes
20. Reading critically—determining the validity and reliability of statements

The San Diego County Reading Research Project was reported in a series of monographs, *Improving Reading Instruction* (County Department of Education, San Diego, California, 1961–1965). The five monographs are: (1) *Report of the Reading Study Project*, (2) *Description of Three Approaches to the Teaching of Reading*, (3) *Teacher Inventory of Approaches to the Teaching of Reading*, (4) *An Inventory of Reading Attitude*, and (5) *Analysis of Pupil Data*.

Results of the research efforts reflected the potential of a way of thinking about reading and instructional materials that was a real alternative to the mainstream of instruction. Interest in the alternative mounted as reports of the project were shared at conferences and through journals. Requests for additional information came from every section of the United States and from many foreign countries. The servicing of requests became a full-time job. The need for a way of working with children's natural language as a base language for reading instruction was evident.

There was no doubt that the curriculum design that emerged from the research studies worked and produced favorable results. But the statement of twenty mainstreams of emphasis was cumbersome and impractical. It had to be refined and simplified if it was to be disseminated on a wide scale.

My move to the faculty of the College of Education at the University of Arizona in the fall of 1963 afforded time for me to study, refine, and continue research. One result was that the twenty original language experiences were reorganized around three major strands for the production of instructional materials published as *Language Experiences in Reading,* Levels I, II, and III (Roach Van Allen and Claryce Allen, Encyclopaedia Britannica Educational Corp., Chicago, 1966–1968).

Strand One emphasizes the use and usefulness of each child's communicating abilities as basic to developing language required for reading. Seven of the language experiences are grouped here.

1. Sharing experiences
2. Discussing experiences
3. Listening to stories
4. Telling stories
5. Dictating words, sentences, and stories
6. Writing independently
7. Writing individual books.

Strand Two emphasizes the study of the components of language that must be understood for independent reading of printed materials. Six of the language experiences are grouped here.

1. Conceptualizing relationships between speaking, writing, and reading
2. Expanding vocabulary
3. Reading a variety of symbols
4. Developing awareness of common vocabulary
5. Improving style and form
6. Studying words.

Strand Three emphasizes the continuing influence of the language and ideas of other people communicated in many forms. Seven of the language experiences are grouped here.

1. Reading whole stories and books
2. Using a variety of resources
3. Comprehending what is read
4. Summarizing
5. Organizing ideas and information
6. Integrating and assimilating ideas
7. Reading critically.

Following publication of *Language Experiences in Reading,* films and other pupil materials open to children's own language began to be marketed for a language experience approach. Professional organizations began to recognize the approach and provide time on programs for its explanation and elaboration. Textbooks for teacher education were published and used in increasing numbers.[1] The approach moved into the mainstream of educational theory and practice in many places.

Language Experiences in Communication is an updated statement of a language experience approach in instruction. Research efforts of educators and linguists, especially at the University of Arizona, indicated needs for changes in the original statement of twenty language experiences. The title of the book itself reflects the most fundamental change. The focus has shifted from *reading* to *communication.* Efforts to learn better ways of teaching children how to read have shifted to efforts to discover ways to develop personal language competences that permit and promote reading. There is no effort, nor any desire, in this book to separate reading from other communicating abilities for systematic, direct instruction. Language in communication processes is kept unified in theory and in instructional examples so that preservice and in-service teachers can understand how to embrace a language experience approach and to interpret it in personal ways. Personalization is as important for teachers as it is for children.

Language Experiences in Communication can be useful in the general education of teachers who highlight reading-language arts. Much of its content is traditional, but it is presented in a new curriculum de-

---

[1] Irene Wesley Hoover, *Historical and Theoretical Development of a Language Experience Approach to Teaching Reading in Selected Teacher Education Institutions,* Ph.D. dissertation, College of Education, University of Arizona, Tucson, 1971.

sign. To the traditional content is added the dimension of personal language production. This addition—an emphasis on the basic value of each child's language—makes the book useful to several special groups in teacher education.

Teachers of special reading classes will find the organization and the suggestions particularly valuable in building self-confidence which is a critical need of many children who have experienced failure and frustration in previous reading instruction. Children who participate in making some of their own books use basic vocabulary for reading and then relate it to reading material produced by others.

Teachers of children whose home-rooted language is not English can develop a program within the curriculum rationale that permits them to participate successfully. They can communicate their ideas in multiple ways while they are acquiring the English necessary for reading.

Teachers of children with learning disabilities will find the book of great value in that many discussions suggest the development of communicating abilities that do not require skills in reading print and in writing. Children who will never be good readers of school reading can learn to communicate effectively and happily.

Guidelines and examples of classroom organization that do not require continuous ability grouping are included. *Interaction* is stressed. *Isolation* is minimized. The goals are centered around the idea that every child will be able to relate personal experiences and personal language to all reading. Speaking, listening, writing, and reading are interrelated in instructional suggestions just as they are in life experiences.

This text presents a way of thinking about learning language for reading that most successful teachers have thought about and used to some degree. Few have had a structure for teaching in that way over a sustained period. Their deep feelings and beliefs have been submerged by programs and procedures that leave out the real language of learners. That structure is presented here with the hope that all teachers who love children's language will find success in using their language in a basic program for reading-language arts.

R. V. A.

Acknowledgments

The assistance of many individuals over a period of many years made this book possible. I am deeply grateful to all of them.

In my early teaching experience my elementary principal, Elva Fronabarger, set an example and gave counsel that set my thinking about children and learning in the direction of a language experience approach. Graduate studies at the University of Texas under the direction of Dr. Henry J. Otto, undergirt my teaching experience and provided a research base in curriculum that has sustained me through the years following 1948.

During the time that I was on the faculty of Southern Methodist University, teachers and administrators in the Dallas, Texas, area illustrated for me what was possible when personal language was incorporated into reading instruction. This was followed by a period in Harlingen, Texas, where I had an opportunity to work with an outstanding staff in the pursuit of a true alternative in reading for children whose first language was Spanish. It was during this time that the first statements of curriculum design for a language experience approach were uttered but not published. To all the Dallas and Harlingen associates I express my profound gratitude.

Hundreds of teachers and staff associates in San Diego County contributed to the ideas that I have been able to formulate into the curriculum design of this book. Without their help and dedication this work might have faltered. High praise goes to those who did not give up a good idea when counterforces were critical and unfriendly.

The administrative staff, colleagues, and graduate students in the College of Education at the University of Arizona have contributed immeasurably to the development of the present version of a language experience approach and to the production of this book. Dean F. Robert Paulsen and Dr. Milo K. Blecha, Head of the Department of Elementary Education, have given personal support and provided blocks of time for research, writing, and field studies which were necessary. I thank these associates and others too numerous to mention.

Professional associations in which I am an active member have supported and encouraged my work on the language experience approach presented in this book. Dr. Russell Stauffer, University of Delaware, organized a Language Experience Approach Special Interest Group within the International Reading Association which has brought attention to this alternative program to educators throughout the world.

Leaders in the National Council of Teachers of English, the Association for Childhood International, and the American Association of Elementary/Kindergarten/Nursery Educators have been generous in involving me and my ideas in publications and programs. I am thankful for the opportunities they have provided to spread the ideas basic to the understanding and acceptance of this book.

My early writing of books came about because of invitations from colleagues who exhibited interest and confidence in me and my ideas. Dr. Helen Fisher Darrow invited me to write *Independent Activities for Creative Learning* (Teachers' College Press, New York, 1961) with her. Next, Dr. Dorris M. Lee asked me to work with her in the preparation of a basic statement relating language to reading. This work was published as *Learning to Read through Experience* (Appleton-Century-Crofts, New York, 1963). To Helen and Dorris I am grateful.

The work that Claryce, my wife, and I did with the staff of Encyclopaedia Britannica Educational Corp. in developing teacher and pupil materials is the strongest influence on the preparation of this teacher education text. There are too many men and women in that organization in all parts of the United States and Canada to risk mentioning any by name. Each one, in some way, has helped educators realize that it is possible to implement a language experience approach as a basic curriculum that includes reading. These educators, in turn, have worked diligently to model the approach. They have been generous to me with feedback, examples of pupil work printed in this text, and photographs which enhance the meaning and attractiveness of the book.

In the preparation of this manuscript professional readers and editors, especially James Walden, Indiana University, and Roselmina Indrisano, Boston University, have been helpful with comments. My special thanks goes to Dr. Harry T. Hahn at Oakland University, Rochester, Michigan, for his dialogues that went far beyond his written comments. He was a true friend to point out possibilities omitted in the early phases of the manuscript.

All the members of my family have been understanding, supportive, and involved in the work that made this book possible. My children, Lynda, Larry, and Elva, have engaged in research, typing, proofreading, and many household chores which made possible the early writing that Claryce and I did. We love them and appreciate their contributions reflected in this book.

R.V.A.

To Claryce

Contents

Part One
A Language Experience Approach to Teaching Communication

The thoughts that pass through our minds are captured in language. The form of the language may vary widely. It may be hieroglyphics on the walls of a cave or printed lines in a newspaper, music notations of a composer, the dots and dashes of the telegrapher, the imitating sounds of a baby, or the lyric expression of a poet. But all are the attempts to communicate meaning through symbols.

A language experience approach in education is recognition in daily practice that learning is based on the background and experience of the learner and that his efforts to communicate that experience may take many forms. For communication it is the recognition that each student brings to school a unique language personality. Teachers strive to preserve this language personality at the same time that certain common understandings about how other people communicate effectively are habituated. The language experience approach in curriculum is developed around three major strands.

Strand One: an emphasis on experiencing communication in natural ways

Strand Two: an emphasis on the study of communication that helps a person to be literate in our society

Strand Three: an emphasis on ideas and on language as other people use it to communicate their ideas

The three strands are:
——experiencing communication
——studying communication
——relating communication of others to self.

They are developed into a statement of curriculum rationale with twenty substrands. These substrands have been selected because they have more potential for promoting effective communication than have others that might have been selected. They are interpretations of the rationale developed from the research results of the San Diego County Reading Study Project at the end of 1963. That study continued through 1965 and was a part of the U.S. Office of Education First Grade Reading Studies (Bond, 1967). The rationale used in that series of studies and in early language experience approach publications was a research-oriented statement directed to the question of which language experiences available for instructional programs are the ones that have the most to contribute to reading development.

The present statement of the curriculum rationale in this book reflects the results of study, research, and implementation of the reading emphasis, especially through the use of the *Teacher's Resource Books* of *Language Experiences in Reading, Levels I, II, and III* (Allen and Allen,

1966–1968). These materials were developed around the original curriculum rationale of San Diego County Reading Study Project. Their
use in thousands of classrooms revealed that some of the topics submerged in that early statement needed to be highlighted. It was the
successful communication experiences of the learners, regardless of
the form, that seemed to release them to pursue language learnings
that led to reading. To portray visually, to dramatize, to sound out
and sound off, and to explore in self-expressive ways yielded a positive self-concept that permitted the learners to deal with the more specific goals of language learnings that have been a part of traditional
school programs.

The statement of curriculum rationale that follows in Chapter 1
reflects the new insights into the values of creative communication for
the total school curriculum. The specific application of the rationale to
language development is elaborated in the other chapters of Part One.

1. Sources of a Language Experience Approach in Communication

The goals of a broad communication-based approach to learning cannot be stated as listening goals, speaking goals, writing goals, and reading goals. Skills and abilities in these areas are essential, but to organize an instructional program around them per se is to fragment communication experiences in ways that require integration at some future time. To integrate learning into personal and meaningful behavior requires the skills of an advanced scholar. To ask young children to perform this intellectual operation is to ask for the impossible—except by chance in a few cases. Further, it requires that teachers who understand communication processes use valuable time to put back together what did not need to be separated in the first place.

The basic question is not whether we teach listening, speaking, writing, and reading but whether we deal directly or indirectly with communication experiences. These experiences must be ones that make a difference in an individual's ability to communicate ideas and feelings and to be influenced by the ideas, the language, and the feelings of others.

The Curriculum Rationale for a Language Experience Approach which follows outlines some of the abilities that have been identified as useful in general communication. The rationale reflects specific attention to those language experiences contributing to abilities in reading. The topics of the rationale are elaborated in Parts Two, Three, and Four.

Instructional programs that leave communication abilities and skills integrated are distinctive in some ways from traditional programs that separate an area such as reading for continuous, direct instruction. These distinctive characteristics are enumerated in this chapter and should be understood prior to using the instructional suggestions that follow. Classroom applications are included to illustrate how teachers keep the communicating skills integrated during instruction.

Curriculum Rationale

Strand One: *Experiencing communication* emphasizes the employment of multiple media that are natural and normal ways of self-expression—talking, painting, singing, dancing, acting, writing.

1. Sharing ideas orally—talking about topics that are self-selected and of personal interest; telling or illustrating on a purely personal

basis something that may or may not be related to classroom activities.

2. Visually portraying experiences—using art media and scrap material to explore combinations for the sheer pleasure of observing what happens; representing what one observes, imagines, or understands in abstract as well as in realistic forms; illustrating what someone else has thought and said in such ways that those ideas are internalized or interpreted (not copied); creating new schemes for ideas.

3. Dramatizing experiences—creating and re-creating with voice and body movement the feelings and ideas of others as well as the roles that are impossible in real life; putting self in other's place; communicating without words through pantomime; interpreting facial expressions, gestures, posture, and tone of voice.

4. Responding rhythmically—using self-selected body movements to illustrate meanings from sounds of music, sounds of language, and personal feelings; moving to predetermined patterns with rhythmic accompaniment; illustrating meanings through body rhythm and dancing.

5. Discussing and conversing—talking about topics, as they arise, in ways that require more mature skills than oral sharing; interacting with what other people say and write by altering contributions to fit into discussions and conversations around a theme.

6. Exploring writing—learning and using in conversational situations such topics as letter recognition, letter names, letter formation, letter orientation; copying dictated stories on paper and on a chalkboard; writing of own ideas using appropriate forms of alphabet letters to represent sounds of language; contacting, in a natural setting of writing, language characteristics such as capitalization, punctuation, standard spelling, sound-symbol relationships; observing the writing process when dictating.

7. Writing individual books—writing and publishing in many forms and for many purposes; editing and illustrating publications; using pupil-produced publications in the reading program.

Strand Two: *Studying communication* emphasizes an understanding of how language works for individuals, learning alternatives offered for natural speech patterns, understanding sound-symbol relationships, acquiring vocabularies of the form-class words and of high-frequency structure words.

8. Recognizing high-frequency words—developing awareness that English contains many words and patterns common to all speakers

and writers; mastering the words of highest frequency for sight-reading and correct spelling; using the high-frequency structure words of English in meaningful relationships to other words in sentences.

9. Exploring spelling—contacting and mastering regular and irregular phoneme-grapheme relationships during processes of writing and reading; making adaptations of personal pronunciation and standard spelling; using phonetic analysis when applicable; mastering frequently used words that defy phonetic analysis.

10. Extending vocabularies—increasing listening, speaking, reading, and writing vocabularies of words and word clusters that pattern in language, such as nouns, verbs, adjectives, and adverbs; adding new meanings to known words; recognizing and using known words in new and creative ways; creating new words for nonsense and fun talking and writing.

11. Studying style and form—profiting from listening to reading and studying well-written materials that reflect the ways in which authors express their feelings, observations, and imaginings in beautiful language; increasing sensitivity to varieties of styles and forms of expression; replicating artful forms of self-expression such as couplets, quatrains, cinquains, haiku, letters, and diaries; sensing the humor of passages; differentiating poetry from prose; expanding sentences with descriptive words and passages.

12. Studying language structure—pronouncing and understanding words through processes of analysis and synthesis; developing meanings by stringing language sounds into sentences and portions of sentences; using affixes to extend meanings of time and number; responding to rhyming and rhythm of language; recognizing the repetition of some syllables in many words; studying specific topics of structure such as use of prepositions, determiners, pronominal references, and subject-verb-object relationships.

13. Reading nonalphabetic symbol systems—responding to the meanings of symbol systems that are not represented by the alphabet, such as clocks, dials, maps, numerals, and graphs; responding to primary readings in the environment, such as weather, plants, human emotions, color, texture, size, shape, taste, and smell.

Strand Three: *Relating communication of others to self* emphasizes the influences of the language and ideas of many people on the personal language of learners as they browse and read many types of books, see and hear films, listen to records and tapes, listen to music, enjoy fine arts prints and photographs, handle sculpture and discuss it, and add to their personal repertoire of self-expression abilities.

14. Listening to and reading language of others—hearing and reading the language of many authors through stories and poems; responding naturally with new words and sentence patterns as illustrated by authors; comparing and contrasting personal ways of saying things with those of authors.

15. Comprehending what is read—understanding what is heard or read; following directions; reproducing the thought of a passage; reading for detail; reading for general significance; understanding words and their meanings in context.

16. Organizing ideas and information—using various methods of putting ideas from multiple sources into an overall concept that can be reported, such as picture painting, collage, montage, sculpture, making games, composing music, and construction; planning and producing stories with sequences of ideas, multiple characters, and settings; planning and writing poetry in predetermined patterns; classifying briefly the stated ideas of others.

17. Assimilating and integrating ideas—using listening and reading for specific purposes of a personal nature; extending personal meanings and using the new meanings in self-expression as a result of reading stories, viewing films, listening to recordings; talking about things *like* and *not like* what has happened; seeing and hearing experiences elaborated and extended in many ways.

18. Searching and researching multiple sources—finding information on topics of interest and on assignments by using interviews, reference books, tapes, films, filmstrips, observations, and other ways available when information is needed.

19. Evaluating communication of others—determining the validity and reliability of statements; sorting out and evaluating the real from the imaginary; sorting out assumptions from facts; recognizing an author's purpose and point of view; recognizing styles that include exaggeration, sarcasm, and humor.

20. Responding in personal ways—illustrating confidence and technical skill in responding to communicative efforts of others without duplicating them; performing personally as a result of influences from many sources without specific reference to the sources of those influences; reflecting humanistic qualities of an author, an artist, a teacher, a composer, an architect, a musician,

a scientist, and any other contributor to society who is dependent on creative self-expression for survival.

Linguistic Base

Growth in language that permits and promotes *reading* is a major goal of a language experience approach. Reading is never treated as something apart from language and thought. The existing language of each child is used as the base for building language competence required for reading printed materials. A continuing emphasis is placed on the individual use of language to produce reading material so children can observe and experience language relationships that work for them. Language is treated as a unique human experience which can be valued, kept through writing, and then reconstructed through reading. No child's language is rejected as inadequate because rejection cannot change real language and cannot prevent its becoming "reading" when it is recorded without alphabetic code; in fact, rejection may handicap children with divergent language at the time when literacy skills of reading and writing are required in school tasks.

Reciprocal relationships of linguistic structures of phonology, syntax, and morphology are believed to be basic to language growth that results in the reading of print.

——Phonology is the aspect of language that relates to the production, by human beings, of meaningful sounds and sound patterns when communicating. It is the oral code that is decoded through processes of listening.

——Syntax is the aspect of language that relates streams of sounds and print representations of those sounds into sentences and meaningful parts of sentences in connected discourse.

——Morphology is the aspect of language that relates to the awareness and use of word formations such as inflections, derivational forms, roots, affixes, compounds, and contractions.

Figure 1 illustrates the potential for reciprocal relationships of linguistic structures with the three strands of the curriculum rationale. As children live and learn in situations in which they hear the language, use it in syntactical arrangements, and understand the subtleties of word structure, they increase their abilities to communicate in multiple ways, understand how language works for them, and profit from contact with the language and ideas of other people.

The conditions that enhance and accelerate language learnings are

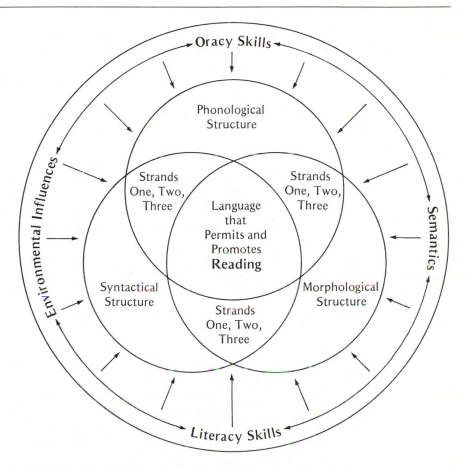

FIGURE 1 *Linguistic Base for a Language Experience Approach*

on the outer design of Figure 1. They suggest by their placement that teachers must be cognizant of and able to deal with

    ——environmental influences—the social climate of the classroom

    ——oracy skills—talking and listening to talking

    ——semantics—personal meanings that learners bring to language, compared and contrasted with meanings inherent in the ideas and language of others

    ——literacy skills—reading and writing.

Language that permits and promotes reading is acquired when the following conditions are orchestrated in the planned program.

1. Skills of phonology, syntax, and morphology are developed, modified, and extended in each of the three strands.
2. The skills inherent in the linguistic structures are related to oracy as well as to literacy, and the interrelationships occur in a meaningful environment of communication.
3. The teaching method for language growth in a language experience approach is basically interactive.
4. Children acquire competency with their own language during the time they are relating to language as other people use it.
5. As children grow in the communicating powers extending beyond nonverbal behavior, they search constantly for personal meanings that relate to the meanings held by other people.
6. Language in a societal setting is the language that yields pleasure and purpose for human beings.
7. Children seek their own meanings through purposeful communication that is not dependent on print but that does not exclude print.

A language experience approach, when implemented, accepts the fact that children learn to speak according to whatever models are available. This fact is extended into reading and writing. Teachers operate on the assumption that if a child can acquire meaningful and communicative oral language without "talking lessons," that same child can relate to the printed forms of language without "reading lessons." Reading and writing—literacy skills—emerge as basic linguistic structures mature and interrelate. Detailed suggestions for programs that foster the relationships are in Parts Two, Three, and Four.

Reading Instruction

Implementation of the curriculum rationale of a language experience approach can accelerate growth toward reading when that is a major goal in the instructional program. The growth is not considered to be the result of "teaching reading" in the conventional sense. Reading is the result of the interaction of language learnings within the three strands of the curriculum rationale as illustrated in Figure 2. A theoretical application of that model suggests that at any point at which these learnings overlap, reading results. The perfect reader would be one who had related the strands in the curriculum rationale so completely that the three strands merge into one. In between the perfect reader and the beginning reader are multiple ways of working in an

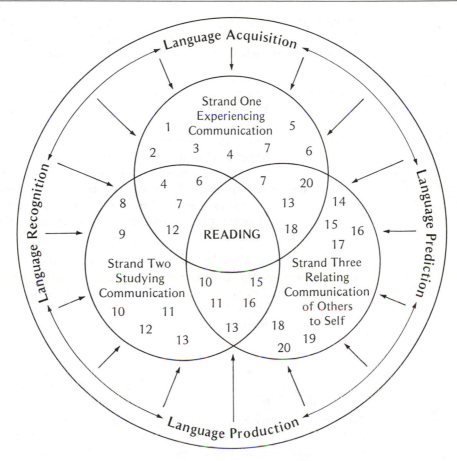

FIGURE 2 *Reading in a Language Experience Approach to Teaching Communication*

Strand One: Experiencing Communication

1. Oral sharing of ideas
2. Visual portrayal of experiences
3. Dramatization of experiences
4. Responding rhythmically
5. Discussing and conversing
6. Exploring writing
7. Writing individual books

Strand Two: Studying Communication

8. Recognizing high-frequency words
9. Exploring spelling
10. Studying style and form
11. Studying language structure
12. Extending vocabularies
13. Reading nonalphabetic symbol systems

Strand Three: Relating Communication of Others to Self

14. Listening to and reading language of others
15. Comprehending what is heard and read
16. Organizing ideas
17. Assimilating and integrating ideas
18. Searching and researching multiple sources
19. Evaluating communication of others
20. Responding in personal ways

educational setting to accelerate the overlap. The instructional objective is one of planning and implementing programs that include some emphasis from each strand each day. The major ideas that interlock in the model are:

Strand One: The child communicating in multiple ways with multiple media using personal ideas and personal language

Strand Two: The child studying the components of language that have most to do with the reading process and learning how those components work for self and others

Strand Three: The child being influenced by the language and ideas of many people so his or her personal language changes in the direction of that found in most reading materials.

In Figure 2 *READING* is at the center to indicate its importance as a stated goal even though it is not the focus of direct instruction. As indicated, instructional programs are generated on the outer parts of the model. They feature four major classes of activities: language recognition, language acquisition, language prediction, and language production.

Language Recognition

Emphasis on recognition skills for reading is traditional. Phonetic analysis, structural analysis, acquisition of a sight vocabulary, and other recognition skills are repeated over and over in most reading instructional programs. In a language experience approach this same emphasis on skills is maintained. A major difference between it and conventional programs is that in the language experience approach the teacher trusts the children's own language to illustrate the characteristics of language that are fruitful in developing recognition skills. They are helped to see relationships between their own language and the printed language of others. Through processes of comparing and contrasting their own dictated and written productions with those of others, they experience language recognition skills and understandings such as the following ones.

——The words they use frequently are the same ones other people use frequently.

——Many of their own words begin with the same sound which is represented in writing with the same symbol or symbols.

——Many of their own words end with the same sound which is represented with the same symbol or symbols.

——Any sound they can speak can be represented with the letters of the alphabet.

——Changing one letter in a word can change its pronunciation and meaning.

——Consonants and consonant clusters usually represent the same sound each time they appear at the beginning of words.

——Vowels represent a variety of speech sounds.

——Some syllables appear over and over in everyone's language.

——Many words rhyme with others.

——Sometimes two or more words are combined to form compounds.

——Sometimes two or more words are contracted, or shortened, with an apostrophe to show where the sounds and letters are missing.

——Abbreviations can be used in the place of some whole words when they are known by just about everybody.

——Sometimes words that sound alike in speech have different spellings and different meanings.

——People who read and write find the same letters written in many different forms.

——Capitalization and punctuation are signals in writing that help in oral and silent reading.

Recognition skills are developed as children communicate in multiple ways, but it is through writing and the processes of editing manuscripts for publication that much of the direct instruction is done. Recognition skills are reinforced and extended as children use those discovered in their own writing when they are reading from others. The most basic skills are illustrated in both instances. They are characteristic of the language of every child and are reinforced through language study activities. Seldom-used skills are discussed and taught when needs arise.

Language Acquisition

There is a continuing emphasis on developing substantial inventories of words that children will find in reading materials throughout their lives. In speech and writing they collect and use words, phrases, and sentence patterns that highlight the concepts that

——everything has a name and most things have many names

——there are many ways to express ideas of movement with language

——descriptive passages require the use of words and phrases to distinguish characteristics such as color, size, shape, texture, sound, taste, smell, feeling.

——language is useful in contrasting and comparing the known with the unknown to clarify meanings and to generate new feelings and attitudes.

Children use words of structure in their sentences and participate in activities which result in developing a sight vocabulary of words that occur frequently in the language. They learn that they can create new words and new ways of saying things for special occasions and for special effects.

Children contact and acquire vocabularies new to them through activities that involve singing, chanting, listening to reading, listening to recordings, viewing films and filmstrips, listening to stories and poems, acting out stories and poems, choral reading, and playing vocabulary games.

Literature selections with patterned language are used for repetition of language that might not be characteristic of home-rooted language but might be characteristic of reading materials that the child will encounter throughout life. Also, they provide models for self-expression through new writing patterns.

Priority is given to the acquisition of vocabularies of the form classes: nouns, verbs, adjectives, and adverbs. Those words are gathered in from the real experiences of children as they view their world in new ways, with new purposes, and with a teacher who mediates language so every child can

——hear language in new and meaningful contexts

——say things with new words and new language patterns that become permanent through use

——write with an ever-increasing repertoire of personal language resources

——read from any sources with as much pleasure from how the author says things as from what she or he communicates.

Language Prediction

Selections for listening and reading in a language experience approach include those with repeating patterns and dependable lines. These selections permit children to predict and repeat words, phrases, and whole stanzas without seeing the print. They learn to anticipate language and language patterns that repeat frequently in reading materials. This familiarity and assurance permits them to read printed materials with confidence not available when only words are emphasized. From beginning levels and continuing throughout life, they use these predictive abilities to read silently at a speed faster than speech. They know and anticipate what is coming in printed portions and use recognition skills to confirm or deny their predictions.

Characteristics of language such as alliteration and rhyming promote predictive abilities. Poetry with repeating lines and patterns is important in a language experience approach. The visual impact of patterns in printed material is helpful in releasing children to try to read new materials. They can observe that only a few words are different as they move along with the reading. Much of the print is repeated. In poetry the patterns of rhyming words usually give some clue to new words at the end of lines.

Choral reading is useful in establishing the phonological structure of patterned stories and poems. Once the sound pattern has been established, the words that follow can be predicted with a high degree of certainty. An able oral reader usually introduces a pattern and then invites others to join in chorus when the language repeats. When printed copies are furnished, breaks in the pattern keep readers alert to the use of recognition skills to check out predictions.

Many patterned stories and poems with a high degree of predictability can be used as models for writing. Personal interests can be expressed within the patterns through the substitution of nouns, verbs, and descriptors associated with a new topic. Several personal productions with the same pattern afford reading material that repeats the structure vocabulary of language while it permits the use of a wide range of form-class words.

Chanting games and singing songs that repeat language patterns provide needed practice in trying out new ways of saying things atypical of personal language. This practice prepares children to recognize those patterns in print and to predict the flow of language.

Procedures for judging the relative difficulty of reading materials can make use of predictive abilities. Random samples of a selection can be reproduced with a pattern of words missing, such as every fifth word as in the cloze procedure. Children read to supply the words. If they reproduce as many as 50 percent of the same words used by the author, they can be judged to read the material with independence. Less than that indicates that they might need to read that material in an instructional setting.

Older children who read well can increase their predictive abilities by marking out in printed passages all words except the nouns, verbs, adjectives, and adverbs. When they read the passages orally to a small group, the listeners can retell the story using full sentences. Through this procedure they realize that a few words carry a heavy load of meaning and that certain classes of words merely support the mainstream of ideas so they can be expressed in sentences. Conversely, the group can read all the words except the nouns, verbs, adjectives, and adverbs to find that all semblance of meaning is missing.

Predictive activities begin with preschool programs and continue throughout the school program. They serve as a companion to recognition abilities. Together, prediction and recognition enable readers to communicate with an author through the use of minimum visual clues. They promote comprehension-centered reading.

Language Production

Individual books, class books, language study activities, dramatic productions, musical productions, and art displays grow out of the implementation of the language experience approach to teaching communication. It is to be hoped that some of the pupil-produced materials will become useful in the reading curriculum.

Pupil-produced books and reading charts reflect familiar vocabulary and current interests. They are significantly different from other reading instructional materials. Because the content and language are known to the authors, they can become the teachers of their books. When original manuscripts are read orally by their authors, emphasis can be placed on effective interpretation through reading rather than on recognition skills. Predictive qualities are built into the language of the author and do not need to be given in repeating language patterns to be remembered. Children are influenced by the ideas and the language of others, but they need to integrate those influences into a new, personal language for speaking and writing. Creative production, especially creative writing, offers opportunities to try out new language.

Production in many media is emphasized. No child is denied the opportunity to share thinking because of poor language recognition abilities. Everyone is expected to communicate in numerous ways and to associate most means of communication with speech and writing.

The reading of printed materials is introduced through procedures of "reading" the real environment of people and things. Imagination is encouraged in the process. Experiences are reflected through art media, acting, and talking. Some of the talk is recorded and reproduced through reading from time to time. Children gain a firm grasp on the notion that their ideas, expressed with words, can be written. What is written becomes reading. As they mature enough to compare and contrast, they come to realize over and over the following points.

——The words they use to write about a topic are much the same as those used by others.

——The sounds they make are recorded by writing with an alphabet that is the same for everybody.

——What other people write about comes from real experiences or from imagination.

——Many authors share their ideas in a sequence.

——Characters must be described so listeners and readers can form a mental image of them even though they have never seen them.

——The settings of stories must be described so listeners and readers can form a mental image of them even though they have never been there.

Editing of manuscripts to be used in the reading curriculum is a significant and necessary part of the production process. Children learn the fine points of reading through editing their writing just as they learn the fine points of writing through the reading of well-written materials. The reciprocal relationships between writing and reading are emphasized and internalized through the many production activities of a language experience approach to learning communication.

Distinguishing Characteristics

A language experience approach to teaching communication offers some alternatives to traditional language instruction, especially as instruction relates to the curriculum called reading. Some of them follow.

1. The oral language background of each child continues to be used throughout the grades as a basic ingredient in word recognition and vocabulary growth. Children are expected to hear and say words and sentence patterns many times before and during the acquisition of abilities and skills required for reading print.

2. Vocabulary controls are viewed as being in the language itself and in the language background of each child. Words of high frequency are expected to be used by all children who are producing dictated and written material. The ones of highest frequency will occur most often in all children's language. Recognition of these words in all reading, not just in the reading textbook, accelerates the acquisition of a basic sight vocabulary.

3. The introduction of reading vocabulary is accelerated for most children. Rather than selecting words for repeated drill, teachers develop an understanding of the major classes of words that all people use to communicate.

4. The major emphasis in organization is on individualization. There is no need, or any desire, to separate children into ability groups within the classroom for direct instruction in reading skills. Grouping is for specific purposes. Learning centers permit children to be dispersed for their work so the teacher can devote direct teaching time to identified problems and needs. The teacher's role shifts from one of managing ability groups to one of interaction in communicating processes. Needs of individuals are identified as teacher and pupils talk, write, sing, play games, paint, and read together. Diagnosis is continuous.

5. More than other experience programs, a language experience approach to teaching communication has a basic framework of language experiences to serve as a screening device for selecting activities and events that contribute to the development of communication skills and attitudes. Once teachers internalize the three major strands and the twenty substrands (listed in Figure 2), they can select materials and develop a learning environment for reading that is efficient and has the variety of choices necessary for the wide-range abilities of pupils.

6. The direct teaching program in word-recognition skills, including phonics and phonetic analysis, is closely related to writing and spelling activities in which children deal with the language letter by letter, syllable by syllable, and word by word. Minimum time and attention are devoted to figuring out words during the reading activities. Teachers know that the accompanying oral language and written language activities will feature direct instruction on sound-symbol relationships.

7. The concept load of meaning in reading material is eliminated when the child uses personal writing to learn to recognize words. He knows the content of his materials, whether dictated or written

independently. Comparison studies of children's writing and the writing of others provide a base of confidence for children to believe that they can read what others have written.

8. Children with backgrounds of experience and language that are extremely divergent from the typical story content of reading texts are not placed at a disadvantage. From the beginning and continuing through the grades, they deal with familiar ideas and language that is theirs. This is an advantage for the child with superior language development just as it is for the child with a limited language background. All children have an opportunity in the approach to see their own speech recorded through writing. Most of them learn at an early age to write their own ideas in their own language for purposes of making reading material for themselves and others.

9. Children gain some knowledge of the structure of the English language as they repeatedly experience the relationships of alphabet letters to their sounds. They see these relationships running through sentence patterns that are useful in expressing their ideas.

10. A wide variety of books is necessary for a language experience approach to teaching communication. Stories in basal readers, trade books, supplementary texts, books in the content fields, and current publications such as newspapers and magazines are useful. Books that children produce are required in the reading curriculum.

11. Multisensory materials are used extensively. Films, filmstrips, recordings and tapes, photographs, art prints, musical compositions, and the whole world of real things become essential materials in the program. They form a base for vocabulary acquisition and growth.

12. Children express themselves in multiple media as a part of the basic curriculum. They talk, write, respond with body rhythms, use art media of all types, and act out roles of other people. Their personal, individual ideas are valued in any form of expression that is selected for communication. They do not have to wait until they are good readers to participate fully in the educational processes. Poor readers have a place while they acquire necessary abilities to improve.

13. Reading is treated as a process of reconstructing oral language that has been written. The pattern of thinking about reading which is internalized by each child is that ideas can be spoken, then written, then reconstructed through reading.

14. Improving communication is viewed as the art of raising the levels of sensitivity of each child
   ——to one's environment, including the language environment
   ——to relationships between oracy and literacy
   ——to writing as a means of making reading materials
   ——to multiple sources of information and inspiration
   ——to multiple forms of response to ideas and feelings.

Teachers live with children in a learning environment where sensitivities are raised to focus on print in such a way that reading is a natural and normal result. Children do not need lessons in "how to do it." They all have personal needs developing which require reading, and they learn how through the many reciprocal relationships that exist for them.

Some Applications by Teachers

Attitudes of Personal Success

Janet Jones teaches in Buena Vista School which is located in an area where some of the children have limited language backgrounds and some have very good oral language. She knows that no one set of prepared materials can meet the needs of all the children in improving their communication abilities. Consequently, she does not look for such materials. Rather, she tries to choose a wide range of language experiences that will meet a variety of needs without making children feel that they belong to an unworthy group. She avoids teaching procedures that designate some children as low achievers and build in them perceptions of "not being able to."

According to Mrs. Jones, each child who enters her class has a language personality different from that of every other one in the classroom. She is determined to preserve some of that individuality at the same time that she builds understandings and skills which will aid in communication. To do this, the procedure from the first day requires the individual to express personal thoughts, aspirations, ideas, and ideals. This the child does through speaking, painting, writing, and other media. The teacher works with the children to help them move from oral and pictorial expression of their ideas to expression through writing. The language experiences involved are not separated from the act of reading in Mrs. Jones's classroom. She finds it impossible to remove the basic instruction in reading from the real, personal language of the children who are finding their own words, sentences, and stories in the classroom environment. To accommodate the wide range of language development, Mrs. Jones has some activities that meet her criteria for good experiences for children.

> ——The activities require that each student apply his personal language to each activity.
> ——They invite the child to engage in thinking on a personal basis.
> ——They draw on the past experience and the imagination of each child.
> ——They require a minimum of preparation on the part of the teacher.
> ——They place the teacher in the role of a resource person rather than the "keeper of the keys to knowledge."
> ——They involve inexpensive products which do not need to be saved from year to year.
> ——There is assured success at some level for every child.

Some of the activities follow.

Making Reading from Talk

In her classroom talk is a basic ingredient for developing other communication skills—listening, writing, and reading. She finds that most children have an abundance of talk that can be used in making reading. Her procedure is:

1. Children are asked to express ideas of something seen, heard, imagined, or wished for with a simple crayon drawing. The children are asked to fold back 3 or 4 in. of the drawing paper at the bottom so that it can be saved for writing.
2. A group of eight to ten children works with Mrs. Jones at a time, telling the group about their pictures.
3. After each story Mrs. Jones asks each child to select one or two things for her to write under the picture. In this way she has an opportunity to edit some of the gross errors that are made in free speech. This technique also reduces the amount of dictation she takes from one child.
4. As she writes each sentence at the bottom of the picture, she talks informally with the children about what she is doing. She identifies words, invites children to tell her the names of letters, talks about words that begin alike, words that end alike, and words that are alike.

5. She proves that anything they can say can be written down with the twenty-six letters of our alphabet and that a person who knows how to read can tell what someone said without hearing her or him.

6. The stories of each group of eight to ten children are bound into books with construction-paper covers that have the titles and the names of the authors on them.

7. The books are read by the group on the following day and by other groups after that. Children are treated as authors and as contributors to study materials. Their talk is utilized in helping them understand more about their language. Skills of writing, spelling, and word recognition are being initiated. The integrity of each child is being preserved.

Dictation and Independent Writing

At no set time are the children in Mrs. Jones's class expected to move from dictation of stories to independent writing. She listens for the first suggestion that a particular child can do independent writing. She knows from past experience that as soon as one child makes a commitment to write, others start writing to follow. In the period of transition she encourages children to use their full language power in many classroom activities because she knows that their writing will be somewhat limited. She does not want them to feel that what they write is the only important language contribution they make to the class.

Two or three times a week Mrs. Jones takes dictation in front of the whole class. This is usually done in relation to a picture painted by a child and volunteered for discussion. It is different from the type of group experience chart that is used for reading development. Mrs. Jones's purpose is to talk with the children about the structure of written English. The talk is informal and points up understandings essential for progress in doing independent writing. She calls attention to such things as letter formation, sounds represented by letters, capitalization, punctuation, sentence sense, organization of ideas, and use of descriptive words.

Mrs. Jones usually emphasizes one or two things during a dictation period. She gets her clues for needed discussions and illustrations by observing and listening to children as they work and play. She helps children gain understandings without her having to do excessive direct teaching and grading of writing products. The dictation activity gives her an opportunity to keep reviewing necessary items.

Writing at Home

As soon as a few children present Mrs. Jones with crumpled "masterpieces" which they have written at home, she begins giving them blank paper to take home for writing. She usually staples ten or twelve sheets of newsprint, 9 in. by 12 in., together for this purpose.

She then brings a file box into the room with a folder for each child in it. The folder is to keep the stories written at home. Each day as children bring their stories, they read them to the class and then file them. The folders are arranged in alphabetical order so that the children have a good experience with that system.

When the number of stories is too great to allow each child to read, the procedure changes to one of letting children file their stories until they have a certain number (usually ten), and then the child is asked to choose one or two to read to the class. The stories are stapled into a book with a construction-paper cover and placed in the classroom library. Thus Mrs. Jones supplements the book table with dozens of personal books of interest to the children because the authors are in the classroom. She also finds that parents become interested in the development of writing and spelling skills and gain some understandings of the many-faceted learnings in which the children are engaged.

Vocabulary Expansion

With the great range of language development represented in Mrs. Jones's group, there is need for vocabulary growth experiences that are not too discouraging for the less-able children yet have a challenge for others. In searching for ideas for activities to promote vocabulary growth, she has found several that meet her criteria.

At times during the school year, a bulletin board is reserved for children to contribute similes they have heard, used, or read. They usually illustrate their work for the bulletin board.

"As soft as cotton."
"As round as a pancake."
"As big as an elephant."

A class book is usually in progress in which children record rhymes they think up. Sometimes Mrs. Jones makes a blank book with an attractive cover; she might call it *Make a Rhyme.* Children make sense and nonsense rhymes for the book.

"A fish in a dish."
"A cat with a bat."
"A frog on a log."
"A bee in a tree."
"Kites fly way up high."
"Very soon it will be noon."

Some children never get beyond this stage of rhyming, while others begin to write couplets and simple poems.

What Did You See?

Almost daily Mrs. Jones has a picture or a filmstrip without words which she uses as a means of helping children improve their ability to describe their environment and their feelings about people. She chooses material that lends itself to wide interpretation so that she will get a variety of responses. Sometimes she uses this material with small groups; at other times she uses it with the total class. She feels it is good for the immature children to hear what the more mature ones say about what they see. After the filmstrip has been shown to a group, it is added to the collection of individual viewing filmstrips for the Viewing Center.

The class takes short walks in the school neighborhood to observe interesting things around them. Mrs. Jones believes that children will learn to see more in their environment if they have names for the things they see, have words to describe the movement they observe, and can describe some aspects of what they see.

What Did You Hear?

A very quiet activity that changes the tempo of the class routine is one that is used frequently. Mrs. Jones asks the children to get quiet enough to hear what is happening out-of-doors. They put their heads on their desks and listen carefully. Then they tiptoe to whisper to Mrs. Jones what they have heard. She keeps a record of what they tell her and reads the list to the class. Sometimes the children will challenge the response of someone, so Mrs. Jones insists that they report only what they have heard.

Along with this activity Mrs. Jones has a Listening Center with earphones for eight children at a time. In the center she keeps recordings that give children a variety of listening experiences. When she adds something new, she may ask the first group of listeners to tell the class what they heard. In her collection she has music, songs, poetry, stories, songs in Spanish and French, records with different musical instruments, and other materials that build listening skills and provide models of excellent oral reading.

I Am Thinking

Children need to understand the use of modification in the language if they are to become efficient and effective in oral and written communication and appreciative of the writing of others. Mrs. Jones wants the children to have many informal oral experiences on which to build a strong foundation. She will say, "I am thinking of a *river.*"

The children respond first with adjectives to modify—up to three.

river
wide river
wide, winding river
wide, winding, dirty river

A child can add a prepositional phrase that Mrs. Jones introduces by using an appropriate preposition. "I am thinking of a wide, winding, dirty river *with* . . ."

The next child might respond, ". . . with a boat."
Then the children can modify again.

boat
white boat
clean, white boat
small, clean, white boat

Mrs. Jones might finish the sentence, ". . . tossing on the waves." She does not want to draw out the activity with any one word to make the responses too difficult for the children. She wants each one to participate at a comfortable level of vocabulary development.

Dramatizing Stories

Stories are read or told in the classroom every day. Mrs. Jones views this activity as basic to the language development program. She extends the listening and telling experiences through dramatization of stories.

Mrs. Jones likes to use many of the favorite stories of children. She will read a story such as "The Three Billy Goats Gruff." Later she will tell it. Then she may help a group of children to dramatize it. To do this the children need to visualize

——the characters

——the setting

——the characteristics of the actors

——the conversation and action of the story.

In the dramatization the teacher serves as the narrator at first, but later the children take turns in this role. No child is too immature to participate in dramatization. The timid, shy child who serves as scenery or is an animal with no speaking part in early productions is sure to grow and to be included in speaking parts as she or he experiences the success of dramatic production.

Sometimes Mrs. Jones uses simple puppets to dramatize stories. She finds that the experience of manipulating a puppet often helps a shy child to become less self-conscious in audience situations. The more confident child usually makes an excellent narrator or stage manager.

Using Bulletin Boards

Mrs. Jones likes to have attractive and useful bulletin boards in her classroom. To her the most attractive ones reflect the ideas, concerns, and productive efforts of the children. She also thinks that children should assume responsibility because by so doing they have to deal with communications problems beyond the common ones of speaking and writing. They have an opportunity to practice skills in

——choosing a main idea

——using a few words to convey a great deal of meaning rather than using complete sentences

——using color and design to carry part of the message

——emphasizing ideas with color and size of letters and background.

One technique that Mrs. Jones has found to be effective is to place a caption on a bulletin board and ask children to fill in with paintings, cutouts, and captions. She uses titles such as:

Where Do You Live? (Children draw their homes and write their addresses.)

Who Are You? (They draw self-portraits and write their names.)

Birds in Our Community. (Paint or cut out birds and write their names.)

People at Our School. (Children draw portraits of school personnel and write names and positions.)

Mrs. Jones knows that every time something new is added to a bulletin board, most of the children will try to read what is there.

Self-understanding

When Ralph was asked to teach a group of children ten to fourteen years old who had been unsuccessful in learning to read, he was assured freedom to work with the group. He could not bring himself to believe that all these children were unable to learn to read. He believed that if he would value each child as a human being and provide valid purposes for reading that made sense to the pupils, they would respond with reading skills commensurate with their abilities. Since he believed reading skills emerge as a result of a fully developed communications program, Ralph decided reading would not be taught as a separate skill at a special time of day. He felt that better attitudes could be developed through activities requiring self-expression rather than remembering answers to questions that the pupils did not ask and that had no meaning to them. His teaching rationale had three major emphases.

——Highlight the child's own language, faulty as it may be.

——Help each child to understand something about how the English language works for individuals.

——Bring each child in contact with the ideas and language of authors, to agree or disagree, like or not like, extend with personal experiences, modify to meet specific situations, and interact in the multitude of other ways through which good authors have helped people to live a more abundant and interesting life.

The ideas used by Ralph to implement his goals illustrate how a teacher strives for *attitude growth first* and *skill development second*.

Ralph developed a system of reading buddies in his class. He felt that his defeated readers needed to develop confidence in reading many, many books at a level on which they could achieve. Knowing they would never read the easiest books in the library, he asked the first-grade teacher to assign one of her pupils as a reading buddy to each of the children in the ungraded classroom. The purpose was for each first-grader to become an audience for oral reading by the older students. The plan was a tremendous success.

Ralph had an individualized instructional program in all curriculum areas; when a first-grader came to visit his buddy with a book to read, it did not disrupt the program. The relationship grew; the two classes took field trips together so that each first-grader would have an individual guide. This plan gave real incentive to the older children to read in order to prepare for the trips. As the younger children got to the point at which they were interested in dictating long and involved stories, the older children took dictation and read the stories back to the young children. Some of them illustrated and bound the stories into hard-back books and placed them in the school library. They were having a real experience with language at a level they could handle successfully. Ralph was available to help when needed, but he was thrilled to see the level of responsibility his students would assume when they wanted to do a good job and were involved in a personal relationship with another human being that was satisfying to them.

The taking of dictation and reading was such a success that Ralph decided to use this interest to extend the skill program. He had noted that many of the errors in recognition and spelling occurred with high-frequency words. In place of futile drills, he engaged members of the class in writing books for young children to read. He introduced the idea that simple sentences are usually based on a formula of high-frequency words plus the names of people and things. He gave each class member a personal copy of a list of words of highest frequency. He helped the members to see that if they would list some names of people and some names of things, they could make many sentences using only the words on the short list of 300 words printed on just one page.

In order to keep the full language of the students as part of the classroom activities, he encouraged each one who was going to write a book to tell his story with his full language. Sometimes the stories were taped, and sometimes they were written. But he wanted the authors to understand that they possessed more language power than was necessary to write a simple story. He also wanted them to see that if they wanted to reduce the number of words, they should take out descriptive passages. This descriptive language was transferred to illustrations.

There were busy days as the classroom was transformed into a publishing house with authors, illustrators, editors, printers, binders, and general managers. Days flew by as the class brought in dozens of books from the library to use for ideas and models. They read and reread books, not in order to learn how, but to learn enough about how authors used the English language to write simple stories.

As the books were finished, bound copies were taken to the classrooms of the younger children. The author was invited to read the book first and then to leave a copy for the classroom library. Books from the Publishing Center had been produced in multiple copies, so there was a book for each of the classrooms to which the author was invited.

The response of the younger children was terrific! Almost suddenly the "dumb kids" were being recognized as worthy, contributing members of the school community. The level of reading achievement of the children at this point was not the real concern of Ralph. He was much more interested in their obvious gains in being able to—and wanting to—read. He knew that the group in his classroom could learn many things and read with interest and effectiveness if he continued to work with them on a basis that made sense to them.

To extend the information and ideas of the students in ways other than listening and reading, Ralph began to show films without words. After viewing one, he would engage the class in discussing what they saw in the film and guessing what the producer was trying to say with the pictures. Then they would view the picture and listen to points of agreement and disagreement with what they had decided. The follow-up discussions were full of meaning and characterized by high interest. The students were not placed in the untenable position of always trying to remember what someone else said; they were interacting with ideas—theirs and someone else's. Their points of view, imaginings, information, and prejudices were valued as beginning points for learning.

Some films had no text—just background music. These were used for vocabulary development. As the viewing was taking place, children were formulating words to describe what they had seen. The same emphasis was used with filmstrips of cloud formations, textures of wood, flowers, water, ships, automobiles, airplanes, rockets, and other items of interest. Ralph was not seeking *the right answers* but was trying to elicit as many different answers and responses as possible. He wanted the students to learn from experience that in a free, intelligent society we have need for many different answers to the same questions and problems and the ability to assume personal responsibility for what is said. Each child was experiencing the satisfaction of being a human being.

Ralph experimented with a program of student government in his class. All the children were accustomed to a school situation in which someone else had made the major decisions about proper behavior and the right ways of doing things and in which they were often reprimanded for disobeying the rules. Ralph had a strong impression that his students did not understand the reasons behind most rules; scolding had been tried and found wanting. He decided on a program of action—and his experiment in student government was begun.

First, the class engaged in discussions of the different ways that people govern themselves. Ralph read to them and brought books and articles to the classroom for the students to read. They viewed films on government operations and began to make some decisions about how a classroom might be governed. As the plans were formulated, Ralph had serious doubts about the effectiveness of the operation, but he let the students carry through. He was pleased to see them busy with reading and writing, no one excusing himself because of inability to read.

As the children began to realize that their ideas of self-government were not working, they wanted someone to tell them that they had failed. Instead of providing this satisfaction, the teacher helped them analyze their problems and recommended helpful materials. He brought some simple interpretations of the United States Constitution and read with them so that he could lead in a discussion of the differences between their government and a constitutional form of government. The result was an effort to try to draft a constitution for the class. This was not viewed as a lesson, and previous success in class enterprise led the class to believe that they could succeed again. Reading, writing, and spelling experiences were abundant—and so were heated discussions. Ralph was observing a group of children working on their own problem and using communication skills in a functional situation without fear of defeat.

An activity in critical reading was inspired by a collection of newspaper articles with headlines that might be interpreted in many ways. On a bulletin board with the caption Headline Stories, Ralph tacked articles with the text folded up under the headline. Any student could write a story with one of the headlines as a title. At intervals after several students had written articles, the newspaper stories were unfolded. Those who had written to the headlines had first chance at reading the newspaper stories. Sometimes the stories were read aloud to the class along with some of the student stories. At these times

Ralph led the group in discussing the fact that the same words do not mean the same to everyone who reads them. What had happened to us before we read them has something to do with what we understand when we read. The clippings along with the other stories were made into a book for all to enjoy.

Among the many ideas for understanding the nature of language that were used in the class, a study of figurative language and idiom was of greatest interest to the students. Ordinary objects were brought into the classroom to be viewed with an element of distortion. Students observed a carrot, potato, flower, and other items while looking through a goblet that was thin at the top and thick at the bottom. They used magnifying glasses, stood on something high and looked down, and looked at things from underneath them. Ralph kept a record of language he heard and then shared some of it with the students, helping them to see that things can be described effectively by saying they are *like* something else that we know about. When he read aloud stories and books, class members would frequently point to the use of figures of speech in effective writing.

It came as something of a surprise that all the students used idioms in their spoken language. They had not been aware that in English many things cannot be literally interpreted. The class made a book of idioms and illustrated it with nonsense drawings. Some of the idioms were:

He's getting in my hair.
His goose is cooked.
Go fly a kite.
He burns me up.

Another interesting word study was thinking of multiple meanings for words. The class made a book, *Words with More Than One Meaning*. Each child illustrated a page with a drawing that interpreted a sentence copied from the collection on the chalkboard. The following were among them:

A fish has scales but can't sing a note.
A potato has eyes but cannot see.
A river has banks but no money.

The activities associated with writing books for young children gave most of the students confidence in writing, but descriptive language was lacking. Much of what was written was sterile and flat. Hearing good language from the best authors failed to bring the desired improvement. Ralph helped the class to understand how one can modify the noun or pronoun with other words that alter the meaning and clarify the idea. Pupils then reworked a sentence or a paragraph of their own writing, adding appropriate adjectives.

After they could see the effectiveness of adding adjectives, the class used the same method in modifying the verb. The pupils went through a story each had written, adding an adjective and an adverb to each sentence. This activity resulted in added interest in good writing and helped the students to appreciate good descriptive passages as Ralph read to them and to be aware of good writing by authors they were reading. They developed a real appreciation for the best authors. Reading had become for them a process of interacting with the language of authors and of using reading to extend meanings and for ideas that would help them to express their own thoughts in better language and with more clarity.

This was the goal of their teacher!

Selected References

Allen, Roach Van. "How a Language Experience Program Works." In *A Decade of Innovations: Approaches to Beginning Reading,* edited by Elaine C. Vilscek. International Reading Association, Newark, 1968.

————and Claryce Allen. *Language Experiences in Reading, Levels I, II, and III.* Encyclopaedia Britannica Educational Corp., Chicago, 1966–1968.

————. *Language Experiences in Early Childhood.* Encyclopaedia Britannica Educational Corp., Chicago, 1969.

Ashton-Warner, Sylvia. *Teacher.* Simon and Schuster, New York, 1963.

Aukerman, Robert C. *Approaches to Beginning Reading.* John Wiley & Sons, New York, 1971.

Bond, Guy L., and Robert Dykstra. "The Cooperative Research Programs in First Grade Reading Instruction," *Reading Research Quarterly*, 2, 4 (1967), 5–126.

Chomsky, Carol. "Write First, Read Later," *Childhood Education,* 47, 4 (March, 1971), 296–299.

Cox, Vivian E. "Reciprocal Oracy/Literacy Recognition Skills in the Language Production of Language Experience Approach Students." (Ed.D. disertation.) University of Arizona, Tucson, 1971.

Dunne, Hope W. *The Art of Teaching Reading: A Language and Self-Concept Approach.* Charles E. Merill, Columbus, Ohio, 1972.

Goodman, Kenneth S. "Effective Teachers of Reading Know Language," *Elementary English,* 51, 6 (September, 1974), 823–829.

Hahn, Harry T. "These Approaches to Beginning Reading Instruction: ITA, Language Experience and Basal Reader—Extended into Second Grade," *The Reading Teacher,* 20, 8 (1967), 711–715.

Hall, MaryAnne. *Teaching Reading as a Language Experience*. Charles E. Merrill, Columbus, Ohio, 1970.

Houston Independent School District. *A Summary of the Major Findings in the First Year of Title I Experimental Reading Programs*. Research Services Department, Houston, Texas, 1972.

San Diego County, California, Superintendent of Schools. *Improving Reading Instruction*. The County Department of Education, San Diego, California, 1961–1965.

Monograph 1. *Report of the Reading Study Project*

Monograph 2. *Description of Three Approaches to the Teaching of Reading*

Monograph 3. *Teacher Inventory of Approaches to the Teaching of Reading*

Monograph 4. *An Inventory of Reading Attitude*

Monograph 5. *Analysis of Pupil Data*

Serwer, Blanche L. "Linguistic Support for a Method of Teaching Black Children to Read," *Reading Research Quarterly*, 4, 4 (1969), 449–468.

Smith, James A. *Adventures in Communication*. Allyn & Bacon, Boston, 1972.

Spitzer, Lillian K. *Selected Materials on the Language Experience Approach to Reading Instruction*. (An annotated bibliography.) International Reading Association, Newark, 1967.

Stauffer, Russell G. "The Effectiveness of Language Arts and Basic Reader Approaches—Extended into Third Grade," *Reading Research Quarterly*, 4, 4 (1969), 468–499.

———. *The Language-Experience Approach to the Teaching of Reading*. Harper & Row, New York, 1970.

Wilkinson, Andrew. *The Foundations of Language*. Oxford University Press, London, 1971.

Language as it is considered in a language experience approach is not restricted to symbolic expression through the use of the letters of the alphabet. It includes symbols that the mathematician uses to express his thoughts about the universe, those that the musician uses to express his beliefs about life, and those that the actor might use to interpret the thoughts and feelings of other human beings.

In any of their forms language symbols serve as a means of communicating the significance of human experience, and in our teaching of language we must never separate the beauty of living and the meaning of the universe. This is so because language itself is not a subject; it is rather a medium through which the thought of the world passes and the vehicle in which knowledge moves. To separate language from what it stands for, to pull symbols away from their meanings, and to teach about the symbols without teaching about the experience would be an empty sort of task.

Language serves as a thought medium, and it serves as a means of communication. To try to determine which aspect is more important is fruitless, but it is well in our teaching of language to place more emphasis than has been done in the past on language as a thought medium—to total communication. This emphasis requires that more attention be given to self-expression through many media but especially through oral and written creative expression. It also requires more attention to language experiences that illustrate the reciprocal relationships between listening, speaking, reading, and writing. When language is taught as a thought medium, the curriculum is individualized and personalized rather than standardized. It becomes a human language experience which follows some guiding principles.

1. Children vary greatly in rate and extent of language growth.

Growth in language, as with all other growth, shows wide deviation among children. Of the various means of caring for these individual differences, the most practical and effective way seems to be personalized teaching or working in small flexible groupings within a larger setting of broadly conceived activities for learning centers. In this book the suggestions will center around the development of learning centers in the classroom where children will disperse for independent work on an assigned or on a self-selected basis, thus freeing the teacher to work with individuals and with small groups.

2. Systematic instruction and practice in language skills are based on children's needs as revealed in their purposeful language activities.

Although communication skills and abilities are best taught in context, there is need for follow-up, direct teaching, and practice to automatize the language skills. But these procedures are productive only after a need for the use of such skills has been demonstrated. Whenever a need for a specific skill or for correcting a definite error is evident, that is the time to present a developmental lesson or a suggestion leading to practice periods that help to internalize the skill. The direct teaching is on any of the language skills shown to be inadequately used. It is at this time that this textbook can contribute most effectively.

The time for systematic instruction will be discovered during observation and consultation. Discovery may occur during an individual conference or after reading notes jotted down when the teacher is observing children working in various learning centers. The important point is that time should be taken for specific teaching of the language skills currently needed in the activities as they are being carried out. Approached this way, direct language practice and teaching are not isolated but are closely related to children's actual experience in communication.

3. Language activities should evolve from children's actual need to communicate.

The need to communicate may arise out of any classroom experience or any school subject. Thus the teacher should always be alert to recognize every opportunity throughout the day for having children use the means of communication that are important to them. The more lifelike and natural the situation is, the wider is the variety of forms of communication that will be employed. In an integrated school program or through participation in broad instructional units, children have the opportunity for the *functional use* of every type of communication necessary in normal daily living. Such a program interrelates all aspects of the school day.

Language in School Activities

Up to the time that children start school, their entire life has, with little suppression, been one of experimenting with and practicing spoken language to build meanings out of experiences. But starting with the first grade, there is likely to be a change. At this point the teacher, faced with the necessity to give formal instruction, may almost immediately begin the intensive teaching of reading of printed symbols, thus limiting opportunity for spoken language. The spoken language that does occur in connection with reading may become word calling rather than meaningful interpretation of experiences. The symbols with which children are dealing in written language do not represent the thought of which they are capable. Only as the child at all levels of the elementary school is encouraged to continue self-expression through the spoken word is there in the classroom environment the raw material out of which refined written language evolves and multiple forms of creative expression emerge. Speaking and writing reinforce the reading program, and reading of good writing enriches the speaking and writing programs.

Reciprocal relationships of oracy and literacy skills in an instructional setting of the language experience approach were studied by Vivian E. Cox (1971). She used available research to guide the study toward the application of language-learning generalizations.

1. The linguistic competence that the child brings to school becomes the basis for elaboration and modification of further language learnings through instruction (Strickland, 1962; Loban, 1963; Menyuk, 1971).
2. Language learnings occur best in compulsory situations that require interaction between adults and children (Lefevre, 1970; Wilkinson, 1967).
3. Literacy is a reflection, a modification, and an extension of oracy (Ruddell, 1967; Wilkinson, 1967).
4. Natural constraints unique to the English language occur phonologically, syntactically, and morphologically (Naom Chomsky, 1965; Loban, 1963).
5. Reciprocal interrelationships exist between the receptive and productive components of language in terms of skills of recognition and prediction (Wilkinson, 1971; Cazden, 1968).
6. The sense of recognition and prediction comes from meaning-bearing patterns, not vocabulary. This sense is evident in every sentence (Smith, Goodman, and Meredith, 1970; Lefevre, 1964; Loban, 1963).
7. The focus on meaning-bearing patterns highlighting the form classes is more important than the focus on structure words which are roughly equivalent to words of highest frequency (Strickland, 1962; Lefevre, 1970).
8. The flexibility of usage of language patterns is more important

than the frequency of their occurrence (Strickland, 1962; Loban, 1963).

9. In language arts instruction the child's functional vocabulary is more important than his specific vocabulary (Lefevre, 1970; Naom Chomsky, 1965).

10. Experience in personal authorship builds bridges from oracy to the reading aspect of literacy (Hildreth, 1964; Burrows, Jackson, and Saunders, 1962).

11. Linguistic connections in the reading process are established through multiple auditory experiences which build an awareness and appreciation of the English language—its rhythms, tunes, and patterns (Strickland, 1969).

12. Success in language arts instruction is optimized in instructional programs that place equal emphasis on the interrelationships of the audiolingual and manual-visual processes (Stauffer and Hammond, 1967; Vilscek, Cleland, and Bilka, 1967).

A philosophy that revolves around the reciprocity of oracy and literacy skills implies that there will be a total communications program, not merely a few language lessons. The thinking that is involved in all classroom activities and the language that conveys it should be considered together. Many opportunities arise during the day for the development of language abilities, and the teacher has the choice in each instance of taking time at the moment or of setting aside another time for clarifying meanings, referring to language books, or doing necessary practice. In this way language development can be related directly to the ongoing activities of the classroom, and a language experience approach is implemented.

Improving Language Usage

Although a classroom may have an ongoing, all encompassing, and seemingly rich program in which language is related directly to the culture in the room, there will be islands of difficulty where stranded children need assistance. Children with handicaps of speech or hearing, those who are retarded, and children who come from non-English-speaking homes or homes of limited English usage may often need special help. For these children improvement in language will come largely through hearing good language spoken and through having many firsthand experiences that interest them and provide stimulation to speak and write, using the language that they possess and are extending. Oftentimes growth will seem to be unusually slow because of the difficulty of teaching in the face of a child's particular personal or environmental limitations. For the teacher this approach to the difficulty implies a unity of goals in language usage for all children but not a uniformity of instruction. It is this *unity* without *uniformity* that the language experience approach rationale seeks to illustrate.

A child's language will closely reflect the usage he encounters at home and in his neighborhood. To apply a single standard of usage to all children in a classroom is to overlook the fact that accepted usage varies among social groups; thus a child's usage will be right for him because it is the language of those who matter most to him. In spite of this variation, many children will rise above the language usage levels of their homes and neighborhoods. Part of this improvement will come about because of what happens in the classroom and because of the attitude of the teacher toward the nature of language. Improvement will continue to the extent that the learning environment of the children is one that stimulates the selection of personal goals within the evolving culture of the classroom. The culture will change as the learners have an opportunity to make intelligent choices from alternatives offered by the teacher and by instructional materials.

Children will improve in the mechanics of language when teaching provides them with meaningful experiences out of which their understandings can grow. This fact is apparent when we consider that in children's oral language the dynamics of meaning is usually sufficient to take care of the equivalent of punctuation. Most children punctuate well as they speak, but they need help in seeing how punctuation is written down to express differentiations in meaning. Similarly, sentence sense is more clearly related to a child's understanding of what he desires to say than to his knowledge of grammatical rules. The improvement of sentence sense is a goal of instruction for all children, while we may limit the teaching of the complexities of grammar as a discipline to those who use much writing as a medium of expression.

In addition to developing children's abilities in speaking and writing, we must teach for improvement in listening if we are to have a rich and balanced program of language development. Modern forms of communication make the ability to listen increasingly important. Listening experiences are no longer direct ones in which there is opportunity to react and ask questions, to test one's own understanding of what has been said, and to check the validity of the speaker's ideas. Today we habitually listen to remote sources, such as newscasts, which we can test only in our minds by critically evaluating ideas as we listen.

Reading is highlighted in a language experience approach—not as lessons in "learning how to," but in natural sequences of moving from seeing "talk written down" to doing independent writing, to comparing and contrasting one's own language in print to that of others, and then to using and enjoying the ideas and the language patterns of other authors. Much of the mechanics of the curriculum in traditional reading programs is dealt with in the writing program of a language experience approach. Writing with independence requires that the student know sound-symbol relationships, common patterns of spelling, syllabication, word order in sentences, and other aspects of language structure that have been assigned to *reading* because of the limited emphasis on writing in the curriculum. Significant progress in reading is not possible without these understandings of structure, but they are functional in instruction in written expression much more than they are in reading.

Sequence in School Language Programs

Reliance on mere language maturation is an inefficient and uneconomical way to approach language improvement. Rather, the teacher uses as a guide what has been learned through research and study about the language development of children.

Research by linguists interested in the relationships of language acquisition to reading and writing abilities continues to pile up evidence that it is futile to place children in highly organized reading instructional programs prior to their acquisition of oral language that includes basic structures reflected in reading material. Paula Menyuk (1969) and Carol Chomsky (1972) present evidence that language acquisition precedes reading of printed materials. Patricia Van Metre (1972) used the schemes developed by Carol Chomsky for judging levels of complexity of syntactical structure in a study of third-grade bilingual students. She found that both bilingual and monolingual children who scored in the bottom quartile on standardized reading achievement tests lacked a functional use of language that Chomsky (1969) found to be characteristic of most children by the age of five. Conversely, she found that bilingual and monolingual children who scored in the top quartile in reading achievement had, without exception, functional use of syntactical structures that are characteristic of most children by the age of ten.

Studies by Kellogg Hunt (1964) and others listed in Selected References of this chapter substantiate the point of view that a priority item in planning any language instructional program is planning for language acquisition. This view is in sharp contrast with programs that place recognition of printed words in a position of priority.

In this book some of what we know about language acquisition is presented in such a way that a sequence of language experiences, ranging from those requiring the least to those requiring increasing maturity and experience, is suggested for the teacher. This sequential guide does not suggest lessons as such but provides the teacher with a framework for screening suggestions from all sources and for evaluating progress in the process of maturing in language facility. An attempt is made to describe a sequence of language learnings that are intertwined with the thought processes of children. The philosophy is maintained throughout that the language and thought of children are inseparable. They emerge together. A little of one parallels the other, until they reach maturity side by side and are intertwined inseparably.

The experiences related in this book have been selected, not with the intent that the teacher will attempt to duplicate them in classroom teaching, but rather that they are rich with ideas for helping boys and girls improve their abilities in communication with a focus on reading and writing. The creative teacher will find innumerable ways to adapt and utilize ideas from materials presented here and will add to these by keeping a record of valuable experiences developed with students. The effectiveness of the language program depends on the creativeness with which the teacher uses ideas from this book and from other sources, on interest in and understanding of boys and girls in the class, and on continual striving to improve all aspects of communication.

Linguistic Principles for Teachers

Classroom teachers implementing the basic philosophy of a language experience approach in communication learn to function as linguists during the process of instruction. They become students of human speech. They learn to listen to variations in pronunciation and speech patterns. They manifest positive attitudes toward differences in speech. This method is in sharp contrast with attitudes and programs that tend to obscure or try to eliminate differences as if they were a plague.

A prime responsibility of the teacher is to illustrate and demonstrate continuously the relationships between speech and writing and reading. There is a central focus:

Speech is the language!

Writing is an imperfect representation of that speech!

Reading reconstructs the written portion of speech!

With this central focus there is a changed and changing attitude toward children and language. Those with limited language are valued as class members. Those whose first language is not English can illustrate differences and provide a learning environment for contrasting and comparing different ways of saying the same thing. Those with dialects that are significantly different from the language characteristic of school textbooks are helped to see unity in meanings (through speech) and at the same time to see wide gaps in spelling and reading.

Some aspects of language engendered by a linguist's attitude are identified in *Linguistics in the Elementary Classroom* (Los Angeles County Department of Education, 1965).

1. Language is a creative activity of each person.

The language of each person is a bit different from that of every other person in the world. Each child brings his different language to school. It is all he has. The teacher must value it and help him to understand how his oral language relates to written language. A learning environment with repeated opportunities for each child to contrast and compare personal language with that of other people is provided by teachers who have the attitude of a linguist.

2. Language patterns are well learned by the time a child is five or six.

Even though their grammar and pronunciation are usually faulty, children are using a variety of sentence patterns at the time they start school. Teachers listen to this variety of patterns and record it in writing. They talk about things that are alike and different in the way we talk. They do not attempt to control vocabularies for purposes of teaching a sight vocabulary. They avoid the use of materials that might cause regressive tendencies in children's language—materials such as preprimers of the basal series.

3. Language habits, once learned, change slowly.

Children do not change their oral language patterns as a result of lessons. Lessons are used to expose children to alternatives, but if any significant change is made, it will be made as a result of *choice*. Teachers with the attitude of a linguist work to provide intelligent choices for language change.

4. The writing system, or code of English, is alphabetic and has certain inadequacies.

The symbols used to reflect the sounds we make in talking do not have any sound in them. A linguist would never say "What sound does *b* make?" Human beings make the sounds of words and sentences, and each person has to develop understandings of how his sounds can be written.

Phonics is a language study that is flexible in the use of an alphabet to record human speech, not a study of a system that is the same for everybody. As children dictate and write in a language experience approach, they experience phonics in a functional setting, especially if from the beginning stages they are writing along with reading.

5. Language is changing continuously. It has a history.

Both meanings and pronunciations of words change. Children working with a linguist get excited about the changes and are interested in adding words to the English language. They learn that they can make up new words, say them, write them, and then test the writing to see if another person who has not heard the sound can reproduce it by looking at the printed form. This type of experience is fundamental phonics.

6. Language varies with age, socioeconomic group, and the geographic region of the speaker. This is dialect.

The use of a standard alphabet and standard spellings of words has not erased the dialects so widespread in our country. Dialects persist because there is not a one-to-one correspondence between the sounds of speech and the sounds represented by the symbols of the alphabet. There is a bit of difference which a linguist values in children, especially when exploratory spelling is a mirror of unusual dialects.

7. The concept of correctness is replaced by a concept of alternatives in pronunciation, word choice, phrasing, and construction.

When teachers view reading as an extension of personal language, they are not concerned with uniformity of self-expression. In the same sense that they value the variety of ideas reflected by children in their paintings, they value the variety of ways in which children say and write things. Gross errors in grammar are modified through ear training which includes listening to many voices talking and reading and extensive participation in unison and choral language experiences which permit children to try out new ways of saying things in full voice and with confidence that they will not be singled out for corrections. Many alternatives are available from which children can make correct choices. Each child, in effect, develops a wardrobe of languages—one suitable for home, one for school, and one for the peer group.

Selected References

Ainsfeld, Moashe. "Language and Nature in the Young Child." In *The Psycholinguistic Nature of the Reading Process,* edited by Kenneth Goodman. Wayne State University Press, Detroit, 1969.

Berko, Jean. "The Child's Learning of English Morphology." In *Psycholinguistics: A Book of Readings,* edited by S. Sapoeta. Holt, Rinehart and Winston, New York, 1961.

Burrows, Alvina, Doris Jackson, and Dorothy Saunders. *They All Want to Write.* Prentice-Hall, Englewood Cliffs, N.J., 1962.

Cazden, C. "Three Sociolinguistic Views of the Language and Speech of Lower Class Children—With Special Attention to the Work of Basil Bernstein," *Developmental Medicine and Child Neurology,* 10 (October, 1968), 600–611.

Chomsky, Carol. *The Acquisition of Syntax in Children from 5 to 10.* Research Monograph No. 57. The M.I.T. Press, Cambridge, Mass., 1969.

———. "Stages in Language Development and Reading Exposure," *Harvard Educational Review,* 42, 1 (February, 1972), 1–33.

Chomsky, Naom. *Aspects of the Theory of Syntax.* The M.I.T. Press, Cambridge, Mass., 1965.

Cox, Vivian E. "Reciprocal Oracy/Literacy Recognition Skills in the Language Production of Language Experience Approach Students." (Ed.D. dissertation.) University of Arizona, Tucson, 1971.

Durkin, Dolores. *Phonics, Linguistics and Reading.* Teachers College Press, New York, 1972.

Eisenhardt, Catheryn. *Applying Linguistics in the Teaching of Reading and the Language Arts.* Charles E. Merrill, Columbus, Ohio, 1972.

Goodman, Kenneth S., and James T. Fleming (eds.). *Psycholinguistics and the Teaching of Reading.* International Reading Association, Newark, 1968.

Hildreth, Gertrude. "Linguistic Factors in Early Reading Instruction," *The Reading Teacher,* 18 (December, 1964), 172–178.

Hunt, Kellogg W. *Grammatical Structures Written at Three Grade Levels.* NCTE Research Report No. 3. National Council of Teachers of English, Urbana, Ill., 1964.

Labov, William. *The Study of Nonstandard English.* National Council of Teachers of English, Urbana, Ill., 1970.

Lefevre, Carl A. *Linguistics and the Teaching of Reading.* McGraw-Hill Book Co., New York, 1964.

———. *Linguistics, English and the Language Arts.* Allyn & Bacon, Boston, 1970.

Loban, Walter D. *The Language of Elementary School Children.* NCTE Research Report No. 1. National Council of Teachers of English, Urbana, Ill., 1963.

Los Angeles County Department of Education. *Linguistics in the Elementary Classroom.* Los Angeles County Superintendent of Schools Office, Los Angeles, 1965.

McNeill, David. *The Acquisition of Language: The Study of Developmental Psycholinguistics.* Harper & Row, New York, 1970.

Menyuk, Paula. *Sentences Children Use.* The M.I.T. Press, Cambridge, Mass., 1969.

———. *The Acquisition and Development of Language.* Prentice-Hall, Englewood Cliffs, N.J., 1971.

Ruddell, Robert B. "Oral Language and the Development of Other Language Skills," *Research in Oral Language,* edited by Walter T. Petty. National Council of Teachers of English, Urbana, Ill., 1967.

Smith, E. Brooks, Kenneth Goodman, and Robert Meredith. *Language and Thinking in the Elementary School.* Holt, Rinehart and Winston, New York, 1970.

Stauffer, Russell G., and W. Dorsey Hammond. "The Effectiveness of Language Arts and Basic Reader Approaches to First Grade Reading Instruction," *The Reading Teacher,* 20 (May, 1967), 740–746.

Strickland, Ruth G. *The Language of Elementary School Children: Its Relationship to the Language of Reading Textbooks and the Quality of Reading of Selected Children.* Bulletin of the School of Education, Indiana University, Bloomington, 1962.

———. "Children's Language and Their Reading." In *Some Approaches to Reading,* edited by Nila B. Smith and Ruth G. Strickland. Association for Childhood Education International, Washington, D.C., 1969.

Van Metre, Patricia. "Syntactic Characteristics of Selected Bilingual Children." (Ed.D. dissertation.) University of Arizona, Tucson, 1972.

Vigotsky, L. S. *Thought and Language.* The M.I.T. Press, Cambridge, Mass., 1962.

Vilscek, Elaine C., Donald L. Cleland, and Louise Bilka. "Coordinating and Integrating Language Arts Instruction," *The Reading Teacher*, 21 (October, 1967), 10.

Wilkinson, Andrew M. "Oracy in English Teaching," *Elementary English*, 45 (October, 1967), 743–747.

———. *The Foundations of Language*. Oxford University Press, London, 1971.

Children learn best what they want to learn. The teacher's task, then, is to work on the wants of children—to create in each child the desire to know and the desire to act on knowledge. Teaching with this orientation is the art of improving children's sensitivity to their human and physical environment so that they can see more, hear more, feel more—discover the extraordinary in the ordinary—and so that they can communicate their thoughts with the clarity, the enthusiasm, the versatility, and the exactness that interest an audience.

Most children do not learn something before they have developed an interest in it through personal experience. Some degree of meaning must be present before a child can add new meanings, especially those meanings that are technical or that come from printed materials.

We therefore take advantage of children's natural curiosity which is present and operating all the time. Of equal importance is remembering that each child has a natural language, faulty as it may be, and that new language learnings must be related to *that natural language*.

Because of the wide range of natural language abilities expressed in an assortment of dialects, it is impossible to propose a standard program in communication skills and abilities for children of any age or grade level. Rather, it is the responsibility of the professional worker in education to be familiar with the wide range of possibilities for dealing with children. No matter what skills and abilities are selected for emphasis or what experiences are introduced into the learning environment, they should be for the purpose of helping each child develop competence to

    ——communicate effectively with others

    ——progress successfully in school

    ——meet efficiently those tasks involving speaking and writing in daily living and in life-lifting situations

    ——use effectively the listening and reading opportunities to compare and contrast her or his own ideas and language with those of others.

Concepts for the Child

The *one big responsibility* of a teacher at any level of instruction is to help each child to conceptualize, to habituate, and to internalize a few truths about self and language. Some of these truths are enumerated in the *Teacher's Resource Guide, Language Experiences in Reading, Level I* (Allen, 1974).

I can think about what I have experienced and imagined.

Experience and elaboration of experience beyond reality are foundations on which communication is built. There can never be any *reading*—or writing, speaking, or listening—apart from an experiential background which furnishes

——a sound system—phonological structure
——an ordering of the sound system—syntactical structure
——a system of selecting clues to meaning—morphological structure
——personal meanings derived from total life experiences
——semantics.

All of these conditions are met in normal life prior to any attempt to develop literate skills of reading and writing.

I can talk about what I think about.

The thoughts and the meanings behind the thinking of each child become the basic ingredient for a program of improving communication in multiple forms of expression. The thoughts and the language of other people will, it is hoped, influence the learners as they hear stories and develop independent reading abilities, but they are not basic to the beginnings of new literacy. Meanings are inside—not outside—the learner. They are always present and seek expression through human sound mechanism.

What I can talk about I can express in some other form.

The forms for the expression of ideas vary a great deal, but in most school situations they are illustrated as children talk, write, paint, dramatize, model, and construct. Some of these same forms are used to reproduce the ideas of other people through specific assignments, but such activities are in another category of conceptualization. Painting and writing remain the most used and the most personal forms of recording meanings from speech, but all other forms are important and necessary if most of the children are successful in improving communication.

Anything I record I can recall through speaking or reading.

Experiences with body motion, art media, and writing with the letters of the alphabet help children to recognize that one form of expression is much more precise than the others and gives more specific clues about the thinking of its creator. *Good writing*—with wide-range vocabulary and skillful use of figurative language—conveys meanings that are almost identical with those intended by the author. But the abilities required for effective written communication do not emerge from lessons. They emerge as each child moves back and forth between writing and the less specific media of communication—painting, drawing, dramatization, role-playing, construction, rhythms, and others—and the whole development is hinged on oral communication that originates with the desire of a thinking individual to share his ideas.

I can read what I can write by myself and what other people write for me to read.

Once children arrive at the point at which personal writing without copying occurs, reading that writing becomes a natural, automatic language experience. The thoughts are theirs, the language patterns are natural and normal, and the total vocabulary is familiar. It is from this type of personal writing experience that the reading of what others have written can be launched successfully and enthusiastically. Regardless of dialect differences, most of the words used by children and by other authors will be the same. The major differences that occur are in the positions in sentences of form-class words—nouns, verbs, adjectives, and adverbs. Once children recognize the similarities in their writing to that of others, they lose the fear of not being able to reproduce verbatim the language of others. They view reading as a communicating experience with persons not present.

The children who from the beginning relate speaking, listening, and writing to the reading process are the ones who can carry on a conversation with an author, listening inwardly to what is said, agreeing and disagreeing, accepting and rejecting ideas, and integrating their own ideas with those of the author. Thus, for them, *reading* is not a separate study in school but a natural part of activities dealing with sending and receiving messages: *communication*.

As I talk and write, I use some words over and over and some not so often.

Most children enter school with a large speaking vocabulary. They use the words of highest frequency in the language with ease and with a variety of meanings. The control of the words of high frequency, which has been practiced in reader series in recent years, is a control of the vocabulary that most children use with great ease, flexibility, and confidence. These words tend to be the *structure words* of English—all those that are not *form-class words*. Approximately three hundred of these words cluster at the top of any list of rank order based on frequency of use (Carroll, Davies, and Richman, 1971). The instructional task is not one of control but one of helping children to
——recognize the visual forms of the words they use naturally through observing language recorded when presented in dictation
——realize that all in the class tend to use many of the same words
——recognize that all people who write use the same words in talking and writing.

As I talk and write, I use some words and clusters of words to express my meanings.

Most of the meanings in language are conveyed by words that name things, express motion, action, or both, and describe by limiting or expanding color, size, shape, texture, sound, taste, smell, feeling, contrast, and comparison.[1]
Most words in these classes can be shifted to different slots in sentences to express different meanings.
He fell on the ski *run.*
The new car *runs* quietly.

---

[1] Roach Van Allen and Claryce Allen, *Language Experiences in Early Childhood,* Encyclopaedia Britannica Educational Corp., Chicago, 1969.

The *runny* syrup was supposed to be jelly.

Children who acquire a wide-range vocabulary of nouns, verbs, adjectives, and adverbs through personal use develop abilities to predict their use in reading materials because of inherent meanings. They can check their predictions as soon as they know sound-symbol relationships of initial letters in words, some common endings, and some high-frequency phonograms (-*in*, -*it*, -*on*, -*or*, -*at*, and others). By adding *predictive skills* to *recognition skills,* they increase speed and efficiency in the reading process (Wilkinson, 1971).

**As I write to represent the sounds I make through speech,
I use the same symbols (letters) over and over.**

Teaching children to symbolize their speech sounds rather than trying to get them to assign a sound or sounds to symbols selected by the teacher is to use an experience approach to teaching phonetic elements of the language. This method is a way of recognizing in practice that every human being communicates by means of a unique sound system. No two are identical. Every person who writes must relate print to speech and then see relationships to an infinite number of variations. Phonetic understandings are developed from a "say it" to a "see it" sequence. This sequence ensures that the understandings are applied to the *real language experiences* of each individual, including skills in listening, speaking, word recognition, and spelling.

**Each letter of the alphabet stands for one or more sounds
that I make when I talk.**

At first the teacher records the oral language of individuals toward developing this understanding. As children write independently, this understanding matures to the point of including the many variations inherent in the English language. The variable phonetic system of English requires that children learn the elements of phonics by use of procedures that emphasize the *oral* prior to the *written* aspects of the language. As they begin to recognize that every word begins with a sound that can be written with a letter or letters, the children experience a breakthrough to the magic realm of reading and writing. Their learnings continue as they develop an awareness of such language characteristics as common word endings, syllables, consonant blends, digraphs, diphthongs, and other aspects of word structure. These understandings become a long-range learning experience which continues unfinished throughout life (Durkin, 1972).

As I read, I must add to what an author has written if I am to get full meaning and inherent pleasure from print.

Usually there is more to a story or poem than is written. Written forms have always been imperfect representations of what an author knows and feels.

If an author was telling a story, he would add to it, supplying sound effects, hand movements, facial expressions, and intonations which are impossible to print but which enhance the written form. To add these dimensions is the responsibility of the reader. The ability to add these pleasures to reading comes not from direct lessons but from repeated experiences in personal writing which are extended into story telling, dramatization, choral speaking, pantomime, and discussions.

Concepts for the Teacher

It is not enough for the teacher to begin by helping each child to conceptualize a few simple truths about language in the communication process (Hodges and Rudorf, 1972). Every teacher has a fundamental responsibility to establish a conceptual framework as a guide in selecting activities, experiences, materials, and evaluation procedures. This framework will guide him or her in establishing goals for individuals without losing the unity of the instructional program. Lack of uniformity becomes a diminishing problem when the teacher works within a conceptual framework such as the following one.

The basis of children's oral and written expression is their sensitivity to their environment both within the classroom and in the world at large.

The continuing responsibility of the teacher is to help children at all levels of ability to be increasingly aware of the world in which they live—to listen, to talk about it, to observe it in many ways, to write about it, and to represent their feelings and their facts with many media.

Freedom in self-expression—oral and written—leads to self-confidence in all language usage including grammar, punctuation, capitalization, and spelling.

When children work with and rework their own language, they gain significantly in understanding the strengths and weaknesses of that language. The reworking of other people's language in the form of exercises makes little or no difference in the self-expression aspects of language.

Skills such as letter formation, word recognition, spelling and phonics, and style and form can be developed more meaningfully from the child's own language than from a continuous round of exercises using someone else's. The raw materials of language instruction, then, must come from the natural language of each child.

A natural flow of language develops in children engaged in programs of instruction based on personal patterns and meaningful vocabulary.

The flow proceeds in steps like the following.
   ——Children's written expression flows easily from their oral expression. At first experiences are recorded as they dictate to the teacher or another adult and observe the process of making reading from talk.
   ——Motivation for improving language form and usage comes as children's writing is published in books, magazines, and newspapers for others to read.
   ——As children continue to write, their forms of expression are influenced by the things they read and by expressions they relate in storytelling, dramatization of stories, and choral speaking. Good reading material leads to good language usage.

Interaction, the only process through which language matures, is promoted through the use of numerous activities, experiences, and devices.

Activities such as making class books, listening to stories, storytelling, sharing, dictating to each other, and writing in patterns of simple poetry help children build confidence in expanding ideas and in refining language skills (Moffett, 1973). The classroom is viewed as a *laboratory* of language experiences extending through the day. Good experiences add depth of meaning to social studies, raise thoughtful questions in science, individualize interpretations in art and music, promote accuracy in mathematics, and provide freedom of expression in creative writing. Language is the cement that holds the total curriculum together. The classroom is truly a laboratory for experimenting with and exploring language.

Utilization of the child's own language as one of the bases for reading instruction results in a high degree of independence in writing and reading.

At all levels of the elementary school, children should have frequent opportunities to read their own writing to the total class, to small groups within the class, and to other groups within the school.

When children are reading their own writing, the concept load of the reading material is reduced to zero. In preparation for oral reading, they can devote their energies to clarity of expression, effectiveness of presentation, interpretation of punctuation, and other details necessary in good reading. During the process sensitivity to well-written materials of others increases and appreciation for our best authors develops.

How children view themselves during the process of acquiring reading skills and attitudes does make a difference in the level and the quality of achievement. How teachers view relationships of language acquisition to reading achievement makes a difference in the development of a learning environment and in the selection of teaching strategies and materials.

A Classroom in Action

Molly Baker has a language-centered class. She believes that if children are to communicate effectively and efficiently, they must first be helped to recognize that language is useful. Various activities can give children experience of language's usefulness. Talking and dictating give depth of meaning to art and construction activities. Listening, viewing, discussing, making books, and reporting convey the meanings in social studies, science, and mathematics. Planning, learning new words and new meanings of old words, talking, and careful listening add spirit to singing songs and playing games.

To achieve her goal of demonstrating to children the usefulness of language, Molly Baker has simple guidelines:

——variety of activities to assure success

——direct teaching of language recognition skills

——influence on children from outside-of-self sources to be utilized

——structure through learning centers.

She knows that for any planning period—usually one week for her—she should choose some activities from Strand One, featuring ideas and the natural language of the learners, some activities from Strand Two, featuring language study, and some activities from Strand Three, featuring language and other communication devices available through books, art prints, photographs, films, recordings, music, and sculpture.

Variety of Self-expression Opportunities

Each day there is opportunity for some children to engage in oral sharing on topics of purely personal interest. What is shared may or may not be related to ongoing lessons in social studies and in sciences. Molly Baker feels that each time children assume responsibility for sharing their ideas they may be revealing interests and extending responsibility as group members.

Boys and girls engage in discussions every day. They respond and react to each other and to the rich environment of the classroom. In this setting Ms. Baker is alert to identify topics that seem of interest to many children. She never lets a week pass without devoting some time to the development of more and more mature discussion skills. The discussion topics come from her observation and from items of current interest suggested by the children.

In the discussion situation Ms. Baker is not asking questions and seeking responses. Rather, she is developing a talking-listening situation in which she is seeking interaction between pupils and between pupils and teacher. She helps the children to see that as they make contributions, they may have to alter their ideas as new information is brought out by others. This requires each participant to be a careful listener to all contributions. Listening is a more mature skill than is just answering questions.

Ms. Baker recognizes the value of developing oral discussion skills as a base for writing and reading. Children gain confidence and the ability to develop a theme or topic orally as she helps them to conceptualize along these lines.

———*Writing is a record of oral language.* If they can talk about something, they can write about it. She illustrates this point by taking dictation or by summarizing a discussion on the chalkboard or on a chart.

———*Reading is often a discussion experience with a person not present.* We listen with our inner mechanisms to what the absent author has to say. In between the lines we agree or disagree, change our minds, extend our information, enjoy, and add our own experiences to those of the author. As she reads to children, Ms. Baker seeks responses that help them to feel that they are having a discussion with the author.

In planned discussions the teacher is in a good position to help children clear up some of the gross errors in speech patterns, especially in the use of common words. At a planned discussion time, Ms. Baker feels that her role as far as correcting is concerned is different from the role she plays when children are engaged in oral sharing on a purely personal basis.

Molly Baker encourages children to write their thoughts. She helps them to feel that the only limitation on writing is their speaking and thinking ability. If they can think about something, they can talk about it. If they talk about it, they can say the same thing in writing. What they write makes reading material for themselves and others.

In this way language is visualized, and reading vocabularies are extended beyond the level of controlled vocabulary presented in most reading material developed for young children. Their own stories are true and make-believe, fact and fantasy, poetry and prose. The offerings of the children are collected in books for the Reading/Research Center.

About once each month the children in Ms. Baker's classroom publish a magazine. It represents the kind of writing that children can do on their own. The magazine is managed by a staff of editors and reporters elected each month. They collect the copy for their assigned sections such as stories, poems, pictures, puzzles, art, fashions, jokes and riddles, news, and any others that an editor is interested in developing.

No specific time is set aside for the production of magazine material. The editors tell the class something of what they have in mind, and invite contributions by anyone interested. They attempt to use all contributions and edit them carefully. They do not change the ideas and the special way a child might say something, but they do try to keep a high standard of correctness in their magazine.

Even though all the children like to write, they enjoy expressing their ideas in other ways, too. A favorite choice is painting at the easels. Four easels are ready for work all through the day. Often a child who cannot think of anything to write begins painting, and an idea emerges. After the painting there is something to say or write. Ms. Baker has found that children who talk and write in relation to their paintings tend to paint with more purpose and produce things meaningful to others. Paintings are displayed in a prominent place for others to enjoy and interpret.

Teaching of Language Skills for Mastery

Molly Baker does not have a regular plan or any semblance of a schedule when she does direct teaching of the relationships between skills of writing and reading. Rather, she tries to keep in mind some instructional guides appropriate for young children and teaches as opportunities arise.

There is a strong conviction that if specific word-recognition skills are developed, they must emerge as a natural language experience. The technical aspects of the skills must be subordinate to the role of helping support the major concepts and generalizations about them. These theories must be observed and discussed because individuals are having personal language experiences requiring their application.

In Ms. Baker's case the word-recognition skills that some children (but not all) are expected to cope with each year include:

——recognition that some words are alike, some words begin alike, and some words have the same endings

——ability to use the names of letters of the alphabet in talking about writing words

——ability to recognize one's name in print

——ability to recognize most of the words of highest frequency wherever they are found

——ability to write or dictate one's ideas in a variety of ways and for a variety of purposes

——recognition of some of the words in the environment—popular brand names used in advertising, signs in the community, names of stores in shopping centers, labels in the classroom, and simple captions that are obvious

——read with some independence simple stories and patterned poetry.

Ms. Baker wants each child to perceive of *self* as a reader and a writer as well as a speaker and a listener. She makes charts of cutout words that many children are sure to recognize, and has a reading time that assures success for all.

Some of the oral reading time is spent in pointing out interesting words authors use to describe things that they are writing about. Ms. Baker discusses the variety of ways in which authors begin sentences, their use of more than one descriptive word at a time, their use of action words, and other aspects of good language that might be used by children. She believes very deeply that children should live in a classroom with wide-range vocabulary as a part of their experience. In these ways she balances any influence that might come from the use of controlled vocabulary readers.

Influences from Outside-of-self Sources

Ms. Baker reads something from good literature to the class each day. She suggests that the children listen for a variety of purposes other than for simple comprehension. She expects a quality of feedback that is not typical of workbook questions and answers. The children are encouraged to make responses recalling their own everyday experiences. They share their hopes and desires as a result of listening. Their imaginations are heightened as they project themselves into fuller ranges of thought under the guidance of a good author who uses words in ways that are not characteristic of their home language.

Ms. Baker tells stories that serve as an example of how authors begin a story, develop a plot, and come to an ending. She also reads stories suitable for children to retell. As she works with children on storytelling, she gives them real experience in expressing ideas in thought units, using colorful and descriptive language, developing ideas in sequence, choosing good action words, and reproducing words, phrases, and sentences used by other authors. All of these experiences are essential for success in reading print for meaning. She is convinced that a child who cannot tell a story is a very poor risk for success in reading one.

In one corner of the room is a "secret place" where children may record stories that they have read or written. When a child is ready to record, he or she hangs out a sign that announces, "Quiet Please, Recording." When the sign is hung out, everyone is exceptionally quiet.

At the end of the day recordings are played back. The children listen to the stories very intently and comment on such things as good sentences, story content, oral expression, choice of words, new words that have never been used in a story in the room before, and the interpretation of someone else's language to make the stories sound real.

Children enjoy sharing ideas gained from reading by visualizing a story in a series of colored slides made from their own paintings and drawings. Pictures are mounted on cardboard of the same size for the photography. Some children write a summary of the story and read it as the pictures are projected on the screen. Others tell the story without any script. Sometimes several children work together and read the parts of characters. Other times they tell stories, using the same set of pictures. They try to see how many different stories they can find in the same pictures.

The thrill of seeing the pictures enlarged on the screen seems to be incentive to enlarge on the story itself—to read between the lines. Children who are reluctant to write a story of any length find that they can retell stories that interest the class and are satisfying to themselves.

Structure That Opens Up Communication

Within the classroom organization she has developed, Molly Baker uses multiple resources to open up communication for all children. Some of her plans are listed here. (See Figure 4, page 88.)

1. Major language goals are selected for a minimum of one week of emphasis. They are chosen from the three major strands of a language experience approach.
2. Activities relating to the goals are developed for four to six learning centers.
3. Learning centers that need to be activated or continued are identified, and necessary materials are listed.
4. Some type of evaluation is planned for each stated goal.
5. The type of teacher-pupil contact best suited for each activity is identified.

6. Lesson plan sheets are charted to check
    ——the extent to which the twenty language experiences of the rationale have been included over a period of four to six weeks
    ——the variety of activities planned in terms of the needs of children to work with other children and with the teacher
    ——the frequency of change in learning centers needed to keep them interesting to children who learn the stated objectives with ease
    ——the extent to which evaluation procedures deal with the stated goals for instruction
    ——the use made of new ideas, new materials, and fresh, creative experiences.

Selected References

Allen, Roach Van. *Teacher's Resource Guide, Language Experiences in Reading, Level I.* Encyclopaedia Britannica Educational Corp., Chicago, 1974.

Austin, David F., Velma B. Clark, and Gladys W. Fitchett. *Reading Rights for Boys: Sex Role and Development in Language Experiences.* Appleton-Century-Crofts, New York, 1971.

Carroll, John B., Peter Davies, and Barry Richman. *Word Frequency Book.* Houghton Mifflin Co., Boston, 1971.

Durkin, Dolores. *Phonics, Linguistics, and Reading.* Teachers College Press, New York, 1972.

Hodges, Richard E., and E. Hugh Rudorf. *Language and Learning to Read: What Teachers Should Know about Language.* Houghton Mifflin Co., Boston, 1972.

Lamy, M. W. "Relationship of Self-Perception of Early Primary Children to Achievement in Reading." In *Human Development: Readings in Research,* edited by I. J. Gordon. Scott, Foresman and Co., Chicago, 1965.

Lee, Dorris M., and Roach Van Allen. *Learning to Read Through Experience.* Appleton-Century-Crofts, New York, 1963.

Moffett, James. *A Student-Centered Language Arts Curriculum.* Houghton Mifflin Co., Boston, 1973.

Purkey, William W. *Self-Concept and School Achievement.* Prentice-Hall, Englewood Cliffs, N.J., 1970.

Quandt, Ivan. *Self-Concept and Reading.* International Reading Association, Newark, 1972.

Wilkinson, Andred M. *The Foundation of Language.* Oxford University Press, London, 1971.

Zimet, Sara Goodman. *What Children Read in School.* Grune & Stratton, New York, 1972.

The central idea of classroom organization for a language experience approach to communication is constant alertness to ways of realizing the possibilities each child has for communicating. These possibilities are countless: hearing self and others saying things and reading the "talk" of others; writing and appreciating the authorship of others; painting and understanding the ideas and feelings of others who have painted; and reading orally and silently to interpret the ideas and feelings of authors.

The goals of the approach can be achieved only by those who use multiple methods and materials (1) to help each child experience communication in a variety of situations, (2) to study the aspects of communication that produce refinement, and (3) to relate the communicated ideas of others to personal experiences.

Closed systems of organization required of highly organized and highly structured programs cannot be used because they devalue the personal language of the learner in favor of language from outside sources which are already selected, printed, and purchased. For this reason it is important that anyone who embraces the philosophy of a language experience approach understand some of the fundamental requirements of planning and organization, although no one can tell another *exactly* how to develop a language experience approach classroom.

Each teacher must come to grips in a personal way with
——the basic philosophy
——the curriculum rationale
——the learning center organization
——the use of multiple materials.

He or she must sort out those aspects of the program that can be implemented with the fewest violations of the basic goals. Decisions and choices are made after consideration of human values inherent in the growth of communication abilities. Time to consider, to reflect, and to evaluate is needed. Independence to create something different, to compare and contrast, and to arrive at valid conclusions is necessary.

An organization that promotes communication is one that balances like a mobile in motion constantly. For every emphasis on creative self-expression there is a balance of studying specific skills that enhance communication. For every product of the individuals in the classroom there is an influence from outside sources that reflects excellence.

Language Laboratory Organization

Children's communication skills, including word-recognition skills, are developed through numerous activities, experiences, and devices. To increase the chances of success for more children, every teacher must know and use multiple ways of working with class groups and individuals.

The classroom is operated as a language laboratory that functions throughout the day and involves language learning in all curriculum areas. The laboratory is characterized by two major streams of organization: (1) *direct teaching* activities in which the teacher assumes responsibility for identifying and extending language concepts, and (2) *learning centers* where children can go by choice or by assignment to engage in many forms of self-expression. Some activities should bring them in contact with the ideas of other people communicated in many ways. Others should be open to their own ideas and ways of expressing them.

The two major streams are interwoven in actual practice because one is impossible without the other. Direct teaching of a set of language skills should usually be extended and exercised in one or more of the learning centers. On the other hand, observation of student performance in the learning centers will often suggest skills and abilities that need to be called to the attention of the whole class or of a small group. The individual work and the small group work necessary to the program are possible only in an environment that provides for ongoing learning centers for children who are not involved in the direct teaching experience. Some learning centers are established as continuing centers for the school year; others are temporary for a special study or season. Some that are used most of the time are:

——Discussion Center
——Arts and Crafts Center
——Cooking Center
——Discovery Center
——Music Center
——Dramatization Center
——Game Center
——Language Study Center
——Reading/Research Center
——Viewing/Listening Center
——Writing/Publishing Center
——A Quiet Place.

Learning Centers for a Language Laboratory

The *Discussion Center* is an idea as much as it is a place. It is the center where the teacher is usually in charge, and it may be activated several times a day. It is a time for the teacher

  ——to demonstrate new games and other activities before they are placed in the learning centers

  ——to introduce new patterned language selections and practice them with the group before the activities are placed in the learning centers

  ——to read to children from children's literature and to discuss the ways in which authors express their ideas

  ——to stimulate children to discuss topics of interest, and to hear their responses in a large group setting.

Children use the Discussion Center as a place

  ——to read creative productions to the class

  ——to show paintings and other art products

  ——to present plays and other forms of dramatization developed in other learning centers

  ——to share personal ideas and experiences, using their home-rooted language in a friendly setting without fear of ridicule.

The teacher and the children together use the Discussion Center as a time and place to evaluate progress and participation. Together they might decide

  ——how to improve the movement of pupils from center to center

  ——how to increase participation in playing games

  ——how to find characters for dramatizations that are to be produced

  ——how to reduce the level of noise during activities

  ——how to take care of housekeeping activities.

The Discussion Center is such a vital part of the learning center organization that there is limited value in developing other centers with activities unless there is a Discussion Center that permits the teacher and the children to keep the organization running smoothly. A teacher who opens up learning opportunities to all children through dispersal of those activities throughout the environment must have a time and place to keep information flowing and movement under control.

The *Arts and Crafts Center* is a vital ingredient in the language-learning environment. It serves as a launching pad for oral language expression. From oral language comes writing and reading in natural, personal forms. Ideas never expressed before germinate as children apply paint to paper, model with clay, cut and tear paper, and arrange a variety of materials into a collage. Ideas that are difficult, if not impossible, for many children to gain from reading are grasped in paintings, sculpture, and crafts. These ideas, once spoken, are basic to further development of writing and reading.

The activities of the Arts and Crafts Center are recreational in many cases and should be done for the sheer pleasure of the doing. These do not have any planned language follow-up activities.

The Arts and Crafts Center must be a treasure house of creative materials that are available for the children and the teacher. Essential materials should be provided by the school; other materials are furnished by the children and their parents from items that are usually thrown away.

Art exists in all aspects of the learning environment and is not just one place in the classroom. It is a part of the Writing Publishing Center when books are being illustrated. It is in the Dramatization Center when puppets are being made and costumes are being created. It is a part of the Game Center when activities are being illustrated, and can be a part of all the other centers as they are developed to be visually attractive.

The *Cooking Center* more than any other language development center assures the use of words of all the major classifications—names of things, how things move, the descriptive categories of color, size, shape, sound, smell, taste, touch, emotions, contrast, and comparison. These words linked with the structure words of English assure a full language-learning environment when cooking is used as a language enrichment activity.

High motivation is built into cooking activities. Children are anxious to participate and get involved in follow-up language experience as well as in the tasting and eating activities. They will read recipes for exact meanings and will follow the sequence of ideas presented because they learn that not to do so will yield failure in the product.

Cooking is an activity in which parents can be involved in a meaningful way. They can supervise activities and check on pupil participation. Also, they can demonstrate the preparation of foods indigenous to their ethnic groups.

The Cooking Center produces opportunities for eating together and for the development of the language of courtesy and manners. Children can invite parents, school personnel, and other groups to share the foods they prepare. In doing this, they learn to entertain others in conversational settings.

The *Discovery Center* highlights the acquisition of the language used by scientists, engineers, architects, musicians, artists, teachers, and other people whose work is dependent on their views of how people and their physical environment are related. This center always features the language of the names of things, of how things move, and of all descriptive categories. In addition it encourages the acquisition of the language of contrast and comparison as children look at things from new perspectives.

The Discovery Center needs a variety of materials and locations. It can be inside with microscope and magnifying glass for students to look at collections of plants, insects, and minerals. It can be outside where students can observe clouds, the effect of wind, rain, the motion of machines, the sounds of nature and of machines, and the natural habitat of birds and insects. At all times there should be a discovery box or bag containing things for children to shake, rattle, feel, and listen to. They can guess how many, what shape, the texture, and the contents of the box or bag. At times the Discovery Center can be closely related to the Cooking Center and the Music Center.

The *Music Center* is where the rhythm and rhyme of poetry forms might be introduced with drums or sticks that can be used to beat out the rhythm of language. Any assortment of materials to excite curiosity is appropriate.

The *Dramatization Center* gives children repeated opportunities to try out new ways of thinking about themselves and others. They pretend to be characters that they have heard or read about, and assume the language of those characters. This acting requires the use of language structures and vocabularies that can never be characteristic of normal conversation and discussion; yet it involves the language of reading materials which will be encountered over and over.

The Dramatization Center should be located where there is some storage in shelves or in boxes. Hats, shoes, masks, tools, puppets, and other items permit children to change characters in a flash. Children are encouraged to play school, fly an airplane, fly into space, and be a barber, a nurse, a medical doctor, a beauty parlor operator, an auto mechanic, or any other character that gives them an opportunity to use informal language in new settings. Puppets must be available to encourage children to try out sounds and expressions not typical of their normal conversation.

The production of shows in a puppet theater brings children together to plan and form friendships through cooperation and rehearsals. The use of the puppet theater also provides a functional setting for extending the work of a group of children to others as they invite parents, school personnel, and different class groups to view their productions. Recognition of this type of activity strengthens the self-image of children and permits language to grow in multiple ways.

The *Game Center* is a place where children reinforce many skills that are introduced in other settings. It is where there is a great deal of disciplined language learning and where the discipline of behavior is practiced within a recreational setting.

Wide-range ability grouping is useful in the Game Center so that children who already know a language skill can play with those who need specific help in order to learn the games. Games to practice language skills might include classification games, racing games with a master board and spinner, sets of cards games, and puzzles of all kinds.

Some of the games are produced commercially, and others are made by the teacher, the children, and parents. When children make their own, in the process they give attention to specific details and purposes and organize the information so that it can be understood by others. A level of correctness not typical of most activities for children is required.

Making and playing games creates in the learning environment a spirit of mutual helpfulness and friendship. These activities serve as an outlet for creative expression and satisfy needs of many children to engage in some successful endeavor each day.

Children in upper grades who need to review basic language facts of reading and spelling can learn to play games and become the tutors of young children who need supervision in order to play.

A *Language Study Center* in the learning environment is a place where a wide range of activities is available for exploration and practice. The materials for direct instruction are usually introduced in the Discussion Center and then placed in the Language Study Center for assignments. They remain there for self-selection.

This center deals with many skills and attitudes toward language. A major category is *word study*. Emphasis is on abilities to anticipate the pronunciation and meaning of words through context clues, root words with affixes, letter combinations that occur frequently, other phonetic skills, and use of aids similar to dictionaries.

Another major category of activities at this center deals with *lan-*

guage structure. Emphasis is on abilities to anticipate meanings from clues in sentences, paragraphs, chapters, and stories (sequence of events).

A Language Study Center provides continuing opportunities for the acquisition of a sight vocabulary of structure words and at the same time undergirds the need to anticipate the place of nouns, verbs, and descriptive words in English sentences. This emphasis might be considered *functional grammar* in contrast with formal grammar studies.

The center can be a place in the room where children go to do their assigned work in language study, or it may be a place where they can check out materials and do the work in any part of the classroom.

The *Reading/Research Center* is central to the operation of the program and is usually a highly visible one. Its purposes are to furnish a variety of materials for children to browse and read and to provide stimulating activities for children to engage in for practice and review of basic reading skills.

The teacher's conference with a child about reading is related to the center. Through it the child's general abilities in silent and oral reading are assessed. Activities are designed so the child at conference time can demonstrate abilities or lack of them in a friendly, personal setting and then plan with the teacher some things to do to improve or to explore new reading skills. Over a period of time the teacher will suggest a wide range of activities and keep a record of progress.

The Reading/Research Center as a place in the learning environment should have materials available for developing activities that review reading skills already introduced: vocabulary skills, comprehension skills, study skills, word-recognition skills, silent reading skills, and oral reading skills.

The Reading/Research Center is also a place where children go to browse as a recreational or as a study activity. It should contain a wide variety of books in a minimum of four categories: (1) books for recreational reading, (2) books in which children can locate information, (3) books developed specifically to help children be better readers, and (4) books written by children in the class and in the school.

The Reading/Research Center should be a comfortable place with rugs, mats, and pillows where children can sit on the floor and relax while browsing. Tables and chairs are useful but not necessary for the center.

The Viewing/Listening Center is one where reading and writing skills are not required for effective participation. Here there is usually high interest and success. Children learn many things as they listen to stories and music recorded by different voices and view filmstrips, films, flat pictures, fine art prints, and other materials.

Books with accompanying records should be available at all times. Children whose oral reading is halting and slow can learn to follow along the print as they listen to recorded models of good reading. Books and records can be provided in more than one language. Tapes can be made by parents and by older children who are good models of oral reading.

The Viewing/Listening Center should be considered a recreational center as well as a study center. A collection of filmstrips, study prints, and recordings should be available with no assignments attached. Children who lack competence in literacy skills should be encouraged to learn from the audio and visual communication materials and to profit from exposure to new ideas.

The Viewing/Listening Center is usually in a specific place in the classroom. The location has to be near electric outlets. Audio-visual equipment and materials are part of the resources required for effective operation. Some that are desirable are: record player and records, tape recorder and tapes, filmstrip projector, motion picture projector (or access to one), photographs and other study prints, fine art prints, camera, and continuing collection of pictures and records brought by pupils.

The *Writing/Publishing Center* is a place where children find many resources and much motivation that promote self-expression through writing. Alphabet and numeral models are available as long as children need them for improving handwriting and for learning new letter forms when publishing books and posters.

Enjoyment is a key idea for the Writing/Publishing Center. The mechanics of writing never overshadows the pleasure of recording ideas in creative and clever ways. The publishing emphases in the center afford reason for editing manuscripts that are to be published in multiple copies for others to read. The raw writing of children is to be valued and encouraged at all times.

The publishing adjunct to the center is where children work to refine original manuscripts before they are reproduced and bound into substantial bindings. They may work individually to proofread their own writing, or they may work in teams with assigned responsibilities to read for one or more kinds of errors. The editors have conferences with the authors to make suggestions for revisions toward improving the original manuscript before it is published. Manuscripts that are shared orally by the author and are not selected for publication need not go through editorial procedures. Most manuscripts in the classroom will fall into this category.

Ongoing publications in the Writing/Publishing Center might be newspapers, magazines, class books, and series of books that individuals write. Periodically a book will be selected for editing and binding for the school library.

A Quiet Place can be a designated place in a classroom or an idea that makes possible individual relaxation in self-selected places in the learning environment. A designated area can be set off by a screen, book shelves, a small rug, a large pillow, or a comfortable chair. The purpose is to offer children a place and a time to relax, contemplate, and rest. The one essential requirement is that everyone understands that there is to be no disturbing talking or noise.

A Quiet Place provides for rest on the basis of individual need as contrasted to enforced periods where everyone is required to rest at the same time. Alternate times for activity and rest meet basic needs in a learning center arrangement. Constant activity can destroy the notion of the organization, and children become uproductive and unruly. Those who appear to need discipline may have a deeper need that can be met with a few moments of peaceful relaxation.

Beautiful objects such as paintings, art prints, photographs, flower arrangements, special books, interesting rocks and shells, and other things that appeal to the senses attract children to A Quiet Place where they can be happy alone. Space to lie down and stretch out is desirable. A nap is permitted and in some cases encouraged.

The ultimate in accountability for the successful operation of a learning center organization is realized when the teacher can slip away to A Quiet Place for a moment of peace and quiet and all the children honor that need.

Learning Centers for the Three Strands

When the basic curriculum rationale for a language experience approach has been internalized, the learning environment can be organized in a way alternative to that outlined in the discussion Learning Centers for a Language Laboratory. This organization is planned around the three strands.

Center One: Self-expression activities for personal communication
Center Two: Language study activities for understanding how language works, especially for writing and reading
Center Three: Language influence activities that bring learners in contact with the language, the ideas, and the multiple means of communication used by many people

Within each large center for a *strand* there can be subcenters for special emphasis and special needs.

Center One: oral sharing and discussing
                art expression in its many forms
                creative writing
                creative dramatics
                responding rhythmically to music
Center Two: games that review language skills
                language study activities
                dictation experiences for language
                study
                mechanics of writing
                editing manuscripts
Center Three: books for browsing and reading
                reading instruction
                viewing filmstrips and films
                listening to recordings of stories and music
                puppets as story characters

When the learning centers representing the three strands are used, students can be divided into three groups of approximately the same size. They must be groups of heterogenous ability in which at least one member can understand and/or read directions well enough to keep the group as independent as possible.

While children are working in the strand learning centers, the teacher can work with a group in a center or with individuals apart from the learning centers. The dispersal of students for independent and small group work frees the teacher to work as a consultant, a diagnostician, an observer, and an evaluator.

Evaluation of Classroom Organization

Classroom organization for a language experience approach can be evaluated in ways that yield scores useful in planning for improvement. Although there are many intangibles in a creative program, at many points visible evidence reflects an implementation of the curriculum rationale as stated in Chapter 1 and expanded in Chapters 5 through 24.   They are:

1. Evidence shows that the real language of the learners is valued by the teacher and used by the teacher in building children's skills for communication.

EXAMPLES

——Children participate freely and comfortably in their home-rooted language.
——The real language of children is used as part of the room environment in reading charts, posters, talking murals, and books they have written and published.
——Children are free from the fear of using incorrect language to express themselves.
——Space and time are provided for children to communicate their ideas through many arts and crafts media and through dramatization, puppets, rhythmic activities, and discussions.
——Tapes that are recordings of children's own language are included in the listening activities.
——Edited and unedited stories and poems written by the children are part of the oral reading program.

2. Evidence shows that a language study program reflects to a degree the real language of the learners.

EXAMPLES

——The dictated speech of children is written by adults so the children can observe how the alphabetic code works for them.
——Speech-to-print relationships are discussed in informal and friendly ways that permit the internalization of a phonics system for one's own dialect.
——Children have conversational abilities to discuss the mechanics of language when writing and reading.
——The room environment reflects an emphasis on the increase in vocabularies of nouns, verbs, adjectives, and adverbs.
——The room environment reflects an emphasis on the development of a sight vocabulary of high-frequency words.
——Alternatives are offered children whose speech patterns are significantly divergent from the language patterns usually found in printed materials.

——Children participate in editing manuscripts for publication of their stories and poems.

——Children learn to read a variety of symbol systems.

3. Evidence shows that children are influenced by the language and ideas of other people to the extent that their own language is growing.

EXAMPLES

——Many books are available for recreational reading, browsing, locating information, and improving reading skills.

——Books written and published by the children are a part of the classroom library.

——Films and filmstrips bring children who are not necessarily good readers in contact with the language and ideas of others.

——Books with records and/or tapes of the printed text are available to children to provide models of good reading and enjoyment of the ideas of others without their having to be good readers.

——Oral language activities include language patterns of authors that may not be typical of the home-rooted language of the learners.

——Art prints, musical compositions, sculpture, and other creative products are available for individual interpretation.

——Children have opportunities and resources for research on topics of interest.

Scales for rating levels of implementation of the curriculum rationale are included in Appendix A. One scale is for kindergarten classrooms where reading print and independent writing are not emphasized. Another is for classrooms where reading print and independent writing are goals.

Rating scales provide scores that can be interpreted in light of the goals for the program. Some possibilities for use of the scores are for self-evaluation by individuals and/or teams of teachers, for external evaluation by a principal or supervisor, and for cooperative evaluation through conferences that compare and contrast teacher self-evaluation with evaluation by an observer using the rating scale.

To date use of the rating scales indicates that children in classrooms where teachers score highest are those who tend to score highest on reading achievement as judged by standardized tests. What happens is that children in a high-scoring environment find reading and reading skills in multiple places and in multiple forms in

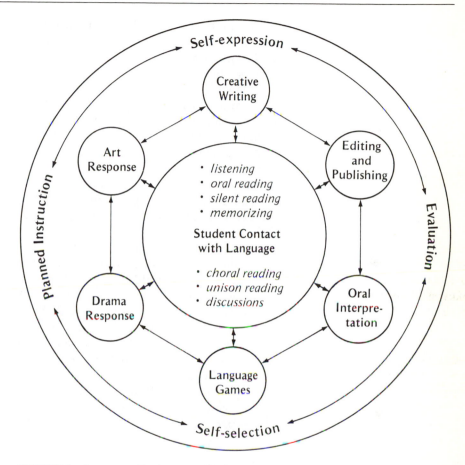

FIGURE 3   *Language Environment and Reading*

the classroom. If they fail to understand in one setting, another set-ting is available. The interrelations of language and an environment that promotes reading achievement are illustrated in Figure 3.

Basic Ingredients of a Schedule

The basic ingredients for a language experience approach are derived from all aspects of communication—listening, speaking, writing, and reading. The oral language background of a child is a basic ingredient in word recognition; other communication skills branch from this one. In a language experience classroom the thinking of each child is valued, regardless of how limited it is. Thus, children are encouraged to express their thinking in many forms but especially in oral language. Oral language can then be represented in written form by a teacher or by a child, to be reconstructed (read) by the author and others. Reconstruction leads to reading the written language of others from a variety of sources, which in turn should influence the thinking and oral language of the reader so that spelling, writing, and reading improve. This recycling of language in its many communicative forms assures language growth toward reading.

The continuing responsibility of the teacher is to help children at all levels of ability to become increasingly aware of the world in which they live—to "talk" about it in many media and to relate their observations and impressions to their own experiences. The instructional schedule provides time for the teacher to

—read to the children some children's literature every day
—guide the children in reading or reciting something in unison
—discuss topics of interest with children
—tell stories from real and imaginary experiences
—read *with* individual children each day
—record language that expresses feelings and ideas from the Arts and Crafts Center
—encourage children to write for recreation
—serve as a consultant to publishing projects
—use multisensory materials.

Read to the group of children some children's literature every day.

Reading to children is basic reading instruction. They must have an opportunity to hear the way hundreds of authors say things. The ability to listen to other people's language is prerequisite to any level of silent reading.

Various arrangements can be made for oral reading. Frequently the teacher will read to the total class. Children must view the teacher as a *reader* if they are to profit from reading instruction by that teacher. Skills in oral reading should be illustrated over and over by the person who is teaching those skills to students.

Other arrangements can be made. The teacher can invite children from the intermediate grades to specialize in oral reading to younger ones. These children need not be the highest achievers. Teachers will work with them to prepare the reading before meeting with the younger children. Some reluctant readers of sixth-grade material profit from reading simple stories and poems in effective ways.

Many classic stories have been recorded by outstanding actors. Some stories are available on filmstrips with accompanying records. A Viewing Listening Center can be developed to use these materials so children can profit from excellent models of oral reading.

Guide the children in reading or reciting something in unison.

Children deserve to join voices in a successful language production experience. The poor and reluctant readers have a special need to open up and read with confidence.

Choral reading is essential for the development of confidence in oral reading. Children need coaching in voice modulation, pause, emphasis, stress, and pronunciation. These abilities can be illustrated and practiced in choral reading situations without embarrassing individuals.

Unison reading prior to individual oral reading assures children that they can say the words. It also builds a background of meaning impossible to acquire from poor oral reading.

Reading songs in a group prior to learning to sing them provides an opportunity to build rhythm into reading. Chants also have rhythm helpful in reading and can be learned in unison reading and reciting.

Discuss topics of interest with children.

Deepening sensitivity to people and events is an ongoing goal of a language experience approach. Children must be helped to talk about the things they observe, hear, and read about. They must hear words they have never heard before if they are to extend reading vocabularies. Seldom can children reconstruct printed words that they have never heard. How can they hear an increasing number of words without some organized discussion on topics of interest? How can they be expected to comprehend through silent reading something that they cannot understand through discussion?

Discussions in which children are invited to add their thinking to topics, interact with the thinking of others, argue, change points of view with new information, prove points with facts, and seek other information to substantiate positions can be a help in seeing relationships between discussions and silent reading. Children come to view an author as an absent person who has something of interest or importance to say. They develop interest in trying to carry on a discussion with a person who is present only through print. As in a live discussion the reader will agree and disagree, like and dislike, be happy and sad, accept and reject, expand and abandon. To ask most children to develop these sensitive, personal skills *only* through silent reading and follow-up activities is to relegate many to failure in the very areas in which we are making tremendous investments of time and energy.

Tell stories from real and imaginary experiences.

Telling a story calls for important reading skills. It requires an understanding of sequencing of events, portraying character, establishing setting, and organizing plot. A child who has grasped these abilities will probably have less comprehension difficulty in silent reading than one who has not had a chance to explore these abilities in informal ways.

When a language experience approach is used, there must be time and opportunity for oral composition of stories in addition to the sharing of events and the discussion of topics of interest. A teacher or a child might tell a story and let other children act it out in pantomime. One child might tell the beginning of a story and let several children give personal endings.

A tape recorder is needed for children to record stories which can be used in the Viewing/Listening Center. Occasionally one of the stories might be good enough to be transcribed and published as a book for the library. Children need visual evidence of the relationship between being able to construct a story orally and being able to reconstruct someone else's story by reading it.

Read *with* **individual children each day.**

Reading with individuals and small groups is a continuing opportunity for the teacher to demonstrate ability and interest as a participating reader rather than as a monitor of children's reading. During individual conferences the teacher can make a deal to read a sentence, a paragraph, or a page alternately with the student. This interaction highly motivates improved reading. The proximity of demonstration by the teacher and performance by the student is reflected in greater achievement and more interest in improvement. The experience can result in meaningful follow-up activities for the student.

Children who write and publish books should be honored by having the teacher read the book effectively with the author. Prior to a scheduled reading to the whole class by the author, the teacher can demonstrate effective strategies for presentation which may or may not be imitated by the author when reading.

**Record language that expresses feelings and ideas
from the Arts and Crafts Center**

In a language experience approach art expression is essential at all levels. Young children paint so they can have reading lessons. Painting is a part of reading. This concept is in contrast with classroom organizations in which children are permitted to paint if they finish their work and have been quiet. Painting breeds thinking. The germ of an idea that emerges at an easel or with other art material can be expanded through talk, can be written once it is said, and can be read once it is written.

Art expression materials are as essential in intermediate grades as in primary grades. Children need to feel that they can express their ideas in many ways and with multiple media. Many student authors illustrate their writing. Some team up in an author-illustrator combination. They continue to view art expression as a way of saying things to others and see relationships between different types of writing and different types of art.

Abstract paintings might be compared with nonrhyming poetry. In both instances the producers invite the viewer or listener to bring personal thinking and experiences to the work, to add to it, and to interpret it. They leave room for *you* in their work. This concept is an essential skill in the interpretation and reflection of reading done silently. It is doubtful that the skill will ever be matured through silent reading alone.

Encourage children to write for recreation.

A Writing/Publishing Center is as essential in a classroom using a language experience approach as is a Reading/Research Center. The Writing/Publishing Center can be a place where children go to write or a place in the classroom where materials are stored for children to select and take to their seats to use. The important idea is that children must be given a continuing opportunity to choose writing just as they are encouraged to choose reading by providing a classroom library. Both centers are essential for language development. One emphasizes the child's expressing personal ideas with personal language; the other emphasizes the child's interacting with the ideas of authors and being influenced by their language.

In setting up a Writing/Publishing Center there are minimal essential supplies:

——paper in a variety of sizes, colors, shapes
——lead pencils, pens, colored pencils, crayons, felt-tipped pens, and a typewriter
——reference works such as spelling lists of words indexed by topics such as seasons, a variety of dictionaries ranging from simple to complex, collections of words by categories of color, size, shape, texture, action
——motivators and stimulators to help children decide on something to write
——pictures that suggest beginnings, endings, or middles of stories
——blank books with cover titles that invite children to write about what they observe in the world
——language study folders in which children can illustrate their understandings of such language elements as compound words, contractions, figures of speech, idioms, words with more than one meaning, alliteration, rhyme
——comics with blank talk balloons so that children can make up and write in talk for the sequence of pictures
——phrases and sentences that make good story beginnings
——models for practicing handwriting, especially printing, to make publications attractive and easy to read.

Ready access to the Writing/Publishing Center by children is necessary. The schedule for selecting writing should be much like the schedule for selecting recreational reading. The treatment of the results of the choice should be much like that of the treatment of what a child learns while browsing in the Reading/Research Center. There should not be strict accountability for what happens, but frequently products from the writing center can be published for the reading center.

Serve as a consultant to publishing projects.

An essential ingredient of a language experience approach is a continuing program of publishing the work of students. At beginning levels children paint to represent ideas and then dictate labels, sentences, and stories to accompany the paintings. As they develop skills in handwriting, they do their own writing with the teacher's help and with the aids in a Writing/Publishing Center.

Teachers of very productive children can extend the publishing program by asking older boys and girls to take dictation and make stories into well-bound books. A few children who have difficulty writing can illustrate what others write. Some classes of older children make sturdy blank books which young children can use. Sometimes mothers will aid in typing and binding.

Older children can form a publishing company for the purpose of producing newspapers, magazines, and books. In addition to the tasks of authors and illustrators, they assume responsibilities for editing, proofreading, making layouts, binding, and distributing the products. Some classes have been very successful in projects of writing and illustrating books for young children to read.

Children should have frequent opportunities to read their own writings to the entire class, to small groups within the class, and to other groups in the school. The child who is reading personal writing is using material that has a zero meaning load. Nothing is new in the content. Thus, attention in oral reading can be devoted to clarity of expression, effectiveness of presentation, interpretation, punctuation, and other necessary details that make listening to oral reading a pleasure.

Motivation for improving language form and usage comes as children's writing is read by others. Pride in published works stimulates young authors to seek language forms that will be understood by others. They are also influenced by what they read and what others read to them.

As children express their own ideas, they may become interested in finding out, through reading, what other people think and say about topics of interest to them. Wide reading, in turn, can stimulate individual authorship.

We must remind ourselves continuously that *the way a child feels about herself or himself and reading is more important than any method or material.* To be an author and to understand processes of publishing have been found by many teachers to build strong links between a child and the authors she or he will come to know and respect.

Use multisensory materials.

Language skills are extended and ideas are refined as students listen to tapes and records. They will be able to hear the many ways in which people say things at the same time that they are learning to view print silently and hear the message through inner listening mechanisms. Hearing a variety of people talking and reading can help children develop an ear for varied speech patterns.

Reading skills of interpretation and of extending meaning can be promoted by the use of films. Students view the films with the soundtrack turned off and then discuss their own perceptions and derived meanings before listening to the commentary of the film. Progress in maturing language skills is accelerated as students form bases for contrast and comparison of their own ideas and language with those of others. An added variation is to show a portion of a film, stop it, and ask students to predict what will come next.

Filmstrips without words printed on them can be used over and over as guides for children's language development. The teacher shows the filmstrip, shows it again a frame at a time, and lets children make the commentary in terms of what they see in the pictures. Several versions are made, and then one of them is taped to use with the filmstrip. The accompanying recording, if there is one with the filmstrip, is played only after the children have invested much of their own thinking and oral language in making a commentary. This procedure builds confidence in the use of their own language at the same time that they are making progress in recognizing the language of other people—in hearing it and recognizing it in print.

Patterns of Teacher-pupil Interaction

The language experiences suggested here can be used by the teacher in three basic patterns of classroom organization, singly or in combination, depending on the nature of the work of the day.

PATTERN 1: THE TEACHER WORKS WITH THE ENTIRE CLASS

This pattern works well for
—reading aloud to children
—children reading their stories or other compositions aloud
—children composing stories orally
—discussing topics of interest by the class
—extending experiences through films, filmstrips, and follow-up of field trips
—introducing and demonstrating games to go into learning centers
—singing songs and chanting rhythms
—choral reading and unison reading
—conducting seminars on the development of various skills.

PATTERN 2: THE TEACHER WORKS WITH SMALL GROUPS

This arrangement works well for
—completing activities initiated in the large group
—teacher taking dictation from one child while others observe and listen
—children reading to each other without teacher supervision
—teacher reading with a child or a small group of children
—giving special instruction in skills to some children identified as needing it
—playing games to practice skills
—teacher choosing appropriate books
—viewing filmstrips
—listening to records and tapes
—editing manuscripts for publication
—producing puppet shows
—dramatizing a story.

PATTERN 3: THE TEACHER SERVES AS A RESOURCE PERSON FOR INDIVIDUAL AND INDEPENDENT ACTIVITIES

This arrangement works well for
—suggesting ideas for writing individual books
—helping with spelling

——furnishing words for independent readers

——helping choose and organize an independent activity

——conferring about reading progress and setting up new goals

——conferring about writing progress and serving as editor in chief prior to the publication of manuscripts

——playing games with a child who needs strong reinforcement and direct teaching

——taking dictation from children who are too shy to talk before a group.

Learning situations must be organized in ways that permit children to view themselves as worthy and able to succeed in communication tasks of increasing difficulty. They must feel the success of working alone, of working with other children of like ability, and of working with those whose abilities are significantly different from theirs. They must have repeated opportunities to read what they write to small groups and to the total class. Occasionally they should have an opportunity to read aloud something they have prepared for the enjoyment of the whole class.

A language experience approach does not require, nor does it recommend, grouping students by ability as a standard procedure for organizing the class for instruction. Such a school practice—one that usually makes reading achievement *the measure of success* in the early grades—highlights lack of success and may destroy the child's self-image as a reader rather than improve his or her reading skills. This same self-image is all that the child has available when developing other communication skills. The goal of providing opportunities and experiences for success by the largest number of children is met with flexible groupings that emphasize children's success and accept the fact that every child individualizes reading whether we plan for it or not.

Program Planning

Program planning for a language experience approach is enhanced by a few basic guidelines that insure implementation of the curriculum rationale.

1. Select activities from all three strands for each planning period. Plans may be on a daily, weekly, or other time basis. Over a month or six weeks, plan to extend learnings in the twenty sub-

strands of the rationale. (See Figure 2, page 13, for a list of strands with substrands.)

Details of the three strands and twenty substrands are in Chapters 5 through 24; they include explanations, examples, and summaries of the skills and abilities to be developed.

2. Plan for flexible groupings to meet the needs of children in the total class setting, in small groups, and for individual exploration. Every day there should be opportunities for children to participate in a total group activity and to spend time on individual interests. Most of the small group activities emerge to meet special needs felt by children or identified through teacher-pupil conferences.

The same activity, such as viewing a filmstrip, might be used for the total group one day and then be available in a learning center for individuals and small groups over several days.

3. Activate learning centers that best serve the language concepts being emphasized. Five or six learning centers usually serve the needs of a class group, but more can be activated if the purpose of them serves goals of the instructional program.

Some centers such as those involving art, reading, and writing are used most of the time, but materials in them need to be changed to keep them fresh and meaningful.

Suggestions for developing and using learning centers for language growth can be found in *Language Experience Activities* (Allen and Allen, 1976), a companion to this book. In it is a detailed presentation of language concepts that need to be developed. The stated concepts are illustrated with activities for multiple learning centers.

4. Select evaluation procedures appropriate to the objectives of the instructional program. Informal check lists can be made from the summaries of skills and abilities at the ends of Chapters 5 through 24. Criterion-referenced tests can be constructed with items from those summaries as guides for test items. Personal conferences can be used to evaluate progress for many of the objectives. Standardized tests can be useful in gathering information to serve as a basis for comparing and contrasting information gathered from more informal sources.

The program planning chart (Figure 4) illustrates a way of recording decisions for a program. It can be duplicated as it is or enlarged to

Name _____ Class _____ Dates _____ to _____

Theme or language emphasis: _____

Activities from the Three Strands	Classroom Organization *			Learning Centers Activated † (with materials and equipment needed)	Evaluation ‡			
	TC	SG	I		In	CR	St	PC
Experiencing communication								
Studying communication								
Relating communication of others to self								
Other activities								

*TC—total class
 SG—small group
 I—individuals

†Learning centers available: Discussion, Arts and Crafts, Cooking, Dramatization, Game, Reading/Research, Viewing/Listening, Writing/Publishing, A Quiet Place

‡In—informal inventory
 CR—criterion reference
 St—standardized test
 PC—personal conference

FIGURE 4   *Program Planning Chart*

include other items. A collection of plans for a year's work becomes a valuable professional resource that can be shared with other teachers. It also serves as evidence of program development in any study of accountability.

Selected References

Allen, Roach Van. *Teacher's Resource Guide, Language Experiences in Reading, Level I.* Encyclopaedia Britannica Educational Corp., Chicago, 1974.
———— and Claryce Allen. *Language Experience Activities.* Houghton Mifflin Co., Boston, 1976.

Barbe, Walter B. *Educator's Guide to Personalized Reading Instruction.* Prentice-Hall, Englewood Cliffs, N.J., 1970.

Barth, Ronald S., and Charles H. Rathbone. "The Open School: A Way of Thinking About Children, Learning and Knowledge." *The Center Forum,* vol. 3, no. 7. Center for Urban Education, New York, 1969.

Billings, Zelpha W. "The Self-Selection Classroom." *Keeping Up with Elementary Education,* vol. 15, no. 3. American Association of Elementary-Kindergarten-Nursery Educators, Washington, D.C., 1970.

Carswell, Evelyn M., and Darrell L. Roubinek. *Open Sesame: A Primer in Open Education.* Goodyear Publishing Co., Pacific Palisades, Calif., 1974.

Darrow, Helen F., and Roach Van Allen. *Independent Activities for Creative Learning.* Teachers College Press, New York, 1961.

Douglass, Malcolm P. "Does Non-Grading Improve Reading Behavior?" In *Thirty-First Yearbook, Claremont Reading Conference,* edited by Malcolm P. Douglass. Claremont Graduate College, Claremont, Calif., 1967.

Dyson, E. "A Study of Ability Grouping and the Self-Concept," *Journal of Educational Research,* 60 (1970).

Featherstone, Joseph. *Schools Where Children Learn.* Liveright, New York, 1971.

Howes, Virgil M. *Informal Teaching in the Open Classroom.* Macmillan Publishing Co., New York, 1974.

National Association for the Education of Young Children. *Open Education, the Legacy of the Progressive Education Movement.* National Association for the Education of Young Children, Washington, D.C., 1970.

Ramsey, Wallace Z. (ed.). *Organizing for Individual Differences.* International Reading Association, Newark, 1970.

Rogers, Vincent R. *Teaching in the British Primary School.* Macmillan Co., Collier-Macmillan Canada, Toronto, 1970.

South Carolina State Department of Education. *Learning Alive.* The State Department of Education, Columbia, S.C., 1973.

Spodek, Bernard. *Open Education.* National Association for the Education of Young Children, Washington, D.C., 1970.

Voight, Ralph C. *Invitation to Learning—The Learning Center Handbook.* Acropolis Books, Washington, D.C., 1971.

Weber, Lillian. *The English Infant School and Informal Education.* Prentice-Hall, Englewood Cliffs, N.J., 1971.

Wilson, Lois Fair. "The British Infant School: A Model for Early Education." In *Thirty-Fifth Yearbook, Claremont College Conference,* edited by Malcolm P. Douglass. Claremont Graduate College, Claremont, Calif., 1971.

Part Two
Experiencing Communication

Strand One emphasizes "the employment of multiple media which are the natural and normal ways of self-expression—talking, painting, singing, dancing, acting, and writing." To be communicative through self-expression activities, children must rely on themselves. They must come to realize that no one else can *really* communicate for them. Each has uniqueness, his or her own style. A responsibility of the school is to preserve this individuality, this uniqueness, at the same time that progress is being made by children in assimilating our language heritage and societal expectancies. Teachers of communication through self-expression recognize that fluency and flexibility in language help children to make a happier adjustment to life and to ideas and feelings within them. Language skills foster confidence and personal opportunity. They help children to understand and appreciate classmates. Language values are the values that relate to all effective teaching-learning situations. Some of these values are described below.

1. Creative language experiences provide for individual differences.

Children think and reason differently. They have varying abilities, interests, drives, and talents. Teachers who live and work with children soon realize that each must be dealt with differently. They realize that children work best when their tasks and responsibilities are appropriate to their age and abilities and are flexible enough to permit individual ways of thinking and working.

A well-developed program of oral and written communication provides richly for individual differences. The children develop a style of expression typically their own. As the adults in their lives let them know that they appreciate their style and value their ideas, children gain confidence and extend their efforts to produce something that is truly theirs.

Teachers must guard against preconceived ideas about what children's language should be—how it should be spoken, written, dramatized, or painted. It is their task to create the learning environment in which spontaneous language expression can flourish. The attitude of teachers will contribute to language experiences which either express individuality or show that unfortunate similarity which reflects teacher dominance.

2. Creative language experiences develop imagination.

All children are endowed with the power of imagination—the power to form mental images. This resource is available in every classroom at no extra cost, but somehow in the process of what we call education, the power of imagination diminishes as other facets of personality are developed.

Teachers working with children must be careful not to destroy or discourage the imagination of children. As children work to increase their abilities in oral and written communication, they should have great freedom to draw on their imaginations for content, settings, situations, and characters. Through imaginary characters and plots children can express their inner concerns and feelings with a sensitivity and a frankness that are seldom reflected in assignments involving real characters and settings. Dramatizations and all forms of creative writing invite children to maintain and to continue to develop their powers of imagination.

3. Creative language experiences build self-confidence.

Children must rely on themselves when they are engaged in creative language production. They must search in their own storehouses of experiences and use the skill and knowledge that they possess when they use their own language to solve speech and writing problems.

Evidence of pleasing results gives children a feeling of satisfaction. A measure of success from something of their own thinking inspires them to other achievements. It helps to set personal standards rather than to be judged always on the basis of uniform standards, rivalry, or competition. Some measure of praise may be used by adults to build self-confidence, but it must be used wisely. Strong and exaggerated praise can be damaging. Children may recognize its falseness or become discouraged by the fact that they cannot live up to the high expectation implied in the praise. Self-confidence is strengthened through the gratification a person derives from completing a task in a way that meets personal standards.

4. Creative language experiences provide for emotional expression.

Children need socially acceptable outlets for their emotions. They need some dramatic ways to do this so they can observe the response of other people. Dramatization and creative writing depend on the expression of emotions for an important part of their power to communicate. When the emotions of children are deeply involved with their subject, whether oral or written, their output will contain an element to which others can respond. Masterpieces in writing are usually expressions of basic emotions to which people have long responded.

In creative language experiences, children have to combine their ideas and experiences with their emotional attitudes. As they do this, they must select words and phrases and put them in appropriate arrangements that will communicate feelings. All these processes help children express their emotions in orderly and acceptable ways.

5. Creative language experiences develop the aesthetic sense.

Although emotional and social improvements are valid goals of rich language programs at school, they must be accompanied by goals that build appreciation for quality and beauty in speech and writing. As the level of awareness to the beauty around them is raised, children increase their delight in the treasures of the world near them. Through their work in writing children gain the power to distinguish quality in the thought and expression of others who have described the world as they see it.

Children need exposure to the great works of literature of the past and of their own time. Oral reading by the teacher or by the child who is a good reader is a good way to provide the exposure to which most children can respond. Few young children can do the reading themselves and get sheer enjoyment from artistic language. They need oral exposure.

Children who have engaged in much writing about their own ideas and have experimented with many forms of writing are the ones best prepared to appreciate good writing when they encounter it. Whether or not a child becomes an author is hardly the major consideration. Every person needs to be able to make quality judgments and selections of reading material in everyday life.

6. Creative language experiences deepen appreciation of other people.

An aspect of the language process that focuses on the thinking of individuals and on uniqueness of expression is the opportunity for children to appreciate the work of others in the classroom. A child who has struggled to communicate ideas—orally or in writing—is appreciative of other children who have solved their problems in a variety of ways that bring pleasure. He or she expects and looks forward to diversity of self-expression and is released from the shackles of believing that *correctness* and *conformity* are synonyms.

7. Creative language experiences bring balance to educational activities.

Children need the educational balance of a program that takes into account their creative powers at the same time that they are learning the fundamental skills of handwriting, spelling, the mechanics of English, and reading. They need time to consider their own ideas, feelings, and aspirations. Independence to create something different is a necessary balance to the kinds of learning that require children to arrive at the same solutions. Both play a part in helping children improve their oral and written communication.

A child who has developed the ability to communicate effectively through many forms is one who derives greater satisfaction from dealings with other people than does the child who lacks necessary communicating abilities. There is scarcely a school activity that does not depend on personal communication for its completion. Even school activities of the rote-learning type imply that the learner brings to the task certain communicating abilities not required for immediate responses. The child in most instances is assumed to be able to talk, to portray visual ideas, to act out, to respond rhythmically, to discuss, and to write.

The whole world of ideas is tied up or freed according to man's ability in personal communication. In spite of the heavy emphasis in schools on the ability to read what others have communicated through writing, the reading act must be followed by some form of personal communication before it is fulfilled. The reading act is extended and enhanced in direct proportion to the reader's ability to transpose the ideas of another into some form of personal communication such as speech, writing, art, and drama. To replicate the words used by an author through a process called oral reading is the minimum ability of a beginning reader. The mature reader communicates with the author with no real attention to the "words" used. *Ideas* are taken in through gobs of words. These ideas can then be communicated at appropriate times through many forms.

Teachers who develop a personalized curriculum capitalize on opportunities to release children to discover and exercise a variety of communicating skills and abilities. They do not think of anyone as belonging to a certain grade level or age group. They become familiar with the range of abilities described in this book. To this they add their knowledge and abilities in personal communication, their experiences as persons and as teachers, their judgment, and their observations of individuals and groups who communicate effectively.

From these resources teachers determine which resources available to them support appropriate forms of communication in the learning environment. This does not mean that teachers step aside from the responsibility of definite planning. Rather, it means that when they plan for skills and practices for higher levels of proficiency, a basic ingredient of such planning is attention to personal communication experiences as outlined in Strand One of the Curriculum Rationale for a Language Experience Approach.

FROM THE RATIONALE   Oral sharing of ideas—talking about topics that are self-selected and of personal interest, telling or illustrating something on a purely personal basis that may or may not be related to classroom activities.

The experience of verbalization as well as the verbalization of experience is essential to the education of most human beings. Both require oral interaction within some kind of a language community. When the close language group of a child changes from the home and neighborhood to a classroom setting, the need for verbalization increases, but often the opportunity decreases. The traditional school emphasis on the acquisition of the literacy skills of reading and writing has overshadowed the need for the oracy skills of speaking and listening.

Literacy skills and oracy skills enjoy a reciprocal relationship in an educational setting and must be thought of as reinforcing each other. Teachers using a language experience approach do not decide whether reading is more important than speaking or vice versa. They plan for both! They are aware that growth in oral communication is likely to represent growth in reading also. An application of the Cox Language Analysis Scale (Cox, 1971) yielded results indicating clearly that the *quality* of oral language production is related significantly to a young child's growth in reading skills and abilities. Children whose oral language production reflected a high level of mastery of the basic elements of phonological structure, syntactical structure, and morphological structure were the same children who read with minimum instruction. At the other end of the continuum, children who ranked low on the quality scale did not read even with maximum instruction. Since Cox's work was a feasibility study to determine if oracy-literacy information useful to teachers could be collected, the results merely serve to keep alive the need for all teachers to include *oral sharing of ideas as basic in all instructional settings.*

When an instructional program that includes an emphasis on oral sharing of ideas is planned, some basic questions can be kept in mind as guides: (1) What is oral sharing of ideas? (2) Why have oral sharing of ideas? (3) How does oral sharing of ideas work in a classroom? (4) Which oral activities are stressed in a language experience approach?

A summary of skills and abilities is presented at the end of this chapter. The items are stated so that they can be used to construct informal preassessment and postassessment inventories as well as criterion-referenced tests.

What Is Oral Sharing of Ideas?

Oral sharing of ideas is basically a "getting acquainted" experience in communication. Topics are self-selected, and timing is flexible enough to extend from the first greeting of the morning to the last good-by of the afternoon. Time can be organized but it need not be. Topics can be suggested but must not be mandatory. Freedom to use personal language is a prerequisite for oral sharing of ideas.

The oral language that children bring to school is a personal possession which, more than anything else, represents *who they are*. To deny the use of natural, home-rooted language is to deny children the right to function as the persons they really are. To degrade it is to degrade the person. To cast negative reflections on it is to cast negative reflections on the child and the family heritage that that language represents.

Oral sharing is a process of opening up communication between child and teacher and of the child's establishing rapport with the peer group. In the process the child reveals interests and aspirations, fears and doubts. At the same time the child shares influences that come from reading, observing, and imagining and reflects home-rooted language with attendant strengths and weaknesses. Often the child tries out new ways of saying things. In this way the process furnishes anecdotal material to the teacher for follow-up instruction and evidence of children's growth in the quality of their language.

Oral sharing of ideas is the most basic process in communication available in classroom settings, and it may be the most basic language experience that feeds the growth of reading abilities. It balances literacy skills with oracy skills. Both are essential in communication.

Why Have Oral Sharing of Ideas?

The way children feel about themselves during the process of learning reading and writing is more important than any method or material. Studies in self-concept and school achievement, which are summarized by Purkey (1970), show such strong relationships that it is impossible to do intelligent planning for instruction without an emphasis on the enhancement of *self*.

Since language production, both oral and written, can be a process of self-enhancement, it deserves a place in basic instruction and should not be reserved for a "sharing time" or for special occasions.

Before and during the time children are engaged in personal author-ship, there is little chance that a teacher can identify the language needs of a child apart from regular planning for her or him to com-municate in natural ways in the learning environment. How else can a teacher gather clues?

Some children have unusual pronunciations for words that occur frequently in reading.

CLUES FOR INSTRUCTION

Unison reading and choral reading can emphasize phonological struc-ture that is characteristic of reading materials but not characteristic of the oral production of the child. Chants and games which repeat lan-guage patterns give practice in pronouncing words. Recording read-ing and talking on tape provides immediate feedback for evaluation.

Some children use syntactical structure that will never be available for replication in readers.

CLUES FOR INSTRUCTION

Sing songs and play games that repeat sentence patterns standard in reading instructional materials. Chat with the child during dictation; offer alternatives rather than corrections. Select sentences to repeat during *reading to* the children. Ask children to read in natural lan-guage patterns what has been written and dictated.

Some children elaborate with descriptive words which reflect a literacy quality not characteristic of reading instructional materials.

CLUES FOR INSTRUCTION

To avoid causing boredom during the acquisition of basic reading skills, add descriptive language to the printed portion of the ma-terial—a color word or a size word to each sentence where appropri-ate, a phrase telling why or where. Make use of the full language power of the learner by substituting orally new nouns and verbs that make meanings more specific or language more creative. Encourage dictation and writing that use the quality of language characteristic of spontaneous expression.

Some children are confident in language situations even though their progress in reading is slow.

CLUES FOR INSTRUCTION

Read with the child during conferences—"You read to me, I'll read to you." Schedule time at the Viewing/Listening Center for following a printed text while listening to a recording of it that is a good reading model. Arrange for the child to read from personal authorship activities. Keep self-image positive through use of puppets and dramatization. The power is there. The language connection to reading has not been made yet.

Some children use a variety of sentence patterns when engaged in spontaneous expression but write with a limited number.

CLUES FOR INSTRUCTION

Remove the glory of being able to read every word correctly. Reduce emphasis on readers with limited examples of sentence patterns. Relate writing more to speech production than to replication of reading books. Introduce poetry patterns, such as those of the haiku and cinquain, to force artful writing with a limited number of words. Read books of literary merit with repeating patterns that can be followed orally and that might serve as models for artful writing. Use dramatic play to keep language power functioning and alive during periods of learning specific skills.

Some children pronounce only portions of words that reflect tense and number.

CLUES FOR INSTRUCTION

Pronounce word endings that have meaning in language when reading with children. Model the whole word. Make games with root words that have meanings changed by adding sounds represented by *s, -es, -ing, -ed, -er, -est*. Write dictation on the chalkboard. Erase all endings that have language meanings. Read the passage in unison. Restore the endings and discuss the improved meaning.

Only a few examples have been discussed to illustrate why it is important for teachers to hear individuals talk in natural ways. There is no substitute for gathering the information that a teacher must possess in order to do intelligent planning.

How Does Oral Sharing of Ideas Work in a Classroom?

Informal conversation is the key to all other oral sharing. From the time a child enters the classroom and says, "Hi!" the adult-child interaction begins. The teacher might respond, "Hi! That's a new shirt you have on today!"

Such a comment opens up communication. The child has a way of sharing something in a natural way. If something of special interest is noted at this time, the teacher might ask the child to share it with the class later in the day. The sparks that ignite informal sharing are incidental, but they happen all day in classrooms where teachers value children's ideas and children's language. This process could be called planned incidentals.

Shirley has a planned time for sharing each day. Rather than make all the decisions about who will share, she has a committee that locates people, topics, and products that can be shared. The committee is alert at different learning centers, on the playground, and in informal visiting to pick up clues to recommend to Shirley.

Bob wants more participation than is possible when he is listening to one child at a time. He organizes children into groups of four or five for the sharing of ideas and interests. If the group members decide that there is something of great interest to others, they recommend that the whole class hear what they have heard. This multiplier effect involves many children and alerts them to select from their experiences ones that will interest other people.

Joe asks for brief statements of ideas from class members. He takes notes, and when he is aware of widespread interest in a topic, he selects it for further elaboration and discussion. The extended sharing can be done that day or the following one.

Juanita uses the Arts and Crafts Center as a source of oral sharing of ideas. Children who are reluctant to talk may be those who enjoy painting. She selects two or three paintings each day and asks for oral sharing of the ideas of the paintings. If a child does not have anything to say, he or she can choose a classmate to say what a painting means. Sometimes a portion of the oral sharing is recorded and attached to a painting, but Juanita does not limit the oral sharing to what she thinks she has time to write. Frequently, during the process of deciding what, of all that was said, is to be written, oral editing in the form of alternatives can be offered the child whose language is characterized by gross errors. Juanita always writes the child's choice after the alternatives have been offered.

Many children are willing and able to engage in oral sharing from the time they enter school. These children should be helped to improve their oral sharing and encouraged to find many other ways to share their ideas, their feelings, and their daily experiences. Suggestions from the teacher will lead them to understand that they can

—paint a picture to accompany the oral report

—paint a picture and write a simple story to accompany it

—write a report at home and read it to the class. (These reports can be filed and made into a book, *Stories from Home*.)

—imitate a radio broadcast by the use of a toy microphone

—provide a news bulletin board for those who want to write news items, and pin the items to the board

—publish a newspaper or magazine which contains news items, puzzles, poetry, games, and information

—use simple puppets to add interest to an oral report and to entertain an audience

—make book-reporting a part of the spontaneous reporting in the classroom.

Important Activities

Four major classifications of oral language activities are stressed in a language experience approach: (1) spontaneous expression, (2) presentation of dictation, (3) storytelling, and (4) reporting.

Spontaneous Expression

Spontaneous expression is a priceless treasure in any learning situation. It may be the only avenue open in some classrooms for the establishment of rapport that is strong enough to support interaction.

Without interaction it is doubtful that language learnings will move forward. The child who is slow to start reading and writing must be made to feel secure in the learning environment. The acceptance of spontaneous expression is a sure way to establish security. Visiting in the classroom with each other about anything is an "opening up" experience which permits direct instruction in good faith at other times.

The fluent child who would probably be bored with preselected reading materials can have free reign of personal language power in spontaneous expression.

Presentation of Dictation

Children presenting dictation are free to say what they think. Prior to doing any writing, the teacher should encourage the child to tell the whole story or idea. Frequently this presentation is long and involved. One or two ideas can be selected for recording. This procedure gives practice in selecting the main idea from all that has been said.

During the process of presenting dictation, a child may use language that has gross errors or words considered vulgar. If such is the case, the teacher may offer alternatives at the point of writing what has been selected. The alternatives are not offered to correct the child but to build a case for choice. The teacher writes the version the child chooses.

In a language experience approach some child should present dictation for the teacher to record on the chalkboard each day. This can be brief, but it is important that teacher and children have an opportunity to observe and interact with what happens when speech is reduced to print. Emphasis, tone, modulation, pause, and inflections are lost. They remain forever in the speaker and/or reader. But they must be present in the mind for effective reading to occur.

Storytelling

Telling stories and retelling stories are essential oral experiences in a language experience approach. When a child is able, from real experience or from imagination, to choose characters, a setting, and fabricate a plot that contains a climax and an ending, that child has demonstrated the abilities that are required to comprehend stories written by other authors. Until such abilities are developed, reading is likely to remain word-calling. There is no substitute for storytelling in the development of the intellectual base for *reading comprehension*.

The telling of stories, real and imaginary, is as important as listening to them. This creative experience develops audience contact that few language activities can do. It encourages voice inflections, sound effects, physical movements, and language embellishments that lend variety to the usual "reporting voice."

Storytelling about experiences develops such language abilities as expressing ideas in thought units, using colorful and descriptive language, developing ideas in sequence, and choosing good action words. All of these are essential communicating abilities of the person who is successful as a reader of good literature.

Reporting

What one observes and hears can be reported. Awareness of the wonders of nature and of people is the basis for language growth. As one reports, formally or informally, there is need to name things, to tell how they move, and to describe them. Categories of description include color, size, shape, texture, sound, taste, smell, and feeling. The language of contrast and comparison enhances and clarifies meanings. The teacher-pupil interaction during reporting activities may be more specific than at times of spontaneous expression. Topics may be assigned. Common experiences of a class group may be reported. Children may assume different roles when reporting the same experience—from the viewpoint of a scientist, an artist, a teacher, an architect, or a musician or from any other viewpoint possible because of an interest or an experience.

As children mature in reading abilities and interests, much of oral reporting may be related to self-selected and self-assigned reading. Such reporting can be unscheduled as well as scheduled. In addition to reporting bare facts from print, children should be expected to add: What else might the author have said if he could be here? What was hinted but not said? What would I have said or done under the same conditions? Other topics appropriate for personalizing and illustrating their influence on the reader can be woven into a report.

An important aspect of sharing and reporting is the ability to communicate accurately and with organization that the listener can follow. In the beginning stages these abilities can be developed and strengthened through questions that the teacher might ask: Did you really see or hear what you reported? Do you think that the other children understood your explanation? Did the people in the class listen while you gave your report?

Good reporting can also be stimulated by
——holding brief oral evaluations at the end of the day
——summarizing what happened in committee work
——describing how a construction project was carried out
——cooperatively planning the major activities of the day
——telling how to play games.

Older children begin to learn to organize their ideas and thoughts by outlining or by listing major points of emphasis. They recognize that the purpose of reporting to the class is to supply information needed by the group as a whole, and so they try to give their reports, either oral or written, in a manner both clear and interesting to the audience.

Skill in reporting increases as the teacher guides the children
——to recognize and define problems
——to gather materials and evaluate their importance according to the problem
——to take brief notes and organize them in logical sequence for presentation.

Abilities developed through sharing and reporting emphasize the value of individual contributions. These experiences characterize the real difference between a society that develops individuals who assume responsibility for contributing to the thought of its citizens, and a society that seeks to teach its youth by rote what officials deem important. Sharing experiences provides the openness, the motivation, and many of the ideas on which other language abilities are developed.

Summary of Skills and Abilities for Sharing Ideas Orally

SHARING AND REPORTING

——Shares ideas and experiences with class and others
——Presents simple reports to class on observations, trips, reading, and other experiences
——Strives for accuracy and clarity in reporting

——Shows increasing skill in making announcements and explanations
——Increases skill in organizing and summarizing ideas to report
——Recognizes need to report in appropriate situations
——Selects interesting, worthwhile material to report
——Uses appropriate illustrative material to convey ideas more effectively
——Uses notes and simple outlines for oral presentations
——Cultivates as a speaker clarity of speech, pleasing voice, and good posture
——Realizes need for presenting accurate information, giving source of data

STORYTELLING

——Relates events in proper sequence
——Uses voice effectively to portray story
——Selects stories appropriate for the audience
——Develops an easy, natural manner for telling a story
——Develops skill in interpreting mood and characters of a story

ORAL LANGUAGE TECHNIQUES

——Attempts to speak correctly
——Grows in ability to pronounce commonly used words correctly
——Tries to speak clearly and distinctly so others will hear and understand
——Extends and refines vocabulary
——Uses complete sentences and logical sequence of sentences in expressing ideas orally

Selected References

Allen, Roach Van, and Claryce Allen. *Teacher's Resource Book: Language Experiences in Early Childhood.* Encyclopaedia Britannica Educational Corp., Chicago, 1969.

Cohen, Dorothy. "The Effects of Literature on Vocabulary and Reading Achievement," *Elementary English,* 45 (February, 1968), 209–215.

Cohen, S. Alan, and Gita S. Kornfeld. "Oral Vocabulary and Beginning Reading in Disadvantaged Black Children," *The Reading Teacher,* 24, 1 (October, 1970), 33–38.

Coopersmith, Stanley. *The Antecedents of Self-Esteem*. Freeman and Co., San Francisco, 1967.

Cox, Vivian E. "Reciprocal Oracy/Literacy Recognition Skills in the Language Production of Language Experience Approach Students." (Ed.D. dissertation.) University of Arizona, Tucson, 1971.

Erwin, Susan M. "Imitation and Structural Change in Children's Language." In *New Directions of Study of Language*, edited by E. Lenneberg. Institute of Technology Press, Cambridge, Mass., 1964.

Loban, Walter. *The Language of Elementary School Children*. National Council of Teachers of English, Urbana, Ill., 1963.

McDavid, R. I., Jr. "Social Dialects: Cause or Symptom of Social Maladjustment." In *Social Dialects and Language Learning*, edited by W. Shuy. National Council of Teachers of English, Urbana, Ill., 1965.

McNeill, David. *The Acquisition of Language: The Study of Developmental Psycholinguistics*. Harper & Row, New York, 1970.

Menyuk, Paula. *The Acquisition and Development of Language*. Prentice-Hall, Englewood Cliffs, N.J., 1971.

Piaget, Jean. *The Language and Thought of the Child*. Harcourt, Brace and Co., New York, 1926.

Purkey, William W. *Self-Concept and School Achievement*. Prentice-Hall, Englewood Cliffs, N.J., 1970.

Ruddell, Robert B. "The Effect of the Similarity of Oral and Written Patterns of Language Structure on Reading Comprehension," *Elementary English*, 42 (April, 1965), 403–410.

———. "Oral Language and the Development of Other Language Skills." In *Research in Oral Language*, edited by Walter T. Perry. National Council of Teachers of English, Urbana, Ill., 1967.

Rystrom, Richard. "Dialect Training and Reading: A Further Look," *Reading Research Quarterly*, 5, 4 (1970), 581–599.

Tatham, Susan M. "Reading Comprehension of Materials Written with Select Oral Language Patterns: A Study of Grades Two and Four," *Reading Research Quarterly*, 5, 3 (1970), 402.

Vigotsky, L. S. *Thought and Language*. The M.I.T. Press, Cambridge, Mass., 1962.

Weaver, Wendell W., and Albert J. Kingston. "Modeling the Effects of Oral Language upon Reading Language," *Reading Research Quarterly*, 7, 4 (1972), 613–628.

6. Visually Portraying Experiences

FROM THE RATIONALE

Visual portrayal of experiences—using art media and scrap material to explore combinations for the sheer pleasure of observing what happens; representing what one observes, imagines, or understands in abstract as well as in realistic forms; illustrating what someone else has thought and said in ways that internalize or interpret (not copy) those ideas; and creating new schemes for ideas.

In a language experience approach children have freedom to use their own ideas and subjects. They express them in personal ways and with a variety of materials. Children, when portraying their ideas and experiences visually, need freedom to choose and to organize in creative and personal ways. There is no need for them to compete with other children or to reproduce with exactness what someone else has already produced as they might do in oral reading.

This does not imply that no skills need to be taught as children progress through developmental levels of expression with art media. Since art is not totally intuitive, direct instruction and modeling of processes and techniques are important. Skills, as well as freedom of expression, are necessary if art is to contribute to language growth. The attributes of creativity are essential in both forms of communication. Concepts of both art and language must be translated into performance. Reading must be a natural extension of painting.

Attributes of Creativity

Productive experiences useful in a language experience approach link the development of skill with other attributes of creativity. The teacher is aware of those attributes and encourages their development along with skills in visual portrayal. Dr. Viktor Lowenfeld (Lowenfeld and Brittain, 1964) discovered and named eight attributes of creativity during seven years of research at Pennsylvania State University. They are:

—sensitivity to problems
—fluency of ideas
—flexibility
—originality
—redefinition
—analysis

——synthesis

——coherence of organization.

The Lowenfeld attributes are closely related to creativity in language processing.

1. Sensitivity to problems

No creative work is possible unless it is based on a sensitive experience. Thus, enhancing sensitivity to problems is a responsibility of every teacher of *language as an art*. The teaching task is one of helping learners refine their sensibilities so that they use their eyes not only for seeing but for observing, their ears not only for hearing but for listening, and their hands not only for touching but for feeling.

Sensitivities to different materials and media—to be able almost to predict what will happen when two colors merge or when a piece of wood is polished—may contribute to a refined sense of language to the point that one can in reading predict what an author's next words are before seeing them. This is the ultimate reading skill.

2. Fluency of ideas

The practicing of fluency in the visual portrayal of experiences is common in every classroom where the same material is used for different purposes. The more fluent children become in the use of their crayons, the more creative they will be. To promote greater fluency both in the choice of experiences and in the use of materials is a basic part of education.

Verbal fluency and ideational fluency go hand in hand. The ability to think of a number of synonyms is indicative of the verbal fluency essential for mature and literary language.

3. Flexibility

No creative process is fully utilized if it does not take advantage of the many "happy accidents" that occur. Flexible children can make adjustments to changing situations in the creative process and adapt their expression to what happens. They are not dependent on predetermined patterns, such as those in coloring books and workbooks which are stiff and unproductive of the creative thinking process.

Constant shifting of the mind and of the productive efforts of individuals marks them as creative. This characteristic is apparent in language when a person edits oral language, uses exclamations and other forms of incomplete sentences in creative ways, uses regional dialects for effect, and varies speech patterns to depict characters with different personalities.

4. Originality

Our respect for individuals in their differences and reactions is basic to a democratic society. Art experiences, more than most others in the classroom, allow for and value "uncommonness of responses." In doing so, they make a significant contribution by stressing originality and by strengthening the self-image of children.

Conformity may in certain instances be a social necessity. Language production, especially in writing and spelling, requires a level of conformity that is not characteristic of visual portrayal, but in writing the uncommon ideas and arrangement of words can be recognized and valued as healthy growth toward effective citizenship.

5. Redefinition

The ability to rearrange and redefine materials for new purposes is an important aspect of any creative process. The nature of experimentation is to rearrange existing materials, ideas, and facts in new combinations. In visual portrayal when a child takes a pipe cleaner and fashions it into the design of a person, the material has been redefined. When children use known words in new arrangements such as in haiku or limericks, they move away from the rigidity of right definitions toward redefinitions.

6. Analysis

In analysis we start with the whole and arrive at details. Without arriving at details, it is impossible for children to penetrate the notion of differences in man and the environment. Experiences rich in perception involve analysis which activates new feelings and new information that make experiences meaningful.

Attention to details in art—color, texture, contrast, center of interest, and flow—builds a base for the analysis of language. Children who lack experience in analyzing such items as paintings, sculpture, and photographs are seldom prepared to engage in phonetic analysis, structural analysis, and syntactical analysis. Analysis of art should precede analysis of language and accompany it throughout the educational experience of children.

7. Synthesis

To synthesize is to combine several elements to form a whole. To combine several objects or parts of objects and give them new meaning or create a new impression is an activity that continues through the visual portrayal of experience. Collages, montages, and mobiles require synthesizing abilities; in fact, every creative work involves this ability to some degree.

Fluency and flexibility in synthesizing tasks with art material reflect abilities required for reading and writing. Combining sequences of sounds into words (spelling) is a synthesizing task. Arranging words into a sentence requires the same ability. Gathering ideas from an author and arriving at a statement of the main idea or major purpose is an example of synthesis. Since no one can read and write without some measure of this ability, to extend it through visual portrayal of experience is to build a firm base for more technical requirements.

8. Coherence of organization

Coherent organization is the part of creativity that most closely relates to authorship and to reflection of comprehension. It is characterized by economy—the capacity to express the utmost with the least means and effort. What is left out—the white spaces—is as important as what is filled in.

Coherent organization is not prescribed or arbitrary. It may be intrinsic to an individual work and to no others. It may be more inherent to the complete integration of thinking, feeling, and perceiving than to the elements in art or in writing. It is an essential part of any liberal education that enables one individual to communicate in multiple ways with other individuals who relate the organization of the presentation to self.

The Lowenfeld attributes are useful for planning and evaluation when they are associated with a communication program in which art is vital and language as an art is essential.

A language experience approach in communication links art expression and language production in an inseparable relationship. Art, in its broadest sense of visual portrayal, is a launching pad for oral language. After oral expression the processes of writing and reading follow naturally. Art serves as a recreational attraction when children may just "mess around." Through this type of activity many discoveries are made which can lead to fruitful productivity. Self-esteem and confidence can be built through art expression that reflects personal ideas and feelings. Children whose home-rooted language is not English can consider their thinking to be on a level equal with that of those whose language is English. Art provides a continuous opportunity at all levels of education for successful experiences in school without requiring reading and writing or even speaking.

From Concept to Craft

Self-expression in art increases awareness of the elements of composition—line, depth, color, texture, form. As children have experience in using many media, they use these elements in various ways and combinations. The natural conversation accompanying these experiences requires the use of words of the form classes—nouns, verbs, adjectives, and adverbs. The classifications of descriptive words used most frequently in literary selections are those that are used most often in talking about the processes and products of art—color, size, shape, texture, feelings, contrasts, and comparisons. Repeated experiences with the elements of art contribute to goals of visual expression, the unified whole with each part contributing to the intended effect. Repeated experiences of talking during the process and of responding to the product should build a language base that permits language production at a literary level.

Young children draw, paint, and sculpture forms representing their visual images of real and imaginary subjects. Usually they do not plan the arrangement of forms but place them in the pictures or mold them in accordance with immediate importance. This lack of prior planning does not in any way detract from the value of self-expression with media. To deny children the exploratory phase of art would be like denying speech until they can speak with poetic expressions.

Older children may be aware of creating a design, having a center of interest, developing rhythm in the work through repetition of form and color, and applying all the elements of composition with a selected medium. This development takes place gradually and should always be accompanied with freedom of expression through experimentation.

Teachers who provide time and space for visual portrayal of experiences as a basic ingredient of the communications program are guided by fundamental concepts that help the teacher select activities contributing to language growth.

1. To express self in artful ways, a child needs to be encouraged to invent, to improvise, and to fabricate.

SOME POSSIBILITIES FOR PROJECTS

Assemblance offers children a chance to arrange common materials such as boxes, buttons, paper rolls, and other objects in pleasing and uncommon ways. Color and design with paints unify assemblage.

Tissue paper overlay with its color and transparency blends magic into the art of creating many hues and values from the variety of colors and shapes of paper torn for the overlay effect.

Finger painting provides opportunities to use fingers, hands, and parts of the arm to apply and distribute paint on a glazed piece of paper.

2. To see many solutions in a problem and to choose one to develop is a needed ability in communication.

SOME POSSIBILITIES FOR PROJECTS

Colored chalk can be used on wet paper to create a color wonderland. Children respond to its ease of application and immediate representation of something bold and bright—a dragon, a field of flowers, a design of flames, the spirit of a circus. Chalk on newspapers yields instant designs suggested by the arrangement of print.

Sand casting with a variety of tools for making impressions in wet sand and a variety of objects for embedding before pouring plaster offers a chance for directness and expressiveness in a rather primitive way but one that cannot be duplicated exactly by anyone else.

Limited palette paintings with crayons, watercolors, or tempera interpret a subject in one dominant color and mixes of that color to achieve depth and form. It is a way of varying interpretations of a subject rather than of reporting photographic details. Variation can be achieved by cutting colored photographs from magazines, choosing portions of the same basic color, cutting shapes, and arranging them into a design.

3. To arrange parts into a design with unity or togetherness is an ability children develop for realistic and abstract representation.

SOME POSSIBILITIES FOR PROJECTS

Collage is a process of forming artistic compositions by placing items such as cloth, buttons, seed, braid, string, and cardboard in an arrangement and gluing them down. Dabs of color and some related lines are usually added to unify the design. Collage techniques can be observed in the work of famous artists such as Braque and Picasso. Collage is a way of doing something unusual with the usual.

Paper-and-paste projects, especially those dealing with abstract designs, provide practice in arranging for contrast, line, rhythm, and form. Arranging and rearranging are practiced before the cut or torn forms are pasted for the design.

Traditions of other cultures, such as the Mexican piñata and Japanese origami, might encourage children to experiment and to get involved in paper creations of their own.

With freedom and encouragement children naturally apply themselves to the pleasing experiences of tearing, cutting, pasting, building, and shaping constructions.

4. To bring sharply differing elements into harmony through design and color is a required ability for an artist.

SOME POSSIBILITIES FOR PROJECTS

Texture painting with sand, cornmeal, eggshells, and other textured materials can be used to change all or part of the surface of a painting. Children who use textured materials are redefining their use and thinking in new directions about materials for self-expression.

Carving is a subtractive process, the opposite of modeling, and is achieved by children as they experiment with cutting, scratching, and gouging with simple tools. Results yield contrasts in light and shadow, in bright and dull, in smooth and rough.

5. To translate a word or words into a visual representation is a required ability.

SOME POSSIBILITIES FOR PROJECTS

Tempera painting is a form of communication that most young children can deal with before they can write for themselves. Later the pictures become illustrations for the written word rather than the story itself. Easels and supplies for tempera painting should be available in every language experience approach classroom. Freedom of expression with tempera paint is as significant as the illustration of a word or a story.

As children observe their world in order to paint the things in it, they are able to see variety. A tree is not always green; clouds are not always white; the sky is not always blue. They minimize stereotypes and maximize multiple ways of expressing an idea or a word.

Crayon is usually the first medium for art that children use. It should be encouraged for the expression of ideas and for illustrating.

Clay modeling is a process of working from lumps, slabs, or coils to create three-dimensional objects. Clay can be kneaded, rolled, stretched, cut, joined, pinched, and pulled. Some of the products are fired in a kiln. But much clay work is a series of new beginnings; children decide on one thing after another as they create objects with clay.

6. To enjoy art, one does not depend on oral statements but on feelings generated by the total effect of the process and product.

SOME POSSIBILITIES FOR PROJECTS

Paper sculpture is the shaping of paper by rolling, folding, pleating, or wadding to achieve structural designs. It can be fringed, curled, and punctured for decorative effects. It has no set rules but a lot of new starts as one procedure leads to another. The product may be discarded, but the process has value enough to sustain the activity.

Paper laminating is a process of applying strips of paper dipped in wet paste to a framework such as newspaper coils, chicken wire, boxes, bottles, and balloons. There is continuous evaluation of the need to build up areas as the form becomes an animal, a totem pole, or a mask.

Drop-dry-draw is a process of dropping thick or dry tempera on very wet paper. The paint "explodes" and runs together. After it dries, the child decides what is there—real or imaginary—and outlines it with a marker.

Doodlings drawn with crayons and pencils can be filled in with color and a few features to represent feelings such as love, happiness, and fear, to create imaginary creatures, or to make pleasing designs.

7. To represent what an artist sees or imagines when handling natural materials requires minimum adjustments.

SOME POSSIBILITIES FOR PROJECTS

"Art is in the eye of the beholder" applies constantly as children see the shapes of animals, machines, and people in rocks, branches, driftwood, seedpods, shells, and clouds. Some natural materials need a little carving, scratching, or painting to bring out features and to highlight areas for a center of interest. The similarities observed require acute visual perception.

Collections of look-alike objects foster the use of figurative language in the classroom—similes, metaphors, and personification.

8. To exaggerate an idea is permitted and promoted in art activities.

SOME POSSIBILITIES FOR PROJECTS

Mosaics are surface pictures made by inlaying in patterns small pieces of colored glass, stone, seed, cardboard, or other material. Whatever its subject—animals, birds, people, a landscape, insects—a mosaic should have a strong center of interest around which the remainder of the design is built.

Murals usually exaggerate a few major objects or ideas by making them big and bold. Supporting ideas are small and subdued in comparison with the major ones. Murals can be painted with tempera, chalk, or crayons. Paper sculpture can be attached to give depth to major ideas. Cut paper adds boldness to areas to be emphasized. A mural is, in effect, an outline of an idea for an essay or other language production.

9. To make things more pleasing to the eye, all people share the desire to create and decorate them.

SOME POSSIBILITIES FOR PROJECTS

Stitchery is a process of combining materials and placing decorative stitches on them. It involves tactile experiences of manipulating and choosing materials of various textures, types, and sizes. It is a way of making pictures that is used all over the world.

Basket weaving is an ancient craft which still has appeal today. The process of working out individual shapes and designs is a challenge to creativity. The craft is excellent for eye-hand coordination.

Weaving consists of threading strips of material such as yarn, string, cloth, or paper (the weft) over and under, back and forth, through strips of material laid out in parallel rows and held firmly at both ends (the warp). The weaver develops an artistic design by utilizing the elements of color, value, texture, and pattern. The processes employed by children will help them to appreciate the skill and artistry of weavers of all time and from all over the world.

10. To show motion with static materials is an ability developed by children.

SOME POSSIBILITIES FOR PROJECTS

Puppets of all kinds—paper bag, sock, finger, laminated paper, stick— can transport a child to a land of fantasy and make-believe. Materials are chosen and arranged so that motion is possible in the use of puppets in language activities. The personality and voice of a puppet can be transmitted by the feelings and voice of a child. Puppets help children try out new ways of saying things.

Mobiles hang in space and seem to float in the air if their creators have related each part to the whole in such a way that there is balance of the space-line-form concept. Unity of design permits mobiles to be ever changing as they move. They are just like a well-written story or poem that is ever changing for its readers.

From Painting to Reading

Self-expression with paints is frequently the most advanced form of communication available to children, with the possible exception of speaking. Since speaking by all the children all the time is impossible in school situations, other forms of communication must be available.

1. Painting is linked naturally with talking.
   A child paints and then talks about the painting.
2. Talking is linked naturally with writing.
   A child paints, then talks, and then writes or lets someone else write some—but not all—of what has been said.
3. Writing is linked naturally with reading.
   A child paints, then talks, then writes, and then reads or has someone else read what has been written.
4. Reading what one writes is linked naturally with interest in what others have written on the same topic.
   A child paints, then talks, then writes, and then reads what has been written. She or he finds that in most cases many people have written on the same topic. This other writing can be listened to or read for a comparison of and contrast between authors.

Painting is a launching pad for reading in a communications-based program.

CLUES FOR INSTRUCTION

Keep a painting center supplied all the time for self-selection and for assignments. A limited number of colors can be provided for any one day. Four or five is enough.

Designate a place in the classroom for completed pictures if they tell a story. (All paintings do not have stories, and those that do not are as valuable as those that do.) On the same day of or the day following the completion of pictures, listen to the stories related to them.

When taking dictation, extract one or two sentences to write. If, however, the child does independent writing, help in the selection of the portion to be written. On the day following, read aloud or let the authors read what has been written. Invite other children to read the whole story or any portion they can sight read.

If possible, locate and place in a convenient place stories on identical topics for children to browse and read. Most reading series have stories on topics typical of what many children write. These books do not need to be easy enough for children to read to be valuable for browsing and locating words.

Display the paintings and stories so that they are available for reading and for sources of words for writing. Children who talk and write as an extension or as a summary of an idea expressed with paints are usually those who learn to read and write early and with confidence. They do not have to wait until they have a vocabulary of sight words from someone else's book; they don't have to wait until they have developed the skills of phonetic analysis; they don't have to sit quietly in the wilderness of round-robin reading by poor and halting readers. Children bring to the painting-writing experience such personal investment that they seek the dividend of reading and find it in familiar ideas and in familiar language. As they observe their presentation of dictation, they get a beginning in personal writing to the extent that very early they begin to express themselves through writing as well as through painting. But in the majority of cases, painting comes first.

Once writing in relation to painting occurs, children doing the writing can read almost verbatim what is written and grasp the original meaning. After that comes the reading of what other children have written. With a little guidance in helping children see that most of the words they use are the same as those used by other children, this step is easy and natural. The authors are present to help with the reading. The teacher is free to work on other tasks—not tied down to a small reading group, telling words and monitoring behavior. Following guidance in comparing the words in personal writing with those in books, newspapers, and magazines, some children launch into reading simple books without reading lessons.

Teachers in working with children who even into the intermediate grades have delayed reading development can use the same motivational procedures and language strategies to build enough self-confidence that reading is possible. Without a measure of self-confidence, which is reflected in self-expression, it is doubtful that any child will learn to read.

CLUES FOR INSTRUCTION

Older children can produce books for younger ones. Picture books are appropriate and require attention to a sequence of ideas. Easy reading books focus on vocabularies of high-frequency words. Nouns in the stories can be illustrated.

When descriptive words or passages are eliminated to reduce the number of words and the length of sentences, the descriptions can be preserved in the illustrations.

Authors who read their books to young children learn to engage them in discussions of the illustrations, using vocabularies of color, size, shape, texture, sound, taste, smell, and feelings.

Summary of Skills and Abilities for Visually Portraying Experiences

PERSONAL ENJOYMENT AND APPRECIATION

——Uses a variety of art materials to express ideas
——Chooses art activities for recreation
——Enjoys artistic products of others
——Experiments with art media
——Appreciates and uses the art of other cultures
——Enjoys the processes of art whether or not the product is worth keeping
——Decorates own belongings to make them more pleasing to the eye
——Reports on visits to galleries, art shows, and art museums

LANGUAGE RELATIONSHIPS

——Talks informally about own art products and processes
——Can tell stories about some of own paintings
——Can choose main ideas for dictation or writing of stories for some of own paintings
——Uses descriptive categories of words in talking and writing about art—color, size, shape, texture, feelings, contrast, comparison
——Uses words of motion when talking and writing about art—painting, carving, weaving, pasting, scratching, cutting
——Uses names of things in talking and writing about art

——Chooses books about art and artists for recreational reading
——Represents a main idea in a work of art
——Can produce paintings to represent a sequence of ideas
——Uses art to illustrate own books
——Uses art for bindings of own books
——Uses art to display poems in the classroom
——Illustrates ideas gained through reading
——Illustrates ideas gained through listening
——Makes puppets to assist in telling stories—those read and those original
——Creates new characters and new situations for stories
——Uses figurative language such as similes, metaphors, and personification in making observations

PERSONAL REPRESENTATION

——Uses art in several working centers of the classroom—writing, science, mathematics
——Participates in art for special days, seasons, events
——Can select appropriate art media for communicating ideas and feelings
——Uses abstract art for self-expression
——Creates imaginary characters and creatures
——Fabricates a unified work from a variety of scrap materials
——Experiments with many media
——Chooses materials independently to satisfy self-expression needs
——Observes and represents the things of the world in a variety of ways—close up, far away, with shadows, distorted, exaggerated
——Highlights one object in work of art to create a center of interest
——Can judge things that go together to achieve harmony of design
——Sees look-alikes in natural materials such as branches, rocks, seedpods, clouds, plants

Selected References

Allen, Roach Van, and Claryce Allen. *Teacher's Resource Book: Language Experiences in Early Childhood.* Encyclopaedia Britannica Educational Corp., Chicago, 1969.
Association for Childhood Education International. *Let's Make a Picture* and

Let's Create a Form. Association for Childhood Education International, Washington, D.C., 1969.

Darrow, Helen, and Roach Van Allen. *Independent Activities for Creative Learning.* Teachers College Press, New York, 1961.

Dunn, Hope W. *The Art of Teaching Reading: A Language and Self-Concept Approach.* Charles E. Merrill, Columbus, Ohio, 1972.

Feldman, Edmund B. *Art as Image and Ideas.* Prentice-Hall, Englewood Cliffs, N.J., 1967.

Lowenfeld, Viktor, and W. L. Brittain. *Creative and Mental Growth,* 4th ed. Macmillan Co., New York, 1964.

Mattil, Edward L. *Meanings and Crafts.* Prentice-Hall, Englewood Cliffs, N.J., 1965.

Meilach, Cona, and Elvie Ten Hoor. *Collage and Found Art.* Reinhold Publishers, New York, 1964.

Morine, Harold, and Grace Morine. *Discovery: A Challenge to Teachers.* Prentice-Hall, Englewood Cliffs, N.J., 1973.

Packwood, Mary M. (ed.). *Art Education in the Elementary School.* National Art Education Association, Washington, D.C., 1967.

Riendeau, Betty. "Since Children Are Creative—Involve Them in Reading," *The Reading Teacher,* 22, 5 (February, 1969), 408–413.

Snow, Aida Cannarsa. *Growing with Children Through Art.* Reinhold Publishers, New York, 1968.

South Carolina State Department of Education. *Learning Centers: Children Alive.* State Department of Education, Columbia, S.C., 1973.

FROM THE RATIONALE   Dramatization of experiences—creating and recreating with voice and body movements the feelings and ideas of others as well as roles that are impossible in real life; putting self in other's place; communicating without words through pantomime; and interpreting facial expressions, gestures, posture, and tone of voice.

Dramatic play is an activity in which the children express spontaneously a complete identification with the world as they see it and feel it. They portray in a doing-thinking-feeling way their impressions of persons, places, objects, and situations. Dramatic play promotes improved expression of concepts of self; it transposes the child from her or his world of being to one of pretending to be; it provides experiences of feeling to take to reading; and it develops an interest in drama as a means of interpreting ideas gained through reading.

Self-concept and Self-expression

Dramatic play or dramatization is a natural activity of children, taking place in the classroom, on the playground, and at home. The classroom version of dramatic play, however, is a far cry from yesterday's classroom *dramas*. The most noticeable difference is the spontaneity of today's children engaged in creating their own plays. They have to have ideas before they can create. They must learn how to express their ideas in three-dimensional form in order to dramatize them.

For the majority of children it is important to express most of their deepest feelings through vicarious experiences. In order to express the difference between being generous and selfish, brave and fearful, happy and sad, successful and failing, a child can become a character in a play and show real feelings. One experience in expressing such concepts leads to confidence in other forms of self-expression and to continued interest in dramatizing an idea. As children play a great variety of roles, new interests are aroused and new problems are faced. These new aspects require the use of more and varied materials and additional information in order to express clearly the basic ideas or situations. When used as a base for reading, the experiences in drama provide a backdrop for identifying and understanding characters that can never be understood from real-life experiences only.

Both aggressive and timid children benefit from the opportunity to express themselves in dramatic productions. In addition to being an aid to speech production and refinement, realistic dramatic training improves listening, reading, and writing skills. It calls upon the same basic mental abilities required for listening with comprehension; it exercises the same skills used for organizing that are gained from silent reading; and it develops fluency and flexibility as an attribute requisite to creative writing. Yet all these skills and abilities can be developing without, or prior to, the acquisition of reading and writing skills. Dramatic experiences can keep learners in touch with language that is full and beautiful during processes of learning specific literacy skills. It can furnish teachers valuable clues for planning direct instructional activities for the future.

CLUES FOR INSTRUCTION

Begin role-playing and sociodrama with known and familiar situations. "Show what happened" is an easy way to introduce dramatization following an oral sharing of events. Maybe a second or a third character will be needed. Choose from volunteers, and a cast is ready to perform. Spontaneity and natural language are key demands of this type of drama.

Move on to situations in which children act out roles calling upon them to decide their own obligations to others and to show how they can respect their rights and feelings—an adult in charge of children on an excursion, a baby sitter for an evening, the captain of a losing team, the chairman of a business meeting where controversy rages, a person who observes a dishonest act, or the discoverer of something new that could be of great benefit to mankind. Choose roles that are known to have parallels in reading selections planned for the near future.

As children have the opportunity to act out many roles, some will realize that their own thoughts, feelings, and actions are not unique. With a little guidance they will realize that most stories and poems deal with common, ordinary thoughts and situations much like their own. Artist-authors say what they have to say about ordinary things with extraordinary language. It may be that dramatization will offer some children their first reason to say things in new ways that open up opportunities for them to function as authors. They are not likely to write anything they have never thought *and said*. They are not likely to read with comprehension anything they have not felt nor experienced to some degree. They must have some basis on which to make comparisons and contrasts, or the message of an author might pass by them. Dramatization can provide many of these bases.

Children who have frequent experiences in dramatic play, socio-drama, and other forms of creative dramatics tend to display an interest in the dialogue that they find in reading; they may want to organize a series of events into a play and provide a plot. They find satisfaction and enjoyment in working individually or as a member of a group in creating dialogue and directions for puppet shows, for plays, and for radio, television, and motion picture scripts.

As children mature in their ability to dramatize ideas, they
——become more sensitive to the use of voice and gesture in expressing shades of meaning and "think" these voices and gestures as they read
——are more interested in viewing films and listening to recordings
——adapt their own stories into plays for the stage or puppet theater
——are aware of the close relationship between dialogue, action, costumes, and stage settings.

Dramatic play and dramatization activities give clues to students about their world and who they are in that world. Those who participate *identify* some of the things they need to know about themselves, their families, their friends, and about work.

Dramatic interpretation helps children to *relate* these clues to many situations that they will find in reading, listening to recordings, and viewing films. Dramatization helps them to *revise* these clues as they get to know the world better through observation, exploration, discussion, expression of their own ideas, and development of abilities to communicate these ideas through speaking and writing.

This process helps them to become more mature, self-reliant, self-actualized individuals, able to function as literate citizens. They can understand, appreciate, and tolerate the varied points of view and feelings of others, and they can express their own points of view and feelings effectively and in a variety of ways.

From Being to Pretending-to-Be

In dramatic play children consciously pretend that they are someone else. They extend their feelings, explore some of their emerging thoughts, seek relief from some of their frustrations, and live in the future as they become animals, people from another planet, persons earning a living, parents, teachers, and other characters who give them an opportunity to experiment with experiences and ideas before an audience.

Sociodrama is another creative technique of pretending. In spontaneous dramatic action children identify themselves with some particular personality described in some specific life situation. The acting is called role-playing. Sociodramas are not written or memorized because their primary purpose is to open up new levels of awareness of how people feel and why they behave as they do in a given situation. A simple form of sociodrama is to describe a true-to-life happening, stopping at the climax before the problems are resolved. Children can then choose various roles and create their own outcomes for the story. In doing so they can reveal their own feelings about the problem or the situation at the time when they are pretending to be someone else.

Pretending-to-be requires the use of voice inflections and vocabulary not typical of home-rooted speech. It offers repeated opportunities for children to practice using language they have never used before. It extends experiences in oral language production toward a match with what is found in many reading materials.

CLUES FOR INSTRUCTION

Guide children in the selection of parts representing all ages of people—from the oldest to the youngest. Offer parts in dramas that are set in a variety of places—from large cities to remote areas. Choose drama situations that give children an opportunity to act as persons of different racial and ethnic backgrounds. Tap the unlimited resource of the unknown and the unexplored—the imaginary world of childhood.

As a thinking reader every child will encounter a great variety of situations in silent reading. To have acted a part builds a base of experiences that is helpful in making reading a thinking process. Pretending is basic to reading.

Dramatization and Reading

From their earliest days of listening to reading, children can indicate a level of understanding by simply acting out characters. This ability and interest can be continued and utilized in school to the advantage of students and teachers.

Zella likes to tell stories. She announces a story and identifies the characters. Children volunteer to be the characters before they hear the story. As she tells the story, the characters pantomime their parts. They have to listen carefully and think fast of ways to show actions and feelings. The audience gets emotionally involved in observing the characters in action.

Bess likes to read something of children's literature each day. Her selections include many that can be acted out. After a few times of demonstrating the procedures, she makes cards for the Dramatization Center so that groups of children can work independently. The cards have names of the characters. Children can choose by distributing the cards and can change characters by changing cards. A copy of the story is usually available for checking on details, but children are encouraged to use their own versions and interpretations in line with the general outline of the story.

Simple props might be used. They can be developed rapidly and added to the usual supply of hats, coats, shoes, scarves, and other items in the Dramatization Center.

In Bess's class children who perform poorly in oral reading situations that require exact replication can participate freely and effectively in the dramatization of stories.

Oliver plans a theater-in-the-round at least once a week. One student has permission to prepare the play. The story to be acted out is kept a secret. The student director reads it as many times as necessary for him or her to learn to tell it with ease and clarity. Props are prepared ahead of time. Characters are usually volunteers. They move to the center of the room, and the audience sits around the edge. The storyteller begins and the action starts. Most of the time the characters have never heard the story before. Their actions are spontaneous. Sometimes the story is enacted several times with different sets of actors.

Oliver knows that this dramatization experience keeps children reading for specific purposes and forces them to gain an awareness of stories that have setting, characters, action, and plot that are appealing to others. Oral interpretation of stories is improved significantly, and listening skills are sharpened.

Mary likes to extend the ability of children to make personal interpretations by reading a story together with them and then by changing the setting from a cold to a hot climate, from California to

China, or from a small town to a big city. She might even change male characters into female characters and vice versa, people into animals, or old people into young people. Students assume the roles and act out the parts spontaneously. Such activity highlights some of the major features of well-written stories and helps students to read with greater interest and increased meaning.

The unfinished story is used frequently by Juan as a stimulus for dramatization. He has a collection of stories with beginnings that are sharp and clear. He reads to a point of high interest and then lets small groups of students act out an ending. Sometimes he puts the printed version of the unfinished story in the Dramatization Center so that there will be time to work out dialogue and props. Following the presentation of several versions of the story ending, he places copies of the finished story in the Reading/Research Center. No comments are necessary to interest students in reading it. They *must* find out the author's ending.

The Teacher and Dramatization

The experience of dramatization as well as the dramatization of experience is an integral part of a language-centered classroom. Whether or not children are unable to reproduce or reflect ideas gained from listening, reading, or both may not be as significant as the fact that they participate in activities that permit them to try being someone or something other than self. It is through such experiences in communication that some psychologists believe that self is enhanced (Bills, 1959; Carlton and Moore, 1971). If this theory is true, then teachers have an obligation to create learning environments that permit and promote dramatization. To retell a story in action is *not* a primary goal of dramatization in a language experience approach classroom. Rather, the goal is to give children repeated opportunities to live through situations—to discover and improvise.

Some essentials guiding a teacher's point of view and understanding of dramatization in learning situations that promote language growth for reading follow.

ESSENTIAL 1: A FRIENDLY RELATIONSHIP IN WHICH RAPPORT IS ESTABLISHED BETWEEN TEACHER AND CLASS

Mutual respect is fostered when the teacher is able to enter into problem-solving situations as a learner. Experiences must be shared, desires must be revealed, ideals must be shared, and stands on moral judgment must be revealed but not set up as the right ones. There is no need for children to enter into personal problem-solving when the end result is always judged as right or wrong. The process of entering into possible solutions is the goal. In such situations language production is real and natural. Teachers can gain clues from the performances that will guide in future encounters, but they cannot gain the privilege of passing final judgment.

ESSENTIAL 2: AN ATTITUDE OF ACCEPTING CHILDREN'S LANGUAGE AS IT IS

In dramatization there is no need to monitor the correctness of language. A major goal for the teacher is one of creating opportunities to hear raw, natural language coming from a "free spirit." No program of language instruction can be individualized until the chief planner knows individual potential and problems. Such information does not come from pencil-paper diagnostic tests or from listening to oral replication of someone else's language through reading. It comes only when the individual is free to be self or to act as someone else.

ESSENTIAL 3: AN UNDERSTANDING OF THE ESSENTIAL INGREDIENTS
THROUGH WHICH DRAMATIZATION FUNCTIONS

Dramatization, like other art forms, is dependent on contrast and comparison. There can be no drama without contrasts in stillness and motion, silence and sound, and darkness and light.

A classroom does not need the equipment of a theater to provide actors with the resources necessary for a dramatic production. A Dramatization Center does need to have items for producing a variety of sounds not made by human voices. A flashlight or a lantern made of cardboard is all the equipment necessary for a shift from darkness to light when children are acting. Flicking an electric light switch might be enough. Motion is inherent in children's activities, but it may be refined with suggestions and practice in using hands, feet, facial expressions, and body motions to interpret a wide range of feelings.

ESSENTIAL 4: A WILLINGNESS TO PARTICIPATE IN THE
EXPERIENCE OF DRAMATIZATION

Children deserve to work *with* the teacher rather than *for* the teacher. Natural situations arise as new techniques and materials are introduced at the Dramatization Center. Beyond this teachers must take character parts when stories are read for dramatization. In many classrooms it is essential that sometime the teacher assume the role of a person who speaks with incorrect grammar and with a regional dialect. In some situations the teacher should be a character whose behavior is intolerable. Children who dramatize other character roles with the teacher come to understand the teacher as another human being with problems like theirs.

ESSENTIAL 5: AN AWARENESS OF LANGUAGE CONCEPTS THAT CAN BE EMPHASIZED AND EXTENDED THROUGH DRAMATIZATION

Numerous objectives for dramatization can be enumerated (Woods and Trithart, 1970). Among these are
—the joy of being involved with others in human experiences
—the understanding of self
—becoming self-directed
—discovering and selecting values to live by
—developing unique human potentialities
—developing interest in reading
—developing appreciation for well-written literature.

But the major purpose of dramatization in a language experience approach is that of extending language power in a variety of situations. Teachers are not satisfied to listen as one child after another replicates the language of someone else and to call it reading. They are not satisfied to let one child who raises a hand and begs for a chance to give an answer to a question answer for the whole class. Teachers in a language experience approach need to
—hear children express themselves orally in an environment of free language usage
—hear each child adjust his or her own language to fit a variety of characters
—observe expressions of feeling toward known and unknown situations
—mediate language growth toward the occasional use of literary language
—orchestrate groups of children into productions reflecting the influence of artist-authors and producers—phrases, sentences, rhymes, songs, and rhythms that fit naturally into spontaneous drama.

Summary of Skills and Abilities for Dramatizing Experiences

DRAMATIC PLAY

—Participates freely and willingly in dramatic play
—Is spontaneous and natural in oral expression

——Can enact what she or he sees and hears

——Uses language appropriate to the character being portrayed

——Uses hands, feet, facial expressions, and body to interpret characters

——Uses conversation with another person to further the action of the play

DRAMATIZATION AND READING

——Shares favorite poems and stories with others

——Shows originality in the interpretation of stories, poems, music, and dramatizations

——Helps to plan and participate in class TV and radio programs

——Uses incidents in stories for dramatization

——Plans and participates in puppet shows

——Creates original plays with plot, characters, and setting

——Repeats words and phrases of characters in stories when dramatizing them

——Interprets characters by hearing them read by others

Selected References

Austin, David F., Velma B. Clark, and Gladys W. Fitchett. *Reading Rights for Boys: Sex Role and Development of Language Experiences.* Appleton-Century-Crofts, New York, 1971.

Bills, R. E. "Nondirective Play Therapy with Retarded Learners," *Journal of Consulting Psychology,* 14 (April, 1959), 140–149.

Carlton, Lessie, and Robert H. Moore. *Reading, Self-Directive Dramatization and Self-Concept.* Charles E. Merrill, Columbus, Ohio, 1971.

Cohen, S. Alan, and Gita S. Kornfeld. "Oral Vocabulary and Beginning Reading in Disadvantaged Black Children," *The Reading Teacher,* 24, 1 (1970), 30–38.

Combs, Arthur W., and Donald Snygg. *Individual Behavior.* Harper & Row, New York, 1959.

Cox, Vivian E. "Reciprocal Oracy/Literacy Recognition Skills in the Language Production of Language Experience Approach Students." (Ed.D. dissertation.) University of Arizona, Tucson, 1971.

Harris, Peter (ed.). *Drama in Education.* The Bodley Head, London, 1971.

Kelley, Earl C. "The Fully Functioning Self." In *Perceiving, Behaving, Becoming.* Association for Supervision and Curriculum Development, Washington, D.C., 1962.

Phillips, B. "Anxiety as a Function of Early School Experience," *Psychology in the Schools,* 4 (1967), 335–340.

Purkey, William W. *Self-Concept and School Achievement*. Prentice-Hall, Englewood Cliffs, N.J., 1970.

Rinquest, Sharon. *A Creative Dramatics Guide, K-6*. Nebraska State Department of Education, Lincoln, Nebr., 1968.

Rogers, C. R. *Counseling and Psychotherapy*. Houghton Mifflin Co., Boston, 1947.

Woods, Margaret S., and Beryl Trithart. *Guidelines to Creative Dramatics*. D.O.K. Publishers, Buffalo, 1970.

Responding rhythmically—using self-selected body movements to illustrate meanings from sounds of music, sounds of language, and personal feelings; moving to predetermined patterns with rhythmic accompaniment; and illustrating meanings through body rhythm and dancing.

Rhythmic responses are basic to every person's communication. As a nonverbal form they are as significant in many cases as the verbal forms that may or may not accompany them.

The printed word can only imply basic body responses, but most literary works draw on our experience background of self-expression through rhythmic experiences. Movement is so basic to life experience that every sentence spoken or printed has a verb in it or one implied.

Because the printed word can only imply basic rhythmic responses, it is difficult to imagine that a person who has not experienced those responses in some meaningful way can ever read literary works with meaning. To assume that because children move freely, they understand and engage in a wide variety of rhythmic responses is to assume what is not true for many of them. To assume that they have words for the hundreds of movements of man, animals, machines, and the elements is to assume what is not true for most of them.

Many children in our schools are shy and inhibited about expressing themselves with their hands, feet, fingers, toes, and body. They have been made to feel that to be still and quiet is a virtue of highest priority for success in school. It is a sad commentary on our school programs that these shy children, along with all the others, are expected to enter into reconstructing the meanings of cold print that does not reflect the language or ideas of anyone and to call it reading! These procedures and behavioral objectives are administered to children without the slightest inventory of their level of self-confidence in expressing personal meanings in sounds of music and in sounds of language. Some schools thrust what they call self-selection reading programs on children who have never had an opportunity in the school setting to learn how to self-select a simple body rhythm when listening to music. Simple inventories usually reflect the fact that children who lack the self-confidence and self-concept needed to make personal responses to music are the same ones who cannot remember words, cannot reply to questions of meaning, and cannot decide which book to read when given a choice.

Is it any wonder that our schools are embarrassed by a multitude of reading failures who are being rescheduled daily into classes taught by remedial reading teachers? For most children the basic needs are not centered in remedial reading but in the basic life experiences that undergird the output and intake of language. Activities that center around rhythmic responses to music and to language can contribute to the needed base. They are basic to reading in a language experience approach.

Language Development through Rhythmic Response

The language of movement, which is essential for speaking, writing, and reading in sentences, can be fostered and refined through rhythmic responses. The words of movement and their meanings can be learned in other ways, but efficient instruction links the actual movements to the words. These words of movement, when experienced and verbalized, can be used for writing and will be recognized in reading to an extent not possible without meaningful interpretation. Some of the ways in which children develop language through rhythmic response are:

——moving to rhythmic music
——pantomiming with body movements while listening to music
——creating body movements to express feelings
——playing singing games and chanting
——responding to films without words
——responding by writing.

Moving to Rhythmic Music

Through instructions and demonstrations children acquire a repertoire of responses from which they can select some that could become personalized at later times.

CLUES FOR INSTRUCTION

Practice rhythms for the following body movements when they are appropriate to a story or song:

clapping of hands	slapping of abdomen
clicking of tongue	swinging of arms

rocking of body	jumping
marching	running
skipping	galloping
hopping	swimming

Use basic rhythm later as children move and make sounds of animals and machines. Without direct instruction in relation to the words they depend on, imitation of the movement or a variation on two or three movements combines into a meaningful interpretation in the mind of a child.

The teacher as an observer can obtain clues to which children can synthesize related elements into a meaningful whole. This ability is the same as that required for recognizing words in print (reading) and recognizing the relationship of sound to alphabet letters in words (spelling).

Teachers can participate by actually helping children to move to the rhythm of music rather than by just moving while music is playing. They can clap the accents and be a partner while a child claps, marches, or tiptoes. They can improvise, experiment, vary, and create. They can build rapport in a success situation which will be extremely valuable when the child faces a failure situation in language recognition skills.

Pantomiming with Body Movements While Listening to Music

Responding without talking gives children a chance to interpret meanings at a beginning level as well as at the advanced level used by actors. Pantomime promotes relaxed interpretations. It permits the teacher to introduce verbs that may be new to some children. It builds confidence in self-selection which will be useful and necessary as reading and writing activities become increasingly independent ones.

CLUES FOR INSTRUCTION

Children listen to music with different tempos and to music that creates a variety of moods. The teacher or the children can follow spontaneous directions while listening. The children can sit in a circle on the floor and follow the directions with individual interpretations.

The leader might say:
"Use your hands and arms only.
Keep the rest of your body still.

Wave
  stretch
    twist and turn
      cup fingers
        fly
       fling
      flutter
    shiver and shake.''
''Now move your hands and arms as you think they should move to this music.''
''Use your feet only.
  Wiggle your toes
    pull toes up tight
      stretch feet back and forth
    relax your toes.''
''Now choose your own way to move your feet to the music.''
''Stand up and move your legs and feet. Keep the rest of your body as still as possible.''
''Bend your knees
  lift one foot an inch from the floor
    kick forward
      kick backward
    dangle one foot in the air
  stand on tiptoe.''
''Choose your own way to move your feet and legs as you listen to the music.''
''Move your whole body.
  Whirl
    glide
      slump
        collapse
      stiffen
    vibrate
  grow high
wilt.''
''Let the music tell you how to move your hands and arms, your head, your feet and legs, your whole body.''

After there is evidence that some children can select body responses to interpret many meanings, small groups can be organized to interpret specific situations such as those found in stories that they are hearing and reading.

CLUES FOR INSTRUCTION

Children can sit or stand as they interpret a situation without saying words but with feelings for the meanings of words.

Standing: walk in space
run down a crowded sidewalk
cross a busy street
swim across a pool
throw a baseball
sweep a floor

Sitting: hold a frisky kitten
eat hot food
watch football on television
fuss with someone
brush your teeth
paint a picture

As children respond, comment on individual participation. Use verbs that may be new to many of the children but ones that they are likely to encounter in listening to and reading stories.

"Maria is nimble as she walks in the crowd."

"Tony thrusts his arm out when he swims fast."

"Jose puckered his lips when the soup was too hot."

"Sue scrubbed her teeth vigorously."

The comments are not for the purpose of teaching the words directly but of exposing children to the large number of words used to tell movement.

When responding rhythmically on command, children may hear verbs new to them. Demonstrations will be needed but should be done in the spirit of helping children enhance feelings of being able to respond with motions and with words that are rapidly becoming their own.

Creating Body Movements to Express Feelings

Vocabularies of words of feeling and emotions can be learned through direct instruction but should not be so set that children are right or wrong in their interpretations. Meaningful vocabularies of words of feeling are essential for listening to and reading stories with characters. Words such as *wicked* and *joyful* can set the meaning of a whole story. Contrastive words such as *angry* and *happy* are keys to comprehension in many stories. They can be significant even though they occur only once in a story.

In real life persons express their feelings with body movements as well as with words. The two are linked together in meaningful expression. They are recorded in print which becomes reading.

CLUES FOR INSTRUCTION

Say a word of feeling or emotion. Ask the children to do something with their faces, their arms and faces, or their whole bodies to express the feeling as they say the word. Keep repeating the word together softly in a rhythmic pattern in order to intensify efforts to reflect feelings of words such as *afraid, proud, troubled, sad, selfish, peaceful, lonesome, loved, bashful,* and *pleased.*

Read stories, listen to recorded stories, or listen to stories on film. Listen for words that tell how people feel. Choose one character for each child. Express the feelings of that character with facial movements, hand movements, and body movements without talking. If the children enjoy this exercise, let them trade characters and listen again.

Play recordings of music with or without songs. Talk about feelings the composers may have wished to express in certain passages. Move to the music in ways that express widely varying feelings about the compositions—dance, act, or whirl. Interpret with movements of the entire body or with just the hands or face the feeling of gaiety, gloom, happiness, or sadness. Try to find some of the same words in stories.

Playing Singing Games and Chanting

Play, sing, and chant in order to link rhythmic responses to language. Since the rhythms of language repeat over and over, children who know one set of words to a rhythmic pattern can substitute others that may be more meaningful to them than the original ones.

CLUES FOR INSTRUCTION

Traditional singing games such as "Farmer in the Dell," "London Bridge," and "Skip to My Loo" can be used as starters, but most music textbook series include many singing games from around the world. Each game is likely to repeat a basic language pattern found over and over in reading. For each pattern, words can be substituted to vary the language to the interests and background of the group while keeping the rhythm of, for example, "Farmer in the Dell":

"The teacher's in the room. . . ."
"The grocer's in the store. . . ."

Through the process of the substitution of words to basic rhythms, the language and ideas of any group of children can be used for rhythmic responses. One tune can serve many sets of words.

Diane had a challenge to teach children with a limited background in English. Most of them lived in Spanish-speaking homes. She kept singing songs with them until she found one that most seemed to know. When she tried "Happy Birthday," she got an encouraging response. The children could sing this song in English. Diane brought her bongo drums to school for the children to play as they beat out the rhythm and sang "Happy Birthday" to each other. She wrote the words of the song on the chalkboard with wide-open spaces between the lines. As children beat out the rhythm on the drums and with fingers on their tables, she invited them to say other things in the same rhythmic pattern. She listened until she heard one that would work and wrote it between the lines of "Happy Birthday." The children would read along as they sang the new versions.

Rene said,

"Crazy crashday to you,
Crazy crashday to you,
Crazy crashday, dear Evel,
Crazy crashday, to you."

Barney said,

"Happy rainday to you,
Happy rainday to you,
Happy rainday, dear Wormy,
Happy rainday to you."

Within a week sixteen versions had been recorded on reading charts. They were duplicated and made into "Happy Readers." The children were launched into a reading program with rhythmic language that almost forced them to keep going. The beat, the sound, the choral production, and the use of familiar topics provided easy reading material which children could identify as theirs. They were not learning to read a foreign language but their own.

Responding to Films without Words

Films without narration but with background music are useful in guiding children to respond rhythmically.

CLUES FOR INSTRUCTION

A series of films without words such as *Magic Moments* (Encyclopaedia Britannica Films, 1969) has background music which gives children ideas for making their own films. "Bang!", one of the series, can be shown one or two times with the soundtrack playing. The soundtract can then be turned off, and the children can find things to use as instruments to play in an orchestral accompaniment. The results are sometimes astonishing when children are helped to sense when their instruments can add most to the music.

"Fantasy of Feet," another *Magic Moments* film, can be used for interpretive dance. Since there are no words for listening, each child is free to move to the music. The motion pictures offer suggestions which may not be typical of past performances. Extension of experience in selecting rhythmic motions without predetermined patterns is promoted with this type of film.

An introduction from a film on the movements of feet can be followed by direct instruction through demonstrations and experimentation.

What can feet do?
——dance with heavy feet, light feet
——make rhythmic patterns—fast-slow, forward-backward, slide, tap, heel-toe
——move like those of a football player, of a basketball player
——dance to rhythms that are characteristic of certain places—Mexico, Hawaii
——pretend they are magic feet
Listen to the music while viewing "Magic Hands" or "Join Hands, Let's Go," from the *Magic Moments* series—
——show many ways to say "Let's go!"
——play "Follow the Leader" using hand motions
——play charades

——pantomime activities such as sewing, playing piano, directing traffic

——pretend your hands are magic

Responding by Writing

When children reveal their thinking while listening to music, there can be no denying that experience backgrounds enter into what is heard. Uniform responses are neither possible nor desirable. Comprehension that reflects diversity is personal and is a precious commodity that must be fostered and valued.

Georgia played a recording of selections from *The Nutcracker Suite*, by Tchaikovsky, to seven-year-olds at the end of first grade. The only instructions were: "Think about anything you wish while you listen. You may write one of your thoughts when we have finished." Here are some of the results:

——"The music made me think of party girls dancing in a faraway land." Gale

——"The music made me think of my kitty cats." Brian

——"The music made me think of Saturn and the stars and Mary, God, and angels." Betsy

——"The music made me think of where the Romans lived and where they danced. And sometimes they played over a pot and snakes came out." Tony

——"The music made me think of mermaids swimming in the ocean." June

——"The music made me think of turtles digging in the sand." Kevin

No one can deny that the experiences, backgrounds, and interests of the children entered into their responses to music.

Children bring to a reading experience the same backgrounds and interests that they bring to an experience in listening to music. They use these experiences in comprehending. Unfortunately, in many reading programs responses have been predetermined and recorded in workbooks and tests. Children are expected to arrive at uniform responses almost to the exclusion of diverse ones. Because of this tradition it is imperative in a language experience approach that avenues such as those afforded by music be kept open and available. It may be through these avenues that the language personalities and the courage to make personal responses grow strong enough to overcome the effects of the convergent thinking required for success in narrowly conceived reading programs.

Debbie, a ten-year-old in a central city school, listened to "Morning" from the *Peer Gynt Suite* by Edvard Grieg. Afterward she wrote to the rhythm of the music a song that she called "Raindrop Dance."

> Playing among the winds is fun,
> Swaying gaily 'neath the sun,
> Opening, ringing, sounds of gladness,
> Telling the world of happiness,
> Ringing softly in the streets,
> Making joy for plants it meets.

Rhythmic sounds had released Debbie to write in a way that was not characteristic of her speech. What she said about rain was rather ordinary. The way she said it was extraordinary—poetic.

Listening to classical music does not require a musical background. The reason certain selections are classical is that there is a message and a feeling in them for everyone. They release thoughts and language. They have the power to bring up from memory mental pictures of past experiences. They build a rhythmic sense of expression not typical of conversation and discussion experiences.

Elva did not require a specific listening experience to respond in writing to her feelings and observations when in sixth grade. Music had become such an integral part of her life that she was able to write the following.

Music Everywhere

> There's music in the air,
> There's music everywhere,
> Music in the wind as it
>   blows through the trees,
> Music in the chirp of a bird,
> Music in the night when the
>   crickets sing.

So listen,
And you can hear
Music in the air,
Music everywhere.

Composing Music for Language

Children who memorize poetry and create their own poems can enhance the language with melodies that highlight the rhythmic nature of English. Exploratory work in musical composition leads to refinements which may be published for performance. A Music Center can be developed with instruments such as tone bells, an autoharp, tone blocks, and a piano. As children learn to repeat poetic language, they can be encouraged to try to find a melody for it. Most of what results is never recorded, but occasionally a melody is created that is worth keeping. Teachers who are unable to record a melody in writing can often find a volunteer student or teacher to do so. Also, many children in intermediate grades learn to record simple melodies with minimum instruction. Specific suggestions are available in music programs. The important idea for the language program is one of supporting, through real experiences, the facts of rhythm, melody, and repeating patterns in poetic language.

Sara wrote "My Bunny," and the teacher helped the entire class to get involved in composing a melody for it. They used an autoharp and a piano to try out possibilities. The teacher recorded the melody on the chalkboard and called attention to the repeating patterns. The children could see that some measures were repeated several times and that some chords on the autoharp were repeated over and over. These discoveries helped them to read and sing rhyming poetry.

Ramon composed a poetic statement, "Butterflies." His teacher encouraged him to find a melody that would help him to say what he had to say in a melodic way. Ramon needed practice in sounding out English pronunciations. His composition gave him and all members of his class a chance to hold on to syllables and words far in excess of any reasonable practice in oral reading.

By the time Anita and Danny were in junior high school, they had written poetry and composed music many times. They combined their talents to present "When All the World's Asleep" as an observa-

My Bunny

Once I had a bun-ny, whose name was Cuddles.

And when it rained, he liked to jump in puddles

When he got all dir-ty, he'd wash himself with care. He's

such a pretty fel-low my cuddly, cuddly hare.

Butterflies

Butterflies hare beautiful wings. They

seem to have wings that sing. They

fly in the sky ver — y high.

When All the World's Asleep

Anita Posey

Danny Harris

Where do insects go at night when all the world's asleep?

Where do bugs and butterflies and caterpillars creep?

Turtles sleep in-side their shells; the robin has her nest.

Rabbits and the sly old fox have holes where they can rest.

Bears can crawl in-side a cave; the lion has his den.

Cows can sleep in-side the barn, and pigs can use their pen. But

where do bugs and butterflies and caterpillars creep, when

ev-ery-thing is dark out-side and all the world's a- sleep?

tion they had made from a science unit. They did not answer their question, but they extended it with a composition that has obvious design, structure, repetition, and simplicity. They took an ordinary question and did something extraordinary with it. In the process they tried out, explored alternatives, revised, and probably just messed around until the patterns fell into place. Through the process of composing music to accompany the poem, both elements were refined. Through sharing the poem through song, all the class members participated successfully in oral reading.

Rhythmic Response through Choral Speaking

Choral speaking is the oral interpretation of poetry and prose by a group of persons. As children hear poems and join with each other and the teacher in repeating refrains or favorite parts, they are beginning choral speaking. This can gradually develop into the interpretation of poetry by several or many voices in unison and can thus become a form of group dramatic interpretation. The principal purposes are:

——the use of creative forms for expressing rhythms, emotions, and moods

——assurance that every child can join in effective oral production of someone else's language

——practice in reading with emphasis, pause, and voice modulation that aids in and adds to meaning

——enjoyment of oral reading of poetry

——satisfaction from participation in effective performance.

Choral speaking can help to develop self-assurance by giving timid children a chance to function as a part of the group. It can improve voice quality, careless speech, and faulty English patterns without singling out one child for humiliating correction. It can increase vocabulary by making new words a happy experience. It can develop children's ability to read aloud effectively and with understanding.

Those children who plan the interpretation themselves get the most from choral speaking. They experiment with various effects, compare, evaluate, and try again before deciding on a pattern of presentation. If the children like, understand, and grasp the mood of a poem, they will tend to adapt their voices to its feeling, tone, and meaning and will give a genuine treatment of it. They will also develop a sensitivity to poems that lend themselves best to choral speaking. These are usually poems that have a marked rhythm, contain a chorus, refrain, or recurring effect, and are full of contrasts in mood and rhythms.

A fourth-grade class became interested in jungle animals as a result of viewing films, reading, and listening to music. At first they wrote their responses and feelings in the form of individual poems. Then they used rhythm instruments to imitate sounds they might hear. After painting some pictures to express their ideas, they were ready to compose a class poem which all could contribute to and all could enjoy. The result was "Jungle Daze," a poem they interpreted with many variations of solo parts, sound effects, tempo, stress, and voice inflection. They never did try to finalize the way to say the poem in a chorus but continued to make adaptations as long as they used it.

Jungle Daze

Very early in the morn,
Before the break of day,
Little creatures of the forest
Come down to springs to play.

Slowly, carefully, one by one,
And later two by two,
They get together in groups
To ask each other: "What's new?"

Now the sky is clear.
Gray shadows have passed away.
The sky is dressed in brilliant colors,
Like a Spanish shawl so gay.

I hear bigger animals coming.
Their steps are drawing near.
The rhythm of their feet
Is sounding loud and clear.

Trees fall, bushes are crushed
When the huge elephants come.
Their slow, big, clumsy feet
Sound like the beat of a drum.

Monkeys above are chattering
And swinging from limbs of a tree.

To me they are castanets clicking.
They seem to say: "I'm glad that I'm free."

Softly, quietly through the tangled jungle
The great cats go.
Like the jingle of the tambourines
Their noisy cries chill me so.

Alligators crawling on muddy banks
Make a gyro sound,
And through thick swampy waters
Go swimming round and round.

Pythons, cobras, boa constrictors
Are great jungle snakes.
They frighten me as they come along,
Like maracas, they make me shake.

Very gently the rains began
Making sounds like rhythm sticks.
Faster and faster the rains came down
Like claves, played fast and quick.

I am caught in the spell of the jungle.
Something has happened to my feet.
I keep time to the enchanting rhythm,
With its steady, pulsing beat.

There is a fire within me burning,
Burning so wild and free.
"Oh! I'm glad that I'm alive.
This is pure ecstasy."

Like the fire turning to ashes,
I grow tired and stop with a moan.
I look for the forest creatures round me,
And find that they have flown.

Now the jungle day is ending.
The sky in gay colors shines bright.
Soon their brilliant shades will be fading,
For the day has turned into night.

Choral speaking can be used with the youngest children as a language activity. It helps them to listen for their parts, to remember what they are to say, and to interpret words and word patterns. Activity poems are also suitable for the youngest children because the group can do the actions while the teacher or a few children say the poem. Later the children can progress to poems with choral refrains, with the teacher doing most of the reading and the children coming in as a chorus on the refrain. A further step is for the children to take more of the parts, including the solo. More elaborate forms can then be introduced. Cumulative chorales are those that begin with a few voices with more being added as the poem develops until all are included.

A good procedure with older children follows.
——The teacher reads a poem aloud, asking children to form word pictures in their minds as they listen.
——Following the reading the children describe their impressions.
——Mimeographed copies of the poem are used to guide discussions about word meanings, punctuation, and interpretations of certain words.
——The poem is read again with children performing the action—walking to the rhythm or tapping the rhythm on their desks as someone reads the poem.
——Solo and group parts are designated and tried for effect.
——Parts are assigned and memorized.

When children feel the words in a poem, join in the rhythmic production, hear the pattern of sound, and understand the meaning, memorization is almost automatic. Most children will memorize the whole selection even though they may participate in only portions of it during the performance. For that reason it is important to select poems that will build language flexibility and versatility which are not common in the natural speech of the children but which are useful in silent, independent reading—especially reading that young children will do in the future.

Summary of Skills and Abilities for Responding Rhythmically

LANGUAGE DEVELOPMENT

——Increases vocabulary of verbs as a response to rhythms
——Uses phrases and sentences that reflect understanding of basic vocabulary of motion

——Imitates movement of animals and makes accompanying language sounds

——Imitates movement of machines and makes appropriate language sounds

——Responds to music listening by writing thoughts, interpretations, and feelings

——Composes simple rhythms to accompany poetry

——Locates and reads the verbs in sentences

——Responds rhythmically to words of movement

——Pantomimes meanings of common words

——Substitutes words to fit basic rhythms of chants and games

RHYTHMIC RESPONSE

——Selects movements for hands, head, feet, and body while listening to music

——Moves in rhythmic patterns to music for marching, skipping, galloping, and other motions

——Improvises, experiments, and creates rhythmic interpretations

——Creates rhythmic responses to nonverbal films

——Composes simple rhythms to accompany poetry

——Knows and responds rhythmically to games and chants that repeat language patterns

CHORAL SPEAKING

——Joins others in reciting poetry with choir

——Takes solo parts in choral speaking

——Plans own interpretations

——Directs choir in interpreting poetry

——Shows an awareness of rhythmic structure by composing poetry for choral speaking

——Demonstrates creative interpretive oral language skills—pause, modulation, emphasis, stress

Selected References

Allen, Roach Van, and Claryce Allen. *Teacher's Resource Book: Language Experiences in Early Childhood.* Encyclopaedia Britannica Educational Corp., Chicago, 1969.

Anderson, Paul S. *Language Skills in Elementary Education.* Macmillan Co., New York, 1964.

Arbuthnot, May Hill. *The Arbuthnot Anthology of Children's Literature*.   Scott, Foresman and Co., Chicago, 1961.

Arnstein, Flora J. *Poetry and the Elementary Education*.   Appleton-Century-Crofts, New York, 1962.

Association for Childhood Education International. *Songs Children Like: Folk Songs from Many Lands*.   Association for Childhood Educational International, Washington, D.C., 1958.

Bernstein, Leonard. *The Joy of Music*.   Simon and Schuster, New York, 1962.

Brown-Azarowicz, Marjorie Frances. *A Handbook of Creative Choral Speaking*.   Burgess Publishing Co., Minneapolis, 1970.

Daniels, Elva S. *Creative Rhythms*.   F. A. Owen, Danville, N.Y., 1965.

Encyclopaedia Britannica Films. *Magic Moments: A Series of Non-Verbal Films*.   Encyclopaedia Britannica Educational Corp., Chicago, 1969.

Fletcher, Helen Jill. *Action Songs*.   The Educational Publishing Co., Darien, Conn., 1961.

Joyce, Bruce, and Marsha Weil. *Models of Teaching*.   Prentice-Hall, Englewood Cliffs, N.J., 1972.

Morine, Harold, and Greta Morine. *Discovery: A Challenge to Teachers*.   Prentice-Hall, Englewood Cliffs, N.J., 1973.

Sheehy, Emma D. *Children Discover Music and Dance*.   Teachers College Press, New York, 1968.

Walsh, Gertrude. *Sing Your Way to Better Speech*.   E. P. Dutton and Co., New York, 1955.

York, Mary E. (coordinator). *Music for Nebraska Elementary Schools*.   State Department of Education, Lincoln, Nebr., 1968.

FROM THE RATIONALE   Discussing and conversing—talking about topics as they arise in ways that require more mature skills than oral sharing; and interacting with what other people say and write, altering contributions to fit into discussions and conversations centering around a theme.

Since the fundamental business of public education is to train youth for active and worthwhile participation in the democratic way of life, any skill or experience that will contribute to one's ability to earn a living, to social competence, to civic competence, and to the willing and intelligent exercise of the privileges and responsibilities of citizenry cannot be denied the right to a place in the curriculum of our schools. One of these skills that has been recognized but slighted in emphasis is the art of conversation, including participation in group discussions. Even though it has been neglected in the past, educators are coming to the realization that conversation is a cooperative enterprise that furnishes the only proved method for intelligent and rational solution to community, social, economic, and political problems.

Conversation is the greatest weapon we now possess in our skirmish with the world. We are depending on it to attract friends and repel enemies, to take the place of fire and steel in settling differences, to buy and sell, and to spread the propaganda of democracy.

Conversation brings us more pleasure than dancing, golfing, going to the movies, or eating a favorite dessert. It not only brings pleasure in itself but also keeps memories alive of past pleasures. We would enjoy few activities if we were denied the satisfaction of talking about them.

Too many teachers continue to practice the policy of suppressing oral expression activities of children, preferring to judge their reactions through written expressions; but others are aware of the need for a well-planned program built around realistic goals. For these teachers some broad abilities have been selected, and specific suggestions about them are given. The abilities to be developed are:

——to have something to talk about
——to offer enthusiastic participation
——to have a pleasing vocabulary
——to observe common courtesies in conversation
——to choose appropriate topics
——to be a good listener.

Something to Talk About

Obviously, there is no need to teach discussion and conversation abilities when there is nothing to talk about. But any classroom with normal children living in a rich environment affords something to talk about. From the kindergarten and continuing on through successive years, children come to realize and recognize that ideas for discussion and for conversation come through

——keen observation

——listening to other people talk

——wide reading

——experience that school life affords.

To utilize the experiences of children in periods of planned discussion and in periods of free conversation is the responsibility of all teachers. Children consider all their content subjects as sources of information for conversation and discussion. An excursion or the viewing of a film for a class in social studies or science usually initiates talk among children, and the teacher takes advantage of such an experience to stress the abilities required for adequate conversation about the subject. In doing this the teacher has put discussion in its proper place in the curriculum. Assigned topics do not inspire students to talk as much about the things they know and want to share with others as about topics that grow out of everyday school life.

Jerry watches for items of interest to his class. At least once a week he arranges the learning space so that when the children arrive there will be designated spaces for them to sit together and talk. Labels are arranged on the carpeted floor for topics that are listed at the entry on a poster with the headline "Let's Talk." In order to control size, tickets are placed in pockets opposite each topic on the poster. A ticket admits a student to a certain group. When all tickets for a topic are gone, students must select other topics. Popular topics are repeated. Children in the class anticipate the topics and try to keep abreast of current events through newspapers and news reports on TV and radio.

At the end of most school days Julia invites all the children to sit comfortably on a rug to talk about what happened and did not happen during the day. Children are encouraged to talk about things they did in the learning centers. When a child reads a book or a poem is completed, the group discusses it. Problems and ideas that need attention the following day are discussed. Behavior is a topic that comes up frequently. Children know that they can and must solve these problems together. The teacher is not the dictator of behavior but the administrator of policies developed through discussion by those concerned.

Enthusiastic Participation

Since enthusiasm is usually evidenced by naturalness, children will use their natural language when they are enthusiastic. Thus the goal of enthusiastic participation in oral language is met

——when children whose home-rooted language is characterized by gross errors speak naturally in discussion

——when children whose first language is a distinct dialect use it in conversation

——when children whose home language is not English use combinations of two languages when participating.

In classrooms where the children and the teacher live together and love each other enough to speak freely of their deepest feelings, alternative ways of saying things must be accepted.

Evaluation sessions follow frequently when enthusiastic participation is a goal of planned discussion sessions. These sessions are ones that are concerned about alternatives in speech rather than about correctness. The teacher does not pose as the one final authority but participates in illustrating one or more ways of saying things.

Significant changes in oral language occur by choice—not following lessons (Hodges and Rudorf, 1972). Choice implies alternatives. Through enthusiastic participation in discussions and conversations, alternatives are illustrated in a meaningful way. A look at those that have been useful in the class may be a means of opening up choices for children who need to make significant changes in personal language if they are to enter into the mainstream of education and American life.

Marie invites older children and adults to her class of young children to discuss hobbies, topics of special interest, and occupations. The invitation states specifically that they are coming for a discussion, not a lecture. In preparation for the discussion the children talk about how they can participate and not about what questions to ask. Following the discussion, there is a period of evaluation at which time the group can discuss levels and quality of participation as well as the importance of having some information in order to participate. Marie feels a special responsibility to comment on enthusiastic participation on the part of children whose language needs massive refinement. She feels that instruction in refinement is futile for most of them apart from easy and enthusiastic participation.

Oscar reads something of his own choosing to the class almost every day. He uses short selections that he can read with enthusiasm. Then he leads a discussion centered around the main point or the writing style of the author. He demonstrates a feeling of ease and good personal involvement in this activity which takes from five to seven minutes. He searches for materials well written in black dialects, in regional dialects, and in language characteristic of ethnic groups represented in the class. Also, he collects recordings of stories and songs illustrating many English dialects from the United States, Australia, Great Britain, Wales, and other places where English is the official language. His goal is to involve every student in discussion, regardless of the quality of the home-rooted language he or she brings into the classroom. Oscar feels that one of the reasons he is there is to listen, to diagnose, and to offer alternatives. He cannot diagnose apart from hearing natural language.

Pleasing Vocabulary

Having something to say and enthusiasm for saying it is not enough. Our choice of words and the way we use them mark us for what we are. Persons with meager vocabularies find self-expression difficult, while those with a broad vocabulary find themselves at ease among friends. Teachers do not expect perfection in the use of words that are difficult and strange to children, but they strive to develop rapport strong enough that children do not fear to try to use words that they have never used before.

Simplicity and clarity are the keys to better language and are practiced by teachers in what they say and in the books they give children to read (Yardley, 1973). Children are taught the basic principles of semantics rather than a list of meaningless words. They are led to realize that words do not represent things but that words represent thoughts. The eyes, ears, and hearts of youth are trained to recognize the tricks of language.

Many people are led to believe that the large vocabulary is the one full of "big" and unusual words, but children should be encouraged to avoid affectations of speech when there are direct and meaningful ways of communicating. Outlandish phrases, unusual syntax, and vogue words should be evaluated against a backdrop of alternatives. Some children may use them because they lack other means of expressing themselves.

This possibility is substantiated in a research study, *A Word Count of Spoken English of Culturally Disadvantaged Preschool and Elementary Pupils* (Sherk, 1973). Sherk and his staff conducted the study in Kansas City and found that the quantity of production was not a true reflection of the quality. Children in his study tended to use the same words over and over. Their inventory of nouns, verbs, adjectives, and adverbs was extremely limited when compared with lists generated from a broad segment of the population. Children with this problem do not possess personal language power that permits them to function in school tasks, especially in tasks of reading language as it is produced in written form. They must have many opportunities to try on a wardrobe of new words in a pleasant, easy environment. The acquisition of language may be a need greater than being able to recognize and analyze a few words from a simple reading text.

Margaret maintains a Word Wall as a part of the language resources available for talking and writing. One part of the wall is a changing list of common nouns extended with synonyms and near synonyms. (Examples: *house*—cottage, dwelling, apartment, hovel, mansion, abode; *horse*—filly, mare, colt, pony, stallion.) For adjectives she takes a common color word and extends it with words of shade and hue of that color. (Example: *red*—crimson, pink, ruby, coral, burgundy.) Children listen and watch for additions to the lists, and some keep individual handbooks of words that extend their vocabularies for talking and writing about ordinary things.

George likes to walk and to talk while walking. He chooses a category such as "shape words" and walks with the class, letting each student keep a list of the different shapes observed. On returning they compile a master list and place it in the Writing/Publishing Center in a form in which it can continue to grow. After a few experiences with his class with shape, texture, color, sound, and motion vocabularies, he offers to let his class members serve as "walkers and talkers" for groups of younger children. They go in one-to-one groupings to help the other children observe the unusual things in their world and to learn multiple words to describe what they see. The older children serve as secretaries for the younger ones and leave lists of words and interesting phrases for bulletin boards and books that the children create.

Observing Common Courtesies in Conversation

Everyone knows the desirability and importance of observing common courtesies in conversation and discussion. The rude, abrupt, and discourteous person is soon eliminated from a group and left alone, wondering why he or she has no friends. Some instruction in acquiring the knowledge and ability to practice common courtesies in talking with others can reduce the number of such cases in a school.

There are many ways to teach these abilities, but the most effective ones are derived from actual conversation practices that are noted and evaluated by the group. School social affairs offer opportunities for this instruction. Children can be brought together with adults or with other children whom they don't know as well as those in the immediate group in order to create a greater need for social competence in their talk. Activities can be planned and made an integral part of the school program toward fostering social skills and courtesies in conversation.

Many desirable abilities and attitudes can be named in connection with this topic; the list below includes some of the most useful and desirable of those to be derived from the teaching of conversation and discussion:

— how and when to interrupt the person talking
— how to disagree with the speaker's statement
— not to be too demonstrative
— not to monopolize the conversation
— to avoid unpleasant topics
— not to whisper in the presence of others
— to include all members of the group in one's remarks
— to express likes and dislikes moderately
— not to be too personal
— to speak in a well-modulated voice
— to avoid futile argument
— to be considerate of persons entering the group after conversation has begun
— not to hurt the feelings of others

——not to repeat needlessly

——to greet and to take leave of a host graciously.

Anna has developed a Cooking Center over several years. With the help of parents who gave trading stamps, she has acquired the equipment needed to serve party refreshments as a follow-up of the cooking experience. Children plan a party appropriate for what they cook, and invite guests from within the school or from outside. Sometimes another class will be invited; at other times only three or four special guests will be honored. Anna uses these occasions to develop the language of common courtesy in real situations rather than in workbook lessons. Dramatic play is used in practice, and the children evaluate progress in their abilities to carry on conversations with guests after each party.

Anna feels that language changes and improves when the environment in which it occurs changes and improves. She has collected beautiful dishes and serving pieces for the children to use at their many parties. They make decorations for their classroom and are encouraged to wear suitable clothes when guests come. They discuss good grooming and appropriate dress for different occasions and how to adjust their language to various events.

Parents participate and are enthusiastic about Anna's program. They appreciate her efforts to do for the speech of their children what they cannot accomplish at home. Some of them try to follow up the school experiences with occasions to practice the language of courtesy at home.

A place in the Reading/Research Center is devoted to parties, planning parties, and simple books of etiquette. These books would never be assigned as required reading, but they are extremely popular when a party is planned.

Ray uses lunch time to emphasize conversations that are polite and courteous. Host jobs are rotated, and each host can initiate, but not dominate, conversations. Although they are very informal, an effort is made to practice common courtesies and to develop language appropriate for social occasions. Tables accommodate six to eight, and the make-up of groups changes regularly so that the same children do not talk together over an extended period.

The class has an ongoing project of trying out ideas to stimulate good conversation. The children have a chart on which they list some of the guidelines.

——Talk about things that interest people in your group.

——Do not tell secrets during conversations.

——Do not act as though you are smart when everyone knows you are dumb on a topic.

——Do not argue. Change the subject.

——Ask questions that will bring a new person into the conversation.

——Do not talk just to please yourself.

Laura was teaching a group of preschool Papago Indian children when she realized that she was not hearing words of courtesy such as *thank you, please,* and *excuse me.* Even with urging, her efforts seemed fruitless. She felt that the children should learn to use these words before they began their more formal school program, so she enlisted the help of her Indian aide, a college student who spoke Papago and English. Lucia, the aide, confided that there never have been words to say thank you in the Papago language. ''We say it with our eyes,'' she revealed.

Immediately Laura realized that she had been receiving gestures of gratitude every time a child's eyes sparkled at the pleasure of new toys, the attractive classroom, and the good food. She knew that she was participating in a culture that extended courtesies in ways different from her own. She wanted to preserve that culture at the same time that she introduced one new to the children. She became gracious and loving when the children said thank you with their eyes. She imitated them and learned the pleasure of their gestures. She shared her way, too, because she knew that as the children grew older, they would need to use the expressions of both cultures. She built for herself a basic generalization out of the experience: There is no one right way to communicate common courtesies.

Being a Good Listener

Good taste and courtesy lead to instruction about when and where one should not carry on conversations. Almost any public gathering reveals the lack of proper attitudes and training in the art of silence and effective listening—at lectures, sermons, musical performances, in libraries, at exhibits, and at certain times at school. Most everyone concurs in the need to be a good listener, but not everyone accepts it as a guide to behavior. To many people what they say seems to be the only important part of a conversation. What others say is totally disregarded.

Andy encourages the children in his class to prepare programs for the pleasure of others—songs, skits, plays, debates, travelogues, art shows, fashion shows, and musical recordings with live commentary. The programs themselves are important, but of equal importance to Andy is the opportunity they afford to discuss and practice listening courtesies that are appropriate throughout life.

Rachel uses the oral sharing time as a base for discussing and practicing listening abilities. Rather than repeating over and over "Let's be quiet and listen while ——— talks," she speaks with the children about facial expressions that show pleasure or boredom, body posture that indicates participation or "cop out," and quiet attention to the person sharing or quiet attention to something else. The be-quiet-and-listen routine, which she tried for too long, does not satisfy her present goals of developing good listeners for participation in discussions and conversations.

Listening is a participation skill and can best be learned when there is opportunity for group activity. To expect children to perform properly and correctly just because instructions are clearly given is to expect what is impossible for many of them. Dr. Patricia Van Metre, author of "Syntactic Characteristics of Selected Bilingual Children" (1972), expanded an earlier work of Dr. Carol Chomsky (1969). She found that children, both bilingual and monolingual, who were poor readers at the end of third grade were confused consistently when listening to syntactic structures that include Ask/Tell constructions, Promise/Tell constructions, Easy to See/Hard to See constructions, and many constructions that include pronouns.

Brief reflection on listening experiences in classroom settings recalls prominent use of the syntactic characteristics listed above; yet many children who have been in school for three and four years have not mastered the meanings to the extent that they can function with information gained through listening.

The Van Metre and Chomsky studies confirm the long-standing concept of teachers who function as linguists. Listening to language is more than listening to words. Pitch, tone, and volume are added to the syntactic characteristics of language during discussions and conversations. Children who do not participate frequently in situations that involve wide-range listening abilities will be lost when looking at cold, silent print that must be brought back to life through effective reading.

Judith watches for words, phrases, and sentences that undergo obvious changes of meaning when the pitch, tone, and volume of voice is changed. She will say something and then ask the children to interpret it in many ways. She writes some responses on the chalkboard to highlight changed emphasis and meaning.

Mother is here.
Mother is here?
MOTHER is here!
Mother IS here!
Mother is HERE!
Do you think I'll believe that?
Do YOU think I'll believe that?
Do you THINK I'LL BELIEVE that?
Do you think I'LL believe that?
Do you think I'll believe THAT?

As Judith works with discussion groups, she helps them develop sensitivity to the language along with ability to grasp simple meanings.

A child's ability to profit from school experiences and participate in a social life will depend as much on listening ability as on reading and writing abilities. No direct measure of progress may be possible or even necessary, but the teacher can always help by focusing children's attention on the need for careful, thoughtful listening as a basic ingredient in discussions and conversations.

Summary of Skills and Abilities for Discussing and Conversing

CONVERSATION

——Talks informally and easily with classmates, teachers, and other adults
——Increases skill in choosing interesting topics of conversation
——Develops confidence in asking and answering questions and in replying to remarks of teachers and others

——Develops understanding of some of the qualities of a good conversationalist

——Uses conversation in appropriate situations

DISCUSSION

——Participates willingly in planned discussions to learn from others as well as to make contributions

——Takes turns in discussion

——Increases skill in participating in group discussions

——keeps to the point under discussion

——organizes thought in logical sequence

——increases ability to make valid generalizations

——weighs evidence before drawing conclusions

——Practices social courtesies when participating in discussions

——Is not overly sensitive to criticism

——Reacts thoughtfully to the ideas of others; asks pertinent questions

——Develops skill in informal parliamentary procedures

——Evaluates own contributions

USING LANGUAGE COURTESIES

——Practices desirable social courtesies as a speaker and as a listener

——Uses appropriate salutations and greetings and responds courteously to them

——Develops sensitivity to others

——Makes introductions properly and graciously and responds to introductions in a like manner

Selected References

Anderson, Paul S. *Language Skills in Elementary Education*. Macmillan Co., New York, 1964.

Applegate, Mauree. *Easy in English*. Harper & Row, New York, 1963.

Ashley, Rosalind M. *Successful Techniques for Teaching Elementary Language Arts*. Parker Publishing Co., West Nyack, N.Y., 1970.

Bellack, A., and J. R. Davitz. *The Language of Elementary Classrooms*. Teachers College Press, New York, 1963.

Burrows, Alvina T., Dianne L. Monson, and Russell G. Stauffer. *New Horizons in the Language Arts*. Harper & Row, New York, 1972.

Chomsky, Carol. *The Acquisition of Syntax in Children 5 to 10.* The M.I.T. Press, Cambridge, Mass., 1969.

Dunne, Hope W. *The Art of Teaching Reading: A Language and Self-Concept Approach.* Charles E. Merrill, Columbus, Ohio, 1972.

Hodges, Richard E., and E. Hugh Rudorf. *Language and Learning to Read: What Teachers Should Know About Language.* Houghton Mifflin Co., Boston, 1972.

Labov, William. *The Study of Nonstandard English.* National Council of Teachers of English, Urbana, Ill., 1970.

Lee, Dorris M. *Diagnostic Teaching.* American Association of Elementary/Kindergarten/Nursery Educators, Washington, D.C., 1966.

Loban, Walter D. *Language Ability in the Middle Grades of the Elementary School.* Report of the U.S. Office of Education, Contract No. SAE 7287, Berkeley, Calif., 1961.

McCullough, Constance M. *Handbook for Teaching the Language Arts.* Chandler Publishing Co., San Francisco, Calif., 1969.

Moffett, James. *A Student Centered Language Arts Curriculum Grades K-13: A Handbook for Teachers.* Houghton Mifflin Co., Boston, 1973.

Sherk, John K. *A Word Count of Spoken English of Culturally Disadvantaged Preschool and Elementary Pupils.* College of Education, University of Missouri at Kansas City, Kansas City, Mo., 1973.

Smith, James A. *Adventures in Communication.* Allyn & Bacon, Boston, 1972.

Tiedt, Iris M., and Sidney W. Tiedt. *Contemporary English in the Elementary School.* Prentice-Hall, Englewood Cliffs, N.J., 1967.

Van Metre, Patricia. "Syntactic Characteristics of Selected Bilingual Children." (Ed.D. dissertation.) University of Arizona, Tucson, 1972.

Yardley, Alice. *Young Children Learning: Exploration and Language.* Citation Press, New York, 1973.

Zuck, Lois, V., and Yetta M. Goodman. *Social Class and Regional Dialect: Their Relationship to Reading.* International Reading Association, Newark, 1971.

FROM THE RATIONALE   Exploring writing—learning and using in conversational situations topics such as letter recognition, letter names, letter formation, and letter orientation; copying dictated stories on paper and on a chalkboard; writing of own ideas using appropriate forms of alphabet letters to represent sounds of language; contacting, in a natural setting of writing, language characteristics such as capitalization, punctuation, standard spelling, and sound-symbol relationships; and observing the writing process when presenting dictation.

Children develop communicating abilities at an early age as they have rich and varied experiences in spontaneous oral expression, informal conversation, painting and using scrap material to represent ideas, acting out ideas and experiences, and using body motions to respond to sounds around them. Later, as a part of school experiences, children grow into the use of forms of writing with an alphabet to express thoughts and feelings. During the remainder of their lives, all of these communication abilities are joined together for effective communication.

The first forms of writing used by young children may be crude and simple, but they have meaning for them immediately and in some instances represent the same meaning at a later date. These crude forms merge into alphabetic writing as children participate in school programs that value self-expression through writing.

Children must not feel that they have to write correctly in order to begin. On the other hand, they must realize that writing involves difficulties not encountered in oral expression. These appear in the form of handwriting, spelling, punctuation, and other elements of composition. Because writing is not simple does not mean, however, that it is too difficult for young children to explore and for older children to refine. Those who have self-confidence in expressing their ideas in other forms of communication, especially oral language, possess basic abilities for the exploration of writing.

It is important to remember that the purpose in all language teaching is to help children develop their ability to communicate with others and to express themselves with ease and clarity. If we begin too early to stress the mechanical and formal elements of writing or if we stress them at the expense of the quality of thought communicated, then we may very well be creating obstacles and a distaste for writing in the child's mind. Our aim should be to develop a genuine interest in writing and to promote as much writing as we can. Correct form must *serve,* never *rule,* writing. Through many experiences in writing and in reading others' writing, in which correct forms of expression are used and encountered, children will incorporate these forms into their own patterns. To the same end we continue to emphasize oral language expression so that oral development and written development reinforce each other.

Every time there is a writing experience, children must see a purpose for writing. They must feel that they have something to say on the topic, and must want to do the writing. In other words children should not be asked to write unless the purpose for it is clear to them and genuine use is to be made of the writing. There will be many opportunities in daily classroom activities for children to use writing in meaningful ways.

In the context of such actual writing experiences the teacher can help children to develop degrees of control over some of the mechanics and forms of written language and to understand the reasons for them.

Self-expression through Writing

Exploring writing for creative self-expression should never be confused with the teaching of the techniques of writing. These are different procedures, even though one reinforces the other.

Creative self-expression is:
— a flowing of ideas
— the element in human experience that puts current in the magnet
— the element that makes sense of the ordinary flow of day-to-day life
— the part of the school curriculum that recognizes human values and establishes a sensitivity to ideas.

This creative flow must be nurtured and developed. Writing that is displayed and published in artful ways is basic to growth in creative language production in school programs. It is personal and private and requires a level of independence and self-reliance seldom encountered in other aspects of school programs. It does not require an audience or an editor during the process of production. It brings pleasure and satisfaction to the author and, it is hoped, to many who hear and read it following publication.

In order to achieve truly creative writing, it is important that a wholesome teacher-pupil relationship exist and that it result in a classroom environment conducive to personal, creative expression. The teacher must be sympathetic to and understanding of the ideas being expressed and be truly interested in the forms of expression used by children, even though some may be quite divergent from standard forms. Rules of punctuation, spelling, grammar, and handwriting are not used in ways that stifle creative expression.

The establishment of the environment is not a simple matter. There needs to be an air of honest freedom in which the pupil feels willing to pursue ideas. Coercion and trite criticism need to be eliminated. Children need assurance that their efforts will not be laughed at, criticized, or made the subject of too much attention either from the teacher or from their peers. Children must feel secure and know that they will have a friendly and appreciative audience as they talk and read their compositions. The teacher must remember that interest is sustained by appropriate content and use of the writing—not by the mechanics of form.

Since teachers know some of the things that appeal to children, they surround themselves with materials and books that will stimulate concepts and ideas. There is no lack of ideas in a classroom filled with material for searching for answers and new ideas, organizing the ideas into meaningful presentations, and communicating the ideas in many forms.

CLUES FOR INSTRUCTION

Talk with children and let them talk with each other until they have clarified their ideas and organized their thoughts. Encourage oral storytelling to the whole class or small groups.

Provide a tape recorder for children to use for oral compositions. They can play back, make necessary changes, and then write.

Use filmstrips without words as a basis for writing. Children choose names for characters and places and then write the sequence of events into a plot that comes to mind from viewing the filmstrip.

Provide boxes of cards on which are written such stimulators for writing as story beginnings, story middles, and story endings. Copy beginning sentences from well-written stories for the card headed "Sentences to begin stories." Cut interesting headlines from newspapers for "Headline stories."

Children write well and at an early age when they have something to say. They think of personal writing as a natural part of human communication.

From Talk to Writing

Relationships between talk and writing exist, but writing is always an imperfect representation of talking. Writing frequently lacks pitch, tone, emphasis, pause, and juncture. Whereas talk is highly perishable, written records have a degree of permanence. Refined writing represents the communication of thoughts with word order and patterns which are not characteristic of spontaneous expression. It raises language to a literary level.

Procedures vary in instructional programs that help children progress from talk to writing, but a few basic steps are required.

Jane uses a procedure that works for most children. She describes the procedure in eight steps.

Step 1: Children talk about paintings they have made. After the talk Jane writes one or two things a child chooses for recording. As she writes, she talks to herself, not teaching directly but reminding herself in audible sounds that she is using alphabet symbols which have names, that some of the words use capitals for the first letters, that the same letters are used over and over as first letters in words, that some words appear again and again, that some ending sounds tell how many and when. This talk is *about* the symbol system and how it works in writing.

Step 2: Jane reads what has been written and checks it with the child who said it. If appropriate, she asks the child to read it with her.

Step 3: Paintings with dictation are displayed around the classroom at levels that children can reach. With felt-tipped pens children identify language characteristics which are essential to understand for independent writing:
——words that are alike (usually words of highest frequency)
——words that begin alike
——words that end alike
——words with capital letters
——punctuation that is the same
——rhyming words
——other topics appropriate to what is displayed.
Children mark each category with a colored pen. Usually

two and not more than three categories are used at any one time.

Step 4: Words that appear five or more times are collected for a chart, "Words We All Use." This chart becomes a major resource for spelling in the Writing/Publishing Center. It is used for games that develop a sight vocabulary for reading.

Step 5: When a child indicates an interest in writing, her or his dictation is recorded very lightly, and the child traces over the letters. A model alphabet with arrows to show directions for strokes in writing is available in the Writing/Publishing Center.

Step 6: Dictation is recorded with space beneath each line for copying. The writing is large enough so that children have no difficulty copying beneath what the teacher has written.

Step 7: Two or three paintings are put on the chalkboard with masking tape—always from volunteers. Children write on the chalkboard. The class or a group from the class listens to the reading of what has been written. Editorial suggestions are requested; they concern capitalization, punctuation, and spelling. Jane gets children involved in using the vocabulary of writing that she introduced while talking to herself when taking dictation.

After the editing is finished, the author copies the corrected sentence or story on a story strip which can be attached to the painting. Stories are used for unison reading on the following day. Some of them are collected for group story-books which are prepared about once a week and duplicated for all the children.

Step 8: Children write on their own, using resources from the Writing/Publishing Center—spelling lists of words of highest frequency, special lists of words of color, size, and shape, words from the Cooking Center such as those of taste and smell, words from the Discovery Center such as those of sound, texture, and motion.

For children who want to write but who are not able to do so independently, there are sentences to copy, names of children to copy, and short poems to copy and illustrate.

Jane finds that with these procedures most of the children in her first grade can do some independent writing after about two months in class. When talking about writing, they can use the names of the letters of the alphabet, can spell words and understand when someone else spells, and can talk about capitalization, punctuation, and other topics necessary for the process of writing.

Processes of relating talk to writing begin early in school but need to be continued as long as there are children in a classroom who need direct teaching or need to be influenced toward refinement.

Jerry takes some dictation on the chalkboard every day from the eleven- and twelve-year-olds. His purposes are to teach the fine points of editing, to illustrate elaboration, to practice clarity, and to edit reporting language toward literary language.

Volunteers sign up for the dictation. They speak without notes and are limited to two minutes. Jerry hopes that what is said is spontaneous, but some of what is dictated is obviously planned ahead of time to include words difficult to spell and run-on language that challenges his ability to punctuate.

After the dictation has been recorded (with plenty of space between lines), editing procedures begin. Jerry feels that he has a responsibility for identifying areas of emphasis in writing that will help children make progress in their personal writing. In addition to simple mechanics (he makes mistakes deliberately), he goes over the text with suggestions for adding descriptive categories, for using specific nouns in place of general nouns, and for saying the same thing in fewer words. For example, he will lead the group in changing a statement that has ninety to one hundred words into a cinquain of only eleven words. He uses dictation to make points about mechanics of writing without having to correct papers one by one. He knows that the interaction between the students is useful in clarifying ideas and in setting personal goals for improving writing.

Writing that is spontaneous expression is the *base for beginning* personal writing, but it is not the total structure. Strategies for moving to literary forms of writing must be illustrated and made available to children.

Once Dee is assured that most of her eight- and nine-year-old children can write their own ideas in language that is close to their talk, she uses dictation to illustrate other ways of saying things. She suggests rhyming words and records some that the children know. She then introduces rhyming patterns such as couplets, triplets, and quatrains. Rather than assign children to write in these patterns, she provides a common experience such as a picture or a film without words and then takes dictation from the group. Revisions are easy to make on the chalkboard, and the children suggest changes from original presentations until a pattern is illustrated. Nonrhyming patterns such as those of haiku and cinquains are shown. Dee hopes that from the dictation experience the children will gain confidence to use new writing patterns on their own. And they do! They experience oral composition first and then move to writing.

Group Compositions

From group discussion to group composition is a natural sequence in the development of written expression. Recording a group composition is an excellent opportunity to learn incidentally many matters of form that carry over to the independent writing of children. As teachers capitalize a title or the beginning of a sentence, leave a margin, and supply quotation marks, they call attention to requirements of good form. In this way form is taught as a natural part of writing, along with content and organization.

Group compositions, in which children are engaged in writing about something they have seen, heard, or experienced in some other way, lend themselves to the development of fundamental word-recognition skills, including phonics. As teachers engage in chitchat about writing, the word-recognition skills that might emerge include the following:

1. Some words are used over and over, and others are not used very often.

Those that occur most frequently in groups and in individual compositions at any level in school are the same words that occur frequently in most writing. These are usually determiners (words that pattern like *the*), prepositions (words that pattern like *to*), pronouns (words that pattern like *I* and *you*), conjunctions (words that pattern like *and*), question words (words that pattern like *what*), auxiliaries (words that are forms of *be* and *have*), and an assortment of other words such as negatives and words of courtesy.

Other words that occur frequently in one composition but not in all compositions may be nouns and verbs. Sometimes they are adjectives and adverbs. Recognition and spelling of words of highest frequency are essential for any level of independence in writing and reading.

2. Some words begin alike.

The letters of the alphabet are used over and over in the initial position of words. If the first sound of a word is written with a consonant, it is likely to be the same sound-symbol relationship for most words beginning with that letter. This is dependable information for reading and writing.

If the beginning sound is written with a vowel, the sound-symbol relationship is variable. Readers and writers cannot depend on its being the same. The spelling of most words beginning with vowels must be memorized.

3. Some words end alike.

The ends that occur most frequently (*-s, -es, -ed, -ing, -er, -est, -ful,* and *-ly*) change the meaning of root words and may shift their positions in sentences. To recognize them and to understand their significance are essential to comprehension of the finer points of meaning. It is through writing, much more than through reading, that children come to grips with this aspect of language structure.

4. Only twenty-six letters are used to write all the words we use.

Each of the letters has a name that is useful in talking about spelling and in doing reference research. Each letter can be written with numerous configurations and must be recognized in its many forms. Each letter represents one or more sounds when used in writing. Consonants represent fewer sounds than vowels. To know the alphabet and to be able to talk about the names of all the letters are useful in writing. To understand many of the sounds represented by letters and clusters of letters is useful in reading.

5. Some syllables occur over and over in the language.

These syllables, when used with different consonants at the beginning of words and with different endings, form hundreds of words. The most frequent ones are:

at, an, ay, all, am
en, ell, et, ed

in, ill, ing, ight, it
ook, ot, ow, old, oy
un, ug.

These syllables are found in all reading and are useful in the analysis of unfamiliar words.

It is impossible to record group compositions without illustrating the five characteristics of writing and spelling described above. The concepts related to these five must be understood and mastered to a high degree before independent, silent reading is possible.

Since it is impossible for some children to learn them in reading groups, specific attention must be given to them during writing instruction. This instruction is best when it is related to the natural language of children such as that used in recording group compositions. Too much emphasis on correct form without allowing for the personal, dynamic ideas of children can make a wasteland of instruction.

Individual Compositions

Language personality is respected as the teacher works with each child to develop certain understandings and skills necessary for writing. Painting and oral composition often precede and accompany the dictation or writing of an idea so that individual ideas can be kept in the learning environment. This procedure tends to eliminate much of the copying of phrases that young children find in their reading material. It also keeps the self-expression vocabulary of each child involved in the production of reading materials by individuals.

What children may write creatively is difficult to predict because they have to write to satisfy their own purposes rather than just to please the teacher. Creative writing usually results when something needs to be written. Some examples of these needs follow.

Letters that will actually find their way to the intended reader

CLUES FOR INSTRUCTION

Develop a postal system within the classroom with mail-collection places for each person, including the teacher. Encourage communication through letter-writing in a variety of correct forms. Write personal notes to absent members. Write letters to thank people who contribute to the class.

Stories to be bound into books for the Reading/Research Center in the classroom

CLUES FOR INSTRUCTION

Somewhere in the classroom keep two or three bindings to hold individual contributions for books. Keep the titles open to all kinds of interpretations: "Herman and Harry," "What's That?", "What I Discovered," "I Did It." When ten to twelve contributions have been made to a topic, edit them with the authors, bind them into a cover, and place the books in the Reading/Research Center.

When going on field trips, take tape recorders and cameras to record what is seen and heard. Make the materials available for children to use in writing their observations and impressions. Bind the contributions as a report for the Reading/Research Center.

A play to share a good plot or a good idea with the class

CLUES FOR INSTRUCTION

Encourage children to convert films and stories into plays. Select the actors and let them "say" their parts before writing. The written versions of plays that result will represent colloquial language that is easy for children to say and read.

A poem to preserve a beautiful thought

Rocks

Some rocks are round.
A streambed is where rocks are
   found.
Think of the years to get as
   round as that!
Even longer than nine lives
   of a cat.

—Milton, age 10

Mountains at Dusk

. . . The color was the deep purple
of a hot day cooling. . . .

—Ricky, age 11

CLUES FOR INSTRUCTION

Permeate the learning environment with lists of words in categories that help children say and write their observations and feelings in poetic language—color words, shape words, size words, texture words, sound words, taste words, smell words, rhyming words, similes, metaphors. Keep the lists open so that additions can be made. Pause when reading to children to savor a beautiful way of saying something. Keep available as a "poet's corner" a small bulletin board on which children can pin their contributions. Mount a branch from a tree for them to use to hang poetic expressions for others to read; it can be called the Poet's Tree.

A word or phrase to express a feeling about a painting or musical composition

CLUES FOR INSTRUCTION

Place fine art prints or good photographs from magazines in the Writing/Publishing Center. Mount the pictures on a board which has pockets that invite children to write and drop in one-word picture titles (usually a noun), two-word titles (usually an adjective and noun or a noun and verb), and three-word titles (usually clusters of words that include nouns, verbs, adjectives, and adverbs).

For the Viewing/Listening Center prepare a tape of short musical selections which can be numbered. With the tape provide a response sheet inviting children to make one-word, two-word, or three-word responses.

From the first year in school until the last every child needs to feel the thrill of "real authorship." Individual contributions of writing should be treated with appropriate mountings and bindings and displayed to foster a feeling of authorship.

Children who experience authorship many times are likely to be those most interested in other authors. They appreciate good descriptive passages, the beautiful language of good poetry, and characters that seem to live. They can muse with an author rather than always seek to be amused. They know that good writing is not easy. But the satisfaction of having personal ideas accepted, enjoyed, and appreciated builds a strong desire for contact with other authors who have had something to say.

Evaluating Exploratory Writing

There can be no judgment of children's creative efforts that does not first take into account the children themselves and their experiences. The major idea of creative self-expression is that children are encouraged to express their sensations and feelings. The products of such activities represent the child as an individual, not as a poet or an author.

If children write when they really have something to say, they are usually eager to do their best. The importance of ideas and feelings is emphasized in such writing, but if the writing is to be read by others, it must adhere to accepted standards of usage. Most children seek help when they are rewriting something that is going to be published in a class magazine or newspaper, placed in a class book, duplicated for other children, or made into a book for the library. The teacher and other children can help with the mechanics, but they do not tamper with the idea. *Writing must sound like the author.*

Through sharing children's writings in the classroom and pointing out such features as an interesting choice of words, an unusual figure of speech, and the use of sound and color words, the teacher can stimulate the desire to write and help to raise the standards of the entire group.

All products cannot be expected to have artistic merit. No one produces constantly at a high pitch. When something of beauty and quality is produced, the teacher has a responsibility to treat it as a treasure, not as another opportunity to teach a lesson in mechanics and form. Less sensitive and artistic products serve that purpose equally well.

Summary of Skills and Abilities for Exploring Writing

BEGINNINGS OF PERSONAL WRITING

——Speaks with ease and freedom in simple sentences
——Makes use of past experiences and information in conversation
——Enjoys hearing stories and poems read
——Keeps a series of ideas in mind in proper sequence
——Expresses thoughts and feelings in dramatic play, rhythmic activities, and art
——Has the necessary eye-hand coordination to form manuscript letters
——Observes the teacher writing and labeling pictures; asks about letters and words
——Learns to form letters into words for writing
——Discovers that writing can be read
——Develops a genuine desire to write

INDEPENDENCE IN PERSONAL WRITTEN EXPRESSION

——Labels own pictures, things about the room, and other objects
——Participates orally in group compositions as the teacher records them
——Tells a story orally to group as the teacher records
——Dictates own ideas to be recorded by the teacher
——Copies group compositions and own compositions that the teacher has recorded
——Begins to write independently about pictures painted, personal experiences, things liked, and so on
——Is increasingly able to handle language and to make words say what is intended
——Gradually acquires knowledge of the mechanics of writing and applies it in creative writing

INDIVIDUALITY IN PERSONAL WRITTEN EXPRESSION

——Conveys something of self in writing
——Enjoys the creative writing of other children
——Enjoys the work of good children's authors—both prose and poetry
——Experiments with different forms of written expression

—Expands range of written expression by experimenting with many new words, phrases, and figures of speech

—Enjoys expressing self in writing and sharing this self-expression with others

—Develops greater understanding of self and the human and physical environment through writing experiences

Selected References

Allen, Roach Van, and Claryce Allen. *Language Experiences in Reading, Level III.* Encyclopaedia Britannica Educational Corp., Chicago, 1967.

Anderson, Paul S. *Language Skills in Elementary Education.* Macmillan Co., New York, 1964.

Applegate, Mauree. *Helping Children Write.* Harper & Row, New York, 1954.

Ashley, Rosalind M. *Successful Techniques for Teaching Elementary Language Arts.* Parker Publishing Co., West Nyack, N.Y., 1970.

Burrows, Alvina T., Dianne L. Monson, and Russell G. Stauffer. *New Horizons in the Language Arts.* Harper & Row, New York, 1972.

Chomsky, Carol. "Write First, Read Later," *Childhood Education,* 47, 4 (March 1971), 296–299.

Corbin, Richard. *The Teaching of Writing in Our Schools.* Macmillan Co., New York, 1966.

Gillooly, William B. "The Influence of Writing-System Characteristics on Learning to Read," *Reading Research Quarterly,* 8, 2 (1973), pp. 167–200.

Greene, Harry A., and Walter T. Petty. *Developing Language Skills in the Elementary School.* Allyn & Bacon, Boston, 1971.

Hall, Mary Anne. *Teaching Reading as a Language Experience.* Charles E. Merrill, Columbus, Ohio, 1970.

Henning, Dorothy G., and Barbara M. Grant. *Content and Craft: Written Expression in the Elementary School.* Prentice-Hall, Englewood Cliffs, N.J., 1973.

Hodges, Richard E., and E. Hugh Rudorf. *Language and Learning to Read.* Houghton Mifflin Co., Boston, 1972.

Johnston, A. Montgomery, and Paul C. Burns (eds.). *Elementary School Curriculum.* Allyn & Bacon, Boston, 1970.

Lee, Dorris M., and Roach Van Allen. *Learning to Read Through Experience.* Appleton-Century-Crofts, New York, 1963.

McCullough, Constance M. *Handbook for Teaching the Language Arts.* Chandler Publishing Co., San Francisco, 1969.

Moffett, James. *A Student-Centered Language Arts Curriculum for Grades K-13: A Handbook for Teachers.* Houghton Mifflin Co., Boston, 1973.

Newman, Harold. *Effective Language Practices in the Elementary School.* John Wiley & Sons, New York, 1972.

Riemer, George. *How They Murdered the Second "R."* W. W. Norton Co., New York, 1969.

Smith, James A. *Adventures in Communication.* Allyn & Bacon, Boston, 1972.

Tiedt, Iris M., and Sidney W. Tiedt. *Contemporary English in the Elementary School.* Prentice-Hall, Englewood Cliffs, N.J., 1967.

FROM THE RATIONALE   Writing individual books—writing and publishing in many forms and for many purposes; editing and illustrating publications; and using pupil-produced publications in the reading program.

Individual authorship is the culminating experience in communicating abilities that relate specifically to reading. Children who are authors are able:
 ——to capture the gist of an idea
 ——to elaborate and clarify
 ——to organize and put in sequence
 ——to prepare a rough draft of a manuscript
 ——to edit and refine an original manuscript
 ——to page and illustrate a manuscript
 ——to share the product in an exhibit, in a collection with others, or in a book that is bound beautifully
 ——to read effectively and independently to an audience.

The children engaged in personal authorship are those who have immediate and deep needs for reading what other authors have written. They usually read more than others and profit most from reading experiences. They internalize, not only meanings, but style and form. They derive pleasure from clever and creative use of language. They are impressed by the artful use of a few words to express a big idea. They read and reread portions of books and poems that suggest to them new ways of expressing their own ideas.

A child who is writing on a topic browses and reads many books on the topic if such books are available. The difficulty level of the books is minimized when personal need is maximized. Much of the content is predictable; illustrations give clues. A child learns that books are useful prior to the time that they can be read orally "without missing words."

A child who has published a book has tremendous motivation to read other books on the same topic. If the book is bound and placed in a school library on the same basis as other books, the author and friends of the author are interested in what other people have written on the same subject. They search out fact and fiction in order to compare and contrast meanings and the treatment of those meanings. They compare and contrast poetry patterns of an author in their classroom with those of other authors. Reading done by *authors* moves away from a passive, quiet activity which serves often as an escape toward an active, productive experience that influences the ideas and the language of the reader.

An Environment for Authors

Artful teaching is an essential ingredient of learning environments where personal authorship flourishes. The artist-teacher lives and talks with children in ways that increase their level of awareness through new experiences with people and places.

—They observe entirely new things and add words to their vocabularies to describe them.

—They hear things they have not been listening for, and increase their vocabularies so that they can tell about them.

—They give their imaginations free rein and communicate their imageries to their peer group and to adults.

—They increase their interest in and vocabularies for smelling and tasting and for comparing and contrasting.

—They relate the qualities and language of texture, shape, size, and color as they report their experiences.

—They communicate in multiple ways through talking, acting, painting, singing, dancing, and writing.

Awareness is raised as the teacher participates *with* children as reader, actor, artist, and author. New levels of awareness are communicated about the earth, sky, water, animals, machines, plants, and people. All have names; all have motion; all have describable characteristics such as color, size, shape, and texture; most have sounds; some have taste and smell; all can be compared and contrasted with each other.

In addition to the psychological and interactive aspects of the environment, some physical characteristics are required if productive efforts are to be attained with minimum help from a teacher or other adults. A Writing/Publishing Center must be available and well supplied.

The Writing Area

The Writing Area is a part of the Writing/Publishing Center where children go to write; it can also be a place where materials are stored for children to check out and use at a variety of locations.

The ideal Writing Area is developed cooperatively by pupils and teachers as they work together as authors. There are some supplies and components that can be used by all authors and that can be planned and provided for before a class group is formed.

Paper should be available in a variety of qualities, sizes, and colors. Handwriting paper can be in supply for practice in handwriting skills, but it must not be a paper prescribed for authors to use. At all levels authors need a choice of paper, one suitable to what is being written. Large quantities of newsprint are handy for first drafts. The blank sides of printed sheets can be used for original manuscripts. Some classroom groups find a supply of computer print-out paper useful. Others supplement the school supply with end-of-roll newsprint from newspaper publishers and with printer's scrap from a print shop.

Markers of many sizes and colors should be available. Different kinds and colors of pencils, felt-tipped pens in a variety of colors, and crayons of all sizes and colors are needed so that authors can get the desired effect for their manuscripts.

Writing models that show several configurations of capital and lower-case letters can be useful when authors are ready to refine and edit manuscripts. These may be in addition to standard models on which children will practice to improve general handwriting skills.

Spelling aids need to be available in a variety of forms and in several places. Some of these are:

——lists of high-frequency words which develop as children analyze their own dictation and writing to discover the words that all authors use

——lists of name words which accumulate for specific topics or are used frequently by many children

——lists of words of movement that are used as verbs in sentences

——lists of descriptive words such as color, size, shape, texture, smell, taste, and touch

——proper names useful for special seasons and projects

——picture dictionaries that might grow from children's own language

——school dictionaries that offer a major resource for more mature authors.

A Word Wall can be established to hold the lists. During periods of considerable writing activity a Word Wall monitor can be appointed to identify words for spelling. The monitor should be able to read most of the words and should know their general locations on the lists. A student from an older group can be assigned to monitor the Word Wall if no child in a young group is able to do so. This program and activity accelerate the development of vocabularies of basic sight words. Many oral word games can evolve for the practice and review of words for spelling when writing.

Story stimulators and motivators must be provided to aid students who need outside stimulation to start writing. Some are:

— sentences and phrases to begin stories, collected from many sources, written on cards, and filed in random order

— model stories with noun, verb, adjective, and adverb slots left blank for authors to fill in

— story beginnings copied on cards with just enough story to suggest characters, setting, and a hint of plot

— story middles, copied on cards, that can be developed in both directions to tell stories

— story endings, copied on cards, that give a hint of what might have happened in entire stories

— story pictures filed for personal interpretations by authors

— collections of pictures, in envelopes, that include people, places, transportation, food, entertainment, accidents, and special occasions that can be arranged in an endless number of stories

— examples and explanations of riddles and jokes that can be used as models

— headlines from newspapers, mounted on cards, that can be used as ideas for stories and poems.

Children should be encouraged to make contributions to the Writing Area resources. It is their source of help and inspiration, and they must understand what is there and how to use the resources as productive authors. It must not be a place where children go to complete lessons.

Vocabulary enrichment resources must grow as the Writing Area is used, or there is little improvement in the quality of writing. Lists, files, and posters can be started for enrichment resources; some possibilities are:

— figurative language files with examples of similes, metaphors, and personification as used by other authors

— lists of synonyms and antonyms—especially examples of words with two, three, and four syllables that are useful in writing poetry with controlled syllabic patterns

— alliteration aids such as a list of words beginning with the same sound symbols that includes nouns, verbs, adjectives, and adverbs

——rhyming aids that include lists of two, three, and four words with like rhyme

——how to say *said* in many ways as an aid to writing conversation that emphasizes characterization

——how to say *not, yes, please,* and other common words in many ways

——nonsense words that can be used or can serve as examples for making up new words for nonsense writing.

As children mature as authors, each one should develop a personal writing handbook. A writing handbook contains many of the helps listed above for a Writing Area but features aids each author uses frequently. Some authors need a spelling aid such as a list of 500 to 1,000 words used frequently. Others do not need this type of aid by the time they are ready to develop their personal resources for writing. Some authors need many motivators and stimulators; others are self-motivated to translate observations and imagination into stories and poems.

The Publishing Area

The Publishing Area, part of the Writing/Publishing Center, is a place in a classroom or school where children process their original manuscripts through editing, illustrating, paging, copying, and binding into forms for others to use. It may be an integral part of the Writing Area, or it may be at a separate location. Some schools with many authors maintain a Publishing Area for the whole school and invite parents to assist in the operation by supplying materials, typing, and helping with the binding process. In these schools simple binding is done in the classrooms, and only manuscripts that are selected for production in multiple copies go to the school Publishing Area.

The process of selecting manuscripts to be published in multiple copies should be well understood by children. A committee might develop criteria and publish them. It should emphasize that everything that is written does not need to be published in multiple copies. Single, original copies are enough for most of what is written.

Publishing is *the peak experience* in a language experience approach. It truly integrates writing, reading, speaking, and listening. It brings into focus the mechanics of language. It draws on influences from many authors and publishers. It uses graphics as an essential ingredient in the language arts. It can be extended and interpreted through dramatization and choral reading. A language experience approach is impossible to maintain without publishing individual books, class books, individual story charts, newspapers, magazines, catalogues, and recipes.

For these publications supplies and aids are required which may not be typical of other communication and reading programs; some are:

1. Scraps of cloth, cardboard, wallpaper, braid, yarn, and leather for covers and illustrations
2. Contact paper to use in bindings of hard-cover books
3. Sewing equipment that includes a sewing machine, hand-sewing needles, awl, and thread
4. Laminator—a laminating machine or iron to use with laminating paper
5. Typewriters for children and adults to use, especially when making multiple copies
6. Lettering pens for printing with stencils and on title pages and covers
7. Paper cutter to cut cardboard for covers and pages of different sizes
8. Paper punch to cut holes for some bindings
9. Glues and tapes for securing books to bindings
10. Art supplies for illustrating in cases in which the Publishing Area is far removed from the Arts and Crafts Center.

The Publishing Area is of limited value unless children participate. Volunteer adults can help, and older children can work with younger children, but participation in processes and procedures is of great significance when the ideas and language of the children are being made into reading material useful in the school program. Some committees on which children can serve are discussed below.

THE EDITORIAL COMMITTEE The editorial committee accepts original manuscripts and reads them to identify mechanical and technical errors and to make suggestions for improving style and form. Some committees divide responsibility by assigning each member a speciality such as spelling, capitalization, punctuation, sentence sense, or paragraphing. Each specialist reads a manuscript and notes suggestions. Then the committee calls a conference with the author to review the suggestions. The author accepts or rejects the suggestions in terms of the purpose of the manuscript. In some cases the author then takes the manuscript to the editor in chief who is usually the teacher.

After review by the editor in chief necessary revisions are made. Sometimes rewriting is desirable before preparing a manuscript for duplication.

Editing of newspapers and magazines may involve other procedures. Contributors may place their rough drafts in designated places for editors to review. There might be editors for stories, reports, comics, sports, fashions, entertainment, editorials, interviews, puzzles, and any other sections included in the publication. In addition to attention to technical errors, editors have to plan the use of assigned space and recommend alterations to fit spaces.

Round-robin readings of rough drafts may be used as an editing technique for contributions to a class book. Groups of five to six can read each other's manuscripts, marking anything that needs to be changed. When a manuscript returns to the author, it will have been around to every editor and will be ready to rewrite in a refined version.

Never does the teacher serve as *the grader* of papers, offering suggestions for corrections to be made when a manuscript is copied. If the teacher functions as an editor, it is *with the author*.

THE TYPING OR PRINTING COMMITTEE   The author makes two or three carbon copies or cuts a stencil for four or more. Typewriters can be used for making carbon copies or for preparing stencils. Manuscripts can also be prepared with lead pencils on white paper and copied with one of the heat-process machines.

The author may do the typing or printing or may choose a member of the committee to do it. Every committee should have at least one member who can use a typewriter (who is not necessarily a typist). A volunteer parent can be a committee member.

Most children like to try to do some of their own typing, even though they type with only one finger. (It is good spelling practice.) If someone else does the typing, the author, including any of kindergarten age, should be invited to strike a few of the letters to see what happens.

If pencil copies are being made for duplicating stencils, an adult can print lightly in letters similar to those used in the classroom, and the author can trace over the printing with bold strokes.

The author has the responsibility of paging the manuscript and deciding whether the book will be folded and stitched, stapled flat, held with ring binders, or put together by other means. Members of the committee serve as consultants and show mockups of different possibilities.

When preparing newspapers and magazines, each contributor may be assigned space or pages to prepare. The variety in printing and illustrating adds interest to the publication.

THE DUPLICATING COMMITTEE In some schools children learn to operate duplicating equipment to publish their own books, newspapers, and magazines. In others teachers or parents are in charge of the machines. In all cases the author or authors whose work is being duplicated should be able to observe the process at least once. For some children this is the most exciting part of the whole production.

THE ILLUSTRATING COMMITTEE Authors may do their own illustrations, or they may seek help from members of the illustrating committee in the Publishing Area. Children on the committee can offer suggestions for illustrations and read paged manuscripts to make certain that the text suggests an illustration at the point that space is provided for it.

Some member of each illustrating committee should understand the following points.

——Nouns can be illustrated more easily than any other class of words. Since nouns carry the heaviest load of meaning in passages, good illustrations aid in word recognition and prediction of words and phrases. For easy reading materials, all nouns not on lists of words of highest frequency should be illustrated.

——Color, size, and shape words can be illustrated. When materials are edited for easy reading, these words may be eliminated in order to reduce the length of sentences. Their places in stories can be retained through illustrations and oral discussions of the materials.

——Texture words can be illustrated with collage materials and with brush strokes. The tactile experience available from collage illustrations extends vocabularies whether the words are printed or not.

——Taste and smell words can only be implied in most illustrations. (Some "scratch and smell" books are available commercially.)

——Leaves, dried flowers, feathers, and other thin materials pressed between waxed paper with a warm iron make attractive illustrations.

——Abstract designs are sometimes as effective as realistic representations.

Some children like to take their manuscripts home for father or mother to illustrate. The family team is a good unit for working on a publication.

In classrooms where book-length publications are produced for every member, the spaces for illustrations are left blank during duplicating and binding. Each child does his own illustrations after receiving the book. Copies for the library are prepared by the illustrating committee.

THE BINDERY COMMITTEE   Many children volunteer for the bindery committee. They enjoy the process of assembly, sewing or stapling, cutting cardboard and cloth to size, gluing, and pressing.

Most Publishing Areas have models of different bindings with step-by-step procedures to accompany them. An example for a hardcover book follows.

Step 1: Cut two pieces of cardboard ¼ in. larger than the pages of your book.

Step 2: Lay the pieces side by side. Leave enough space between for the book to fit in. The width of a pencil is usually about right. Tape them in position.

Step 3: Place the cardboard over the cover material which has been cut 1 in. larger than the cardboard on all sides. Use any attractive paper, wallpaper, fabric, or contact paper.

Step 4: Bond the cover material to the cardboard with glue or drymount paper. Contact paper has its own bonding glue.

Step 5: Fold down the corners of the cover material over the cardboard.

Step 6: Fold over the edges and glue.

Step 7: Attach your book into the binding with a strip of tape on each side.

Step 8: Print the title on the cover. Print the title, the author, the illustrator, and the date of publication on the front flyleaf. A classroom publishing company might be identified.

Explanations of several types of bindings should be available. Simple, flexible bindings are useful, but they do not last long in libraries.

Volunteer parents are very useful in the bindery. They can furnish materials and assist in making the covers. A supply of covers for standard-sized paper can be made in advance, and the author can choose the binding and attach the book.

A publications program does not need to wait until a Writing/Publishing Center has been established. Simple recognition of a child's language productivity can be given by stapling it to a painting or binding it with a piece of construction paper. But the teacher should have in mind goals that will lead to an emerging environment that stimulates the production of materials suitable for the reading instructional program.

Guiding the Production of Authors

Children in school settings seldom write without some guidance that opens up possibilities for new ways of expressing common ideas. The recording of home-rooted language is only a beginning point for individual authorship. It is the point at which confidence begins to build and choices for new ways of writing are begun. Teachers offer alternatives during the presentation of dictation in order to initiate the attitude toward change and experimentation which is essential to sustain authorship over a period of years.

Freedom to Try

Children must feel free to try; otherwise there is nothing to guide and develop. An openness to efforts and an acceptance of exploratory spelling, punctuation, and sentencing are absolute requirements for budding authors. When this situation obtains, creative efforts such as "Brite Spring" come into the classroom on scraps of paper and with supporting illustrations.

Brite Spring

Once a time it was winter but the people couldnt wate till spring one day the people got an idea paint every thing spring colors. hey! that's a good idea lets do it yea! So they got all colors and started to work it took them seven days to do it but on the next day it relly was spring. But at night it rained and when they woke up it was warmer It was really spring. The people said let's give it a name what shell we name it how about Brite Spring Yes! and from now on the people don't paint it spring and thats how spring go its name.
The End

Children who work in a strong phonics program sometimes develop generalizations about sound-symbol relationships which they use correctly in spelling, but they spell incorrectly. Debbie furnished an example.

My Own Animal Story (*Debbie*)

This story is about Rabbits. do you no iny thing about them I will tell you something thay eat led's and carits and thay can jump hi. . . .

To tell Debbie, age six, that she misspelled the words *no* (know), *iny* (any), *thay* (they), *led's* (lettuce), *carits* (carrots), and *hi* (high) is in effect telling her that she should not use her knowledge of phonics as it was taught directly and effectively. At this stage acceptance and encouragement are high priorities. Children must produce manuscripts before they can refine them.

Some writing is difficult to interpret. Spelling that is used often gives minimum clues, but with the author present to do the reading, acceptance is possible. Salvador gave a good example when he wrote: "dess June he is six picos du munsr sacncis." When he read the story, the sound-symbol relationship cleared up. He read: "This is Johnny. He is sick because the monster makes him sick."

A group of children wrote and illustrated stories following a seal show. Prior to writing they listed words that they might want to use such as:

Words for a Seal Story

seal	woman	play
ball	Sandy	clap
lady	Sam	boys
tricks	magic	girls
fish	ladder	

In addition to the fourteen words that the children suggested following the show, a list of about one hundred words of highest frequency was visible from any place in the classroom. (The children had had phonics lessons in kindergarten and first grade.)

Abel wrote: "I sw a seal played wriz a ball and he make tricks." He read: "I saw a seal play with a ball and he makes tricks."

Harold wrote: "the seal was duen some trics. And the lade sent ot got a nedr seal. And the seal did not no trecs. And the lade hed some segy [sausage] from the seal. And the seal clap hes hons. the seal got up on hes set. the seal et fsh. the fehes wer ded."

Harold's story is easy to read with his exploratory spelling. He made minimum use of the resources provided for spelling. At this point he was personally involved to the extent that his own resources seemed adequate—and they were.

Isabel wrote: "The seal had a ball on his nous. Then he went up the ladder and down the ladder. The seal aet fish and all the doys and girls wour claping." Isabel used the resources but still had a problem of copying from one place to another.

From the class of bilingual children the teacher had achieved major goals.

——Most children felt comfortable writing independently.

——A common experience, the seal show, provided a base for building a speaking, writing, and reading vocabulary.

——Every child could read his own writing.

——What was written was useful in reading. (These children could not possibly read a published book about a seal show.)

——Children who volunteered their stories had them edited and published in a booklet with their own illustrations. One form of editing was to print what was written and then to add how the author read it.

——Children used writing resources that were developing in the classroom to free themselves for independent writing.

Models and Patterns

Language on the literacy level and poetic forms of expression are introduced and practiced so they take hold and become a natural form of expression. To rely on "just anything you want to write" is to deny most individuals satisfying experiences as an author. Teachers use numerous strategies, models, and patterns to introduce ways of saying things without dictating what to say. They develop and keep personal files of successful strategies and resources for individual authorship. A few examples are given here:

1. The sentence starter or the model sentence can launch a series of statements of personal experience or imagination.

   Each child copies the sentence starter and adds a simple statement or a rhyme that is purely personal.

   Mommies are for driving the car to take us places. —Walter

Slippery is—
an icy street,
a wet cake of soap
under my two wet feet.

                    —Debbie

Fluffy is—
the pillow on my bed,
my white poodle, Fee-Fee,
with her pompom on her head.

                    —Lorraine

Spring is a time when grass turns green and trees start to bud. —Gary

Sentence starters provide:

——a structure that is dependable for each author
——repetition of the same sentence pattern with different content in each sentence
——repetition for easy reading
——spelling of many of the words.

Children usually have more to say than just the printed part. They can elaborate on an accompanying illustration and thus keep full language in the classroom environment—naming things, telling how they move, and describing them. Home-rooted dialects are useful and welcomed in oral elaboration even though they may have been denied by the nature of the sentence model. Experience backgrounds are used with only slight variations in words.

Sentence starters and model sentences assure the introduction and repetition of words of highest frequency in the language. When bound into readers, every page repeats target words, but every page is different. There is no need to work on comprehension skills because the authors are present. Recognition skills get full attention when this type of pupil-produced material is used.

2. The projection of self to inanimate objects or to animals helps children say things and reveal frustrations that are not typical of sharing and reporting.

The Cup (*Eileen*)

One day I woke up in surprise and saw that I was a cup. I went downstairs into the kitchen and jumped up on the counter. My mother came down and rinsed out the cup (me). Then she turned on the kettle. Then it boiled and she poured hot water in me (the cup).

level of self-concept Then she drank out of me. Then she went upstairs to lie down. Then Bobby came. He's only three. He climbed up and grabbed me. Suddenly, I slipped out of his hands and broke into pieces on the floor. Mother came down and scolded Bobby for breaking her cup. Who cares? It was only me!

Why I Want to Be a Dragster (*John*)

aspirations I want to be a drag racer so I can be famous. And win a lot of money and stickers. I am interested in mechanical things. I want to be a mechanic, too, so I can fix my own car and I can help people by fixing their things like cars, go-carts, mini-bikes, and cassettes, too.

Floor (*Karla*)

Hi! I'm a floor!
People are always
walking on me.
feelings Sometimes,
I feel like opening up
and swallowing them,
But I don't.

Sunbaked Sand Dune (*Douglas*)

I stand alone in the desert
Looking up at the sky.
I am dry and motionless,
Watching the clouds roll by.
My neighbor is a cactus plant,
personification Old and very big.
No other thing can you see—
Not even a little twig.
You see why I am lonely?
Besides the cactus plant
I am the one and only.

3. Brief descriptions of things usual and ordinary help children use words that are not typical of conversation.

Children can look for any object or word, think of its name, its use, its feelings, its size, its shape, its colors, and other characteristics. Then they can write.

Night (*Geoffrey*)

After the last traces of the sunset,
Night falls like a blanket of black velvet
        covering the world.

Broom (*Kathy*)

It sweeps.
It keeps.
It falls apart.
It's big.
It's small.
It's any size at all.

Jet (*Carl*)

Soaring, roaring, flying
Through the polluted sky.
Turning engines breathing
Black, smokey fumes.

Children who feel good about the simple descriptive passages they write can observe ordinary things and create beautiful statements worthy of publication.

Ant Forest (*Douglas*)

The ant forest is big and green.
To an ant it is a lovely scene.
The dew on the ant trees shines like glass,
But really their forest is a clump of grass.

4. Alphabet books of all kinds promote the development of reference skills, stimulate dictionary use, and provide practice in initial sound-symbol relationships.

Each child can choose a category of some kind like zoo animals in the book *All Kinds of Things from A to Z.* Words for each letter of the alphabet follow along with some illustrations. Older children can serve as secretaries to younger children who need help.

Zoo Animals

bobcat	jackal	rhino
camel	kangaroo	seal
deer	lion	tiger
elephant	monkey	unicorn
falcon	ostrich	vulture
giraffe	owl	walrus
hippo	pelican	yak
ibex	quail	zebra

Other categories can be fruits, vegetables, baseball players, plants, fish, birds, clothes, weather, and work.

Books can be bound and used for reading.

One character can be described in an alphabet series that requires adjectives, verbs, and adverbs to complete a sentence for each letter.

Roadrunner

This is an adorable roadrunner acting angrily.
This is a beautiful roadrunner bouncing bumpily.
This is a cunning roadrunner crowing cautiously. . . .

Attention to the understanding and use of the alphabet can be continued throughout the grades when it is linked to literary writing. It is not considered only for primary grades when research and reference work are required.

5. Alliterative language highlights recognition skills of initial sound-symbol relationships.

Simple statements made around a topic such as piles of presents can involve children in alliterative language.

A jolly, jumping jack-in-the box. —Rosa
A beautiful, big, buzzing bike. —Jerome
A monkey that makes music. —Carmen
A wee, wiggledy wagon. —Ronaldo

Each student can add to a book an illustrated page that is useful in practicing the essential skills of using initial sound-symbol relationships.

Alliteration can be promoted through nonsense writing. The teacher or a child can produce a nonsense title and an introduction. Nonsense statements from other students can follow.

> Is that a cow crunching crackers on the couch?
> There's a thumping and a thrashing,
> There's a crashing and a cracking,
> There's a banging and a bumping
> All over the place.
> Could it be—
>   Bats batting butter in bibs in the bedroom?
> Or a—
>   Goat giggling in the garage?
> Maybe it's—
>   Swans sweating while swimming in sweaters,
> Or—
>   Pumpkins popping popcorn in the pantry.

Each student can add an illustrated page for a book that can be used for reviewing initial consonants and consonant clusters. The pride of authorship inherent in this type of production is enough motivation for active participation in the learning experience.

6. Comics from newspapers are useful in promoting clever and creative language.

Comic strips can be collected, the "talk" can be cut out, the remainder of the comic strip can be mounted in books with one frame to a page or on strips of heavy paper, and then the talk can be restored by the students. The talk written can be their own and may include dialects and gross errors typical of home-rooted language. Often this language is clear, forceful, and creative, and it needs to be recognized as useful in some types of communication.

Some children like to cut out characters from several comic strips they know well, and combine them into one of their own. Those who are able to retain the language and personalities of the characters in new and mixed up settings get results that are entertaining and highly creative.

7. Classic stories and poems are useful as models for language and characterization.

Several versions of "Peter Rabbit" were read before Patricia wrote her own while in second grade. She paged and illustrated her story and bound it into a book for the Reading/Research Center.

Peter Rabbit

Peter Rabbit's mother called him and told him to go to the store to get some lettuce and carrots for dinner.

When Peter Rabbit was on the way to the store, he fell and skinned his knee on a sharp rock. He cried because it hurt him.

Then he got up and went to the store. He was hopping on one leg.

When he got to the store, he got the wrong things because he forgot what his mother told him. He got ice cream and Cokes because he liked them.

I'll bet his mother is going to be mad.

He hopped all the way home with the Cokes and ice cream.

When he got home, his mother looked at him and shouted, "What's the matter, Peter? What happened to you?"

"I fell down on a sharp rock," he cried.

"Oh, you poor baby! I shouldn't have sent you to the store!"

Mother Rabbit carried Peter into the bathroom to fix his knee with a Band-Aid.

And then she looked into the bag and saw the Cokes and ice cream, and she shouted, "Peter Rabbit! I told you to get some carrots and lettuce for dinner!"

Mother Rabbit was mad! She sent Peter to his room and said, "Get your pajamas on and get to bed!" She was mad!

The End

Steve wrote the following after he had participated in a choral reading experience with "This Is the House That Jack Built." He was in the fifth grade, and "The Car That Steve Built" was the first book he ever wrote and published for others to read.

The Car That Steve Built

This is the car that Steve built.

These are the tires that go under the car that Steve built.

This is the body that goes over the tires that go under the car that Steve built.

These are the seats that go inside the body that goes over the tires that go under the car that Steve built.

This is the engine that goes under the hood that's in front of the seats that go inside the body that goes over the tires that go under the car that Steve built.

And this is the car that Steve built.

The End

Neither Patricia nor Steve could have written books of a quality for reproduction and use in reading without some model. "Peter Rabbit" and "This Is the House That Jack Built" are only two among hundreds of titles that are useful as models and patterns for children to use in sharing their own thoughts and interests.

8. Types of literature can be used as models for writing that bring variety into the publications program.

Fables are of ancient origin and are in many reading collections. It is one thing to read a fable well enough to understand it. It is quite a different and more demanding ability to be able to write one. Eric read fables and then wrote one in a sixth-grade class.

The Man Who Grew Peach Trees from His Ears (*Eric*)

Many years ago there was a man who never cleaned his ears. The same man owned an orchard of peach trees.

One winter when the seeds were falling, one seed fell in each of the man's ears while he was asleep. Naturally, the man thought he was deaf.

One night the man took a shower and water got in his ears. About one month later a little green plant grew from each ear. When he transplanted the plants, he could hear again because the plants had stopped up his ears.

The next summer he had grown some fine peaches from his ears.

Never sit under peach trees with dirty ears in the winter.

Short stories can be written by children in elementary grades if they read published ones and discuss their structure as well as their content. Good readers need challenges beyond comprehension exercises. Writing in different literary forms challenges the best of them. Carole, a sixth-grade student who could comprehend almost any story in elementary school readers, extended her understanding and was greatly challenged when she wrote a short story that other children enjoyed and admired enough to request that it be published in multiple copies.

Born Wild (*Carole*)

The black rain clouds had rolled in as I started through the woods looking for my wandering horse. Frightened that it would be a huge spring storm that we have in our part of the valley, I knew I had to get Misty in before it started.

The woods looked dark and angry. The trees tried to grab me as I rushed between them. The wind was against me and a chill went through me. In the distance I heard crashes of thunder. Lightning flashed. Feeling the dampness in the air, I hurried on.

Bending the small trees almost to the ground the whistling wind seemed to say, "Hurry, hurry!"

The wind was growing stronger and I screamed, "Misty, come to me!"

Suddenly before me stood a band of wild horses. Straining my eyes, I looked desperately for the brown colt. It was then that I noticed her huddled with the other horses. Surely she wouldn't have returned to the herd as long as I'd had her! I walked toward her and the horses ran for shelter. Yet she stood there as if undecided whether to come to me or return to the band. Only the stallion, the leader, waited for her decision. She turned toward me, her brown eyes thoughtful as if to say, "I love you, but this must be."

Then she turned and I said to myself, "You belong to the wild, Misty!"

I watched as she and the stallion galloped off toward the gathering of wild horses.

As the rain started it blended in with my tears, but down deep I knew she was born wild and would always live wild.

Many other strategies that are models, patterns, and motivators can be used in guiding children into individual authorship. Some of these strategies are:

——recipes, real and imaginary
——dust jackets from trade books used as covers for bindings that have ready-made titles
——sets of stationery with a series of pictures that can be used as binders for short stories and poems related to the pictures
——autobiographies ranging from simple ones that each child completes by filling in blanks with personal information to more elaborate, original ones
——stories in one language that can be translated into another one and published as bilingual readers
——collections of short poems to be copied and illustrated to accompany an original poem in a book
——stories with blank spaces for nouns and/or verbs that can be copied and filled in with personal information to make each story different
——collections of mounted magazine pictures that can be arranged in many sequences for a story with characters, setting, and plot.

Summary of Skills and Abilities for Writing Individual Books

SELECTION OF IDEAS

——Finds topics of interest in the immediate environment
——Uses classic stories and poems as models for writing
——Extends the concept of the alphabet into book-length productions
——Uses resources in the Writing/Publishing Center for topics
——Selects a variety of literary forms to express personal ideas
——Chooses imaginary and nonsense topics as well as real-life topics

EDITING OF MANUSCRIPTS

——Assumes responsibility for self-editing at a level appropriate to ability
——Participates on editorial committees in the editing of group projects

——Knows how to use spelling resources available in the Writing/Publishing Center
——Can use descriptive vocabulary to elaborate simple language
——Can reduce the length and difficulty of sentences without destroying meaning
——Pages manuscripts for illustrating and printing so that each page has at least one contributing idea
——Edits poetry by spacing and selection of print as well as for spelling, capitalization, and punctuation

PUBLICATION OF MANUSCRIPTS

——Makes a variety of bindings for books
——Participates in the production of class publications such as newspapers and magazines
——Serves on committees responsible for producing finished books:
——the editorial committee
——the typing or printing committee
——the duplicating committee
——the illustrating committee
——the bindery committee

READING PUPIL-PRODUCED BOOKS

——Reads own books to an audience of classmates and to other classes
——Interprets own books with effective oral reading which increases interest and understanding
——Chooses books by other authors in the class for recreational reading

Selected References

Allen, Roach Van, and Claryce Allen. *Language Experiences in Reading, Level III.* Encyclopaedia Britannica Educational Corp., Chicago, 1967.

Anderson, Paul S. *Language Skills in Elementary Education.* Macmillan Co., New York, 1964.

Applegate, Mauree. *Easy in English.* Harper & Row, New York, 1963.

Burrows, Alvina T., June D. Ferebee, Dorris Jackson, and Dorothy O. Saunders. *They All Want to Write.* Holt, Rinehart and Winston, New York, 1964.

Burrows, Alvina T., Dianne L. Monson, and Russell G. Stauffer. *New Horizons in the Language Arts.* Harper & Row, New York, 1972.

Corbin, Richard. *The Teaching of Writing in Our Schools.* Macmillan Co., New York, 1966.

Dunne, Hope W. *The Art of Teaching Reading: A Language and Self-Concept Approach.* Charles E. Merrill, Columbus, Ohio, 1972.

Evertts, Eldonna (ed.). *Explorations in Children's Writing.* National Council of Teachers of English, Urbana, Ill., 1970.

Greene, Harry A., and Walter T. Petty. *Developing Language Skills in the Elementary School.* Allyn & Bacon, Boston, 1971.

Hall, MaryAnne. *Teaching Reading as a Language Experience.* Charles E. Merrill, Columbus, Ohio, 1970.

Henning, Dorothy G., and Barbara M. Grant. *Content and Craft: Written Expression in the Elementary School.* Prentice-Hall, Englewood Cliffs, N.J., 1973.

Hodges, Richard E., and E. Hugh Rudorf. *Language and Learning to Read: What Teachers Should Know About Language.* Houghton Mifflin Co., Boston, 1972.

King, Martha L., Robert Emans, and Patricia J. Cianciolo (eds.). *A Forum for Focus: The Language Arts in the Elementary Schools.* National Council of Teachers of English, Urbana, Ill., 1973.

Landrum, Roger. *A Day Dream I Had at Night and Other Stories: Teaching Children How to Make Their Own Readers.* Watkins Press, New York, 1971.

Moffett, James. *A Student-Centered Language Arts Curriculum, Grades K-13: A Handbook for Teachers.* Houghton Mifflin Co., Boston, 1973.

Riemer, George. *How They Murdered the Second "R."* W. W. Norton and Co., New York, 1969.

Smith, James A. *Adventures in Communication.* Allyn & Bacon, Boston, 1972.

Stauffer, Russell G. *The Language-Experience Approach to the Teaching of Reading.* Harper & Row, New York, 1970.

Tiedt, Iris M., and Sidney W. Tiedt. *Contemporary English in the Elementary School.* Prentice-Hall, Englewood Cliffs, N.J., 1967.

Part Three
Studying Communication

Strand Two of the Curriculum Rationale for a Language experience Approach emphasizes "how language works for individuals." It is different from other language study programs for reading in that children's own stories and poems are used along with those from other printed sources to show the relationships of personal language to printed language. In the process teachers and children are helped to generalize that:

1. The words children use frequently in speech and writing are the same ones that are found frequently in the writing of other people (both children and adults); in fact, they are the same words that appear frequently in the English language.
2. The words used most frequently tend to be words of structure in sentences and are meaningless in themselves. Many of them are nonphonetic. They have to be learned in context and at sight apart from phonic generalizations.
3. There is need to develop a 100 percent mastery of the words of highest frequency for reading at sight and spelling independently.
4. There is a relationship between the sounds of speech and the use of the alphabet to represent those sounds. Understanding phonics helps to master the relationships that occur over and over again in the language. Practice for mastery is provided by the emphasis on writing in a language experience approach rather than on reading.
5. Some adaptations have to be made to allow for personal pronunciation and standard spelling.
6. Language can be acquired through listening and talking during new experiences and through the application of new vocabulary to old experiences.
7. Language grows as one learns the names of things, words of movement, and words of description.
8. Listening to and repeating well-written materials extend understandings of the many ways in which authors express their ideas and feelings.
9. Personal ideas and feelings can be expressed in many literary forms. Readers must know the how and why of the most common forms used in writing.
10. The sentence patterns used by children in talking and writing are very much like those used by authors of reading material. The simple patterns of expression, both personal and otherwise, can be extended and embellished with a variety of techniques.

11. Language structure is closely related to comprehension. The reader has to be able to do more than recognize the words in order to communicate with authors.

12. There is a continuing emphasis in a language experience approach that calls for "reading" of the many nonalphabetic symbols and conditions in the environment. These primary reading abilities are considered to be basic requirements for secondary reading abilities such as those used in reading printed materials.

The study of the specifics of language that contribute to reading are emphasized in a language experience approach. These specifics have been identified over a period of years beginning with the San Diego County Reading Study Project (see Preface) and continuing to the present. They are elaborated and extended in the chapters that follow in Part Three.

Recognizing high-frequency words—developing awareness that our language contains many words and patterns that are common to all speakers and writers; mastering the words of highest frequency for sight-reading and correct spelling; and using the high-frequency *structure words* of English in meaningful relationships to other words in sentences.

Certain words in the English language are used frequently in speaking and writing. These words are listed in classic lists such as the Dolch List of 220 Words and the Madden-Carlson List of 250 Words. A recent elaboration of the idea that some words are used more than others is published in *Word Frequency Book* by John B. Carroll, Peter Davies, and Barry Richman (1971). This work applied computer techniques to earlier works and produced a detailed analysis of our language from the point of view of the frequency of words used in published materials for school use in grades 3 and above.

The list of words of highest frequency in the order of the first 100 from the study by Carroll, Davies, and Richman correlates highly with another computer-assisted study by Alden J. Moe (1973a). Moe studied words used frequently in trade books popular in grades 1 and 2 and listed the 100 used most often, excluding nouns. Seventy-eight of the words are among the first 100 on the Carroll list (this list included nouns), and 21 of the remaining words are included in the second 100 words of the Carroll list.

Another computer-assisted study was done by Dale D. Johnson (1971) at the University of Wisconsin. His list is a basic vocabulary for beginning reading and includes 300 highest-frequency words. Forty-two of the first 50 are among those on the Carroll list which was compiled from school materials from grade 3 and above. Forty-five are among the first 50 on the Allen List of 100 High-frequency Words in Rank Order. The Allen list takes into account words used frequently by children in their dictated stories and personal writing.

The new computer-assisted listings rank words from *the word* used most frequently to those used less frequently. The lists contrast with older ones that presented the words in alphabetic order. The rank ordering makes possible a focus on the first 25, the first 50, and the first 100 as needed in planning for instruction and review.

Nouns as a separate category of words of high frequency for instructional purposes were presented in the 100 Nouns List by Allen and Allen (1969) when they prepared the *Teacher's Resource Book: Language Experiences in Early Childhood*. Moe (1973b) has now produced the list High Frequency Nouns for Beginning Readers. The differences between his list and the Allen list might be attributed to the differences in sources of words. Whereas Moe used trade books popular for grades 1 and 2, the Allens used primary grade readers, primary reading tests, and words from children's dictated stories. The important point of these lists is that they point our clearly that the English language contains a set of *name words* common to life experiences. These words are reflected in all writing and are highlighted in beginning reading materials. Two major resources for teachers of speaking, reading, and writing are now available: (1) words of highest frequency, and (2) nouns of highest frequency.

In addition to the word lists, *categories of descriptive words* that occur frequently were identified by Allen and Allen (1969).

color words	taste words
size words	touch words
shape words	words of emotion
sound words	words of comparison
smell words	words of contrast

The work in identification of words that occur frequently and in categories of descriptive words that occur frequently link reading instruction and the selection of reading materials directly with some of the contributions of linguists. Also, they provide a base for the scientific analysis of pupil-produced reading materials.

The work of John K. Sherk (1973) at the University of Missouri at Kansas City records the dramatic difference between the use of words of high frequency by inner-city preschool children and the use of the words by the population in general. The assumption that reading textbooks with high-frequency vocabulary control can be useful with all children is challenged by this major research report. The Sherk report indicates the need for massive help in the meaningful use of high-frequency nouns, verbs, adjectives, and adverbs prior to and during reading instruction.

High-frequency Words and Basal Readers

Basal readers, as they were developed for elementary schools of the United States in the 1930s through the 1960s, used scientifically controlled vocabularies. The scientific control was one of selecting words from lists of those appearing most frequently in the language and formulating sentences using those words plus nouns. Most of the nouns were proper nouns—names of people and animals.

As early as 1921 Edward L. Thorndike published *The Teacher's Word Book of 10,000 Words,* and by 1931 he had revised the book and extended it to include 20,000 words. Later, in collaboration with Irving Lorge, *The Teacher's Word Book of 30,000 Words* was written (Thorndike and Lorge, 1944).

By 1930 a series of readers with scientifically controlled vocabulary was developed by Cora M. Martin (Martin, 1930). The *Real Life Readers* introduced high-frequency words at a controlled rate and repeated them in stories often enough that they became a part of the sight vocabulary of the reader. The words selected were held together in story form with Bob and Nancy; their ponies, Paint and Dick; their dog, Spot; and their baby calf, Dot. The first book in the series was a primer. Martin expected teachers to work with children to build experience charts, to do choral reading, and to read to children to build vocabularies sufficient to profit from reading at the primer level. It was never her intention that reading experiences would begin with controlled vocabulary materials such as those found in readiness books and in preprimers.[1]

The immediate success of the controlled vocabulary materials set off a wave of publishing ventures that used various interpretations of the controlled introduction of words of highest frequency. Difficulty levels of readers from that point on were judged in terms of the number and kind of words on the high-frequency lists included in the stories. Basal readers which resulted replaced all other reading instructional materials in the mainstream of American education. Along with many success stories came problems that were reported as failures in reading. Children with limited self-confidence in the use of the limited language of the readers were thrust immediately into processes of producing exact replication of the formulated sentences. Those who could not reproduce the concocted language were identified as reading failures.

Since most of the words of highest frequency are the same ones that linguists call structure words or function words, the sight vocabulary that was the target of direct instruction dealt mostly with "words of empty meaning" (Lefevre, 1970). The Allen List of 100 High-

---

[1] Dr. Cora Martin was one of my professors at the University of Texas. I served as her graduate assistant and know her feelings about what happened to her ideas during the 1940s and 1950s.

Allen List of 100 High-frequency Words in Rank Order

1. the	26. had	51. can	76. how
2. of	27. not	52. out	77. may
3. and	28. or	53. up	78. over
4. a	29. have	54. about	79. made
5. to	30. but	55. so	80. did
6. in	31. one	56. them	81. new
7. is	32. what	57. our	82. after
8. that	33. were	58. into	83. most
9. was	34. an	59. some	84. way
10. he	35. which	60. other	85. down
11. it	36. there	61. then	86. see
12. for	37. we	62. these	87. people
13. as	38. all	63. its	88. any
14. on	39. their	64. than	89. where
15. with	40. she	65. two	90. through
16. his	41. when	66. time	91. me
17. at	42. will	67. could	92. man
18. be	43. said	68. your	93. before
19. are	44. her	69. many	94. back
20. you	45. do	70. like	95. much
21. I	46. has	71. first	96. just
22. this	47. him	72. each	97. little
23. by	48. if	73. only	98. very
24. from	49. no	74. now	99. long
25. they	50. more	75. my	100. good

frequency Words in Rank Order (which is given above) contains very few words that pattern in sentences as nouns and verbs. These words, when arranged in sentences so that they repeat over and over, do little to build vocabularies that are useful in gaining meaning from general reading. Materials that feature them do little to help reluctant readers read apart from the reading textbooks.

Serious and massive efforts were made to introduce and develop word-analysis techniques in basal readers, and many schools adopted separate phonics programs. But the problems presented by the focus on nonphonetic words of empty meaning were not overcome to the extent that our reading problem was solved through the application of scientific control of vocabulary.

Studies of disadvantaged readers indicated needs for language development as a prerequisite to reading instructional programs and as a

Allen List of 300 High-frequency Words

a	called	gave	kind	no	said
about	came	get	knew	not	same
above	can	girl	know	now	saw
across	change	give		number	say
after	children	go	large		school
again	city	good	last	of	second
air	come	got	left	off	see
all	could	grade	let	old	sentence
almost		great	letter	on	set
also	day	green	life	once	several
always	days		light	one	she
am	did	had	like	only	should
an	didn't	hand	line	open	show
and	different	hard	little	or	side
animal	do	has	long	other	since
another	does	have	look	others	small
any	done	he	looked	our	so
are	don't	head		out	some
around	down	hear	made	outside	something
as	draw	heard	make	over	soon
at	during	help	man	own	sound
away		her	many		start
	each	here	may	page	still
back	ears	high	me	part	stop
be	end	him	means	parts	story
because	enough	his	men	party	study
been	ever	home	might	past	such
before	example	house	more	people	sure
being	eyes	how	most	picture	
below			mother	place	take
best	far	I	Mr.	play	tell
better	feet	if	Mrs.	point	than
between	few	important	much	put	that
big	find	in	must		the
black	first	into	my		their
blue	five	is	myself	quiet	them
book	following	it			then
both	food	its	name	read	there
boy	for	it's	need	red	these
boys	found		never	right	they
brown	four	just	new	room	thing
but	from		next	round	things
by	full	keep	night	run	think

third	told	us	way	which	words
this	too	use	ways	while	work
those	took	used	we	white	would
thought	top	using	week	who	write
three	toward	usually	well	whole	
through	turned		went	why	year
time	two	very	were	will	yellow
times			what	with	yes
to	under	want	when	without	you
today	until	was	where	word	your
together	up	water			

point for continuing emphasis. Vocabulary control, insofar as high-frequency vocabulary is concerned, began to be viewed as being inherent in the language itself. The reason the same words are high on all the lists is that everybody uses them frequently in speaking and writing. They control the structure of sentences in all dialects and are required in most sentences to mark the appearance of the form classes—nouns, verbs, adjectives, and adverbs—in sentences. The realization that all dialects have the same structure words, regardless of their pronunciation, has released educators to trust children's real language to provide the same emphasis on words of high frequency that has been the priority emphasis in basal reader series of the past.

The Allen List of 300 High-frequency Words (see page 218) grew out of my interest in studying the language children use when they dictate and write stories from their own experiences. The list confirms the fact that they can be trusted to use the same structure words that adults use in communication. Children's personal language can be used in the development of the base language for reading.

High-frequency Words in a Language Experience Approach

The importance and the necessity of developing a sight vocabulary of words of highest frequency are not questioned in a language experience approach and in other approaches offered as an alternative to basal readers. Rather, the sight vocabulary is highlighted as an essential for success. It is the methodology that is different (Lefevre, 1970).

Function of Structure Words

The function of the structure words of highest frequency is included in instruction along with the sight recognition of those words. Most of the instruction is through informal conversation which builds awareness, but children are expected to know that there is a real purpose for the meaningless words. Some of these purposes follow.

1. Some words are determiners. They mark nouns in sentences. In sentences they are words that pattern like *the, a, my, our, this, that, every*.
2. Some words are pronouns. They take the place of and refer to nouns in sentences, but the noun must be implied or stated for clear meaning. In sentences they are words that pattern like *I, he, mine, you, him, she, her, it, we, they, them, many, none, several*.
3. Some words are auxiliaries with verbs to aid in clarifying meanings related to tense and number. In sentences they pattern with verbs. Some are *is, am, are, was, were, may, can, will, should, have, had*.
4. Some words are prepositions. They mark nouns in sentences and often relate to place or position. In sentences they are words that pattern like *of, in, by, on, to, at, from, under, about, over, through, around, up, with, toward*.
5. Some words are conjunctions. They are useful in connecting words with words, phrases with phrases, clauses with clauses, and sentences with sentences. In sentences conjunctions pattern like *and, but, or, yet, because, therefore, however, hence, furthermore, either . . . or, neither . . . nor, if . . . then, not only . . . but also*.
6. Some words signal questions. In sentences they are words that pattern like *who, where, when, how, why, what, which, whose, whom*.
7. Some words are intensifiers. They alter feelings about meanings inherent in nouns and adjectives. In sentences they pattern like *very, more, most, quite, somewhat, just, only, many, some*.
8. Some words are miscellaneous signals. They are used as greetings and courteous responses and to register approval or disapproval. Some of them are *hello, good-by, please, thanks, yes, no, excuse, sorry*.

There are about 300 structure words in English (Lefevre, 1970), and the majority are high-frequency words that can be explained in terms of function at the same time they are becoming sight-reading words.

Children who learn a little of the function of high-frequency words will be able, it is hoped, to predict their presence when they are reading silently, and will read at a speed much faster than the speed of speech.

Ramon provides a supply of columns cut from magazines and newspapers along with a list of 300 words of highest frequency. Reading the columns, the children mark through every word that is on the list. Then they read what is left unmarked. They find that most of the meaning is still there even though they marked through 65 to 70 percent of the words. After that they take another selection of columns and mark through all the words that are *not* on the list. When they read this version, they find that it is devoid of meaning. Children experience the fact that they can recognize at sight the words of highest frequency—65 to 70 percent of all the words—and still miss the meaning. They experience meaning in reading without calling every word.

Suzanne displays dictated stories around the classroom as they are finished. When ten or more are pinned up, she guides the children to identify and mark words they can find in many places in the stories. Every appearance of a word is marked with the same color; different colors are used for different words. When a word has been found five or more times, it is added to a master list, "Words We All Use." In cases of structure words she always reads the form-class words that accompany to make certain that the children know that the structure words, such as determiners, prepositions, and auxiliaries, are always related to others in sentences—"*The* tree . . . ," ". . . *in the* house," ". . . *is* running," "*I* [John] walked . . . ," ". . . *very* big." They usually look at and say structure words in "chunks of meaning."

Teachers who use a language experience approach trust children to use the words of highest-frequency *frequently* and *meaningfully*. They focus on the redundancy of certain words in language that they use for writing and in the language of reading materials. They review over and over the idea that most of the words of highest frequency have no real meaning in themselves but must be linked with names of things, people, and places, with words that tell of movement, and with words that describe. Teachers talk about the fact that most of what we read is made up of high-frequency words plus names and words that tell how things move. They study language function as well as word analysis; in fact, they develop two major strategies: (1) sight recognition of structure words with limited attention to phonetic analysis and careful attention to the context in which the words are found, and (2) decoding abilities of content words of the form classes. The need for the two strategies is well stated by Sarah C. Gudschinsky (1972) when she says:

> One of the frequent fallacies of many reading methods is that contentives (form class words) and functors (structure words) are lumped together in "word recognition" skills. In the unnatural stress and focus given to functors, the beginning reader may fail to recognize them and so lose his comprehension of the grammatical structure. On the other hand, the pupil who learns sight recognition of words as his only strategy quickly reaches the saturation point in the number of new words that he can remember. Or, the development of techniques for sounding out words may founder on the irregularly spelled functors where such techniques are not efficient. The solution is the use of two sets of strategies, dictated by the difference between functors and contentives with respect to their isolability in language.

The use of two strategies in instruction at all levels contributes to fluency and comprehension in reading. Content is understood within a grammatical framework which permits and promotes prediction skills. For children to know *what to expect* in the way of structure is to permit them to focus on content words and read at a rate faster than speech. By contrast, to develop strategies that treat all words as equal in importance in reading is to slow down reading to a laborious pace which decreases interest and denies comprehension.

Yes, words of highest frequency are important in a language experience approach, but teachers are expected to know enough about language structure to treat those that are structure words in the special ways that promote not only recognition but function, fluency, and comprehension.

Nouns of High Frequency

In addition to the concept of *words of high frequency* as basic to reading, a language experience approach emphasizes nouns, or names, in language along with verbs, adjectives, and adverbs. Teachers are provided with lists of nouns that occur frequently, and children are helped to understand their significance in the comprehension of what someone else has written.

A list of 100 nouns was provided in the *Teacher's Resource Book: Language Experiences in Early Childhood* (Allen and Allen, 1969). An English-Spanish version of that list is given on page 223. The list, expanded to 230 high-frequency nouns, includes nouns from schoolbooks for grade 3 and above; see the list on page 225.

Allen 100 Nouns List [a]

A airplane — el avión
apple — la manzana
astronaut — el astronauta

B baby — [b] el niño o la niña
el bebé
ball — la pelota
balloon — la bomba
el globo
bear — el oso
bed — la cama
bee — la abeja
bell — la campana
bird — el pájaro
block — [b] el dado
el bloque
el cubileto
el cuadro
book — el libro
box — la caja
boy — el muchacho
bread — el pan
breakfast — el desayuno
bus — el camión

C cake — [b] el queque
el cake
el pastel
car — [b] el carro
el automóvil
cat — el gato
church — la iglesia
circle — la rueda
el circo
el círculo
clock — el reloj
clown — el payaso
coat — el abrigo
cow — la vaca

D daddy — el papá
dog — el perro
drum — el tambor
duck — el pato

E ear — la oreja
elephant — el elefante
eye — el ojo

F fall — el otoño
fire truck — la bombera
la bomba de incedio
flower — la flor
foot — el pie
frame — el marco
frog — la rana

G girl — la muchacha

H hand — la mano
head — la cabeza
horse — el caballo
house — la casa

I ice cream — [b] la nieve
el helado

J jacket — [b] la chaqueta
la chamarra
jack-o'-lantern — la linterna hecha
de una calabasa
hueca
jelly — la jalea

K king — el rey
kite — el papalote

L leaf — la hoja
letter — la carta

[a] Interpreted for Spanish-speaking children in the Nogales, Arizona, area by Marjorie C. Driscoll, Reading Specialist.
[b] Commonly used.

Allen 100 Nouns List (*continued*)

M	moon	la luna	
	mother	la madre	
		[b] la mamá	
	moving van	el carro de mudanzas	
N	name	el nombre	
	nurse	la enfermera	
O	orange	la naranja	
P	paper	el papel	
	pencil	el lápiz	
	picture	el retrato	
		el dibujo (drawing)	
		la pintura	
	pilot	el piloto	
	policeman	el policía	
	purse	[b] la bolsa	
		la portamoneda	
Q	queen	la reina	
R	rain	la lluvia	
	raincoat	el impermeable	
	rocket	el cohete	
S	sailboat	[b] el barco de vela	
		el velero	
	school	la escuela	
	shoe	el zapato	
	snow	la nieve	
	sock	el calcetín	
	spring	la primavera	
	square	el cuadro	
	stop sign	el señal de alto	
	store	la tienda	

	street	la calle	
	summer	el verano	
	sun	el sol	
	swing	el columpio	
T	teacher	el maestro	
		la maestra	
	television	la televisión	
	tooth	[b] el diente	
		la muela	
	toy	el juguete	
	tree	el árbol	
	truck	[b] el troque	
		el camión	
	turkey	[b] el pavo	
		el guajolote	
U	umbrella	el paraguas	
V	valentine	la tarjeta de San Valentín	
	Valentine's Day	el dia de los corazones	
W	whistle	el silbido	
	wind	el viento	
	window	la ventana	
	winter	el invierno	
	witch	la bruja	
X	x-ray	el rayo équiz	
		la radiografia	
Y	yard	el patio	
Z	zipper	el zípper	
	zoo	el parque zoológico	

Allen List of 230 High-frequency Nouns

air	coat	frog	monkey	river	tail
airplane	cookies	front	moon	road	teacher
animal	corner		morning	rock	telephone
answer	country	game	mother	rocket	television
apartment	cow	garden	mouth	roof	thing
apple	cup	girl		room	three
astronaut		grass	name	rope	time
author	daddy	ground	nest	rose	today
	day	guitar	next		tooth
baby	dime		nickel	sailboat	top
ball	dog	hand	night	school	town
balloon	dollar	head	nose	sea	tree
basement	door	hill	nurse	second	truck
bear	dress	home		sentence	turkey
bed	drum	horse	one	sheet	two
bee	duck	house	orange	ship	
bell				shirt	umbrella
bird	ear	ice cream	page	shoe	
block	earth	island	palace	show	valentine
boat	egg		paper	side	
body	elephant	jacket	part	sister	wall
book	end	jack-o'-lantern	pencil	sky	water
box	example	jelly	penny	sleep	way
boys	eyes		people	snow	whistle
bread		king	pet	sock	white
breakfast	fall	kite	picture	something	wind
brother	family		pilot	song	window
bus	father	lamp	place	sound	winter
	feet	land	play	spring	witch
cake	field	leaf	poem	square	woman
candy	fire	leg	point	stairs	word
cap	first	letter	policeman	stamp	world
car	fish	life	pony	star	
cat	five	light	princess	stop sign	x-ray
chair	flag	line	purse	store	
chicken	floor	lion		story	yard
children	flower	lunch	quarter	stove	year
church	food		queen	street	
circle	forest	man		summer	zipper
city	four	men	rabbit	sun	zoo
clock	fox	miles	rain	swing	
clothes	frame	milk	raincoat		
clown	friend	money	refrigerator	table	

Sources: Primary readers, standardized tests for primary grades, trade books for young children, school newspapers, and accompanying tests for children.

A sight vocabulary without a heavy loading of nouns is of little use in general reading. The acquisition of a noun vocabulary and an understanding of the importance and functioning of nouns in language are required for any emphasis on meaning. Most children who are disabled readers are deficient in their ability to name things, but they are not deficient in their ability to use the words of highest frequency in the sentences they speak (Sherk, 1973). The List of 230 High-frequency Nouns can be useful as a specific guide for teachers and children in the acquisition of highly functional writing and reading vocabularies.

Mary Ann selects three determiners—*the, a, an.* She reads with a small group of children. Every time they come to one of these words, they find the name of something that goes with it. Then she switches to three prepositions—*of, to, in.* Together they find these words and the nouns that go with them. They read the phrases as a unit. This procedure is continued to include determiners and prepositions on the list of 50 most frequently used words. By this time most children are aware of the function of determiners and prepositions and have learned to trust the nouns to carry the load of meaning.

The recognition of nouns and their meaning in context is basic to any progress in comprehension. Proper nouns are marked by capital letters. Common nouns are marked by determiners, prepositions, and some conjunctions and intensifiers. Most of the markers are on any list of words of highest frequency. The Carroll list (1971), which gives the words in the order of frequency, begins with *the, of, and, a, to, in, is, you, that, it.* Seven of the first ten are noun markers, two take the place of nouns, and one functions as a verb auxiliary or as a special kind of verb.

Darrell encourages children to write stories on self-selected topics. He provides motivation in the Writing/Publishing Center and has a publishing program to encourage refinement of stories. From time to time he works with his authors on word analyses of their stories. They use a list of high-frequency words and high-frequency nouns to check the stories to find the percentage of words used from the lists. He expects to find that from 80 to 85 percent of all the story words, exclusive of proper names, will be on the two lists. He then finds a story or a book on the same topic by another author, and selected portions of the book are analyzed. Most of the time these results in terms of percentages are the same as those of his authors. Then they look at other words that may go specifically with the topic. When these are added, a comparison of percentages of agreement may go as high as 90 percent. Children are amazed that most of the words they write are the same ones used by authors who write on the same topics. If they can read by themselves what they write, they can almost read from other authors.

Darrell finds that this approach to teaching reading is much more effective with "turned off" readers than one requiring oral replication of every word of an author (broken only for purposes of decoding by the use of phonetic and structural analysis). He sees coding and decoding as being reciprocal and mutually reinforcing. When working with reluctant readers, he finds that the use of the two sets of words, each of which can be reproduced on one sheet of paper, is an effective way of helping students understand the differences in two classifications of high-frequency words. One serves as markers for content words; the other *is* content words.

Carl is aware that the poor readers in his class need massive help with recognition of high-frequency nouns. He makes card games using the list of 230 nouns. Some are games of classification to promote simple recognition:

foods	parts of body
clothing	seasons
machines	things to play with
animals	family members

Some are games of simple phonetic analysis:

——words that begin alike

——words that have the same vowel sound internally

——words that have the same phonogram, such as *-at, -an, -ing.*

Some are games for contrasting initial sounds with one-syllable words:

——Take the word *car* and say as many words as possible, changing only the first letter.

——Take the word *bear* and change only the last letter to make additional words.

Some extend a high-frequency noun with others:

Old	Young	Animal	Home
cat	kitten	bee	hive
bear	cub	cow	pasture

Carl believes that the selection of nouns of high frequency as a base for language study and word-recognition skills has merit that is not present in just random selections of words. He knows that the base words are found frequently in stories, tests, and in general reading.

Verbs of High Frequency

Most of the discussion of verbs is found in Chapter 16, but one verb occurs so frequently that it must be mentioned in this chapter.

The verb *be* is in a class by itself in English. It is the busiest and most versatile word in the language. Five of its eight forms are found in the rank order of the first 100 words: *is, was, are, be,* and *were. Am, been,* and *being,* the others, are among the first 300 words.

Forms of *be* are used as the only verb (copula) in linking-verb sentences:

Cats *are* animals.

Today *is* Friday.

They are used as verb markers in passive sentences:

The bird *was* killed.

The cars *were* stopped.

They are used as verb markers in active-verb sentences with *-ing* verbs:

We *are* reading.

The plane *is* flying.

They are used in the nearly extinct subjunctive mode:

If I *were* dead, I would feel better.

As far as this discussion on word frequency is concerned, it is enough to say that the forms of *be* occur frequently and must become a part of every reader's sight vocabulary. The words defy phonetic analysis. They are pronounced /iz/, /woz/, /ar/ or /är/, /bee/, /wur/, /am/, /bin/, and /bēing/. Their pronunciation is known by most speakers in school. Their spelling must be memorized, and their recognition must be completely mastered. Their frequency cannot be denied in any examination of writing.

Forms of *have* occur frequently in the language and must be recognized at the 100 percent level of mastery before independent reading is possible. Three forms of *have* occur in the rank order of the first 100 words: *have, had,* and *has. Having* occurs in the first 500.

Just as with forms of *be,* forms of *have* are used as the only verb in linking-verb sentences:

Jerry *has* measles.

The children *had* fun.

They are used as verb markers in passive-voice sentences with forms of *be:*

The plane *has been* flying.

All of us *have been* playing.

They are used as verb markers in active-verb sentences with *-en* verbs:

We *have* eaten dinner.

John *has* written a story.

The above statements concerning verbs must not be interpreted in a way that will minimize the complexity of verbs in language. They are made to point out specific word-recognition responsibilities of teachers which are present because of the words' frequency of occurrence in language.

Descriptive Categories of High Frequency

Words that pattern as adjectives and adverbs in sentences occur in so many relationships to nouns and verbs that few of them are found on lists of high frequency. Even though children use descriptive words in spontaneous expression, when reading materials are developed for them with reduced vocabulary and short sentences, it is the descriptive categories that are eliminated in the interest of easy reading. Since these edited books are among the materials analyzed in preparing the word counts for primary grades, categories of color, size, shape, texture, sound, taste, smell, and touch are found infrequently. However, when trade books are considered and an analysis of children's dictated stories is included, certain categories of descriptive words occur frequently enough to deserve specific attention in a language experience approach instructional program. Color and size are categories that top the list. They are followed by shape, sound, smell, taste, texture, and feeling.

Many teachers who use a language experience approach highlight the importance of descriptive categories by the development of a Word Wall as a resource for sight-recognition games and as an aid to spelling. Along with the "Words We All Use," "Names We Use," and "Action Words" are lists of color words, size words, and other categories of description. The lists are open-ended so they can be extended at any time. They are visible evidence that descriptive words occur frequently in language. The use of the organization around categories of words for vocabulary expansion is treated in detail in Chapter 13.

Enumeration Words of Highest Frequency

Ordinal and cardinal numbers appear on all the lists of words of high frequency. They are essential for communication in school and out of school. In addition to the words of enumeration, numerals appear frequently in printed material. Even beginning readers of print must recognize some of the language of enumeration in order to gain a slight degree of independence.

Games, songs, chants, stories, and poems having to do with counting and the language of enumeration must be included in the curriculum so that children can say, write, and read the language of numbers. The minimum sight vocabulary is:

1	one	first
2	two	second
3	three	third
4	four	fourth
5	five	fifth
6	six	sixth
7	seven	seventh
8	eight	eighth
9	nine	ninth
10	ten	tenth
100	hundred	

CLUES FOR INSTRUCTION

Innovate on Mother Goose rhymes in ways such as:

Original	New Version
One, two, three,	One, two, three,
Four and five,	Four and five,
I caught a hare alive;	I caught a bird alive;
Six, seven, eight,	Six, seven, eight,
Nine and ten,	Nine and ten,
I let him go again.	I let it go again.

Why did you let it go?
Because it bit my finger so.
Which finger did it bite?
The little finger on the
  right.

Why did you let it go?
Because it pecked my hand so.
When you let it go,
Where did it fly?
Into the sky! Into the sky!

Use additive couplets that children can increase and change.
Poems written or adapted by members of the class have all kinds of possibilities.

Five Lively Boys (*Claryce*)

ONE boy is playing all alone,
Then ring-a-ling goes the telephone.

Ron is coming to play with me.
Now Ron and I make TWO, you see.

Ron and I play tick tack toe,
When we hear a knock and there is Joe.

Ron and Joe and I make THREE
To race and climb our great big tree.

Ron, Joe, and I go by for Bill
Now FOUR go out to climb the hill.

Craig comes by on his new bike,
And wants to join us on our hike.

FOUR lively boys and Craig makes FIVE
Who find holes and rocks and a beehive.

Ron, Joe, Craig, and I and Bill
Climb to the top of the nearest hill.

FIVE lively boys see the town below,
Then start coming down fast, then slow.

Ron, Joe, Craig, and I leave Bill at his door.
So now we have only a gang of FOUR.

The FOUR walk along but Craig decides to ride.
That leaves THREE walking side by side.

THREE boys walking till we come to Joe's house.
He leaves us so he can feed his white mouse.

TWO boys now—just Ron and I.
Then Ron says maybe he'd better say, "By!"

ONE tired boy coming in from play.
ONE tired boy who's had fun today.

Some things to do with this kind of poem include the following.

1. Read "Five Lively Boys" using names of boys in the class.
2. Change to "Five Lively Girls" and use names of girls in the class.
3. Choose boys or girls and act out the different parts.
4. Use "Five Lively Boys" as a choral reading.
5. Make cards with 1, 2, 3, 4, and 5 on them, large enough to be seen across the room. Let someone show a number each time that number in the poem is read.
6. Make a collage of numerals 1 through 5 cut from newspapers and magazines.

Read advertisements in newspapers, especially grocery ads, that can be placed on an easel or on the chalkboard for group participation. Go from that reading to sports pages to read scores and team standings. Do not assume that children can read and write words of enumeration and numerals just because they can say them. Include this vocabulary in formal as well as informal instruction.

Professional Treatment of High-frequency Words

Teachers who are professional in their work will know
—which words are of highest frequency
—which of the highest-frequency words are structure words
—which nouns occur frequently
—which verbs need specific instruction
—that most of the words children use in spontaneous expression and in independent writing are the same ones others use when speaking and writing on the same topic.
Teachers who are professional are not dependent on the instructional materials that they have to buy in order to devote the needed

time and effort to the teaching of a sight vocabulary of words and categories of words that occur frequently.

Ardis uses a list of high-frequency words to make open-ended sentences.

This is a _____ .
Look at my _____ .
Come and _____ with me .
I like to _____ .

She discusses possibilities for the completion of sentences; she lists suggestions on the chalkboard. Children copy the model, choose a word from the list or another word they like, illustrate the sentence, and contribute it to a reading text. Each page includes the same high-frequency words for repetition and drill, yet each page is different. Nouns and verbs are selected in terms of interest and experience. Children are encouraged to talk about their illustrations before reading a sentence. Ardis probes with questions that bring out descriptive categories. In this way full language is kept in the learning environment, while a sight vocabulary is being acquired and mastered.

Since Ardis teaches in a school district where she is required to use a state-adopted set of basal readers, she uses the master lists of words in the backs of books she is going to teach as a guide for the words of high frequency to select for the open-ended sentences. After she has introduced the words and used them in open-ended sentences reflecting the children's experience, she finds that following the introduction of a few names, the children can read the books assigned to them with relative ease. Many of them can read a preprimer at one sitting. Such an experience builds strong self-concepts. It eliminates the laborious treatment of reading with materials that have limited meaning and limited vocabulary.

Norma cuts brand names and signs from magazines and mounts them on tagboard cards. Children select cards with words they can read, put a loop of masking tape on the backs of the cards, and stick them on the chalkboard. Then they say and write sentences that include the words on the cards. Most of the words added are high-frequency ones and are used over and over. Norma has found that older children who are reluctant to read beginning readers are interested in generating sentences using words they know as the kernel idea.

Teachers who are professional link structure words with words of content and meaning. They do not emphasize the "words of empty meaning" apart from clusters of words, phrases, and sentences. They are aware that the words of highest frequency are mostly structure words which need continual linkage in order to be useful in reading and writing.

Professional teachers are aware that the majority of nonphonetic words in English are on the high-frequency lists. These words require a treatment in reading instruction that is different from decoding through the use of phoneme-grapheme relationships.

Summary of Skills and Abilities for Recognizing High-frequency Words

STRUCTURE WORDS OF HIGHEST FREQUENCY

——Recognizes at sight the most frequently used determiners—*the, a, an, this, that, my, every, our*
——Understands that determiners are noun markers in sentences
——Recognizes at sight the pronouns used frequently in language— *I, you, he, she, him, her, we, them, they, your, their*
——Understands that pronouns take the place of nouns in sentences
——Recognizes at sight the eight forms of *be—is, am, are, was, were, been, being, be*
——Uses correct forms of *be* in most speaking and writing
——Recognizes at sight the four forms of *have—have, had, has, having*
——Uses correct form of *have* in most speaking and writing
——Recognizes at sight the prepositions of highest frequency—*of, to, in, for, on, at, by, about, up, into, over, down*
——Reads prepositions as integral parts of phrases rather than as separate words
——Recognizes at sight the conjunctions of highest frequency—*and, or, but, so, because*
——Uses conjunctions to connect words in a series, clauses with clauses, and sentences with sentences
——Recognizes at sight question words of highest frequency—*what, when, which, how, who, where*
——Reads question words with appropriate voice inflection
——Recognizes intensifiers of highest frequency—*many, some, more, only, very, just, most*

——Uses intensifiers when speaking and writing to add interest to language

——Recognizes word signals for greetings—*hello, good-by, please, thanks, yes, no*

——Uses words as signals of greeting, courtesy, approval, and disapproval in talking and writing

NOUNS OF HIGHEST FREQUENCY

——Recognizes at sight nouns that occur frequently in reading
    ——names for people
    ——names for animals
    ——names for foods
    ——names for clothing
    ——names of parts of the body
    ——names for weather
    ——names for machines
    ——names for buildings

——Anticipates and predicts names in reading following noun markers

DESCRIPTIVE CATEGORIES OF HIGHEST FREQUENCY

——Recognizes at sight words of high frequency that modify nouns and verbs such as—*little, big, large, small, long, short, hard, soft, light, dark, white, red, new, old, well, very*

——Anticipates and predicts descriptive words when reading

——Uses descriptive categories in speaking and writing—words of color, size, shape, texture, sound, taste, smell, touch

ENUMERATION WORDS OF HIGHEST FREQUENCY

——Recognizes the symbols used for numerals–0 through 9

——Recognizes ordinal numbers used frequently—*first, second, third, fourth, fifth*

——Recognizes cardinal number words that are used frequently—*one, two, three, four, five, six, seven, eight, nine, ten, hundred*

Selected References

Allen, Roach Van, and Claryce Allen. *Teacher's Resource Book: Language Experiences in Early Childhood.* Encyclopaedia Britannica Educational Corp., Chicago, 1969.

Anderson, Paul S. *Language Skills in Elementary Education.* Macmillan Co., New York, 1964.

Burrows, Alvina T., Dianne L. Monson, and Russell G. Stauffer. *New Horizons in the Language Arts.* Harper & Row, New York, 1972.

Busch, Fred. "Basals Are for Not Reading." In *The First R: Readings on Teaching Reading,* edited by Sam L. Sebasta and Carl J. Wallen. Science Research Associates, Chicago, 1972.

Carroll, John B., Peter Davies, and Barry Richman. *Word Frequency Book.* American Heritage Publishing Co., New York, 1971.

Eisenhardt, Catheryn. *Applying Linguistics in the Teaching of Reading and the Language Arts.* Charles E. Merrill, Columbus, Ohio, 1972.

Gudschinsky, Sarah C. "The Nature of the Writing System: Pedagogical Implications." In *Language and Learning to Read: What Teachers Should Know About Language,* edited by Richard E. Hodges and E. Hugh Rudorf. Houghton Mifflin Co., Boston, 1972.

Hodges, Richard E., and E. Hugh Rudorf. *Language and Learning to Read: What Teachers Should Know About Language.* Houghton Mifflin Co., Boston, 1972.

Johnson, Dale D. "A Basic Vocabulary for Beginning Reading," *Elementary School Journal,* 72, 1 (October, 1971), 87–92.

Lamberts, J. J. *A Short Introduction of English Usage.* McGraw-Hill Book Co., New York, 1972.

Lefevre, Carl A. *Linguistics, English, and the Language Arts.* Allyn & Bacon, Boston, 1970.

Martin, Cora M. *Real Life Readers.* Charles Scribner's Sons, New York, 1930.

Moe, Alden J. *High Frequency Words: Word Cards for Beginning Readers.* Ambassador Publishing Co., St. Paul, Minn., 1973a.

———. *High Frequency Nouns: Word Cards for Beginning Readers.* Ambassador Publishing Co., St. Paul, Minn., 1973b.

Sherk, John K. *A Word Count of Spoken English of Culturally Disadvantaged Preschool and Elementary Pupils.* University of Missouri at Kansas City, Kansas City, Mo., 1973.

Smith, Frank, and George A. Miller (eds.). *The Genesis of Language: A Psycholinguistic Approach.* M.I.T. Press, Cambridge, Mass., 1971.

Thorndike, Edward L., and Irving Lorge. *The Teacher's Word Book of 30,000 Words.* Teachers College Press, New York, 1944.

FROM THE RATIONALE   Exploring spelling—contacting and mastering regular and irregular phoneme-grapheme relationships during processes of writing and reading; making adaptations of personal pronunciation and standard spelling; using phonetic analysis when applicable; and mastering frequently used words that defy phonetic analysis.

Spelling is an inseparable part of communication programs that keep speech, writing, and reading related in instruction. Children must spell because in school they write early and frequently. They must learn common spellings of words they write because other students in the class—not just the teacher—read much of what they write. They must learn to edit their manuscripts for correct spelling because many of them are published and become part of the instructional materials. They must develop a sense of obligation to conform in spelling because to do so is a common courtesy as well as a tool of great importance.

Spelling abilities cannot be developed apart from the desire to learn and from feelings about values to self. Children who feel an urge to communicate, who experience the thrill of authorship, and who know the satisfaction of saying something through writing that is important to other people are the ones most likely to be interested in spelling.

Children who are engaged in authorship should be encouraged at all times to try to spell any word they know. They should feel secure in exploring the spelling of new and unusual words and by knowing that resources are available for spelling help during writing and for editing spelling after writing.

Original writing is the primary objective. Correct spelling is a secondary objective, a supporting one.

No attempt is made in this chapter to describe a method of teaching spelling. Rather, the purpose of the chapter is to describe some relationships between oral language production, writing, and reading and to place spelling in a functional relationship to communicating processes.

Spelling in Writing and Reading

Language experience approaches in communication assure so much active involvement in writing that any need to link spelling to reading is diminished to the point of zero. Practices of sounding out unknown words are discouraged in favor of direct instruction in phoneme-grapheme relationships during writing and stressing comprehended sentences during reading.

Spelling requires abilities to discriminate and to produce single letters in single words sequentially. Language is constructed letter by letter, syllable by syllable, word by word. In composition activities spelling is little more than an editing operation within the larger process of creating patterns of original meaning-bearing language.

When *correct spelling* becomes an issue of prime importance, it can hinder the creative process and discourage effective communication. Priorities that establish spelling as an aid to effective written communication rather than as an equal to it are ones that yield manuscripts worthy of being edited and published.

Estelle introduces spelling during processes of dictation. She talks to herself as she writes as if to remind herself of how to spell. In the process the child dictating and other children observing develop an attitude toward spelling that carries over into independent writing.

She invites children to help with spelling. At first she might ask for help with initial consonants because most consonants in initial positions in words have stable phoneme-grapheme relationships.

From there she begins to involve children in spelling whole words. These are usually structure words that occur frequently in language. She hopes that every child will learn to spell the words of highest frequency in an informal, practical setting since many of them defy phonetic analysis.

When one child is ready, Estelle spaces the dictated story so it can be copied directly beneath her writing. Once the process is initiated, one child after another asks to copy. Words in the child's speaking vocabulary are sure to be ones used for the early spelling-writing experiences because they are the ones spoken in dictation.

Words that occur in the work of several children are collected on a chart for spelling review and for sight vocabulary. The chart is kept in a place where the children can use it as a spelling reference from the earliest days of exploratory writing. There are no spelling workbooks or lists on which children drill to make "hundreds on spelling." All work to master the correct spelling of words that are useful in writing.

Chester encourages children to try to write any word they can say when preparing original manuscripts. He helps them to see that most of the spelling errors involve only one or two letters in a word and that if a word communicates the desired sound, it can be edited for correct spelling.

Many children in Chester's class will use first letters and a line—for example: b——, g——, or t—— —to hold space for correct spelling. If the context is strong enough to carry the meaning, the correct spelling can be handled in a few minutes after the flow of ideas has been recorded. Lists of words are provided in the Writing/Publishing Center as aids in editing spelling. Most children do not need to spend time hunting words in dictionaries for spelling. They do not need definitions since they are editing their own writing.

Spelling that is related to personal writing is not haphazard. Every child who writes uses

—words of highest frequency, the correct spelling of which is highly desirable, if not mandatory, in writing

—words that begin alike in phoneme-grapheme relationships

—words with suffixes that appear frequently, that modify meanings (examples: *-s, -es, -er, -ed, -ing*), and that change the part of speech of many words (examples: *-ly, -est, -ful*)

—root words with prefixes that modify meanings (examples: *re-, un-, dis-, bi-, tri-*)

—syllables that occur over and over in words—beginnings, endings, and middles (examples: *an, on, in, ill, all, at, it, ut*)

—each vowel in multiple phoneme-grapheme relationships.

There is no hint in the instructional program that normal children must learn how to make the basic sounds of their native language at school. At school most of them learn how to represent their language sounds with an alphabetic code. This link between speech and written composition involves spelling directly and constantly.

Reading does not require the production of letters and words. Reading does not require the pronunciation of all letters in every word. It does require the recognition and comprehension of entire sentences as meaning-bearing patterns (Lefevre, 1970). Effective reading requires a blending together of sounds which do not distinguish words as such. An understanding of the details and refinement of language represented by an alphabet may yield confidence and self-assurance to the reader, but *it does not equal reading.*

Programs that attempt to link basic concepts of spelling with reading through what most teachers call phonics may deny children an understanding of how their natural language works when written. Language experience approaches build bases for understanding of:

—relationships that blend personal language production with an alphabetic system of writing

——relationships of personal meanings expressed in speaking and writing to meanings of others through reading

——predictive abilities that permit a reader to anticipate most of the printed words and patterns so that the thinking process can be active during reading.

Efforts to teach spelling through reading interfere with the thought-getting process (Russell, 1946). Emphasis on spelling during the reading process can create problem readers who focus on the letters in words rather than on the meanings of words in relation to the thoughts shared by an author.

Language experience approaches provide functional spelling situations enough for the development of spelling skills that in many cases are in excess of normal expectancies (Stauffer, 1969). Active writing situations provide needed practice in spelling, and a continuing program of publishing children's writing for classroom use requires a high level of refinement of spelling.

CLUES FOR INSTRUCTION

Make crossword puzzles, word-step puzzles, homonym games, words-that-begin-alike games, and card games for the Game Center. Develop activities that require an understanding of syllabication, suffixes, prefixes, contractions, and compounds for the Language Study Center. Stimulate children to produce in the Writing/Publishing Center with activities that involve a restricted vocabulary—rigmaroles, alliteration, conversation, riddles, shopping lists, catalogues, rhyming poetry, and other writing forms using language structure that repeats spelling structure.

Functional Spelling

Many occasions arise for spelling in learning center activities. Abundant are natural situations that require spelling for children to express their ideas in writing. Many activities such as those in the Game Center and Language Study Center require written responses and lists of words. Records that go with many activities in the Discovery Center require written responses. Frequently activities in the Reading/Research Center call for personal interpretations through writing. Activities of the Writing/Publishing Center require spelling constantly, and it is in this center that most teachers provide spelling aids appropriate for the group.

Roberta uses frequent walking trips in the school community to introduce children to vocabulary appropriate for writing their observations. She invites a fifth-grade class to accompany her first-grade class and to act as private secretaries. They usually concentrate on one or two categories of words such as sound words, shape words, words for green, and smell words. Master lists are made from the secretaries' records. A copy is published for a chart to go in the Writing/Publishing Center of the first grade, and copies are reproduced to go into the writing handbook which each fifth-grade pupil keeps.

When children write, they are encouraged to use the lists as spelling references. They also have available the growing list "Words We All Use." The combination of visible spelling sources encourages children to spell correctly when writing rather than just to guess.

At the same time Roberta encourages children to attempt to spell any word they need to use. She wants them to feel that their ideas and personal language are more important than correct spelling. By continual demonstration she shows that original manuscripts can be edited if they are to be published.

In functional writing situations in which children are secure in exploring spelling, the teacher has opportunities to observe spelling behavior and to note points that need direct instruction. As children call for help in spelling words, the teacher can ask questions and make points that assist them to generalize certain principles about spelling that are extremely difficult to develop from lists of words that can be memorized.

As children work in various learning centers that require writing, their spelling behavior can be observed, and teachers can visit informally to help them to gain basic insights into spelling and to understand consistency in and variability of spelling patterns.

Basic Insights into Spelling

Basic to children's understanding of spelling are a number of insights that they acquire by instruction by teachers.

——They use an alphabetic system. When they write a word, they write letters to stand for sounds heard when the word is spoken.

——They must listen for the separate phonemes in a word and note the sequence in which they occur.

——They must listen for consonantal phonemes preceded or followed by a vowel phoneme since they are never sounded in isolation.

——They must recognize when one phoneme ends and another begins, even though they usually flow one to another without any breaks.

——They must in spelling take into account their personal pronunciation of words and in some cases learn to voice some phonemes in new ways.

——They learn that the same sound-symbol relationships can exist as beginning sounds, ending sounds, and internal sounds.

——They practice making first sounds of words and then naming the alphabet letter or letters that best represent the sound. They discover that most first sounds represented by consonants are the same over and over and that vowels in the first position represent several sounds.

Consistency in Spelling Patterns

Children who develop phonological relationships between *sounds* and *letters* of the orthography can spell literally thousands of words that they use in oral language because of the consistency of spelling patterns (Hanna, Hodges, and Hanna, 1971). Repeating patterns of sound and spelling occur frequently in syllables such as these that follow.

at	en	in	ook	un
an	ell	ill	ot	ug
ay	et	ing	ow	up
all	ed	ight	old	ull
am		it	oy	

These basic phonograms contrasted with initial sounds represented by consonants generate hundreds of words. When morphological characteristics such as affixes are added to root words, hundreds of additional words can be spelled.

The cues from linguistics provide understandings that permit children to spell most of the words in their oral vocabularies as long as they spell in an open environment that permits exploratory spelling. They may spell correctly phonetically and not use standard spelling: *hi* for *high*, *brite* for *bright*, *thay* for *they*, and *rong* for *wrong*. Such exploration should be encouraged. As a learning problem it is entirely different from just guessing at spelling words.

Variability of Spelling Patterns

Although most American-English spelling is consistent with the sounds, there are exceptions and these must be learned by anyone who is to write for others to read. When children find words that require special treatment for correct spelling, they add them to a growing list of words. They try to locate the place in a word that requires irregular spelling, and find that in most cases one or two letters cause the spelling trouble.

Lists of words with irregular spelling can be placed in the Game Center. Children can be encouraged to use these words to make spelling games to play with friends. A master alphabetic list is provided for the Writing/Publishing Center as an aid in editing.

Linguistic Factors That Influence Spelling

Some linguistic factors that influence spelling during writing processes are phonological, morphological, and syntactical (Hanna and Hanna, 1965).

Phonological factors deal with the position of a sound in a word, with stress, and with internal constraints that certain sounds put on others when pronounced together. (Example: The beginning sound of words like *foot, finger,* and *fat* are almost always spelled with an *f*. At the end of a word it can be spelled *ff* as in *cuff* or *off, gh* as in *cough* or *laugh,* or *lf* as in *calf*.)

Morphological factors deal with word formation and include compounding, affixation, and word groups that have partial phoneme similarities such as *dog, log,* and *hog*.

Syntactical factors that affect spelling deal with words that are pronounced alike (homophones) but differ in meaning, derivation, and often spelling and with words that are spelled alike (homographs) but differ in meaning, derivation, and sometimes pronunciation. The spelling and/or pronunciation of these words can be determined only in context.

Homographs: *tear* on your cheek
tear in the paper

Homophones: *pool* of clear water
game of *pool*
reed instrument to play
read a book

Both homographs and homophones are homonyms. They offer a special challenge to spelling and reading.

Clara composes rhymes and jingles to interest children in some of the linguistic factors in spelling.

For *compound words* she makes cards that suggest the collection of compound words.

Here is a finger.
Here is a nail.
Put them together
You have a *fingernail!*

For *rhyming words* she sets a pattern that children can follow.

This is a pup.
This is a cup.
This is a pup in a cup.

For words of *enumeration* she provides an example for children to follow with their own ideas.

The first cook cooked one cookie.
The second cook cooked two cookies.
The third cook cooked three cookies.
The fourth cook cooked four.
Were there any more?

For *alliteration* she suggests a pattern of adding descriptive words to a base sentence.

This is an ant.
This is an angry ant.
This is an angry ant acting.
This is an angry ant acting atrociously.

Words Lists for Spelling and Editing

Children who can read words on lists are able to improve their spelling by the use of the lists during writing and/or in editing a manuscript. Two lists that can be supplied on an individual basis or on charts in the Writing/Publishing Center are:

1. List of Words for Spelling and Editing.
2. Words Often Spelled and Pronounced Incorrectly.

The List of Words for Spelling and Editing is much like the Allen List of 100 High-frequency Words in Rank Order provided the teacher in Chapter 12 (page 217) and is arranged alphabetically instead of by rank order so words can be located quickly by students.

Close inspection of the list Words Often Spelled and Pronounced Incorrectly will reveal that the majority of the words are in the rank order of the first 300 words used in speaking and writing. This fact highlights the importance of a spelling emphasis that includes memorizing of words as well as an emphasis that generates spelling generalizations useful for the thousands of words not on this list.

Summary of Skills and Abilities for Exploring Spelling

SPELLING IN COMMUNICATION

——Writes original stories without fear of misspelled words
——Writes poetry that uses rhymes and nonrhymed patterns
——Writes directions and instructions for classroom activities
——Chooses writing as a recreational activity
——Uses phonetic information for spelling "correctly" even though it may not be standard spelling
——Edits own manuscripts for spelling before publishing

SPELLING ATTITUDES AND SKILLS

——Uses word-study techniques to study spelling—not just rote memory
——Uses spelling resources when writing and editing
——Is interested in spelling new words
——Desires to spell correctly
——Accepts responsibility for accuracy and legibility
——Has no fear of trying to spell new and unusual words in original writing
——Studies words spelled in unexpected ways to achieve mastery of those used frequently
——Knows and uses basic phoneme-grapheme relationships in exploratory spelling of new words

Words Often Spelled and Pronounced Incorrectly

above	couple	give	machine	ranger	tongue
across	cousin	gives	many	ready	too
again	cruel	gloves	measure	really	touch
against	curve	gone	might	right	two
aisle		great	mild	rough	
already	dead	guard	million		use
another	deaf	guess	mind	said	usual
answer	debt	guest	minute	says	
anxious	desire	guide	mischief	school	vein
any	do		mother	science	very
	does	have	move	scissors	view
bear	done	head	Mr.	sew	
beautiful	don't	heart	Mrs.	shoe	was
beauty	double	heaven		should	wash
because	doubt	heavy	neighbor	sign	weather
been	dove	here	neither	snow	weight
behind	dozen	high	night	soften	were
believe			none	soldier	what
bind	early	idea		some	where
both	earn	Indian	ocean	someone	who
bough	eight	instead	of	something	whom
bread	enough	isle	office	sometime	whose
bright	eye		often	son	wild
brought	eyes	key	oh	soul	wind
build		kind	once	special	wolf
built	father	knee	one	spread	woman
bury	fence	knew	onion	square	women
busy	field	knife	only	steak	won
buy	fight	know	other	straight	would
	find		ought	sure	wrong
calf	folks	language		sword	
captain	four	laugh	patient		you
caught	freight	laughed	piece	their	young
chief	friend	leather	pretty	there	your
child	front	library	pull	they	
clothes		light	purpose	though	
colt	garage	lion	push	thought	
coming	get	live	put	to	
cough	getting	lived		together	
could	ghost	love	quiet	ton	

Allen List of Words for Spelling and Editing

a	between	daddy	fellow	guess	is
about	big	dark	few		it
after	black	day	fifth	had	its
again	blue	dear	finally	hair	it's
all	body	did	find	half	
almost	book	didn't	fine	hand	
along	both	died	finished	happened	jet
alphabet	box	different	fire	happy	jump
also	boy	do	first	hard	just
always	bring	does	fish	has	
am	brother	dog	five	hat	keep
an	brown	done	fly	have	kept
and	but	don't	foot	having	killed
animal	buy	door	for	he	kind
another	by	down	found	head	knew
any		drama	four	heard	know
are		draw	fourth	help	
around	cafeteria	dress	friend	her	language
art	call	drink	from	here	large
as	came		front	high	last
ask	can		full	him	late
asked	can't	each	fun	his	laugh
at	car	early	funny	hit	learned
ate	cat	ears		hold	leave
aunt	chair	eat	game	home	left
away	children	egg	gave	hope	legs
	Christmas	eight	get	hot	let
baby	city	end	getting	house	letter
back	class	enough	girl	how	light
bad	clean	even	give	hundred	like
ball	close	ever	giving	hurt	lips
be	coat	every	glad		little
beautiful	cold	everyone	go		live
became	come	everything	goes	I	living
because	coming	eye	good	ice	long
bed	cook		got	if	look
been	could	fall	grade	I'll	lots
before	couldn't	far	gravel	I'm	love
began	country	farm	great	important	
best	cow	fast	green	in	made
better	cut	father	grow	interesting	make
		feet		into	man

many	oh	rain	sometimes	time	went
may	old	ran	soon	to	were
me	on	read	spring	today	what
meet	once	reading	start	together	when
men	one	ready	stay	told	where
might	only	real	stop	tongue	which
milk	open	red	story	too	while
mine	or	rest	street	took	white
minutes	orange	ride	study	top	who
Miss	other	right	such	town	why
money	our	room	summer	tried	will
more	out	round	sun	trip	window
morning	outside	run	supper	try	winter
most	over		sure	turn	wish
mother	own	said	swim	two	with
mouth		same			without
Mr.	paint	saw	table	under	woman
Mrs.	painting	say	take	until	women
Ms.	paper	school	talk	up	won't
much	part	second	teacher	upon	wood
music	party	see	teeth	us	world
must	pass	seen	tell	use	would
my	past	send	ten	used	wouldn't
myself	pay	sent	than		write
	people	seven	thank	vacation	writing
name	person	shall	that	very	wrong
near	pet	she	the	visit	wrote
never	pick	should	their	vocabulary	
new	pig	show	them		yard
next	pink	sick	then	walk	year
nice	place	side	there	want	yellow
night	play	since	these	war	yes
no	please	sing	they	warm	yet
nobody	pretty	sister	thing	was	you
none	principal	sit	think	wash	young
north	pull	six	third	wasn't	your
not	purple	sixth	this	water	yours
now	put	sleep	those	way	
		small	thought	we	zipper
of	quick	so	three	weather	zoo
off	quiet	some	through	week	
often	quite	something	till	well	

——Makes and uses personal lists of words needed for spelling during writing and editing

——Selects correct consonants or consonant clusters in the initial position of words

——Contrasts initial consonants with common phonograms to form new words (*b*ad, *f*ad, *h*ad, *s*ad)

——Adds prefixes and suffixes to known root words

——Spells correctly words of highest frequency that have irregular phoneme-grapheme relationships

——Divides words into syllables

——Identifies the stressed syllable in multisyllable words

——Knows that vowels represent variable sounds in words

——Uses contractions correctly

——Compounds words to form new ones

——Uses context clues to determine the spelling of homonyms

——Forms plurals for nouns

——Adds correct inflectional endings to verbs

Selected References

Burrows, Alvina T., Dianne L. Monson, and Russell G. Stauffer. *New Horizons in the Language Arts.* Harper & Row, New York, 1972.

Corbin, Richard. *The Teaching of Writing in Our Schools.* Macmillan Co., New York, 1966.

Evertts, Eldonna (ed.). *Explorations in Children's Writing.* National Council of Teachers of English, Urbana, Ill., 1970.

Gillooly, William B. "The Influence of Writing-System Characteristics on Learning to Read," *Reading Research Quarterly,* 8, 2 (1973), 167–200.

Greene, Harry A., and Walter T. Petty. *Developing Skills in the Elementary School.* Allyn & Bacon, Boston, 1971.

Gudschinsky, Sarah C. "The Nature of the Writing System: Pedagogical Implications." In *Language and Learning to Read: What Teachers Should Know About Language,* edited by Richard E. Hodges and E. Hugh Rudorf. Houghton Mifflin Co., Boston, 1972.

Hanna, Paul R., and Jean S. Hanna. "The Teaching of Spelling," *National Elementary Principal* (November, 1965), 19–28.

Hanna, Paul R., Richard E. Hodges, and Jean S. Hanna. *Spelling: Structure and Strategies.* Houghton Mifflin Co., Boston, 1971.

Henning, Dorothy G., and Barbara M. Grant. *Content and Craft: Written Expression in the Elementary School.* Prentice-Hall, Englewood Cliffs, N.J., 1973.

Hodges, Richard E., and E. Hugh Rudorf. "Searching Linguistic Cues for the Teaching of Spelling," *Elementary English*, 51, 9 (May, 1965), 527.

Hulon, Willis. *A Guide to Correct Spelling*. Schenkman Publishing Co., Cambridge, Mass., 1970.

Johnson, Dale D. "Suggested Sequences for Presenting Four Categories of Letter-Sound Correspondencies," *Elementary English* (September, 1973), 880–896.

Lefevre, Carl A. *Linguistics, English, and the Language Arts*. Allyn & Bacon, Boston, 1970.

Logan, Lillian M., Virgil G. Logan, and Leona Paterson. *Creative Communication: Teaching the Language Arts*. McGraw-Hill Ryerson, Toronto, 1972.

Ruddell, Robert B. "The Effect of the Similarity of Oral and Written Patterns of Language Structure on Reading Comprehension," *Elementary English*, 42 (1956), 403–410.

Russell, David. "Spelling Ability in Relation to Reading and Vocabulary Achievement," *Elementary English Review* (January, 1946), 32–37.

Smith, James A. *Adventures in Communication*. Allyn & Bacon, Boston, 1972.

Stauffer, Russell G. "The Effectiveness of Language Arts and Basic Reader Approaches to First Grade Reading Instruction—Extended into Third Grade," *Reading Research Quarterly*, 4, 4 (1969), 468–499.

Tiedt, Iris M., and Sidney W. Tiedt. *Contemporary English in the Elementary School*. Prentice-Hall, Englewood Cliffs, N.J., 1967.

FROM THE RATIONALE

Extending vocabularies—increasing listening, speaking, reading, and writing vocabularies of words and word clusters that pattern in language as nouns, verbs, adjectives, and adverbs; adding new meanings to known words; recognizing and using known words in new and creative ways; and creating new words for nonsense and fun talking and writing.

Vocabulary growth goes hand in hand with thinking and human interaction (Piaget, 1959). Early in life children learn that word sounds are associated with the people, things, and happenings around them. They relate to their human and physical environment with sounds they hear others using, and usually acquire abilities to communicate effectively with others through experiences rather than through planned sequences of lessons.

Children extend their vocabularies in both breadth and depth. They acquire a stock of new words as their experiences expand in real life and in vicarious ways. They deepen understandings of language as they learn to use the same word for a variety of meanings and in different slots in sentences. They discover that the same word used as a noun can be used as a verb or an adjective. They discover also that the emotional connotations of words can be expressed through intonation and emphasis.

Meanings attach firmly to words that children find useful in solving problems and in expressing ideas, feelings, and needs. Direct experiences with words are required in order for most children to experience vocabulary growth. "Sitting quietly and listening" is no substitute for active involvement in dramatization, storytelling, conversation, discussion, singing, choral reading, and creative writing. Children must have continuous opportunity to relive and relate experiences that are in turn contrasted and compared with those of others. In the process they find it necessary to enlarge their individual understandings of words they use so as to have terms with some commonalty of meaning for all members of the group. More and more words are needed as children get involved in expressing abstract ideas, such as democracy, cooperation, equality, and respect, that may be outside their real experiences.

Free discussion in the classroom furnishes clues to the teacher for planning vocabulary studies. Through it children reveal correct and incorrect usage, exact and vague meanings, and the need for words that are not available automatically. Words are discussed during reading experiences, vocabulary resources are provided in the Writing/Publishing Center, and the learning environment is permeated with materials that permit children to come in contact with words through records, tapes, filmstrips, films, labels, posters, and a variety of books.

In a language experience approach, vocabulary growth is an all-day, everyday concern. Broad experiences are provided. These experiences generate others so that new words are needed, not for the purpose of learning how to read, but for personal communication. It is seldom, if ever, that a child will recognize in print words that have not been said many times. No amount of phonetic analysis can bring meaning or meaningful pronunciation to words that have not been heard, said, or both.

Changes and progress in reading behavior are related directly to changes in the use of words. Young children usually use words in ways in which meanings are specific. Most of the words convey picturable ideas, such as nouns that mean things actually experienced and adjectives and verbs that express obvious qualities and relationships. Adverbs are seldom used. A survey of children's creative writing will reveal the same characteristics evident in their speaking. Examination of reading materials for young children reflects those same realistic language qualities. Any move beyond the specific to the abstract and artistic qualities of language occurs first in speech and then in writing and reading. According to studies summarized in "The Effects of Two Approaches to Reading Instruction Upon the Oral Language Development of First Grade Pupils" (Giles, 1966), repeated reading of preprimer and primer materials promotes *regressive tendencies* in vocabulary acquisition rather than *growth tendencies*. To avoid this regression, a language experience approach treats reading goals through a scheme of communication that moves

——from thinking →

——through oral expression →

——to writing of personal ideas in ways in which some writings can be used as reading instructional materials →

——to reading the language production of the author →

——through comparison techniques that identify the common vocabulary of all authors →

——to reading what other authors have written.

In the process children find in reading materials a reflection of personal language as it continues to grow. This is in sharp contrast to programs of instruction that limit early reading experiences to materials concocted to repeat words of highest frequency or words that reflect consistent linguistic patterns.

Children who experience a growing vocabulary in a natural setting of listening, talking, writing, and reading move with ease to language that reflects desire, anticipation, evaluation, feelings, and hopes. They use figurative language to link the real to an abstract idea and use connectives such as *unless, because, although,* and *provided that* to express complex relationships. Observations are summarized in abstract as well as in real terms. Experiences in talking, listening, and writing build a firm base for silent reading of the language and ideas of other authors who use abstract vocabulary and artistic forms of writing to express them.

Major emphasis in language acquisition in a language experience approach is placed on extending vocabularies of nouns, verbs, adjectives, and adverbs—the *form classes* of words. There are thousands of words in these four classes, and all sentences are dependent on two or more of them either stated or implied. The three hundred or so words that do not pattern in sentences as nouns, verbs, adjectives, or adverbs—the *structure words*—are included in the discussions of words of highest frequency in Chapter 12.

Vocabulary in Language Production

Statements of general agreement among authorities in linguistics and education that there are reciprocal relationships between oracy and literacy abilities are summarized by Cox (1971). In her study "Reciprocal Oracy/Literacy Recognition Skills in the Language Production of Language Experience Approach Students," Cox sought to determine the feasibility of comparing the quality of language production of children in spontaneous expression, presentation of dictation, and personal authorship. She developed schemes of judging the quality and produced evidence that children who had acquired a large vocabulary of nouns, verbs, and words that are used to describe are the ones who make the most progress in school tasks. The study implies that a heavy emphasis on recognition of words of highest frequency has little to contribute to the quality of speaking, writing, and reading.

The Cox study is an extension of one conducted by Eric Brown (1970), "The Bases of Reading Acquisition," in which he summarized the importance of vocabulary acquisition for reading competence when he wrote:

Recently, the universality of language complexity through maturation has been questioned in relation to educational differences in urban sub-cultures and other low-economic groups. Some years ago it was noted in descriptive linguistics that there were no inferior or superior languages; that all languages, from the bushman's to the European's, were of the same order of structural complexity and all were perfectly capable of communicating the native speaker's every thought, wish, or need. And yet the past few years have seen thousands of educators and psychologists speaking about language deficiencies, lack of concepts, and general verbal destitution in low-economic areas where "non-standard" English is spoken. Because from this point of view "linguistic underdevelopment" is a deterrent to cognitive growth, compensatory language development is the rule of the day in ghetto Head Start and school projects.

Investment in compensatory education for low-social and low-economic groups has failed to produce the desired results as reflected in improved reading achievement scores. Studies continue to be conducted which might point out problems that can be dealt with realistically by educators. One such study was conducted by John K. Sherk (1973) and reported in *A Word-Count of Spoken English of Culturally Disadvantaged Preschool and Elementary Pupils*. His research was motivated by conversations with teachers who expressed concern that many children in their classes did not understand common words used in the classroom by the teacher and by publishers of schoolbooks.

Sherk investigated and over a five-year period collected the spontaneous expression of children in inner-city neighborhoods of Kansas City. He arranged the words alphabetically and according to their function as form-class or structure words. Then he superimposed his list upon one already in existence for middle-class pupils, "Spontaneous Speaking Vocabulary of Children in Primary Grades" (Murphy, 1957).

Students for the Sherk study came from Head Start, kindergarten, and first grades in six elementary schools in the urban area of Kansas City. The only criterion used in the selection of students was that they would talk to the interviewer. Results that reflect on the extent of vocabulary are summarized with the order always reported as Sherk : Murphy.

1. In a corpus of 121,371 words there were 5,080 different words.
2. Respondents spoke an average of 1,500 words in the interview but used an average of 64 different words in the language transaction.
3. Based on words recorded by the interviewer, 74.5 percent of the service words or structure words taught in basal reader programs were present in oral language a minimum of 80 times. All but one (*shall*) of the words on the Dolch List of 220 Words were used.

4. Descriptive words on the Sherk list and the Murphy list were recorded at a ratio of 16 : 100.
5. The list of comparatives was at a ratio of 4 : 22.
6. Words that were used as nouns were on the two lists at a ratio of 67 : 342.
7. Words that were used as verbs (not including forms of *be* and *have* which are included in item 3 above) were at a ratio of 21 : 100.

The Sherk study is a detailed presentation of the general verbal destitution of words of the form classes among children in inner-city environments. It also reflects the early acquisition of the structure words of language. From it and other studies that yield similar results, one might conclude that goals of vocabulary extension must be related to the words and concepts that pattern in language as nouns, verbs, adjectives, and adverbs. So-called vocabulary growth that highlights, reviews, and evaluates recognition of words of highest frequency is *not an extending experience*. Children with the most limited language possess those words in the early years of school. They do not, on the other hand, possess enough names of things, words of movement, or words in the descriptive categories to be able to function successfully in school situations. Added to this complex problem is the larger area of syntactical structure which requires an understanding of the slot a word has in a sentence to make its function that of a noun, a verb, an adjective, or an adverb. Although much of this is intuitive in language acquisition, it is impossible for even the intuitive understandings to function apart from a vocabulary that includes the words in a meaningful context.

Concepts for Vocabulary Development

Vocabulary development is more than adding new words to one's experiences. It means putting concepts into operation through a choice of one or more words from a large repertoire. There are more than 500,000 words in the English language, and many of them have more than one meaning. These can be put together to form idioms which have special meanings. All these add up to millions of meanings.

Schemes for acquiring language other than those that are purely additive must be available to teachers and pupils. One possibility is to use *concepts* that contain a basic truth about language without having to list all the words available for illustrating the concept. Through experience and instruction children can organize their new acquisitions into a framework of words that name, words that state or imply movement, and words that extend meaning through description. A framework of stated concepts is detailed in *Language Experiences in Early Childhood* (Allen and Allen, 1969). Some examples of key concepts follow.

Concepts for Names

1. Everything has a name.
    —Every person has a name.
    —Every object has a name.
    —Most things have more than one name.
    —Many names have an opposite.

CLUES FOR INSTRUCTION

Use names of students to extend vocabulary: *Alfred*—boy, friend, brother, son, grandchild, student, baseball player. Create stories that include all the words on the list.

Choose common nouns and do the same kind of extension. Example: *horse*—foal, colt, filly, stallion, mare.

Provide space on the Word Wall or in a box in the Writing/Publishing Center for children to extend name vocabularies in ways that are useful for authors in the class.

Skim through chapters of books; find and list just the proper names. Then read the material carefully and list the other nouns the author used for the characters.

Read paragraphs, saying aloud *only* the nouns. Point out visual clues for nouns as long as necessary for pupils to master the point—capital letters for proper names and determiners (*the, a, my, our, every, this, that*) for common nouns.

Play games that require the person who is it to describe something without saying its name.

Make available the list of 230 nouns of highest frequency (Chapter 12) as a reference for spelling and for making vocabulary games.

2. Names change.
    —The same name is not used all the time.
    —Names change when we speak of more than one.
    —Our choice of names affects meaning.

CLUES FOR INSTRUCTION

Collect words that change when we talk about a group.

tree → grove	ship → fleet
cow → herd	person → crowd

Make new words by putting two words together to make compounds.

dish	neck
+ pan	+ tie
dishpan	necktie

These words can be illustrated, made into books, and used for easy reading.

Here is a *horse*.

Here is a *fly*.

Put them together.

You have a *horsefly*.

Collect names of baby animals and match names of the grown ones.

pup → dog	kid → goat
foal → horse	calf → cow
	—— → giraffe
	—— → rhinoceros
	—— → elephant

Begin a list of homonyms and leave it open for students to add words that sound alike but have different meanings and spellings.

I—eye	sun—son
mail—male	dear—deer

Introduce a junior thesaurus in order to provide a source of synonyms for writing and for games.

3. Special words are used to express time concepts.
   ——Days of the week, months of the year, and seasons have specific names.
   ——Special days that are holidays have their own names.

CLUES FOR INSTRUCTION

Watch for changes that occur with seasonal changes—plants, foods in the cafeteria, clothing, games.

Pantomime games and activities for children to guess what the season is rather than the name of the activity.

Make "time" books on all kinds of topics.

"TV Time"—pictures and stories from favorite TV programs

"Time Goes By"—pictures and stories of long ago

Collect stories and poems that include the names of days of the week, months of the year, and special holidays. Copy them into books for the Reading/Research Center.

4. Some names are nonsense and fun words.
   —Imaginary creatures can have names.
   —Words can be for pleasure only.
   —Any person can make new words.

CLUES FOR INSTRUCTION

Combine portions of several pictures into new persons, plants, animals, or machines. Make up new names for the nonsense creations.

Encourage children to bring nonsense songs and stories to class. As you sing and read together, comment that many of the nonsense words are nouns, a few are verbs, fewer are adjectives, and *none* are structure words. Help children to arrive at the generalization that language growth occurs when words function in sentences as nouns, verbs, adjectives, and adverbs.

Concepts for Verbs

1. People move.
   —There are words for the many movements of people.
   —Word endings—such as *-ed* and *-ing*—are sound and visual signals to tell the time of action.
   —People can communicate through body movements much of what they can with words.

CLUES FOR INSTRUCTION

Collect pictures of people in motion. Make two lists of words that tell the motion; one will list words that imply the action is happening now, and the other list will imply that the action happened sometime in the past. Notice common endings.

Say words of movement and ask children to pantomime them with body and facial movements as you change the meaning.

Pull—a heavy load
     —weeds from the ground
     —a stubborn animal
     —a tooth

Use a thesaurus to develop extended lists of verbs that have essentially the same meaning. Place the lists on a Word Wall or in the Writing/Publishing Center.

2. Animals move.
   ——Movement of animals is frequently compared with movement of people.
   ——Many words that tell the movement of animals and people are the same.

CLUES FOR INSTRUCTION

Use stories, poems, and songs that invite children to move like animals.

Jump like a rabbit.
Walk like an elephant.
Hop like a bird.
Collect pictures of animals in motion. Label them and bind them into books for browsing and for reviewing words of movement.
running swiftly
leaping high
crawling under
Read animal stories to help children collect words that authors use to tell how animals move.

3. Machines move.
   ——In talking about machines, one frequently uses words of motion.
   ——The noise of machines is made by something that is moving.
   ——Many words of motion have the endings -s, -ed, and -ing.

CLUES FOR INSTRUCTION

Listen to machines such as a pencil sharpener, a lawn mower, and a typewriter. Children tell the motion that the machine produces—grinds, clips, taps, and so on.

Have children make pictures of imaginary machines. Paint them or combine portions of several pictures. Tell how they work. Make up new words to tell the movement of the machines.

Collect pictures of complicated machines, real or imaginary. Ask children to tell what they think happens inside the machines. They will need to use words of motion to talk about the machines.

4. The elements move.
   ——Words of motion are frequently used to describe movement in weather.
   ——Words of movement make ideas more vivid.

CLUES FOR INSTRUCTION

Plan for children to observe weather movements from day to day. On a chart collect words with inflections that indicate tense.

to drip	drips	dripping	dripped
to shake	shakes	shaking	shook

Help children to generalize that a past tense word is often a different word rather than the same word with an inflectional ending. Examples are blew, fell, froze, and flew.

Select art prints that include water, fog, rain, snow, and wind. Let children talk about how the artists showed the movement of the elements. Try out some of the techniques with brushes and with finger-painting—circling, pounding, zigzagging, spiraling.

Choose music with titles that suggest that the composer had in mind the movement of the elements—storm, rain, wind. List words that come to mind as you listen together.

Concepts for Words of Description

Distinctions between adjectives and adverbs are elusive except in terms of function (Lefevre, 1970). The simplest distinction is that adjectives generally modify nouns and that adverbs generally modify verbs. Even the *-ly* ending which is sometimes identified with adverbs does not apply. Many words that usually pattern in sentences as nouns have *-ly* affixed when they are used as adjectives—love, lovely; friend, friendly; mother, motherly. But very generally when words commonly used as adjectives have the *-ly* affixed, they function as adverbs—bad, badly; sad, sadly; rapid, rapidly.

Concepts that promote language acquisition are not dependent on the classification of words as adjectives or adverbs. Rather, they highlight the use of words to modify nouns and verbs in categories such as color, size, shape, sound, texture, taste, smell, feeling, touch, motion, contrast, and comparison. Some key concepts related to descriptive categories follow.

1. Everything can be described.
   ——Things have color, size, shape, and texture.
   ——Some things have taste and smell.
   ——Some things make sounds.

CLUES FOR INSTRUCTION

Walk and talk with children to observe things around them. Choose a category of description such as the shape of things, and look for examples—square, round, oblong, sphere, egg, rectangle, triangle—or choose just one shape such as *round* and find everything you can that is that shape. Choose a letter of the alphabet such as *x* and find as many things as you can that are that shape.

Take imaginary walks into fine art prints. Talk about the colors of things, feelings about experiences, the sounds that might be heard, and the odors that might be smelled.

Make shape books like ears, eyes, noses, hands, and mouths. Write original stories and poems or copy those of others that fit the "sense" of the book. Illustrate with pictures. Write on a subject such as "A World without Smell."

Listen for sounds. Identify their source and try to write the sounds with alphabet letters so that someone who did not hear them can duplicate them. Does a cow really go "moo" or a dog "bow-wow"? Let children listen and explore writing.

Plan tasting and smelling activities frequently. Collect taste words and smell words for the Writing/Publishing Center.

2. Most things can be contrasted and compared with others.
   ——When talking about the size of a thing, we often compare it with something else.
   ——Many words that compare the size of things end in *-er* and *-est.*
   ——The words *like* and *as* are frequently used when making comparisons and contrasts.
   ——Ideas can be shared and meanings extended by contrasting one thing with another.
   ——Speech is a series of contrasting and repeating sounds.

CLUES FOR INSTRUCTION

Cook something. Examine the ingredients and describe them before and after cooking. What that is hard becomes soft? What that is soft becomes hard? What gets smaller with cooking? Larger? Popcorn is easy to cook and excellent for contrasting and comparing before and after cooking.

Listen for similes when reading with children. Collect them for a Word Wall list or for a resource in the Writing/Publishing Center. Help children to recognize that when they hear the words *like* and *as . . . as* that something is likely to be compared.

Relate size to things in everyday living. Children will discover that the size of something is often described in terms of other things seen or known. Lead children to generalize that when we talk or write about size, many of the words end with the sounds *-er* and *-est*. When comparing two things, we often hear the *-er* sound; when comparing more than two, we often hear the *-est* sound— *tall, taller, tallest; large, larger, largest*.

3. Emotions and feelings can be expressed with words.
   ——Emotions and feelings can be expressed with body movements, paintings, and musical compositions as well as with words.
   ——Words of feeling are found in most stories about people.

CLUES FOR INSTRUCTION

Collect pictures of faces of people. Talk about how the people must have felt when the pictures were made. Children will discover that feelings cannot be expressed without words of emotion such as afraid, proud, angry, sad, happy, ashamed, lonesome, upset, and bashful. This class of descriptive words can be collected for children to use when writing.

Make doodle pictures. When a face appears in the doodling, try to describe it with a word of feeling. Do the same thing with finger-painting.

Listen to music without words. Recall personal feelings and list the words to describe them. A list of feeling words on a Word Wall may help children to recall their own feelings while listening. Such a list also serves as a place to collect new words. Some that might serve as a starter list are: *anxious, troubled, pleased, selfish, haughty, annoyed, peaceful, wicked, tearful*.

Read stories with a lot of conversation. Watch for ways in which the authors express the feelings of the characters. Listen for new words of feeling.

4. Authors use words of description.
   ——Some authors paint pictures with words.

—Some authors relive an experience with words.

—Some authors create fantasy with words.

CLUES FOR INSTRUCTION

Have children choose storybooks from a library. Ask them to read until they find a word of color, of size, of weather, or of any other descriptive category. Do most authors use descriptive words in stories?

Collect stories and poems that are word pictures. Read them as they are written and then read them again, omitting the descriptive words and phrases. Highlight the fact that descriptive words are necessary for artistic writing.

Choose a story that is a fantasy. Read it without the descriptive words. Is it still a fantasy or does it seem to become more factual when the descriptive vocabulary is left out? Does an author have to use descriptive words in order to write fantasy stories?

Write stories on any topic with wide space between lines. Pass them around and let each reader add at least one descriptive word or phrase to sentences of the original author. Compare the originals with the edited stories in terms of interest, colorful and vivid language, and, when appropriate, recalling real-life experiences.

Resources for Children

A language experience approach learning environment is permeated with resources and activities for vocabulary expansion. Many of the learning areas have a Word Wall, a Writing/Publishing Center with resources for vocabulary expansion, a writing handbook for each pupil, and writing patterns requiring the use of form-class words.

Word Walls

A Word Wall is usually a portion of wall space devoted to lists of words that children can use when writing. It is a resource with which they can have visual contact without moving from the place where writing is taking place. The various sections of the Word Wall indicate classes of words that children should expect to use when writing. The lists are open-ended and grow as children discover new words that fit into a classification. Usually a word is not added to a Word Wall list until it can be recognized by some child or a group of children in the classroom. At times when several children are writing, one child who can read most of the words can be appointed the Word Wall monitor. That child can point out words for spelling and thus relieve the teacher of the responsibility.

A Word Wall might include:
—an alphabetic list of words of highest frequency
—figures of speech
—idioms
—words of the senses—sight, touch, smell, taste, sound
—synonyms
—antonyms
—homonyms
—words of color, size, shape, and texture
—special words for a holiday or a unit of study
—words of movement
—weather words
—"said" words for introducing and concluding conversation

The Word Wall should be ever changing and always growing. Games that use the lists of sight words increase reading vocabularies.

Vocabulary Expansion in the Writing/Publishing Center

Resources of the Writing/Publishing Center should include books and activities that promote language growth. As children write, they should be motivated to use words new to them and to use old words in new ways. A thesaurus is helpful as soon as children can read some words in isolation and use books arranged in alphabetic order. A beginning thesaurus can be used as early as first grade by some children. A junior thesaurus is useful to the end of the elementary grades. Children who write need variety in the vocabulary they select, and a published thesaurus or one generated in the classroom is helpful for editing as well as for composing.

A variety of dictionaries is needed in a Writing/Publishing Center. Picture dictionaries have some usefulness to children during writing but are more valuable in the Reading/Research Center than in the Writing/Publishing Center. They tend to have familiar words and offer little help in vocabulary expansion. A junior dictionary is essential. Beyond that level specialized dictionaries for areas such as science and mathematics are beneficial.

As lists of words grow on a Word Wall, they can be condensed on cards or in folders and placed in the Writing/Publishing Center. After children have studied, played games, discussed, and learned to read special lists of words, they can use the cards and folders when writing and can add to them when they find new words while reading.

In classrooms where children write poetry with syllabication restrictions, there is a need for lists of words to help in writing and editing. Synonyms can be listed with a range of syllables: *small, little, trivial, miniature.*

A Writing Handbook

Children who frequently write need personal resources for words, for spelling, and correct usage. For them a writing handbook can be initiated as soon as the most basic recognition skills are functional and the child knows how to use an alphabetic list.

The writing handbook should include an alphabetic list of words of highest frequency. These words are for spelling reference and are not considered to be "expanding" to the vocabularies of most children. The list is necessary for children who write in places away from established Writing/Publishing Centers and Word Walls.

Beyond the list of words of high frequency, any category of words that children use often should be available. One or two at a time can be initiated with words furnished as starters. After that the list should reflect the growing vocabulary of each pupil in areas such as: color words, size words, shape words, taste words, smell words, texture words, touch words, action words, many names for the same things, figures of speech, phrases, sentences to begin stories, words of courtesy and manners, names of people and places used frequently, and word substitutes for *said* that are used to introduce and conclude written conversations.

The words in writing handbooks should be different for every pupil. Lists should grow as a result of reading and of real experiences that introduce new vocabulary. The categories listed should suggest to children writing that other authors frequently use words from the same categories they use.

Writing Patterns That Require Form-class Words

Writing activities that require children to know classes of words to fit into a predetermined pattern are useful in vocabulary expansion. Children have the security of the pattern as a guide, but they are free to use any words they know to fill in the pattern. The cinquain and diamante are examples. Others are described in *Contemporary English in the Elementary School* (Tiedt and Tiedt, 1967), in *Sparkling Words* (Carlson, 1968), and *Language Experience Activities* (Allen and Allen, 1976).

CINQUAINS

The pattern: five lines, nonrhyming

Line 1: one word, the name of something
two syllables

Line 2: two words that describe line 1
four syllables

Line 3: three words, an action for line 1
six syllables

Line 4: four words, a feeling about line 1
eight syllables

Line 5: a synonym or a word referring back to line 1
two syllables

This pattern is usually introduced in a modified form that uses the number of words but not the number of syllables. The modified version highlights the use of form-class words—nouns, verbs, adjectives, and adverbs.

Only eleven words are required to express the thought with a cinquain. Children know when they have achieved their goal. Kindergarten children can dictate cinquains as group compositions, or individuals can dictate their own. Sixth-grade students enjoy writing them in the modified form as well as with the syllabic requirement. Variations may be practiced, but there is a base pattern from which to start. It is possible to vary the order of the requirements for the five lines. Cinquains offer a variety of writing requirements from a base, which was published first in 1914 by Adelaide Crapsey in *Verse*.[1]

Some examples of cinquains follow.

---

[1] Manas Press, Rochester, N.Y., 1914.

Children
Cheerful, happy
Playing, laughing, tumbling
Eternal happiness seems theirs
Playground.

—Jerry

Modified forms:

Word Control Only

Squirrel
Quiet charmer
Darts for peanuts
Sits nervously while entertaining
Rodent.

—Claryce

Peppers
Scarlet red
Burn like fire
Quick, agua por favor!
Hot!

—Rita

Syllable Control Only

Flowers
Pretty and bright
Swaying in the cool breeze
A gift that cannot be purchased
Carpet.

—Joe

Cinquain writing maximizes the use of nouns, verbs, and adjectives. It minimizes the use of words of structure. Children can compose them in group situations or on an individual basis before they have mastered English syntax. They are especially useful for children learning English as a second language because they can be used early and can be beautiful expressions of self.

DIAMANTE

The pattern: seven lines, nonrhyming

Line 1:   one word, a noun
Line 2:   two words, adjectives
Line 3:   three words, participles
Line 4:   four words, nouns
Line 5:   three words, participles
Line 6:   two words, adjectives
Line 7:   one word, a noun

Lines 1 and 7 are opposites. Lines 2 and 3 and half of line 4 describe the noun of line 1. Lines 5 and 6 and the other half of line 4 describe line 7.

A diamante challenges the writer to shift the description of one thing to its opposite within a pattern. It brings into play synonyms and antonyms and extends them with descriptive words. Line 4 is a transition line, and frequently the two middle nouns refer to both lines 1 and 7. Examples of diamantes are illustrated on page 271.

Personal Words

A collection of personal words is an easy and natural way of expanding vocabularies and of building a sight vocabulary of words already known.

A good starting point is to cut from magazines and newspapers words that appear frequently on television, in advertisements, and on items in the home and to bring them to the classroom. Children can choose words they can read to paste on charts or into blank books. Older children who have difficulty reading limited vocabulary materials and those who are learning English as a second language can find many words that they can read printed in magazines and newspaper advertisements. For them an extension activity can be created by the teacher's taking a known word or a brand name that is distinctive and writing it in manuscript, in cursive, and on the typewriter. The pupil can try to do the same with known words. These writings can be collected into books for reading and for discussions about language.

When reading to children let each of them listen for *one word* from the story that he or she would like to have in a Word Bank. Write the words on cards for children who cannot do their own writing. Use

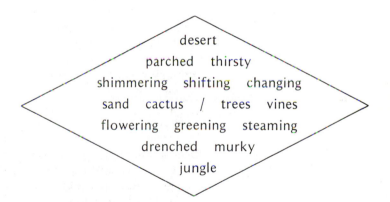

cards to go in files or ones with holes punched in one end for stringing on a metal ring or a shoestring. These words can be reviewed from time to time, and the "unknown" ones removed. Those left can be arranged in alphabetic order; they can be stacked according to the number of syllables; they can be used as a spelling list; they can be arranged by each child in categories that are recognized and meaningful.

Organic vocabulary, such as that described in *Teacher* (Ashton-Warner, 1963), can develop as an ongoing experience. Each child is encouraged to add one word of his or her choice to a word ring or bank each day. The child repeats the word after it is written. The following day the words on the ring are reviewed. Those that are not remembered are removed. This procedure assures every child of a sight vocabulary of known words during processes of learning to recognize words that lack personal meanings.

Summary of Skills and Abilities for Extending Vocabularies

VOCABULARY ACQUISITION

——Develops meanings for new words through experiences
——Develops new meanings for known words through experiences
——Develops understanding of the emotional connotation of words
——Develops understanding of the aesthetic connotation of words
——Acquires a vocabulary for talking about language
——Reacts with meaning to figurative language such as similes, metaphors, and analogies
——Reacts with meaning to idiomatic expressions
——Acquires new words in line with some systematic plan such as one using personal word cards

VOCABULARY APPLICATION

——Uses resources in the classroom for specific word classes needed in writing
——Uses a thesaurus to add variety to writing
——Uses a dictionary to verify meanings
——Develops personal resources such as a writing handbook to aid in writing and spelling
——Can write in patterns that require the use of specified form classes. Examples: cinquain and diamante
——Uses inflectional changes according to context. Examples: dog, dogs; leap, leaps, leaped, leaping
——Uses pictures in context with language patterns that use a variety of form-class words
——Uses the same word in a variety of forms. Examples: beauty, beautify, beautiful; love, lovely, lovable, unlovely
——Makes use of descriptive words to clarify and elaborate mean-

ings: words of color, size, shape, texture, sound, taste, smell, feelings, touch, and motion
——Knows and uses more than one name for the same thing. Examples: mother, woman, female, girl, wife, aunt
——Knows and uses more than one word for the same action. Examples: run, scamper, hurry, race, trot, flee

Selected References

Allen, Roach Van, and Claryce Allen. *Teacher's Resource Book: Language Experiences in Early Childhood.* Encyclopaedia Britannica Educational Corp., Chicago, 1969.

——. *Language Experience Activities.* Houghton Mifflin Co., Boston, 1976.

Ashton-Warner, Sylvia. *Teacher.* Simon and Schuster, New York, 1963.

Austin, David, Velma Clark, and Gladys Fitchett. *Reading Rights for Boys.* Appleton-Century-Crofts, New York, 1971.

Brown, Eric. "The Bases of Reading Acquisition," *Reading Research Quarterly* 4, 1 (Fall, 1970), 56–57.

Carlson, Ruth Kearney. *Sparkling Words: Two Hundred Practical and Creative Writing Ideas.* Wagner Printing Co., Berkeley, Calif., 1968.

——. *Writing Aids Through the Grades.* Teachers College Press, New York, 1970.

Cox, Vivian E. "Reciprocal Oracy/Literacy Recognition Skills in the Language Production of Language Experience Approach Students." (Ed.D. dissertation.) University of Arizona, Tucson, 1971.

Dale, Edgar, Joseph O'Rourke, and Henry A. Bamman. *Techniques of Teaching Vocabulary.* Field Educational Publications, Chicago, 1971.

Deighton, Lee C. *Vocabulary Development.* Macmillan Co., New York, 1964.

Dunne, Hope W. *The Art of Teaching Reading: A Language and Self-Concept Approach.* Charles E. Merrill, Columbus, Ohio, 1972.

Francis, Marjorie. *The Three R's of Language: Releasing Feelings, Reweaving Ideas, Recording Language.* Child Focus Co., Manhattan Beach, Calif., 1971.

Giles, Douglas E. "The Effects of Two Approaches to Reading Instruction Upon the Oral Language Development of First Grade Pupils." (Ed.D. dissertation.) North Texas State University, Denton, 1966.

Greet, W. Cabell, William A. Jenkins, and Andrew Schiller. *In Other Words: A Beginning Thesaurus,* and *In Other Words: A Junior Thesaurus.* Scott, Foresman and Co., Glenview, Ill., 1968.

Lefevre, Carl A. *Linguistics, English and the Language Arts.* Allyn & Bacon, Boston, 1970.

Moe, Alden J. *High Frequency Nouns: Word Cards for Beginning Readers.* Ambassador Publishing Co., St. Paul, Minn., 1973.

Murphy, Helen A. "Spontaneous Speaking Vocabulary of Children in Primary Grades," *Journal of Education,* 14, 2 (December, 1957).

Newman, Harold. *Effective Language Practices in the Elementary School.* John Wiley & Sons, New York, 1972.

Piaget, Jean. *The Language and Thought of the Child,* rev. ed. Humanities Press, New York, 1959.

Sherk, John K. *A Word-Count of Spoken English of Culturally Disadvantaged Preschool and Elementary Pupils.* University of Missouri at Kansas City, Mo., 1973.

Tiedt, Iris M., and Sidney W. Tiedt. *Contemporary English in the Elementary School.* Prentice-Hall, Englewood Cliffs, N.J., 1967.

FROM THE RATIONALE   Studying style and form—profiting from listening to and studying well-written materials which reflect the ways authors express their feelings, observations, and imaginings in beautiful language; increasing sensitivity to a variety of styles and forms of expression; replicating artful forms of expression such as couplets, quatrains, cinquains, haiku, letters, and diaries; sensing the humor of passages; differentiating poetry from prose; and expanding sentences with descriptive words and passages.

Improved self-expression through talking and writing can occur when teachers and children study the style and form of other authors. They listen to, repeat, and practice working within basic patterns which can be expanded and elaborated to express personal thoughts in new ways.

To study style is to study ways of self-expression. Style includes intuitive choices as well as studied ones. In verbal communication it involves choice of words and ways of combining words to express ideas. A child with a rich and varied background has more choices available than one of limited experience.

School programs can accelerate experiences from which children make choices—especially choices of words to express ideas and feelings. They can provide alternatives through direct instruction as well as through self-selected activities. School programs can build confidence in the use of personal styles of language to the extent that a student's writing can be identified by others without a signature, the style being unique to one person.

The element of form is largely predetermined. Literary forms of poetry and prose are well defined. A haiku always has three lines with a total of seventeen syllables. The syllabic pattern of the lines is 5-7-5. Other forms may not be determined as strictly, but they are easily identifiable. Children can use them with a degree of security in that they know when they have achieved a selected form. The content of the form is open to the writer. Also, they can find other authors who have used the various forms and can be influenced by the artistic style of some of them.

Form, as considered here, includes such topics as spelling, punctuation, capitalization, grammar, handwriting, and sentence sense. These elements of form apply to the productive writing of students. They are not treated as lessons but as supports for clear and effective self-expression.

The teacher plays a crucial role in regard to all aspects of style and form. In a language experience approach she or he does not dictate standards and pass judgment on children's creative productions. Rather, alternatives are suggested and illustrated so that students increase their awareness of

——variety in style

——correctness in form.

The teacher uses a variety of influences and provides many models that give a measure of security to children who are exploring their communicative powers.

Some Influences on Style and Form

Influences on style and form come indirectly as well as directly. Some of them are in the hidden curriculum. They are never described, sequenced, published, or evaluated. But they are there in the feelings and in the products of children. They come from sources such as listening to the language of others, interacting with adults during dictation processes, reading from a variety of sources, and participating in seminars on style and form that lead to editing as well as to creative personal production.

Listening children are influenced by the style and form of material read *to* them and *with* them by the teacher. The voice control used when reading aloud brings to life the style of an author in ways that young readers cannot experience when they struggle with recognition skills in order to read.

Words and phrases of a well-written book that are not characteristic of the natural language of children can be effectively interpreted by the teacher and then repeated in chorus by the children. The feel of the voice in interpreting a new language style reinforces it and influences children to use it in their own writing.

Felix wants the children in his class to know that unusual dialects can be effective when used artfully. His speciality in reading to his children, who are mostly of Mexican descent, is reading English poetry and prose that features many dialects—Welsh, Scottish, Irish, Australian, cockney, and black dialects from various regions of the United States. Children participate by repeating creative and clever uses of words and phrases and thus experience artful ways of using language that does not feature standard pronunciation and spelling.

In support of the approach of *reading to* his pupils, Felix includes recordings in the Viewing/Listening Center that feature a wide range of English dialects along with recordings from speakers and singers of Spanish.

Texts that accompany most of the records are written in what appears to be standard English, but when certain people read a text, the interpretation becomes a very personal one. By being exposed to variations in this way, children are encouraged to learn standard ways of spelling and writing at a time when it is very difficult to change their pronunciation of English.

Tina reads something of children's literature to the class every day. She considers this to be *basic reading*. The young children she teaches need massive support in personal language growth if they are ever to read independently.

As she reads, she invites children to say words with her. She specializes in selecting poems and stories patterned in a way that enables the children to substitute new nouns, verbs, and words of description easily and enjoyably. She might read, "This is the house that Jack built." Children respond with new ideas within the language pattern.

"This is the car that Jane drove."

"This is the wig that Mother wore."

"This is the dog that Julian bought."

Tina watches for the influence of this oral participation as she records dictated stories and reads what the children write.

Listening to songs and singing along is another way to influence language. Teachers can draw students' attention to the unique characteristics of different composers just as they do to those of different authors. Many songs lend themselves to changes in wording. Children can use classic language structures as they sing songs of their own experiences and own imagination set to old tunes.

Presenting Dictation

Dictating to someone is an experience that influences a child's style and form. The interaction which is part of the process gives the teacher or another adult an opportunity to offer alternatives to gross errors in grammar, to invite elaboration by asking for words of color, size, shape, and other descriptive categories, and to add phrases that extend meanings by telling where, when, why, and how.

Before students come to school, their speech patterns and general styles of expression are set by the language environment in which they live. At school they are helped to refine their language usage. In a language experience approach the personal style of every child is valued and used, regardless of how divergent it is from conventional expression.

Before writing anything that a child is dictating, the teacher encourages the child to talk spontaneously and freely. After the whole idea or story has been verbalized, the teacher and student may summarize in order to decide what of all that has been said should be written. The teacher does not edit what has been said but occasionally suggests alternatives from which the child can choose. The major concern is one of assuring the student that his or her own style has validity and is valued at this point in language development.

Students watch carefully as the teacher writes and comments on letter form, capitalization, punctuation, spelling (especially irregular spelling), and new sentence beginnings. At the conclusion the teacher reads the dictated story with expression and enthusiasm. The reading model is reassuring to children whose own reading is halting and slow. They know that their own style of saying things can be useful when it is recorded in predetermined language forms.

Dictation can also be useful with older children. A literary form—a fable or a limerick, for example—can be identified, and students can dictate within the form while the teacher writes on the chalkboard. The original version can be edited and then copied from the chalkboard as a model. During the process the teacher has a chance to reinforce the meaning and importance of writing skills, to offer alternatives that change or correct grammar, and to encourage elaboration that leads to clarity and interest. After the writing the teacher has an opportunity to illustrate effective reading.

Reading

Personal reading is an activity that greatly influences style and form. A major danger in the overemphasis of the ability to read the contrived language of many beginning reader series is that children mimic that language in their writing. When that language is used for systematic instruction, it must be balanced with other reading materials and activities that reflect natural language patterns and natural vocabulary. Otherwise children are left on their own to locate, enjoy, and experience the influence of artful writing as a result of their reading. Poor readers may stay in school for several years before they are able to read independently anything worthy of being an influence.

For these reasons children in a language experience approach program write and publish many books and charts that become a part of the basic reading program. These experiences cause them to be interested in reading from a variety of published books for ideas—even before they can read the books orally and pronounce every word. The process of editing original manuscripts for publications useful in the reading program brings children in direct contact with the major aspects of form that are reflected in well-written materials.

Children who select reading for recreation or information usually have time for conferences with the teacher. During the reading conference the teacher can call attention to an author's individual style and effective use of forms of language. This discussion is in addition to the traditional concerns with decoding skills. Children repeat with the teacher words and phrases that may become a part of their personal speech and writing.

Seminars for Editing

The seminar technique is an effective way of helping children to build an awareness of the styles of different authors and to recognize correct form.

Ada keeps informal notes on errors in form that she observes as children write. Periodically she calls for a seminar on a topic of need. She asks children to volunteer original manuscripts that can be made into transparencies. These are projected on the chalkboard so that suggestions for improvement can be written in, discussed, and then changed as necessary. At other times she prepares transparencies with no punctuation or capitalization. Students edit as they discuss matters of form.

Other seminars deal with style. She will furnish a long and involved paragraph and ask for a restatement of the idea in a cinquain or a haiku. This limitation on the number of words or syllables helps children to experience the satisfaction of saying something ordinary in an extraordinary way. This is style in writing. Seminars can be on general style and form as well as on specific topics.

Margie has a special place where children put their stories if they would like to have them used in a seminar. The authors know that other children will make suggestions for changes and that they must be prepared to change or to defend their work.

Because the writing is large, it can be displayed on an easel or on a wall space. Children gather around and listen to the author or the teacher read. Then they comment on strengths and weaknesses. Margie serves as the seminar leader in order to reinforce essential matters of form at the same time that she seeks to preserve individual style. She encourages children to look for ways to improve letter formation, spelling, punctuation, capitalization, grammar, and clarity of meaning. The seminars lead children to avoid writing a story that is totally dependent on an accompanying picture with a beginning sentence such as "This is a . . ." or "Look at my . . ." They learn to use sentences that are clear statements of their ideas: "My horse lives in a barn behind our house" and "Today I found a black seed."

Seminars conducted on a regular basis prepare children for ever-increasing abilities and responsibilities for editing their own manuscripts and for working on editorial committees. Children who lack confidence in making decisions about their writing and that of others have opportunities to listen and participate without being graded. They get ideas to explore and gain insights into style and form which permit them to edit for style as well as for form.

The attitudes of teachers are crucial in seminar techniques. They are not the source of all information. They guide and serve as a reference source. In the final analysis they serve as an editor in chief when manuscripts in the seminar are to be published for use in the reading program. They use the seminar to raise levels of awareness of variety of style and correctness of form. They are hopeful that the technique will lead to free, interesting, and creative writing. At the same time they hope that children will build a basis for the appreciation of effective writing by other authors.

Resources for Children

Children who learn to produce with new styles and in new forms come in contact with new methods of communicating in a functional setting—methods that do not attempt to separate writing, reading, language study, art, viewing, listening, and real-life experiences into discrete categories for instructional purposes. The kinds of understandings that stimulate children enough for them to try new ways are developed in a rich, happy, and varied school and home program. The enrichment is modified, and new possibilities are introduced continually by resources such as:

——reading from a variety of sources
——viewing motion pictures, including those without words
——viewing filmstrips and making original conmentaries
——television viewing with participation
——listening to recordings of music and songs and learning the special language of composers
——following along on recordings that model excellent reading
——viewing art prints and learning the special language of artists
——painting pictures and sculpturing
——growing things
——cooking
——taking care of living things.

A rich learning environment assures children opportunities for choice and generates needs for self-expression. Children who hear and read many types of stories have a background for writing in different forms. Children who hear and say many poems have a background for creating poems.

Much of the approach to original writing in a variety of forms and with styles unique to the authors grows out of an adequate reading environment. There should be much reading aloud to illustrate effective passages. Choral reading and unison reading should be *basic* in the program, assuring that children who are poor readers when reading individually can participate regularly in a successful oral reading experience. They too need to experience the clever and creative ways in which artistic authors record their ideas. The reading aloud *to* and *with* children holds high interest if children focus on goals that relate the reading to growth in understanding style and form as well as in comprehending what is heard. They listen for

——humor in passages
——nonsense words and ideas
——words new to them
——rhyming patterns
——syllabic patterns that repeat
——sensitive passages
——conversation of characters
——sequence of events
——mystery

——implied meanings
——riddles
——jokes
——other characteristics of language that might be useful in their own productions and enjoyable when found in silent reading.

Teachers who are developing in children a sensitivity to style and form find them enthusiastic about trying new patterns of talking and writing. They capture their enthusiasm by helping each child to treat the usual in an unusual way.

The Noun-verb Pattern in Sentences

Martha introduces the study of the noun-verb pattern in sentences with couplets. She illustrates the idea of a quick couplet, and then the children are on their own to write. A book of quick couplets is a natural result.

Babies cry.
I wonder why.

   —Margaret

Birds fly
In the sky.

   —Edward

Frogs jump
From a stump.

   —Jolene

Boats race
For first place.

   —Natalie

Cats meow
For their chow.

   —Helen

After a book is bound and enjoyed, Martha moves on to reading sentences with efforts made to see the noun-verb pattern without looking at the other words. This is an introduction to skimming, but it also forms a basis for evaluating effective, clear writing.

Initial Sound-symbol Relationships

Alfred diagnosed a need for in-depth study of initial sound-symbol relationships in words. About one-third of his fifth-grade class was deficient in and unsure of this crucial skill in word recognition. He used activities that involved the whole class in enjoyable writing, but his goal of improving word recognition was centered on those in need. His technique was to use alliterative talking and writing. He helped the class practice by observing something, naming it, and then writing a sentence or a paragraph using mostly words that begin with the same sound-symbol. The sentences could be pure nonsense in meaning, such as the following.

Ships

Several shining ships sailed south, so Sam shed six shirts sewn by Sophie. Saturday Sophie saw Sam shedding shirts. She shouted, "Samuel Smitherman, should sailors shed shirts sailing south?"

Sam shouted to shore, "Sophie Samantha Smith, shuddup!"

Cindy used the same idea to spark the writing of books as Christmas gifts for parents. Each child named something that would be a good gift for Christmas and described it with one or more words beginning with the same sound and same initial consonant. The books were illustrated, duplicated, and bound with cloth bindings.

Cindy participated in the writing of the words and sentences that held the text together (italicized portions).

Piles of Presents

At Christmas, we'll put out piles of pretty presents.
Which package will you pick?
Maybe there is
    a jolly jumping
    jack-in-the-box,
    a talking teddy bear
    named Timmy
       and
    a tiny train that toots.
What is in the piles of packages?
Pretend, but don't peek!

The Alphabet

Joyce used the alphabet as a scheme for gathering vocabulary following a trip to a living desert museum. Rather than asking each child to tell what she or he liked best, she invited group participation as she recorded responses from A to Z. This is the result.

Desert ABC's

We were surprised to find our ABC's in the middle of the desert!
As we walked and talked together, we found them all.
A was found in agave, ants, and animals of every kind.
B was found in brittlebush, blossoms, bees, birds, and bats.
C was very common—cactus, creosote bush, century plants, cereus, coatimundi, coyote, cactus wren, curved-bill thrasher, and cottontail.
D was the delightful desert itself.
E was a favorite in the little elf owl.
F was the finches we saw everywhere.
G was found in greasewood bushes and a little gecko that ran by our feet.
H was found in a hole by a hedgehog cactus.
I was the insects all around us.
J was the jack rabbit that jumped in front of us.
K was found in the kangaroo rat.
L was found in the lizards—little and large.
M was found in mesquite trees and mice in their dens.
N was nature all around us.
O was the owls flying over the ocotillo.
P was found in paloverde trees and their pleasant shade.
Q was the covey of quails we watched.
R was found in rabbits, rodents, rattlesnakes—and the roadrunners, of course.
S to us was the stately saguaro standing so tall.
T was the tarantula and the tortoise.
U was the utterly unique Desert Museum.
V was found in the vinegarroon.
W was the woodpeckers that build nests in the giant cactus for desert birds.
X was the Mission San Xavier that we could see.

Y was the yucca plant.
Z was our zeal and zest for the Desert Museum.

Jolene knows that children in her class need specific work on alphabetic order for dictionary and encyclopedia work. She encourages them to write sentences or verses using only words that follow alphabetic order. One wrote:

A big critter dived eagerly forward getting himself into Japanese kimono—leaving many new octagonal pieces—quietly roaming—silently teaching us virtues with x-tra young zest.

Teachers who know and use some basic self-expression forms are able to involve children in learning the ordinary topics of school with extraordinary satisfaction.

Patterns for Improving Style and Form

Patterns that offer some security but complete openness to ideas are useful in launching children into new styles of talking and writing. Patterned writing sets bounds but not topics or choice of words.

Some useful writing patterns for children to use in the elementary grades are:

haiku	limerick
senryu	triangle triplet
tanka	quadrangle
sijo	renga

These patterns require children to know how to identify syllables in words, to rhyme, and to select predetermined forms of words such as nouns, verbs, and descriptors. In these forms the syllable is highlighted more than in some others. Its significance in studying language is summed up by Dolores Durkin in *Phonics, Linguistics and Reading* (1972): ". . . the syllable is of basic importance to phonics because it is the unit of pronunciation. In fact, it is on the syllable, not the word, that phonics generalizations focus."

The patterns of writing illustrated in this discussion suggest ways in which children can express their own observations, feelings, and imaginations in styles and with forms they have not been using at home and school. These patterns offer literary quality enough for children using them to move toward an appreciation of the work of artist-authors who write in disciplined forms.

HAIKU

The pattern: three lines, seventeen syllables—nonrhyming

Line 1: five syllables
Line 2: seven syllables
Line 3: five syllables

Haiku is an Oriental verse form of ancient origin. Its simplicity encourages children to say beautiful things in a new way. It is used to express observations and feelings about nature and the seasons. This form highlights the use of words of the form classes—nouns, verbs, adjectives, and adverbs. Some examples of haiku follow.

> Finches and sparrows
> Exchange gossip of birdland
> As they peck at brunch.
>
> —Clare

> Hovering rain clouds
> Gather like timid chickens
> 'Round mountain mother.
>
> —Van

> Winging into flight
> The bold eagle dares to soar
> Beyond the pink clouds.
>
> —Susan

> Slender waterfalls
> From vast snow fields trickle down
> Like long silver threads.
>
> —Elaine

SENRYU

The pattern: the same pattern as haiku. Senryu is used to communicate topics that are not about nature and the seasons. Some examples of it follow.

City skies are dull.
Polluted air lies stagnant.
Can we survive this?

—Carl

Baseball fans screaming
A fantastic catch is made
Another game won!

—Ron

Haiku and senryu require only seventeen syllables to express a thought that could become the main idea for an essay, a story, or a lyric. Children who have never expressed their thinking in these three complex forms profit from the experience of writing in the understandable, simple forms of a known pattern.

Haiku and senryu, as well as other syllabic patterned poetry, require a functional understanding of structural and phonetic analysis—syllabication, prefixes, suffixes, synonyms, contractions. The students must learn to eliminate many words of structure and depend on the reader to think the omitted words when they are useful for the flow of ideas. They focus on the words that carry the heavy load of meaning in communication, and thus build skills necessary for silent reading at a rate faster than speech.

TANKA

The pattern: five lines, thirty-one syllables—nonrhyming

Line 1:   five syllables
Line 2:   seven syllables
Line 3:   five syllables
Line 4:   seven syllables
Line 5:   seven syllables

Tanka is another ancient Oriental poetry form. It is a haiku plus two lines of seven syllables each. Actually, the tanka is older than the haiku, and it is believed that the more popular haiku is just a shortened form of tanka.

The author of a tanka usually expresses five thoughts on a topic. They may include:

——the name of something
——its actions
——its location

——its usefulness
——its beauty
——something distinctive about the subject
——something unusual about the subject
——a comparison
——the color, size, shape, sound, and other features.
Here are some examples of the tanka.

Flowing Fire

Oh, how very still
And how bright the frost today
As wee lights sparkle.
Sunlight lends its flowing fire
To make the ice appear warm.

—Al

Shadows

I focus my eyes
Upon the wall's white surface.
Moving upon it
Are shadows from outside trees.
Oh, so momentarily.

—Yachiyo

In guiding authors to try the tanka, haiku, and senryu, teachers can encourage children to record their observations in natural ways. Then they can count syllables. They will be surprised at how many natural utterances occur in phrases and sentences of five and seven syllables. With a few adjustments most of what is said can be recorded in measures of five or seven syllables. It is as natural for kindergarten children to dictate in these patterns as it is for older children to write in them. But there is something special for most children about poetry writing!

SIJO

The pattern: six lines, each containing seven or eight syllables—nonrhyming

Sijo (pronounced "shē-djō") is a Korean poetry form of ancient origin. Recently it has been translated into English by Peter H. Lee

(1965). In its simplified form popularized for school use, it is much like the haiku and tanka but is not as restrictive. Although it is non-rhyming, internal rhymes occur in much of the Korean verse. Alliteration is used to produce a poetic quality. Observations can be recorded on almost any topic and then edited for the six lines of seven or eight syllables each. Here are examples of the sijo.

Ocean Waves

The ocean waves are endless.
Frills of water flow free.
The weathering winds whip the waves,
Raving, rushing, running.
The waters flow from where to where?
This search surrounds the sea.

—R. V. Allen

Cloud Gazing

Llama turns into a duck.
Duck becomes a small robin.
Camel is loaded to high peak.
Peak grows and becomes a castle.
Huge lion roars into sight.
Long thin cloud covers the view.

—Claryce

Kittens

Some kittens are soft and cuddly.
Some kittens are adventurous.
Some kittens are playful and fun.
Some kittens have stripes and blotches.
The most precious kitten of all
Is my kitten purring to me.

—Patti

Writing the sijo gives children practice in elaborating, sequencing, and comparing. All of these abilities are prerequisite to comprehending when reading what others have written. Besides that, the sijo is a literary form that is easy and pleasurable.

LIMERICK

The pattern: five lines, thirty-four to thirty-nine syllables—rhyming

Line 1: eight or nine syllables— rhyme a
Line 2: eight or nine syllables—rhyme a
Line 3: five or six syllables—rhyme b
Line 4: five or six syllables—rhyme b
Line 5: eight or nine syllables—rhyme a

Usually a limerick follows the syllable pattern of 8-8-5-5-8 or 9-9-6-6-9, but other combinations can be used.

The rhyming scheme requires three words that rhyme and two words that rhyme. It is a triplet split by a couplet. Since limericks are written for fun and nonsense, rhyming words can be created. Some limericks follow.

There was a giraffe from Tobango,
Who wanted to learn how to tango,
But his neck was so long,
That he did it all wrong;
So instead, he learned the fandango.

—Karen

A lad from the city of Troy
Thought that he was quite a strong boy.
He lifted a bale
And let out a wail
That was heard from Troy to Amboy.

—Al

Students who write limericks need collections of rhyming words in the Writing/Publishing Center as well as an attitude for making up words for fun. Writing limericks can create an interest in reading nonsense verse like that written by Edward Lear and Dr. Seuss.

SHAPE PATTERNS

Writing patterns that are designed around shapes have been developed by Iris M. Tiedt (Tiedt and Tiedt, 1967). Among those that bring new style and a dependable form to children's writing are the triangle triplet and the quadrangle.

Margaret

Joanne

TRIANGLE TRIPLET   The pattern: three lines that rhyme

The three lines can be read by beginning at any point of the triangle. The challenge is to say three things on one topic that can be read in any order with essentially the same meaning.

QUADRANGLE   The pattern: four lines, a quatrain

Rhyming schemes can be

a	a	a	a	a	a
a	b	b	b	a	b
a	a	b	a	b	c
a	b	a	c	b	a

The lines are arranged around a quadrangle. They can be read beginning at any corner. The meaning remains essentially the same regardless of where the reading begins. The form requires a great deal of editing unless the author is lucky. This is a useful form for group writing as well as for individual authorship.

RENGA

Renga is a chain of poems written by more than one writer. Two, three, or four writers add to each other's poem. Many combinations and multiple languages are used, such as:

——haiku linked to haiku
——haiku extended to tanka (tanka for two)
——tanka linked to haiku
——tanka linked to tanka
——sijo linked to sijo
——couplets linked to couplets
——quatrains linked to quatrains
——Spanish poems linked to French, linked to English, and so on.

Here is an example of haiku linked to haiku.

Kitten

First Writer: The sleeping kitten
Stretches her body out long
Then curls in a ball.

Second Writer: The waking kitten
Opens her eyes to the world
Then runs to her bowl.

Third Writer: The playful kitten
Leaps on available laps
Then cuddles and purrs.

Here is an example of haika to tanka (or "tanka for two").

Yellow Butterfly

First Writer: Yellow butterfly
Flying through tall seedy grass
Bowing and waving—
Second Writer: Touching each other gently
With an invisible wand.

Here is an example of sijo to sijo.

Zooming in at the Zoo

First Writer: The proud comb is worn very straight.
Piercing black eyes study us.
Peacock walk is stately and slow.
The fine feathers rise and fall
Like a brilliant jeweled fan,
While the neck performs a rhumba.
Second Writer: The gray kangaroo in the zoo
Has perked-up ears on kindly face.
It's turned under from knees on down,
Spreads toes wide when it hops along,
Little legs dangling in front,
Long, strong tail dragging behind.
Third Writer: Tortoise, very, very old,
Lumbers slowly along path.
Black circlets on gnarly legs
Are like small ceramic tiles.
Blackish, brown, and beige shell back
Covered with mosaic patterns.

Here is an example of quatrain to quatrain.

Along the Coast

First Writer: The water's alive with traffic today,
Perhaps 'twill be hard for the fishes to play,
For sailboats and motorboats are sailing the seas—
Some small and some large—doing just as they please.

Second Writer: The water is bursting with waves today.
'Twill be a day for the fishes to play.
Sailboats and motorboats avoid the rough seas.
They let the sea creatures do just as they please.

The renga in the classroom inspires children to contribute to chains of poems with many patterns. Links can be started high on a bulletin board or on a string so that other poets can add to the chain. After a chain of poems has been formed, it can be gathered into a book that is useful in the Reading/Research Center.

Freeing Children to Find New Styles and Forms

The ultimate in understanding style and form is the ability to express one's ideas in multiple ways. Patterned language builds confidence and security, but children must be freed from it and guided to natural ways of saying things in language of literary quality.

Poetry, because of its color, rhythm, and fresh approach to reality or fantasy, has a natural appeal. It frees children of any need to write in ways that are characteristic of their home-rooted language. Instead, they can try out language in ways that are characteristic of the writing of many authors. These writing and reading experiences move children closer and closer to the realization that much, if not most, of their reading is an extension of their own personal language.

When children have many pleasant experiences in hearing poetry and in discussing what it means to them, they are interested in writing creative verses on their own. Class groups compose poems to describe or summarize a common group experience, but the heart and soul of poetry writing is in individual production. Individual compositions may first occur accidentally when young children are dictating their thoughts to the teacher. Simple poems of two lines occur in young children's compositions when their full, free language is used for self-expression.

David, a first-grader, was just beginning to do his own writing when he made an accidental poem:

> The witch was flying and scared the cat
> That was following close behind the bat.

Douglas had never written his ideas in poetic form until he was in the fourth grade. He discovered that he could say things that other children liked very much.

Ant Forest

> The ant forest is big and green.
> To an ant it is a lovely scene.
>
> The dew on the ant trees shines like glass,
> But really their forest is a clump of grass.

Teachers who understand and use poetry help children to extend their style and form through oral and written expression. They encourage children to wonder about things and to ask questions. In a third-grade classroom Cynthia recorded her wonderings in a poem.

Fairyland

> Where is Fairyland?
>
> Over the meadow,
> Or in the stream?
> In the moonlight,
> Or in a dream?
> In a hole,
> Or in a wall?
>
> Or maybe any place at all?

Some children become so interested in poetic forms of expression that they make rhymes for the sake of rhyme making. Michael, a boy in fourth grade, made a poem about writing a poem.

A Poem

I was thinking all the day
About this poem. What would I say?

I thought of an airplane, but that wouldn't do.
Then I thought of something else—a zoo.

Airplanes, cars, boats wouldn't do.
Should I write about monkeys, deer, and things at the zoo?

I thought about that zoo.
I think I'll write a poem about it, that's what I'll do.

I guess this poem took a long time,
But that's how I got this little rhyme.

Most children begin to write their thoughts in poetic forms when they live in a rich environment of poetry. From simple beginnings they want to express more and more of their thoughts and feelings in poetic language like that they have been hearing and reading.

Teachers have a responsibility for bringing into the classroom poetry of many types. Children's interest in poetry is broadened by exposure to varied selections. Their efforts to write their own thoughts in poetic form are increased as they realize that poems are meant to do many things. They come to know that they can read or write a poem

——to paint a picture

The Old House

The house is old and dark
And the trees are like a park.
It is damaged with no care.
Stillness is in the air.
The porch roof sags
And the window shades are just torn rags.
But the house has had its day!
Most things happen this way.

—Douglas, age 10

——to bring laughter with sense and nonsense

The Dogwood Tree

I say, "Did you ever see
Something as odd as a dogwood tree?"
It's green and lacy and white,
And a funny thing—there's not a flea in sight.
It doesn't growl, bite, or scratch,
It's a funny tree you could never match.
It's just green and lacy and white,
And it doesn't have an appetite.
But the funniest thing of all to me
Is, "Why do they call it a DOGWOOD tree?"

—David, age 10

I Want the Truth Now, Goddess Gay!

I was in a plane so high
And I saw a cat come gliding by.
I wore a dress of blue, green,
Yellow, violet, orange and red—
And that cat tore my dress
To colored shreds.
Out the window the pieces flew
And danced in a circle
Up in the blue.
It is the truth!
Up there, see?
That's how the rainbow
Came to be!

—Gay, age 10

——to share a very pleasant thought or deep feeling

Planes

Planes are gliding through the air,
Way out there.
They look at me as if to say,
"Isn't it a lovely day?"

—Paul, age 10

HAIKU SELECTIONS

Low, oh, so low trees
Swaying in the breeze so cool
Shade my cat and me.
                    —Mavany, grade 4

Why is there sunshine?
Why is there rain in winter?
Only God knows why.

                    —Linda, grade 4

—— to tell a story
Randy got an idea from reading a magazine picture story.

A Boy's Dream

I wish I were Shepard, or Grissom or Glenn.
If I were, I'd ride in the sun's fiery den.

I'd feel the great pressure of blastoff and G's,
And all the earth's men looking for me.

The intense sudden blast of power now and then
And I think I might wish I were home again.

Those moments of doubt are now gone away,
Just like an old ship in the sea's mighty sway.

I'd feel the great loneliness way out in space.
Not much like it was back on Earth's green face.

I'd orbit the earth—maybe twenty-two times,
Just like a big clock a-striking its chimes.

When it was all over, I'd fly back home
Like a dog that happened to find a big bone.

Triumphantly with a smile on my face,
Proud as can be to be the first man in space.

                    —Randy, age 12

Literary writing and reading bring together elements of style and form that lift ideas above communication of the common reporting type. It frees children to explore and experiment with language. Fears of being wrong are minimized, and personal thoughts are maximized. The language of authors is valued along with their ideas. Reading joins writing as an artistic endeavor.

Summary of Skills and Abilities for Studying Style and Form

——Interprets literary writing with such elements of voice control as
  ——pause
  ——emphasis
  ——modulation
——Reproduces dialects unlike his or her own
——Substitutes own words in slots in sentence patterns
——Elaborates basic sentences with descriptive words and phrases to denote

color	sound
size	smell
shape	taste
texture	touch

——Chooses correct form when alternatives are presented
——Participates in dictation of a literary form such as a fable or a limerick
——Collects from authors words and phrases that may become a part of personal speech and writing
——Expresses own thinking in patterned forms such as

haiku	limerick
senryu	triangle triplet
tanka	quadrangle
sijo	renga

——Edits manuscripts of patterned poetry for correct form in regard to such requirements as
  ——number of lines
  ——rhyming patterns
  ——syllabication
——Participates in group editing of manuscripts for style and form
——Can identify the noun-verb pattern in sentences

——Uses alliteration as an effective means of expression
——Uses poetry and story forms to express personal ideas that
      ——paint a picture with words
      ——bring laughter with sense and nonsense
      ——share pleasant thoughts and deep feelings
      ——tell real and imaginary stories

Selected References

Applegate, Mauree. *Easy in English.* Harper & Row, Evanston, Ill., 1963.

Burrows, Alvina T., Dianne L. Monson, and Russell G. Stauffer. *New Horizons in the Language Arts.* Harper & Row, New York, 1972.

Carlson, Ruth Learny. *Sparkling Words: Two Hundred Practical and Creative Writing Ideas.* National Council of Teachers of English, Urbana, Ill., 1973.

Durkin, Dolores. *Phonics, Linguistics and Reading.* Teachers College Press, New York, 1972.

Evertts, Eldonna (ed.). *Explorations in Children's Writing.* National Council of Teachers of English, Urbana, Ill., 1970.

Francis, Marjorie. *The Three R's of Language: Releasing Feelings, Reweaving Ideas, Recording Language.* Child Focus Co., Manhattan Beach, Calif., 1971.

Greet, W. Cabell, William A. Jenkins, and Andrew Schiller. *In Other Words: A Beginning Thesaurus.* Scott, Foresman and Co., Glenview, Ill., 1968.

Hall, MaryAnne. *Teaching Reading as a Language Experience.* Charles E. Merrill, Columbus, Ohio, 1970.

Henning, Dorothy G., and Barbara M. Grant. *Content and Craft: Written Expression in the Elementary School.* Prentice-Hall, Englewood Cliffs, N.J., 1973.

Hodges, Richard E., and E. Hugh Rudorf. *Language and Learning to Read.* Houghton Mifflin Co., Boston, 1972.

Lee, Peter H. *Korean Literature: Topics and Themes.* University of Arizona Press, Tucson, 1965.

Logan, Lillian M., and Virgil G. Logan. *Creative Communication: Teaching the Language Arts.* McGraw-Hill Ryerson, Toronto, 1972.

Moffett, James. *A Student-Centered Language Arts Curriculum, Grades K-13: A Handbook for Teachers.* Houghton Mifflin Co., Boston, 1973.

Nixon, Lucile M., and Tomoe Tana. *Sounds of the Unknown: A Collection of Japanese-American Tanka.* The Swallow Press, Denver, 1963.

Paz, Octavio, Jaques Roubaund, Edoardo Sanguineti, and Charles Tomlinson. *Renga, A Chain of Poems.* George Braziller, New York, 1971.

Smith, James A. *Adventures in Communication.* Allyn & Bacon, Boston, 1972.

Tiedt, Iris M., and Sidney W. Tiedt. *Contemporary English in the Elementary School*. Prentice-Hall, Englewood Cliffs, N.J., 1967.

Zuck, Lois V., and Yetta M. Goodman. *Social Class and Regional Dialect: Their Relationship to Reading*. International Reading Association, Newark, Del., 1971.

FROM THE RATIONALE

Studying language structure—pronouncing and understanding words through processes of analysis and synthesis; developing meanings by stringing language sounds into sentences; using affixes to extend meanings of time and number; responding to rhyming and rhythm of language; recognizing the repetition of some syllables in many words; and studying specific topics of structure such as prepositions, use of determiners, pronominal reference, and subject-verb-object relationships.

The essence of a language experience approach in communication is centered on the idea that no child needs a new dialect as a prerequisite for studying language. There is no hint in the approach that, under the guise of phonics, an attempt is made to teach a new dialect that will fit into a predetermined collection of reading materials. Children are not required to develop a new set of speech sounds and a new set of noun and verb endings in order to engage in reading experiences. As is pointed out by Carl A. Lefevre (1970, page 9), ". . . all over the world, adult speakers of diverse English dialects read the sounds of their own speech from standard printed English; dialects of England, New Zealand, and a dozen or so regional dialects of North America."

The student's natural dialect is good enough as a beginning point in an instructional program; but when this premise is accepted by a teacher, there is an obligation on the part of that teacher to understand some general principles and specific details concerning language structure. Each student is expected to discover basic structural elements in his own language and then to contrast and compare them with those of other dialects, especially with those that are contacted through reading experiences.

In this approach any teacher who attacks or appears to attack an individual's dialect is understood to be attacking the person—the family, the language community, and the cultural heritage of the child. Any teacher who attempts to alter through direct instruction or through submission to the learner of materials in a foreign language can inflict irreparable damage to personal language. To do damage is not necessary when it is realized that most children bring to school a personal language which is a prized possession and is necessary for survival in and out of school.

To discover, to understand, to enjoy, to choose change, to respect different dialects, to interact with the ideas and language of printed materials without reproducing the author's sound system—these are goals that teachers in a language experience approach take to a study of language structure.

Dictation Processes

Literacy skills of reading and writing are not prerequisites for introducing elements of language structure when teachers know how to draw upon oracy skills as a basic resource for recording language through processes of dictation. As soon as children can give attention to the writing of what they have just said, they can begin to discover commonalties in language structure—first, among class members and then in printed messages written by other authors. Pleasure from the experience of observing sounds of language recorded in print builds a level of confidence that is necessary for future use of the dictation process to lead children to discover those structures of language common to all language. The dictation experience at any level strengthens three basic language structures that interrelate communication. They are:

> —*phonological structure*—the recognition and study of the sound system of language; how individuals produce streams of sound that others can understand; and how intonation affects meaning
>
> —*syntactical structure*—the recognition and study of arrangements of words to form phrases, clauses, and sentences; how most human beings learn to do this automatically in their native language; and how word order affects meaning
>
> —*morphological structure*—the study of the arrangement and interrelationships of word-building properties of language; and how slight sound signals are recorded to show changes in meaning—inflections and derivations.

Phonological Structure

During the process of presenting dictation, whether in beginning stages or in later stages of development, the sound of the language being written is personal. It is the sound used naturally by the learner. It reflects local dialects and may require special attention for the correct spelling of written forms of language because of the gap between the personal pronunciation of words and the standard spelling of them.

These local dialects or personal forms of pronunciation cannot be dealt with in any text, but they deserve the attention of teachers as long as they may present a problem for children who relate their own sounds to printed forms. Standard spelling is more difficult for some than for others, and each child must come to grips with some of the personal problems involved which may or may not be arrived at through spelling generalizations. The observation of writing from personal sounds accompanied by friendly conversation with an insightful teacher can be a meaningful learning experience that bridges gaps not treated in any text.

To spell it as it sounds may be *right* for some, but it is *wrong* for others. One will say "car," another will say "caa." One will say "father," another will say "fatha." One will say "idea," another will say "idear." Whose speech is right? Fortunately, all are right in the spoken form. It is when that spoken form is written that uniformity is required.

Uniformity of pronunciation is not a valid goal of a language experience approach in communication, but unity of language through uniform spelling is a valid goal. It can be dealt with effectively when processes of dictation are used frequently. The uniform spelling that is achieved is a base requirement for reading skill development.

Phonological structure related to the development of reading skill is clarified and accelerated as children observe and discuss to the point at which they discover

　　—relationships between sounds and letters
　　—roots in words
　　—the derivational affixing system—prefixes and suffixes
　　—the inflectional system—tense, number, and case
　　—the use of punctuation as a substitute for pitch, stress, and juncture
　　—the English sentence in its written forms as a reflection of the English sentence in its spoken forms.

Carla asks children to gather around a series of dictated stories displayed on a wall to talk with the authors and the teacher. In the process she hopes that most of them will discover that many words begin with the same sound. The children find such words, mark them, and then test the generalization by pronouncing them carefully. They discover that most of the words beginning with the same letter also begin with the same sound—but not all. They may discover after a period of time that some words beginning with *a, e, i, o,* and *u,* such as *once, only,* and *out,* have different beginning sounds. The letters *c* and *g* represent at least two different sounds when they are the first letter in words. Other variations may be found to be consistent. The major focus, however, is on the fact that any talk can be represented by the letters of the alphabet.

Dennis watches for sentences that can produce a variety of meanings by changes in voice emphasis. He does this to show that writing is not always a perfect representation of speech. By changing print and punctuation children in his class vary the meanings of sentences.

The dog is dead.

The DOG is dead!

The dog is DEAD?

The dog IS dead!

Syntactical Structure

The ordering of words into sentences, clauses, and phrases is a necessary requirement for effective communication. It is expected when listening. It is practiced when writing. It is the base for the acquisition of language prediction abilities that permit a reader to proceed at speeds faster than speech production.

Listening and speaking processes provide a few clues that are useful in instruction toward language recognition in printed forms. But capitalization and punctuation in writing provide specific clues for automatic and rapid recognition of the flow of language from sentence to sentence.

When children dictate and observe writing of their speech sounds, they acquire an awareness of the place of printed clues and the importance of the place of printed clues that mark syntactical structure. They learn that certain print symbols such as capital letters, punctuation marks, underlining, and paragraphing substitute for the voice control system of speech.

With the professional guidance of a teacher, children develop an awareness of and a sensitivity to characteristics of language that repeat over and over in sentences. They anticipate the name of something when they hear or see in print words that are usually noun markers (*the* or any word that patterns like it, *of* and any word that patterns like it); they get the feeling for and anticipate words of action in sentences that complete the typical noun-verb pattern of English sentences; they anticipate words and phrases of description which modify the meanings of base nouns and verbs; and they observe the writing of many words of structure which have little or no meaning in themselves but which permit the easy flow of speech sounds and give clues that meaning-bearing words are coming.

——When they hear or see words such as *the, this, that, a, my, every*, and *our*, they anticipate the name of something but not of somebody.

——When they hear or see words such as *I, you, he, she, him, her, we, they, your,* and *their,* they know that a meaningful noun has already been said, will be said in the near future, or is implied and understood because of the setting.

——When they hear or see words such as *of, to, in, for, on, at, by, about, up, into, over,* and *down,* they anticipate a noun in a phrase that extends or elaborates the meaning of a noun that is the subject of the sentence.

——When they hear or see words such as *and, or, but, so,* and *because,* they are connecting or contrasting one expressed idea with another—words to words, phrases to phrases, clauses to clauses, and sentences to sentences.

——When they hear or see words such as *what, when, which, how, who,* and *where* as the first words in sentences, they anticipate a question and look for the punctuation mark to confirm their prediction.

——When they hear or see forms of *be* (*is, am, are, was, were, been, being, be*) and *have* (*have, had, has, having*), they get clues of time in sentences.

——When they hear or see words such as *many, some, more, only, very, just,* and *most,* they inflect their voices or intensify their feelings to fit the purpose of the language.

Prior to observing writing with accompanying commentary, some children may not be able to separate their sounds of language into what we call words. They need repeated experiences in observing the letter-by-letter, syllable-by-syllable, word-by-word process of writing what has just been said in order to ferret out understandings of language structure that combine in meaningful sentences of an infinite variety.

Simple sentences are expanded by adding to them answers to questions such as: what kind? where? when? how?

The car stopped.
The racing car stopped.
The racing car stopped in the middle of the track.
The racing car stopped in the middle of the track during the final
    lap of the race.

Suddenly, after three terrifying spins, the racing car stopped in the middle of the track during the final lap of the race.

Meanings are altered by word substitution in stable sentence patterns.

The white cat jumped into my lap.
The *black* cat leaped into my *car*.
The *spotted dog raced* into my *room*.
This sentence structure can remain stable for an infinite number of meanings as form-class words are substituted.

Meanings are controlled by the position of words in sentences.

children   the   teacher   praised   the
What are the sentences?
The children praised the teacher.
The teacher praised the children.

The same word in a different position in a sentence can change the meaning.

The *angry* boy caught the dog.
The boy caught the *angry* dog.

Altering word forms changes meanings in sentences.

Plurals: The boys run after the dog.
              The boy runs after the dogs.
Possessives: The boy's dog was caught.

Morphological Structure

Repeating patterns of sound and of print that convey meaning are evident when dictation processes are in operation. For example, affixes can be noted informally:

——To indicate tense -*ing* or -*ed* are affixed to verbs. Since many dialect groups omit the sounds of the endings when speaking, it is imperative that children studying language have many experiences observing the addition of these syllables in written form. The speech of children from these groups will change slowly, but they can expect to see the correct printed forms immediately and for many years.

——To denote number -*s* and -*es* are common endings. They usually indicate *plural* when affixed to nouns and *present tense singular* when affixed to verbs. As children name things and tell how they move, they will encounter these patterns frequently. Those who do not pronounce them when speaking need many experiences observing the written form and hearing the endings pronounced by a reader.

——Common endings affixed to adjectives are -*er* and -*est*. They are used in comparative situations to describe two or more than two. As with the other common endings many dialect groups omit these in speech. This omission increases the responsibility of teachers to illustrate the complete printed form that children will encounter throughout their reading experience. To pronounce the syllables correctly is not enough for them to know. Understanding the differences in meaning is essential, too.

——Affixed to adverbs -*ly* is a common ending. In the normal processes of presenting dictation, attention will be called to this sound and to the fact that it is used frequently in describing verbs.

The affixing system can be introduced during processes of dictation. Affixes occur in natural speech and can be identified as sounds that are heard at the beginning and at the end of a great many words. Most dialect groups include prefixes in normal speech, but some of them drop sounds that are usually printed as suffixes. Children from these dialect groups profit from the experience of seeing words with the added sound represented because they may not be able to spell some words with derivational endings "like they sound" for a number of years.

It is impossible to deal extensively with the English derivational system because it is very complex for young children. The affixes are much like structure words in that their meanings are abstract. There are so many affixes available to use in thousands of ways that children can only gain an interest in the process and begin to master a few as they present dictation and observe writing. The study may prove fruitful in vocabulary expansion. It provides added interest to procedures emphasizing word recognition and word attack. Once children discover root words that take multiple affixes, they can generate lists, such as:

arm

rearm	armer	armband
armed	firearm	armament
armpit	disarm	arms
unarmed	disarmed	armchair
rearmed	disarming	armor
arming	armory	

Structure with Meaning

A major problem of language instruction, especially the portions designated as beginning reading and corrective reading, is that the meanings of authors do not match the meanings of the learners. Specific language lessons lose their effectiveness—their meaning—because of the mismatch.

Processes of dictation require that teachers use meaningful language passages. They record only the ideas and the language patterns that they hear from the students. The comprehension load of materials developed from this source is *zero* when used for reading; whether or not children can remember words, they can understand that message when someone else reads dictation to them.

The severe problem of the mismatch of language in teaching reading to different dialect groups from the same reading textbooks is eliminated when basic instructional materials are developed from personal language.

In summary, the processes of dictation involve a natural progression from

—*firsthand experience* represented by painting or crayon drawing to—

—*verbalization* or telling of the experience or idea in natural speech patterns to—

—*summarization* or refinement of the verbalization to—

—*observation of the writing act* and listening to an oral description of the processes of spelling, capitalization, punctuation, repetition of sounds, and frequent use of some words to—

——*reconstruction* of the sounds of speech through oral reading.

These dictation processes assure levels of conceptualization of language relationships that are required for significant progress in personal communication. This conceptualization does not occur for many children when someone else's language structure is always used in instruction and when someone else's language is the only important language in school experiences.

When older children dictate and the teacher writes on the chalkboard, the amount of writing is not as significant as the quality of language used and the purpose for taking dictation. Some children are unable to do their own writing. Others are reluctant to do it. Still others are willing to dictate for the sheer pleasure of observing their talk written down. From the teacher's point of view, the process of recording the language of one child while others observe is a base from which to review again and again such language skills as

——basic phoneme-grapheme relationships

——spelling generalizations

——exceptions to generally observed rules of grammar

——sentence structure

——modification techniques

——capitalization

——punctuation

——tense as reflected in the common endings of verbs.

Follow-up seminars give repeated practice in going over original manuscripts to look for ways of improving and editing them for publication. They illustrate the kind of treatment that can reasonably be expected when a child presents a manuscript to the teacher or to an editorial committee for reading and correction prior to publication. These seminars furnish editorial committee members ideas for their work when reviewing manuscripts of children.

Concepts for Refining Language—Usage, Grammar, Mechanics

The abilities required to use the structure of one's language effectively are important in helping individuals to get some kind of order out of their thoughts, in aiding others to interpret speaking and writing, and in reconstructing the ideas and the language of others through reading. The oral communications program is a major contributor to these abilities. The written communication program adds a level of refinement not characteristic of speech. The reading program reinforces and influences the use of language in new and creative ways. It provides easy access to the variety of sentence structures that enables an individual to communicate effectively in spontaneous ways.

Most children, by the time they start school, use all the basic language patterns common to good English speech. They use the simple sentence, the complex sentence, the compound sentence, and modifiers of all descriptions. In the relatively short period of five or six years, children learn this complicated language process with surprising facility for a number of reasons.

——They have been free to imitate what they hear.

——They have been encouraged to try to say new things—to experiment.

——They have received adult praise and approval for what they have said.

——They have found that they can secure many of the things they want by using language.

These same factors should continue to operate in the elementary grades at school. In addition, children should be helped to learn to write their thoughts and use language in its written form to achieve additional goals, such as:

——communicating with persons who are not present—letter writing

——keeping records of school activities

——communicating with the teacher—reports, tests

——recording personal thoughts and ideas

——taking notes on readings and class discussions

——securing things they want and need.

Of equal importance in the school program is contact with the language of many other people through listening and reading. It is in the setting of listening and reading that they can

——hear new words that they want to remember and use

——hear old words used in new ways

——observe the use of capitalization and punctuation by a variety of authors

——form generalizations about sentences and paragraphs

——learn to communicate silently with a person not present.

The abilities required to understand language structure in settings of talking, writing, and reading are usually described as usage, grammar, and mechanics of written language.

All of these function together in actual practice, but for planning a school program, they are usually separated for descriptive purposes.

Usage

Usage may be approached from the viewpoint of mere correctness or from the viewpoint of ways available to help a child achieve clear, accurate, and vivid expression. Correctness is important, but it cannot stand alone in teaching communicating abilities. Usage becomes good as children add to *correctness* an element of *brightness* that helps them select sparkling words and phrases and use exact words and sentences to say what needs to be said as economically and clearly as possible. Creative writing can furnish continuous opportunity for the exploration of methods of using language in personal ways but with conventional restraints enough for others to communicate with the author. Reading seminars that focus on usage in poems and stories, rather than on word recognition and comprehension, can influence children to try new ways of writing and to edit their personal writing toward making it readable.

Malcolm watches for clever and creative expressions in writing by members of his class. Periodically he writes some of the collected items on the chalkboard and invites class members to say the same thoughts in different ways. These discussions offer him an opportunity to teach directly some elements of language usage that could not be taught through procedures of correcting papers.

He will read a sentence, paragraph, or poem. Then he will set a condition for response.

——Say the same thing to a grandparent, to a good friend, to a small child, or to someone else.

——Translate the idea into comic strip language.

——Change a statement into a question or a question into a statement.

——Alter the meaning with voice inflection and emphasis.

Teresa uses basic readers with the six-year-olds she teaches. Their reading material has a minimum number of descriptive words in it. She asks the children to add appropriate descriptive words to printed material such as:

Rex jumped over the fence.
Add a size word.
Rex jumped over the *high* fence.
Add a color word.
Rex jumped over the *high white* fence.

With young children Teresa is increasing the quality of language without adding to the word-recognition requirements.

It is only as children are free from the restraints inherent in re-working other people's language that they begin to feel the personal need for economy and clarity of expression. Correctness of expression may be enhanced when children are asked to retell a story, to summarize, to answer specific questions, to outline, and to fill in blanks, but these abilities do not insure good usage when writers are expressing their own ideas. When individuals have experience in expressing themselves in their own way, the problems of usage become real. They seek improvement that permits them to use variety in their expression.

Myrna knows that her children have a difficult time getting started with stories. They usually settle for "Once upon a time . . ." Rather than teach directly, she has a card file of story beginnings in the Writing/Publishing Center. These are phrases and sentences that she has copied from various sources. Children can flip through them and find effective beginnings for their stories. A few are:

It was a cold, dark night when . . .
Nancy and Sue couldn't believe what they were seeing . . .
After a long wait . . .
A loud noise broke the long silence.
WOW! The time had come!

Language usage seldom improves without the influence of instruction; yet instruction in skills does not assure improvement. You do not get skills by leaving all other aspects of instruction out. Levels of awareness of acceptable usage can be raised when teachers follow a few guidelines.

1. Improved usage is essentially a problem of enlarging and refining vocabulary so that the speaker or writer has alternatives from which to choose.
2. Correctness is not the end of language instruction. Willingness to

participate in useful language activities is far more important. Productive language can be refined, but one cannot refine that which does not exist.

3. The English language is changing. Some traditionally objectionable forms of expression are now acceptable.

4. Language is a living, growing instrument of communication. It must remain flexible and adaptable to a variety of life situations. Every human being needs a "wardrobe of languages" to meet the demands of changing relationships.

5. Standards of acceptable usage vary with communities and with pupils having different capacities. Efforts of teachers to raise the children's levels of usage far above the standards of the community or above individual capacity are usually futile and may be harmful.

6. The usage program should concentrate on a relatively few serious errors, which ones determined in part by the standards prevailing in the community and in part by the basic requirements for success in writing and reading.

7. Improvement of usage requires much oral work. Correct forms of expression must be repeated sufficiently to cause the correct form to sound right.

Grammar

The matter of what to do about teaching grammar in the elementary grades has concerned teachers for a long time. Differing points of view belong to

——those who are convinced from teaching experience and research findings that the teaching of grammar as a systematized body of information does little or nothing to improve the actual usage of young people

——those who insist on grammar as an organized body of knowledge that children must learn in a logical sequence. They continue to measure children's knowledge of grammar in terms of what they know about grammar rules rather than in terms of how well they use it

——those who have devised means of teaching grammar in situations in which grammar really means something to boys and girls.

Some children come to school using good colloquial speech. There are always some, especially in the upper grades, who know good speech but do not practice it. Another group is made up of those children who have had no experience with good speech outside of the school and have little inner drive to acquire it. The children in both groups need many types of social experiences and a highly functional approach to a language environment. Usually these experiences must be geared to improved speech before improved written expression can follow as a natural part of the child's expression.

The following guides should be observed by the teacher in working with children on matters of grammar.

1. The study of grammar is functional when it is derived from a study of errors in usage. It includes training in principles and definitions that may help pupils with difficulties of expression and in the correction of errors.

CLUES FOR INSTRUCTION

Editing procedures connected with publishing a newspaper, a magazine, or a class book furnish raw material for dealing with functional grammar. Children can be helped to use language textbooks and writing handbooks to extend their understandings of needed changes that they recognize from the sound of the sentence. Editors prepare for conferences with authors by knowing the reasons why changes are suggested.

2. In the process of building sentences and paragraphs to express ideas clearly, children notice change of meaning with change of form and position of words, learn how meaning is affected by change in position of various parts of a sentence, and discover classes of words.

CLUES FOR INSTRUCTION

Browse through a dictionary and make lists of words that have many meanings. Choose a number such as fifteen, twenty-five, or fifty to be the number of words required for the list. Some words that will appear are *act, bank, cast, air, block,* and *check.*

Choose one or more of the words for a bulletin board display. Invite class members to contribute sentences using a word as a noun, as a verb, or as a descriptive word. Suffixes may be allowed. This activity proves that it is the position of the word in the sentence that determines its class—not the word itself.

3. The definitions and principles to be developed in the grammar part of the language program are those related to clear thinking and clear expression. They include:

——use of a simple sentence in the expression of a complete thought

——the relationships involved in the expression of a series of closely related ideas in a compound sentence

——the principles underlying the expression of dependent ideas in a complex sentence

——recognition and understanding of the classes of words, such as how adverbs and adjectives add vividness and color to expression.

CLUES FOR INSTRUCTION

Begin with a two-word sentence that illustrates the simple noun-verb pattern (NV).

Birds sing.

Add an auxiliary.

Birds *can* sing.

Add a determiner.

The birds can sing.

Add an adverb.

The birds can sing *noisily*.

Continue to expand.

The *flock of* birds *in our back yard* can sing noisily *when they think it is time for their breakfast.*

Children can write stories using simple sentences. They exchange papers. The first reader tries to add an adjective to each sentence. The second reader tries to add a prepositional phrase. The third reader adds adverbials where appropriate. The fourth reader makes a compound or a complex sentence to improve the effect of the language. The story then comes back to the original author for oral reading to the group.

This same procedure can be used with stories written by younger children and expanded by older children in the school.

4. Grammar work in any of its details is neither concentrated in any grade nor is it presented in isolated lessons. It represents the building of a body of concepts that begin to take form in preschool years and develop gradually through the grades with the pupil's increasing maturity and expanding needs for detailed and clear communication.

CLUES FOR INSTRUCTION

As preparation for reading a story orally, let students skim through it first. One student after another reads aloud only the words that are in the position of nouns in the sentences. Next the children go through and in turn read the words in the position of verbs. Another variation is to read prepositional phrases.

This activity will focus attention on words that are basic to sentence structure and will clarify the difference in the use of a word as a noun and as a verb. Readers will begin to realize that the noun-verb combination carries the bulk of meaning in passages.

5. Formal grammar is not needed by children nor by average adults to carry on their vocational and personal lives. It is the professional tool of the editor, the copyeditor, and the linguistic specialist.

CLUES FOR INSTRUCTION

Plan an ongoing program of publishing that requires skilled editing. Rotate assignments on editorial committees so that every child can participate in a variety of editorial responsibilities during a school year. Plan time for seminars designed to improve editorial skills for the publishing program.

6. The goal of grammar instruction in the elementary school is to help each child to participate with others in all types of activities without being conspicuous and without having to give thought to his or her use of language.

CLUES FOR INSTRUCTION

Emphasize writing as a recreational activity for children. Encourage them to write with personal language. Edit this language only if it is to be used in some published form.

Provide models of several literary forms that children can use in recording their thoughts without having to rely on their natural grammar. Limericks, riddles, couplets, Oriental forms, cinquains, and other forms are helpful.

Mechanics of Written Expression

Punctuation is a matter of courtesy to the reader in making meanings clear. Modern writers take a great deal of liberty with punctuation and capitalization, but there are certain standard forms that all children should know. The beginning understandings of these forms should be taught to children as they become aware of needs for help in making their own writing meaningful to the reader.

The following list is one that teachers can use as a guide for teaching punctuation. The list does not represent a sequence for teaching skills in punctuation, but it suggests the areas of punctuation that children should be familiar with as they mature in creative written expression.

1. Use of a period
   ——at the ends of declarative sentences
   ——after initials and common abbreviations
   ——after letters and figures prefixed to points in outlines
   ——after numerals in lists of words or sentences
2. Use of a question mark following a question
3. Use of a comma
   ——between day of month and year
   ——between name of city and state
   ——after salutation and complimentary close of a personal letter
   ——to replace *and* in a series of words, phrases, and clauses
   ——to separate a direct quotation from the rest of the sentence
   ——following *yes* and *no*
   ——to set off the name of the person addressed
4. Use of an exclamation mark after expressions reflecting strong feeling
5. Use of quotation marks
   ——around direct quotations
   ——around titles of stories and poems; around titles of books and magazines if underlining is not used
6. Use of a hyphen to separate parts of a word split at the end of a line
7. Use of an apostrophe
   ——in common contractions
   ——in possessives
8. Use of a colon after the salutation of a business letter

Capitalization, along with punctuation, is a matter of courtesy to help make meanings clear to the reader. There is some option in the use of capitalization, but there are also some standards of use that children should be accustomed to in their written expression. The following is a list of recommended items that should be included in instruction. They do not represent a teaching sequence.

1. Capitalization of the first word of a
   ——sentence
   ——line of some poetry
   ——direct quotation

2. Capitalization of the important words in a title
3. Capitalization of names or titles of particular
   ——places: schools, streets, cities, states, nations, and important geographic localities
   ——days of week, months, and special days
   ——persons and pets
   ——initials and abbreviations of proper names
   ——organizations
   ——races, nationalities, and school subjects
   ——companies and firms
   ——brands and special products
4. Capitalization of
   ——the pronoun *I*
   ——topics of an outline
   ——the first and each important word in titles of books, pictures, magazine articles, and the like

CLUES FOR INSTRUCTION

Prepare passages with no punctuation and capitalization. Include some passages with direct quotations. Project the passages on the chalkboard, using an overhead projector, and let students supply the mechanics that clarify meaning and increase ease of reading.

Activities for Refining Language Structure

Usage, grammar, and matters of mechanics grow first in speech. It is reasonable to believe, then, that activities that extend and refine language should be related to speech. Some that are available for classroom groups to use over and over to practice the sounds of language prior to writing and reading are:
   ——dramatization of all sorts
   ——puppet shows
   ——choral reading
   ——listening to recordings
   ——listening to and viewing sound motion pictures
   ——singing songs
   ——listening to stories and poems and joining in by saying lines and phrases that repeat over and over.
Children who engage in speech-related activities learn how to control meaning through intonation. In turn they learn how to use punc-

tuation in writing to represent some of that control. They form a basis for choosing the correct order of letters to spell words that have regular phoneme-grapheme relationships. They learn to imitate and use a variety of dialects in speech and to recognize them when reading. They feel their own worth because they know something of how language works for them.

Summary of Skills and Abilities for Studying Language Structure

USAGE

——Develops standards of correct usage as needed and attempts to meet them in the following ways:
    ——increases skill in using correct forms of verbs
    ——names self last (John and I)
    ——avoids double negatives
    ——uses comparative forms of adjectives correctly
——Uses correctly:
    ——subject-verb agreement
    ——forms of pronouns for subject and object
    ——possessive pronoun forms
    ——personal pronoun forms in compound subjects, objects, and predicate pronouns
    ——agreement of pronoun with noun and pronoun antecedents
    ——objective form after an infinitive

GRAMMAR

——Develops an understanding of grammar as "the orderly description of what is said by certain groups of people"
——Begins to recognize and to write sentences
——Realizes that a sentence tells or asks something
——Recognizes the kinds of sentences:
    ——statement
    ——question
    ——command
    ——exclamation
——Develops an understanding of the sentence as a structural unit

——Develops an understanding of the functions of various parts of a sentence

——Develops an understanding of the functions of words that modify and of words that connect

——Develops an understanding of:

——simple sentences

——compound sentences

——complex sentences

——clauses

——Uses correctly regular and irregular verbs

PUNCTUATION

——Develops an understanding that the organization of the sentence, which is indicated in speaking by pauses, inflections, and gestures, is indicated in writing by punctuation marks

——Develops skill in using the period:

——at the end of a sentence

——after abbreviations

——after initials

——after numbers in a list

——Develops skill in using the question mark

——Develops skill in using the comma:

——in copied material

——in dates, addresses, and between city and state

——after the greeting and closing of a personal letter

——to separate parts of a compound sentence

——with items in series

——with an appositive

——after an introductory adverbial clause

——Develops skill in using quotation marks:

——in copied material

——before and after direct quotations

——in more complex quotations

——Develops skill in using the apostrophe:

——in contractions and possessive singular

——in possessive plural

——Develops skill in using the exclamation point

——Develops skill in using the colon:

——after the greeting of a business letter

——in writing time (6:10 P.M.)

——Develops skill in using the hyphen:

——to break words
——to separate parts of compound words
——Develops skill in using the semicolon
——Develops the ability to prepare accurate and attractive written material
——Uses appropriate placement of:
——margins
——titles
——signatures
——indentions
——Checks own work for accuracy
——Proofreads and edits

CAPITALIZATION

——Develops skill in using capital letters to begin:
——own name, names of streets, school, town, and nations
——first word in sentences
——for *I*, *Mr.*, *Ms.*, *Mrs.*, and other words as needed
——proper names, abbreviations of proper names, and titles
——greeting and closing of letters
——first word in the line of some verse
——topics in an outline
——quotations
——key words in the names of organizations
——proper adjectives and regions of a country

Selected References

Applegate, Mauree. *Easy in English*. Harper & Row, New York, 1963.

Carroll, John B. *The Study of Language: A Survey of Linguistics and Related Disciplines in America*. Harvard University Press, Cambridge, Mass., 1953.

Durkin, Dolores. *Phonics, Linguistics and Reading*. Teachers College Press, New York, 1972.

Eisenhardt, Catheryn. *Applying Linguistics in the Teaching of Reading and the Language Arts*. Charles E. Merrill, Columbus, Ohio, 1972.

Fries, Charles G. *Linguistics and Reading*. Holt, Rinehart and Winston, New York, 1962.

Greene, Harry A., and Walter T. Petty. *Developing Language Skills in the Elementary School*. Allyn & Bacon, Boston, 1971.

Gudschinsky, Sarah C. "The Nature of the Writing System: Pedagogical Implications." In *Language and Learning to Read: What Teachers Should Know*

About Language, edited by Richard E. Hodges and E. Hugh Rudorf. Houghton Mifflin Co., Boston, 1972.

Hayakawa, S. I. *Symbol, Status and Personality.* Harcourt, Brace & World, New York, 1963.

Kavanagh, James F. (ed.). *Communicating by Language: The Reading Process.* U.S. Department of Health, Education, and Welfare, National Institute of Child Health and Human Development, Bethesda, Md., 1968.

Lamberts, J. J. *A Short Introduction to English Usage.* McGraw-Hill Book Co., New York, 1972.

Lefevre, Carl A. *Linguistics, English and the Language Arts.* Allyn & Bacon, Boston, 1970.

Menyuk, Paula. *Sentences Children Use.* The M.I.T. Press, Cambridge, Mass., 1969.

Moffett, James. *A Student-Centered Language Arts Curriculum, Grades K-13: A Handbook for Teachers.* Houghton Mifflin Co., Boston, 1973.

Newman, Harold. *Effective Language Practices in the Elementary School.* John Wiley & Sons, New York, 1972.

Smith, Frank, and George A. Miller. *The Genesis of Language: A Psycholinguistic Approach.* The M.I.T. Press, Cambridge, Mass., 1971.

Strickland, Ruth G. *The Language Arts in the Elementary School.* D. C. Heath and Co., Boston, 1951.

Tiedt, Iris M., and Sidney W. Tiedt. *Contemporary English in the Elementary School.* Prentice-Hall, Englewood Cliffs, N.J., 1967.

Zuck, Lois V., and Yetta M. Goodman. *Social Class and Regional Dialect: Their Relationship to Reading.* International Reading Association, Newark, Del., 1971.

Reading nonalphabetic symbol systems—responding to a primary reading of the environment through such elements as weather, plants, human emotions, color, texture, size, shape, taste, and smell; and responding to the meanings of symbol systems that are not represented by the alphabet through such media as clocks, dials, maps, graphs, and numerals.

Reading that is not dependent on alphabetic symbols is as important as that which is, but nonalphabetic reading is usually treated so casually and informally that children do not recognize it as a form of reading. All children who enter our schools have had reading experiences of many types that did not require any sound-symbol relationships with our alphabetic system of representing language sounds. Some of the reading has been with numerals, but most of it has been with symbols that are much less concrete. They have read such things as the faces of people, the time of day, weather, plants, texture, taste, smell, color, size, shape, feeling, sound, and action.

These life experiences are the very foundation of thinking according to the Piagetian theory (Piaget, 1959). This theory purports that spontaneous curiosity can be deadened or hindered in certain environments in which children grow. It must be revived and nourished if children are to reach an operational level that includes print reading. In *Piaget for Teachers,* Hans G. Furth (1970, page 4) summarizes much of what Piaget has to say.

Assuming that many children who come to school are intellectually impoverished but still have enough internal motivation to grow intellectually—as is shown by the fact that their intellects will continue to grow with or without school—what, in effect, is the school offering the child? This is the message that he gets: "Forget your intellect for a while, come and learn to read and write; in five to seven years' time, if you are successful, your reading will catch up with the capacity of your intellect, which you are developing in spite of what we offer you." Mark well these twin conditions: learn reading and forget your intellect. These things go hand in hand. . . .

Reading, like any specialized learning, presupposes a motivation primarily of a different sort from the motivation underlying the child's capacity to think.

Some clarification of the dilemma suggested by Furth is available for language experience approach teachers through a definition of *primary reading abilities* as the term is used at the Claremont College Reading Conference by Peter M. Spencer (1970, page 16).

The process of reading things in the concrete is identified in our conference as *primary reading.* It is primary in the sense that it must precede the reading of symbols for re-presenting things, and it is also primary in the sense that it is fundamental to the giving of meaning and significance to the reading of symbols. Symbols may be likened to maps for ideas but symbols are definitely not ideas. In order for symbols to be effective for mapping ideas and for their expression and communication, it is essential that the symbols and symbol patterns be given ideational meaning by both the one who writes them and by the one who reads them. That which is symbolized must have its origin in direct experiencing. . . .

We must provide for and make use of primary reading both as a way of behavior and as the source of meaning and of judgments of significance. Word symbols are impotent to supply these. Consequently, a program for reading development which is concerned only with skills of word recognition and the analysis of word patterns is inadequate.

Most children need to feel a sense of accomplishment in being able to "read" in their environment and from their experiences. They need to understand through repeated emphasis that most of their life experiences require the reading of primary sources and that some of them require the reading of secondary sources—the reading of printed materials (Spencer, 1970).

Primary sources are among the nonalphabetic reading that children encounter normally and naturally. These sources include the reading of numerals in many forms and in many places such as clocks, dials, and price tags. They include the reading of maps and graphs and also the reading of meaning into photographs and paintings.

All children need to experience primary reading as a part of school programs, but it is essential that children who are slow to read the language represented by alphabetic symbols have repeated opportunities to do so. The reading must be a recognized part of the school program. It must be important enough in day-by-day operations for children to feel a sense of reading achievement when they participate in the activities. Teachers must feel that primary reading sources are major sources for language acquisition. They must experience over and over the fact that language grown from primary sources is useful later in lessons and activities requiring the reproduction of language represented by the alphabet.

Reading Nature's Signals

All children who enter school have had experiences reading signals in their natural environment (Lee and Allen, 1963). Some of them follow.

Weather: Is it hot or cold?
Is it wet or dry?
Is it windy or calm?
Is it cloudy or clear?

Plants:	Are they alive or dead?
	Are they large or small?
	Are they green or brown?
	Are they for shade or food?
Animals:	Do they have fur or feathers?
	Are they domestic or wild?
	Do they hop, run, or fly?
	Do they communicate with people?
Water:	Is it running or still?
	Is it dirty or clean?
	Is it liquid or frozen?
Air:	Is it clear or polluted?
	Is it moving or still?
	Is it warm or cold?
Earth:	Is it wet or dry?
	Is it rocky or sandy?
	Is it farmed or forested?
	Is it ancient or young?

Most experiences in life have a relationship to the reading process. They give meaning to reading. Even though these experiences increase interest in reading and create a need to read printed materials, children in most schools have been made to feel that the reading of print is the important thing for them to learn. They are usually willing to do the things necessary to learn the skills associated with reading and do not complain that they are denied primary reading experiences. In a language experience approach the reading of nature's signals is as basic to the learning process as the reading of print is.

Children who view their world and respond to it through writing in literary forms such as the haiku, tanka, and sijo must be able to read nature's signals and must possess the necessary vocabularies to translate their experiences into communication units that share their feelings with others.

Children encounter references to nature in literary selections so frequently that a knowledge of nature from experience is required for a high level of comprehension. Fortunately, the things of nature are available to all. Travel may be required for extended experiences, but the most basic experiences are local to all and need only to be recognized as a major source for language acquisition that relates directly to print reading.

Dori uses weather as a continuing topic to expand vocabulary and increase interest in reading. Frequently as she reads aloud, she asks the children to listen for the first weather word the author uses. Through this emphasis she leads them to generalize that words that tell about the weather are used frequently by authors. From this experience the children collect weather words for the Writing/Publishing Center and use them to improve their own writing.

She translates the interest in weather into reading by asking children as they report on the day's weather to tell about the weather in other places. They listen to television and radio reports, use weather maps from the newspapers, and watch for news articles that relate directly to weather. Many children with limited interest in reading the usual stories in the school reading curriculum find that they can and that they want to read newspaper accounts and watch television coverage of weather.

Bonita uses the sky as a continuing emphasis in art. She invites children to observe the sky day after day and to try to portray it in its many colors and moods: blue with white, fleecy clouds, dark with rain clouds, lightning flashing from a huge cloud, and a rainbow bending across the sky.

She asks them to remember the sky at times when they are not at school: sunrise with a pink glow, sunset with many different colors, a full moon in a night sky, and a black sky with sparkling light from the stars.

The children make captions for their sky pictures. These include appropriate words of color, size, mood, and movement. They read nature's signals as they increase their vocabularies in meaningful ways.

Bea collects leaves from trees, shrubs, and weeds around the school. She gives one leaf to each child. The child records the name of the plant from which the leaf might have come and draws a picture of that plant. After talking about characteristics that help in identification such as shape, texture, color, and size, the class goes on a "detective hunt" to match each leaf to its plant. There is excitement in finding matching leaves. There is also increased interest in noting the names of plants in the neighborhood and in giving close attention to the characteristics that distinguish them. Visual discrimination is being exercised.

Bea feels that the reading of nature's signals builds a firm base for the study of likenesses and differences in sounds, in words, in letter formations, and in other features that appear consistently when one is engaged in reading print.

Reading Sensory Impressions

Sensory impressions provide a bulk of information from experience that is useful in recalling and applying meaning when reading printed material. Basic to the whole idea of a language experience approach in reading is the notion that reading of print is accelerated by the continuous experience of communicating in many ways what one sees, hears, touches, tastes, and smells. The sound-symbol relationships required for efficient reading are believed to be strengthened through the active involvement of every learner in verbalizing sensory impressions apart from the printed symbols used to record the words of those impressions.

Stephen projects filmstrips with no captions to increase the use of the vocabulary of the senses. He shows the filmstrip once with no comment. During the second showing, children talk in groups of two or more about what they see and feel in connection with each frame. They are encouraged to extend their imaginations to possible sounds and smells; they talk about the texture of things they see; they talk about the taste of things. If there are characters in the filmstrip, children can follow up with a group story or individual stories that include every frame. The emphasis on a sensory response usually results in talking and writing that includes words of the senses.

Sight

Color, size, and shape are among the impressions gained through sight. Sensory impressions are areas of experience for which there are unlimited variations. They are critical to communication in the arts and sciences. Thousands of words have been generated in order to make fine distinctions and to record accurate observations about them. Most of us read these characteristics into life experiences hundreds of times each day. Yet some children come to school with so little oral vocabulary in these areas of description that to teach them to read printed materials that record the sensory impressions of others seems futile. Nonalphabetic reading *must precede* relating the sounds of words to the alphabetic recording of those words.

Narcine has a collection of photographs and paintings on the same or similar subjects. She includes animals, people, houses, mountains, trees, automobiles, and landscapes. Some are very realistic; others are abstract or give only a faint impression. Some are in full color, and others are black and white. Some may be answers to questions in the mind of the viewer; some may seem to ask questions of the viewer.

Each set of pictures is used to stimulate discussion about how each of us views the world in unique and individual ways. According to how we see things, we respond with words that tell the color, size, shape, and relationship of objects or ideas. In order to communicate impressions, many words of the senses are required. Narcine listens and records words used by the children. The lists go into the Writing/Publishing Center for use during creative writing and into the Game Center as resources for making word games that give practice in sight recognition and spelling.

Color, size, and shape concepts are fruitful in developing figurative language because many of the words and ideas are so common that new and uncommon ideas can be initiated through comparisons. Some of these ideas are illustrated by:

as green as new grass
cardinal red
small as a tiny ant
larger than an elephant
an X-shaped design
pointed like a pyramid

Diane provides practice in the concept of size by helping children to arrange objects according to size—books, rocks, blocks, and other objects. Children choose one set of objects and then arrange it from the smallest to the largest. As they talk, they gain practice in seeing the size of things in relation to the size of others. Some of her arrangements call for the use of words such as *small, large, short, tall, long, wide,* and *narrow.*

Jean makes a collection of blank books of a variety of shapes for her kindergarten class. The children cut out pictures of things with different shapes and paste them in the books. From time to time they talk about the different shapes of things as they look at the collection of pictures and read the printed titles of the books.

Bruce takes his class of children on shape walks. For each walk they choose one shape such as *egg shaped*. As they walk around the classroom, around the school, and around the neighborhood, they look for anything with that shape. After a few experiences like this, the children arrive at a generalization that everything they can see has some shape or a collection of shapes. This creates an interest in expanding vocabularies of shape words for the Word Wall and for the Writing/Publishing Center.

Sound

Talking is the making and blending of sounds into meaningful communicating units. Without the sense of sound there would be no language communication. Talking, listening, writing, and reading are so closely associated that if is difficult to understand how some educators amputate reading from talking and writing in order to make it a more important fact in school experiences than the other three. In a language experience approach, reading of print is believed to be a natural result of understanding the relationships of the sounds of language (talking and listening) to the alphabetic recording of the sounds (writing).

Prior to and during the reading of print, children need opportunities to expand and refine their awareness of sounds and to talk of the sensory impressions that are derived from sounds.

Doris teaches first grade in a community where children's awareness of sounds needs a great deal of refinement prior to the time she introduces and uses the phonics program required by the district administration. Some of the things she does to develop sensory impressions and build a meaningful vocabulary to use in talking about sound are:

——to sing songs in unison to give children confidence in sounding words they have never said before

——to imitate sounds of machines, animals, and people doing things

——to tell and read stories with voice changes to represent different characters and moods which children can then imitate by responding to the model

——to listen for rhyming words in rhymes and poems and repeat them

——to play rhythm instruments and talk about the sounds they make such as *scraping, harsh, high, low, clear, jingling, clinking,* and *muffled.*

——to listen for sounds in the environment and name them as the class takes listening walks

——to listen for words that begin with the same sound and to observe the position of the speaker's lips, teeth, and tongue as she or he repeats the first sound of the words.

Eleanor teaches fifth grade in a school that produces many reading failures. The worst failures at the end of fourth grade are grouped in her classroom.

She removes the source of failure in the beginning by removing all printed material. Among the nonprint materials and equipment in the classroom is a collection of instruments that have a scale—piano, autoharp, and tone bells. She works with the children informally and then formally to build confidence in distinguishing such characteristics of sound as high-low, soft-loud, fast-slow, and unpleasant-pleasant. She says a line from a poem, and a child plays it on tone bells. She beats a rhythm, and a child reproduces it on the piano. She teaches a short poem for choral reading and then lets different children accompany the recitation on the autoharp.

Eleanor makes a sound such as a long sound for *o* at a selected point on the piano scale. She then changes to a short sound of *o,* and children try to find the note that registers that sound. She inventories their abilities to distinguish sounds at the half-step level (white to black notes). This is the level of auditory discrimination required to distinguish the *longness* from the *shortness* of the same vowel. It is only then that she begins to introduce relationships of sound to print. The children are interested. New attitudes toward reading are developed. Necessary skills have been plugged in.

Smell

Sensory impressions relating to smell are not as critical in building language meaning for reading as are some of the others, but they are a part of life experiences and include a vocabulary that is repeated over and over.

The vocabulary of smell is available in many places and for all children. Flowers and food have odors that may be familiar to many children, but they may not have words to communicate what they smell.

Marcia includes a vocabulary of smell words in her efforts to introduce children in her second grade to the vocabularies of sensory experiences. Among the things she does to provide real experiences with smell are:

——to make a collection of spice cards by brushing glue on cards and sprinkling some spice on them so that children can pass the cards around and talk about the odors

——to prepare foods, such as applesauce, chile con carne, and gingerbread, with spice in them so that children can taste things with and without the spice

——to make available toilet articles, such as toothpaste, cold cream, soap, cologne, perfume, shaving cream, and after-shave lotion, for children to smell and name the odors

——to dramatize different smell words with facial expressions

——to cook things, such as popcorn, that change odor in the process so that children can smell them before and after cooking.

Thurman has a study each year on advertisements that smell. He encourages children to watch on television and in newspapers for advertisements that have something to do with how something or somebody smells. Children find out that much of selling has to do with the odor of things. When natural odors are not pleasant, ingredients are added to make things more appealing. Children recognize the importance of knowing the meanings of words that have to do with smell.

Taste

Sensory impressions from tasting experiences occur daily, but they do not assure the acquisition of a vocabulary of words of taste that might be encountered in reading. These words can be acquired through classroom activities.

Mary Alice has a Cooking Center in her classroom; it is an integral part of the language development program. Although she teaches some social skills as a result of the cooking activities, her major purposes are centered around language growth.

Language of all the senses is inherent in cooking and eating, but the language of taste is seldom experienced for instructional purposes apart from Cooking Center activities. Some of the ways in which Mary Alice works to develop vocabulary are:

——to maintain a sweet-and-sour chart on which children list words to describe the sweetness or sourness of foods they taste

——to taste foods before and after cooking to compare and contrast taste

——to taste the same food in many forms such as apples—raw, applesauce, apple juice, apple jelly, and apple vinegar

——to have taste talks after school lunches to gather new words for the list of taste words for the Writing/Publishing Center or Word Wall—delicious, pleasant, yummy, tart, and bitter

——to listen for words that tell about taste during the reading of stories and poems.

Walter teaches sixth grade in a school that produces a whole class of reading failures by sixth grade. Walter requested work with the group because he believes that through real experiences he can bring most of the students to a new awareness of the relationships between talk and writing and reading.

Walter's garden is a focal point for real experiences. The garden is adjacent to the classroom and is very much a part of the reading program. He has prepared a basic vocabulary of terms about soil, water, sunlight, cultivation, and harvest. There is the pleasant experience of preparing and eating the fruits of labor from the garden. All senses are involved in cooking the vegetables from the garden, but the preparation, cooking, and eating time is the best time for the vocabulary of taste words to be generated for class study.

What Walter discovers year after year is that the majority of the reading failures can read widely from primary sources and that most of them can read some printed materials. They lack confidence, sensory vocabulary, and a sense of the relationship between personal language and reading. The majority of them are extremely limited in self-expression through writing. In his own way Walter helps them to see the beauty in a young plant, to anticipate its growth, to value its productivity, and to taste its fruits. These experiences, when properly guided, move most of the children close to reading of the experiences of others as recorded in books.

Touch

Our fingers can tell us as much about our surroundings as our eyes do. There is magic in the sense of touch that can release vocabulary useful in responding to sensory impressions throughout life. Vocabulary relating to the sense of touch is found throughout literature to the extent that a person lacking that vocabulary is at a disadvantage in responding to the meanings intended by authors.

Paula helps children to relate the vocabulary of how things feel to everyday life. As they experience the sense of touch and exchange words to describe it, she gathers the words for future use.

——They touch things in the classroom—metal, wood, plaster, glass, crayons, erasers, paper—and talk about how they feel.

——They go outside to feel things—bark, bricks, grass, soil, rocks, wire, water, mud—and say words to tell about their sense of touch.

——They make crayon rubbings of things with different textures and label them for display—screen wire, leaves, stucco, chain-link fences, bricks.

——They collect fabrics of different textures and mount samples for touching in the Discovery Center.

——They make touch collages out of items that have interesting and unusual textures.

——They collect words for the section of the Word Wall devoted to touch words—scratchy, prickly, slippery, chilly, bumpy, hard, soft, gooey, waxy.

Cheryl has a favorite book of poems about touch, *Fingers Are Always Bringing Me News* by Mary O'Neill (1969). She reads poems about the fingers of blind children, baby fingers, old fingers, city fingers, and country fingers. Then she encourages the children in her fifth-grade class to find and read aloud to the group poems and stories that have good touch words in them. The children listen and add words to the collection of touch words in their writing handbook.

Reading Numerals and Numbers

Numerals are everywhere in the environment of children. Most children have some experience in reading them before entering school programs. They can turn the television dial to a channel they want by watching for the right number to appear. They read numbers on houses and streets. They read prices in newspapers and catalogues. They watch the numerals whirl around at gas stations as the pumps record the number of gallons and the amount to be paid. Most of them play games that use numerals in some way. There is no way that an active, involved human being can escape the experience of reading numerals.

Reading Numerals and Numbers in Newspapers

Children can identify numerals they know in grocery advertisements, and they can read the numbers that tell team standings.

Rita collects grocery advertisements enough for each child to have one page. She names a numeral, and children point to the place where they see it. From there she advances to saying the price of something, and children try to find that number on the advertisement. They find the numbers in both large and small print. With the help of the teacher they read numbers along with the names of products.

She also provides a blank book for children to use to paste in numbers they can read. When a book is filled, it is placed in the Reading/Research Center and used for practice reading.

Reading Numerals in One's Environment

Numerals are found in so many places that most children are unaware that the numbers they read automatically are important. Many of their activities are dependent on some use of numbers.

Howard makes a number diary for the Discovery Center. Children record places where they find numbers they need to read during their studies and other activities. The first pages are easily filled with such items as clock, calendar, page numbers, and room numbers. As the days pass, there are fewer entries, but they are interesting and unusual. Children find serial numbers on school equipment, numbers on graphs and charts, and numbers on tickets, and they may find a Social Security number.

After filling the number diary for a week, the children are asked to keep a diary of their own activities for one day—from the time they wake until they go to bed. After they have recorded the activities, they cross out all those that have number concepts in them—time, amount, distance, dials, calendars, and so forth. In this way Howard highlights the fact that numbers play an important part in everyday life.

Numbers in Stories and Poems

From the earliest nursery rhymes a child hears and says, the concept of number is required for understanding. "Hickory, Dickory, Dock," "Baa, Baa, Black Sheep," "One, Two, Buckle My Shoe," and "Rub-a-Dub-Dub" are examples. Most stories and poems require some understanding of numbers and words that stand for numbers, and the ability to read them is assumed.

Karin chooses stories appropriate for reading numbers and number words. Children read silently and list all the number words and numbers in a story. For oral reading of the same story children are asked to skip the words on the lists they have made. They find that many stories lose their meaning when number concepts are omitted.

Helen makes a set of cards with numbers on them for the Writing/Publishing Center. Some are very small numbers, and some are very large. Children draw one, two, or more of the cards and write stories that involve the numbers. They produce scientific stories to include the smallest ones and often use space travel or astronomy as topics that require the largest numbers.

She also uses sets of cards for storytelling. The cards are placed in a paper bag. She draws a card and begins a story that uses the number written on the card. Then another and another draw from the bag in turn and include the numbers drawn in a continuation of the story. An attempt is sometimes made to keep the story realistic; at other times the story is nonsense.

Numbers Everywhere

Walks in a neighborhood, trips to shopping centers, reading newspapers, and viewing films accentuate the variety of ways that numbers are used to make life meaningful. To read the numbers printed and stamped on things is necessary for independence. Children in school need to gain the assurance that they can read the number signals accurately.

Bob encourages children in his sixth-grade class to build a control panel for at least one modern machine each year. They choose a jet plane, a submarine, a spaceship, or some other machine that has a control panel with multiple dials and gauges. They usually begin by studying an automobile dashboard. They see that most panels require the reading of numbers. From there they begin to build a control panel that will register necessary information for their vehicle. During the process they come in contact with meanings represented by numerals in modern transportation systems and in scientific studies.

Jim uses films to focus on reading numerals. Children watch for numbers as they view films. They either call them out or write them down as they see them flash on the screen on highway signs, license numbers, prices of things, street numbers, house numbers, and other places common in almost any environment.

Reading numbers for meaning and for the purposes intended is not automatic. Most children need opportunities to try out their skills, check for accuracy, and try again to make meaningful responses to the use of numbers that they observe in and out of school.

Reading Graphic Aids

Maps, graphs, charts, signs, and diagrams are in the reading environment of children at home and at school. They usually appear in a combination of symbols that includes lines, shapes, dots, colors, numerals, and words. To be able to read them meaningfully as a life experience may be essential for many students; to be able to read them in school experiences may provide basic meanings in curriculum areas such as social studies, science, and mathematics.

The meanings inherent in graphic aids can be developed best when they are used to record and represent real experiences.

——Children can make maps of walking trips and field trips.

——Those who travel during the school year or during the summer months can be encouraged to collect maps of their travels and bring them to class to share. Children can bring letters postmarked at different places and locate the points of origin on a large map.

——Traffic signs that have shape, color, and symbols as a part of the message are available in most communities. Children are usually interested in these and can make miniatures for use in their play in the classroom and on the playground. Some school grounds can be developed with roadways that include the major traffic signs that children will encounter.

——Graphs showing growth of plants, height and weight of children, and scores of games can be a part of an ongoing learning environment. The making and reading of these graphs can be the basic instruction in how to read other graphs.

——Many instructions on how to put things together include diagrams. Children might be willing to bring models to school that have diagrams as a major part of the instructions for assembly. School engineers and custodians usually have diagrams showing how machinery works. Parents who work with diagrams may be willing to show children how they read them in their work.

——Charts showing progress are needed in any school program that is individualized. Charts of classroom duties and learning center assignments can be initiated in kindergarten through the use of color and shape codes. As children learn to read printed symbols, words can be added to the organizational charts.

Reading that does not depend on motions left to right and top to bottom and on alphabetic symbols is so important that it needs to be dealt with directly. Experiences in this type of reading build a base for more complex reading of graphic aids as children study curriculum areas of technical content. They value ways of communicating specific information and relationships that can be expressed effectively without words or with a minimum of words for maximum information.

Summary of Skills and Abilities for Reading Nonalphabetic Symbol Systems

——Reads nature's signals and has vocabulary to interpret meanings from:
  ——weather
  ——plants
  ——animals

——water
——air
——earth
——Reads sensory impressions and has vocabulary to interpret personal meanings from:
    ——impressions from sight: color, size, shape
    ——impressions from sound
    ——impressions from smell
    ——impressions from taste
    ——impressions from touch
——Reads numerals and numbers appropriate for age and grade in the following ways:
    ——recognizes numerals in place value relationships
    ——reads prices
    ——reads decimal and common fractions
    ——uses number reading to achieve daily tasks
    ——recognizes number concepts written with words
    ——interprets number meanings in stories and poems
——Reads graphic aids, such as:
    ——maps appropriate for school studies
    ——traffic signs
    ——diagrams
    ——growth charts and graphs
    ——clocks
    ——calendars
    ——dials
    ——gauges

Selected References

Allen, Roach Van, and Claryce Allen. Teacher's Resource Book, *Language Experiences in Early Childhood.* Encyclopaedia Britannica Educational Copr., Chicago, 1969.

Ashton-Warner, Sylvia. *Teacher.* Simon and Schuster, New York, 1963.

Burrows, Alvina T., Dianne L. Monson, and Russell G. Stauffer. *New Horizons in the Language Arts.* Harper & Row, New York, 1972.

Dunn, Eleanor. *Let's Cook Today.* Child Focus Co., Manhattan Beach, Calif., 1974.

Dunne, Hope W. *The Art of Teaching Reading: A Language and Self-Concept Approach.* Charles E. Merrill, Columbus, Ohio, 1972.

Francis, Marjorie. *The Three R's of Language: Releasing Feelings, Reweaving*

Ideas, Recording Language. Child Focus Co., Manhattan Beach, Calif., 1971.

Furth, Hans G. *Piaget for Teachers.* Prentice-Hall, Englewood Cliffs, N.J., 1970.

Hall, MaryAnne. *Teaching Reading as a Language Experience.* Charles E. Merrill, Columbus, Ohio, 1970.

Hayakawa, S. I. *Symbol, Status, and Personality.* Harcourt, Brace & World, New York, 1963.

Landrum, Roger. *A Day Dream I Had at Night and Other Stories: Teaching Children How to Make Their Own Readers.* Watkins Press, New York, 1971.

Lee, Dorris M., and Roach Van Allen. *Learning to Read Through Experience.* Appleton-Century-Crofts, New York, 1963.

O'Neill, Mary. *Fingers Are Always Bringing Me News.* Doubleday and Co., Garden City, N.Y., 1969.

Onslow-Ford, Gordon. *Painting in the Instant.* Harry N. Abrams, New York, 1964.

Piaget, Jean. *The Language and Thought of the Child,* rev. ed. Humanities Press, New York, 1959.

Sherk, John K. *A Word-Count of Spoken English of Culturally Disadvantaged Preschool and Elementary Pupils.* University of Missouri at Kansas City, Kansas City, Mo., 1973.

Singer, Mary, and Robert B. Ruddell (eds.). *Theoretical Models and Processes of Reading.* International Reading Association, Newark, Del., 1970.

Smith, Frank, and George A. Miller (eds.). *The Genesis of Language: A Psycholinguistic Approach.* The M.I.T. Press, Cambridge, Mass., 1971.

Spencer, Peter M. "Reading in a Geophysical Age." In *Twenty-third Yearbook, Claremont College Reading Conference.* Curriculum Laboratory, Claremont Graduate College, Claremont, Calif., 1958.

———. *Reading Reading.* Curriculum Laboratory, Claremont Graduate College, Claremont, Calif., 1970.

Strand Three of the Curriculum Rationale for a Language Experience Approach emphasizes the influences of the language and ideas of others on the personal language and ideas of children in the instructional program. How to read is minimized in Part Four. The focus is on how others use language. Teachers are helped to see that they can bring students under the influence of many forms of communication so that the children can make choices for changing and improving their own language in flexible and creative ways. In the process teachers and children are helped to generalize along these lines.

1. New words can be acquired and new ways of saying things can be practiced by repeating the ways in which authors write stories and poems.
2. There is no need to wait until one can read printed materials to be influenced by the language of authors.
3. The learning environment with its learning centers is a laboratory for the development of comprehension abilities.
4. There is a continuing emphasis on expressing in a personal way what is learned from a variety of sources. Opportunities for art, creative writing, and drama are available at all times for interpreting ideas gained from listening and reading.
5. Organizational abilities such as those required for comprehending reading can be practiced in a variety of learning experiences that do not require reading and writing abilities—painting pictures, constructing, sculpturing, and making collages.
6. Personal ideas can be organized into predetermined poetry and story patterns.
7. The same basic ideas can be found in poems, stories, songs, paintings, films, sculpture, and photographs.
8. Once personal ideas have been communicated through some media, they can be compared and contrasted with those of other people who have communicated on the same topic.
9. Questions are more important than answers in stimulating one to search out many sources for information.
10. Answers to questions can be found in many places and through many media.
11. Reading success is not determined by the ability to read teacher-selected materials verbatim but by the ability to recognize and use relevant sources that may or may not require excellence in reading printed materials.
12. Those who are not good readers of reading textbooks can participate successfully in a broad-based communications program.

13. The same basic ideas can be communicated as fact or as fancy. There is a need to know the difference.
14. Authors have a purpose for writing *what* they write and *how* they write. Readers must consider the purpose when evaluating the work of an author.
15. The essence of a communications program is the ability to respond in personal ways to ideas without using the exact language of those who originated the ideas.

Children in a language experience approach are helped to build ego strength for communicating in ways that reflect the humanistic qualities of persons in professions who depend on self-expression for survival. This goal is elaborated and other generalizations are extended in the chapters that follow in Part Four.

Listening to and reading language of others—hearing and reading the language of many authors through stories and poems; responding naturally with new words and sentence patterns as illustrated by authors; relating own language to that used by other authors; and comparing and contrasting personal ways of saying things with those of other authors.

Listening to and reading the language of others are inseparable in language experience approach programs. This union of *reading* with *listening to* results from experience and from research.

The experience of most parents and teachers attests to the value of the input of language through a rich program of reading to children. The expanding market for children's literature reflects the concern of parents that children need an exposure to language and ideas that are not indigenous to the family and community where the child lives. Interest in television programs that are designed specifically to engage children in language acquisition has highlighted a need for rich listening and viewing experiences prior to and during attempts to teach decoding skills (that is, discovering the nature of the correlation between printed units and their oral counterparts).

Research that relates listening to language to success in reading suggests that when we improve certain specific skills in listening, those same skills improve in reading (Bracken, 1972). A study by Paul M. Hollingsworth (1967) reported that when the same skills taught in listening and reading in the intermediate grades were tested, it was found that instruction for certain purposes (specific information, main idea, relationships, evaluation of conclusions) did favorably affect the ability of pupils.

Modeling of reading with "read along" and "echo" techniques has been employed by most adults when they read to young children, but studies that seek to relate the technique to the improvement of reading skills are recent. Leif Fern (1972) reported in a study, "The Oral Model as a Strategy in Developmental Reading Instruction," that the use of oral models prior to silent reading yielded the following results.

1. The oral model is effective as an instructional strategy on variables of vocabulary and total reading on a whole class basis.
2. The oral model makes little or no difference to fourth-graders who score at the upper extreme of an achievement test.
3. The oral model is effective as an instructional strategy on variables of comprehension and total reading for pupils who score at the lower extreme of an achievement test.

The work of Fern and the experience of many teachers using a language experience approach raise serious questions about classroom practices that cause pupils to have to listen to inaccurate and boring models during the learning process. Data on modeling of language in reading instruction suggest that pupils should hear accurate and interestingly narrated models.

Theories of reading offer a wide range of choices for practitioners. The variety strongly suggests that there is no *one best theory*. Both psychological and linguistic models are influential on practices in language experience programs. The programs are oriented heavily toward Piagetian theory. David Elkind (1967), in an article entitled "Piaget's Theory of Perceptual Development: Its Application to Reading and Special Education," reiterates the assumption that there are well differentiated stages of development. He bases his study and report on the assumption that the learning process manifested by a child is dependent on his stage of development.

One of the first things a child must learn, according to Elkind, is that printed material is a representation. It is like speech and must be brought into functional use through a variety of sensorimotor methods. It must be introduced through hearing, feeling, looking, tasting, and smelling.

Kenneth S. Goodman (1970) emphasizes that the reading process cannot be fractionated into its component parts for research or for instruction. He sees reading as active information processing that involves graphic, syntactical, and semantic information. Readers, like listeners, are not bound strictly to the graphic information. They respond, not as recoding to speech, but to meanings that are derived from a whole constellation of experiences. Children who have developed strong language patterns tend to impose them on graphic representations regardless of what is printed. They keep the meaning while they make "good errors." His study of miscues (errors that retain or improve meaning) as a valuable diagnostic procedure reinforces the position of language experience approach teachers that children must *hear* variety in language and must practice many forms of language production if they are to be able to process graphic, syntactical, and semantic information from printed tests.

Developing Listening Abilities

Listening is a major aspect of communication and as such is an ability to be extended in a language experience approach. It is an *intake* aspect of communication and requires that the sound signals be produced by someone other than the listener. It is an ability that is close to that of reading print. The chief difference is that when "listening" to the language of others during silent reading, the "listener" must have enough ego strength to "hear without sound." Subvocalization may take place and be helpful in some cases, but the transfer from listening to the sound of language to silent reading is a development in communication that requires much exercise, practice, and confidence. It cannot be assumed that because a child is in the presence of the sounds of language, listening skills that can be related at a later time to silent reading are in operation.

Listening Participation

Listening as a participation skill can best be learned in situations in which every child has opportunities for class participation. It is not the skill of following the teacher's directions. Participation is a more challenging experience than merely being quiet while someone else talks. It can be a part of most of the activities of the school day as group discussions are used as a means of planning, problem-solving, arriving at a decision, and evaluating group and individual enterprises. Such participation requires thoughtful listening to the thinking of others so that there will be a clear interplay of ideas and real thinking together toward achieving the purpose of the discussion. A meeting of minds is difficult to achieve on a mature level, and children need many opportunities to sense the satisfaction that comes when honest effort is made to interact with the thinking and planning of others. This ability is basic to silent reading that is developed to the point that the reader is communicating with an author.

CLUES FOR INSTRUCTION

Disperse learning situations into learning centers so that children have repeated and continuous opportunities to respond to plans and instructions in meaningful ways. Work toward independence rather than dependence on assignments.

Use a portion of each school day for assessment. Help children to discuss the outcomes of plans formulated in group discussions.

Read *with* children each day on an individual or small group basis. Help them to hear how the story goes by taking turns reading orally. Participate in terms of the needs of the children. Poor readers need especially to listen to models of good reading during the process of learning how to recognize printed language. Those who struggle to recognize words seldom "hear" what the author has to say.

Read to children and let them participate from time to time by telling what they think the author would add if she or he was present with them. Help them to understand in this way that the printed part is an imperfect representation of what the author had to say. Help them to feel comfortable in thinking along with an author. Help them to recognize that exact replication of the printed symbols is not the only measure of good reading.

Listen to music selections and discuss the ideas and feelings gained from listening that does not include words. Listen to and view films without words. Follow up with discussions of what was heard and seen when no words were spoken. Relate this type of experience to one of silent reading when the reader has communication clues other than sounds of words as the major resource.

Avoid assigning silent reading of print without some evidence that the children would respond meaningfully if they were to hear the same words. Avoid repeating failure experiences by linking listening and reading as companion abilities in intake communication.

Kinds of Listening

Listening is not just one thing. There are many kinds of listening that the teacher must be aware of if the abilities are to mature and serve the pupil in more and more meaningful ways. Some of the kinds of listening that might be observed and included in classroom instruction follow.

1. Simple listening—hearing sounds without interpreting any particular meaning of the sound:
    - —a car going by
    - —the ring of the telephone
    - —birds singing
    - —water running
    - —wind blowing
2. Discriminative listening—listening to hear and identify the likenesses and differences in sounds:
    - —high-low sounds on a musical scale
    - —soft-loud sounds at the same pitch
    - —long-short sounds of the same tone

——words that have the same beginning sound
——words that have rhyming endings
——words that have the same sound in internal syllables
——words that are the same

3. Listening for information:
——repeating words that tell the names of things when listening to reading
——repeating facts heard when listening to stories
——understanding oral directives well enough to carry them out independently
——recalling incidents from hearing discussions and from listening to reading

4. Listening to organize ideas:
——ability to hear and repeat happenings in the order they were heard
——ability to summarize several points in a discussion
——ability to arrange points from several discussions into a new organization

5. Listening for main ideas:
——understanding the important point of a story or discussion
——discriminating between major points and illustrations to support and elaborate the points

6. Listening for varied points of view:
——developing a sensitivity to the language of agreement and disagreement
——interpreting tones of voice that express controversy, sarcasm, irritation, reasonableness, and perplexity
——watching for basic differences in ideas when listening to discussions

7. Critical listening:
——listening to analyze the purpose of the one speaking by recognizing bias, exaggerated statements, and false connotations
——listening for conflicting ideas by the same speaker
——being aware of propaganda techniques, half-truths, and name-calling

8. Creative listening:
——visualizing characters, settings, moods, and situations while listening
——listening to evaluate films and recordings in terms of personal feelings
——relating ideas in a speech heard on television and mentioned in discussions

——putting several ideas heard on various occasions into a new whole

Other kinds of listening may be more available out of school than in school. Listening for relaxation and enjoyment can be a part of school programs and should be encouraged by suggestions for radio and television listening as a homework experience. Assigned programs for pure pleasure frequently lead pupils to broaden their listening interests and abilities. Such assignments can also make possible a child's having a set time for listening to television that is different from the recreational time of his or her choice and the family's choice.

Listening in Learning Centers

Every classroom experience that includes oral language can naturally and normally be a good listening experience. Listening abilities should be promoted, however, and not left to chance. A variety of activities can be made available in learning centers from day to day as specific assignments or for self-selection (Allen, 1974).

1. Children who work in the Game Center need to listen for specific instructions in order to participate. The instructions can be on tape, read by an aide, or read by one of the group members. Listening to the reading of instructions and rules for games requires a level of attention to specifics that is not characteristic of most listening, but it is characteristic of the level of attention required for reading in some school assignments.
2. Children who work in a Viewing/Listening Center may respond in personal ways to what they hear and see. They can extend ideas to their own experiences with "That reminds me of the time I . . ." kind of response. They do not need to listen at all times just to be able to repeat what they hear. That ability is important, but it is not more important than responding in personal ways.
3. In a Language Study Center children can work on auditory discrimination exercises that require the hearing of words and portions of words that repeat over and over in the language. They can work on sequences of sounds in words, work that will help them to spell correctly. Another activity can be centered around saying the same words or phrases in more than one language.
4. Reading/Research Center activities should include reading to children on as regular a basis as listening to children read. Children need the experience of hearing good models of oral reading in indi-

vidual and small group conferences as much as they need to hear reading for pleasure in a large group setting. "You read a sentence, then I'll read a sentence" or "You read a paragraph, then I'll read a paragraph" establishes a rapport for discussing some of the finer points of reading. This level of rapport seldom develops when the teacher always acts as a monitor of children's oral reading or previous silent reading. Children need effective models for hearing the language of others just as they need to develop skills in word recognition and comprehension.

The Reading/Research Center also affords a place where children and teachers can relate personal language to language in the printed text. The teacher can read a sentence, then ask a child to tell how he or she might say the same thing. If the child's response is somewhat different in vocabulary and in syntactical structure, the teacher will know that reading from that author will be more difficult for that child than the reading difficulty level might indicate. If the child, however, can mimic or repeat the language of the author, then the difficulty level may be diminished.

Listening to reading in a study situation is extremely significant in a language experience approach. Listening to poor readers read poorly as a daily diet of oral reading has no place in the program. Oral reading by pupils that is listened to by a group should be prepared reading. It should not be a public diagnosis of a very private affair between teacher and pupil.

5. The Dramatization Center is a place where children can act out stories and situations they have heard or read. It gives them opportunity to organize, sequence, and interpret characters from literature that are outside their life experiences. Through listening they pick up the feelings, moods, language patterns, and thought processes of characters. Later, as they assume character roles, they repeat in plays the basic content of the story.

The Dramatization Center can be the place where children work on choral readings which they will perform for other groups. They listen to each other and to the total effect of their presentation to make certain that it interprets the selection in a meaningful and dramatic way.

6. A Discussion Center is a place and time where children can read their own compositions to an audience. When there is only one copy of a manuscript, everyone is the audience except the reader who is the author. Oral reading has purpose because there is only one source. Listening in an audience has purpose because there is

no chance that some have read ahead and already know what they are to hear. The teacher becomes a member of the listening audience. This places a responsibility on the reader that is never felt in reading groups in which every child has a book opened to the same reading selection. Poor readers of reading textbooks have an equal chance with good readers of texts in a situation in which original manuscripts are being read by their authors.

7. Singing songs and listening to singing and other music in a Music Center increase auditory discrimination. The experiences also build confidence in producing language with rhythm and rhyme. The center permits children of all levels of reading achievement to participate in language production for listening.

Listening, as with all learning experiences, requires cooperative teacher-pupil aspiring, planning, executing, and evaluating. Together, students and teachers can develop standards for listening to serve as a basis for relating listening to reading. This emphasis should not exclude other forms of listening that add to a person's store of meanings, enjoyment, and appreciation of the world apart from printed sources.

Factors Affecting Listening and Reading

Some factors affecting listening, especially listening abilities that relate to reading, are:

——physical environment
——psychological environment
——emotional factors
——physical factors
——poor language development
——preformed opinions
——high intelligence.

These factors can be dealt with in a language experience approach program that includes flexible arrangements, continuous change of groups, diversified materials, and individualized instruction for specific skills and abilities. Some suggestions for dealing with these factors follow.

1. Physical environment
    ——Furniture is arranged for face-to-face contact between speakers and listeners in large group and small group discussions.

——Speakers stand or speak so their facial and body expressions can be seen by listeners.

——Language from sources other than people talking is provided by tapes, records, films, radio, television, and sound filmstrips.

——Good manners on the part of the audience are studied and practiced to permit listening.

——Oral reading is featured in audience situations with well-prepared reading by students.

2. Psychological environment

——Children perceive themselves as members of the total group rather than as members of an ability group for reading.

——Ability grouping for reading is avoided as a daily, systematic procedure that might diminish the self-concept of children to the point that low self-concept becomes a bigger problem than poor reading performance.

——Mutual trust is promoted as the teacher participates in reading, expressing opinions, and writing on topics along with the pupils.

——Bibliotherapy is practiced when opportunities arise to discuss the self-image of others as reflected in stories and films.

——Divergent thinking is planned to promote participation with no fear of failure.

——Alternatives replace correctness as goals during discussions for problem-solving and critical thinking.

3. Emotional factors

——Daydreaming is utilized as a time when a thought might emerge that can be captured for a poem or a story.

——A Quiet Place is provided in the learning environment as a place where children can retreat into private thoughts with no questions asked as long as they are quiet.

——Children with low status in a group are helped to produce something significant so they can feel like active participants.

——Home influences that might produce barriers to participation in a listening-reading experience are considered in individual conferences at which inventories of progress are discussed.

——Unpleasant associations among children are recognized as barriers to listening and reading that may be assessed as poor reading performance rather than as personal problems that need some positive support.

4. Physical factors

——Hearing loss or limited attention span may be confused with poor ability unless listening experiences are used as clues.

——Low-energy cases can be dealt with as such rather than as remedial reading cases.

——Inability to sit and listen for extended periods need not be treated as severe disciplinary problems when movement among learning centers is possible.

——Instruction in reading skills that involve phonological structure can be adjusted to highlight visual clues for children with hearing problems.

——Auditory clues and a high tolerance for miscues that retain the meaning can be planned for children with visual impairment.

5. Poor language development

——Limited personal language restricts listening to the language of others and needs to be developed in order to improve listening and to permit reading skills to develop.

——Speaking a foreign language at home may limit listening to *English only* in school situations.

——Records and tapes in several languages for all children can provide experiences that might be acute ones if they were provided for only a few pupils.

——Impaired speech that prohibits the reproduction of sounds selected for instruction can be a limiting factor in listening to the language of others.

——Poor auditory discrimination can result from faulty speech patterns that need attention prior to direct teaching of such skills as the ability to distinguish the differences between long and short vowel sounds.

6. Preformed opinions

——Children who hear what they want to hear rather than what was intended function in listening and reading situations quite differently from children who are open to new ideas.

——Inability to integrate new ideas into previous opinions and decisions limits listening and comprehension abilities.

7. High intelligence

——Uniform expectancies and materials can promote in children of high intelligence a level of boredom that prohibits their listening over and over to what they have known for years.

——Requiring children of high intelligence to read and listen to reading in ability groups promotes regressive tendencies in attitude and school performance (Purkey, 1970).

——Environments with learning centers offer diversity of activities to accommodate high intelligence in a natural and normal way.

——Children who think ahead of the main ideas of a topic can be furnished an audience to hear their ideas and views.

These environmental and experiential factors require the teacher's thoughtful attention. Variety of experiences is required for the variety of abilities in listening and reading. Particular abilities planned for one group or for one individual can stimulate interest in others. Influences planned for one child may extend to others who may not have appeared to be ready for them. Each situation, when dealt with honestly and with trust, can extend to others, as children set personal goals for improving their abilities in listening and reading.

Reading and Telling Stories

Reading aloud and telling stories to children are basic reading instruction. Both are required as ongoing activities in a language experience approach. In this approach children must hear language as it has been recorded by many authors. They are expected to communicate with authors early in the program. It is difficult to imagine that they can communicate when reading silently forms of language that they have never heard. Listening to language of authors is a basic language experience which can be implemented by teachers as they read aloud and tell stories to children (Allen, 1974).

Reading Aloud

Regardless of the wide range of individual differences in a classroom, it is unusual to find a child who does not like to hear stories and poems read aloud. Each can listen as if the reading is a personal affair between student and teacher. Each can feel that there is an opportunity in the classroom for establishing relationships between stories or poems and experience.

Gary sets aside fifteen minutes a day for reading aloud. Occasionally he might have to extend the time because stories are not written for timed reading. He tries to choose stories and poems that can be read in the time allotted because he feels that the total effect of a story or poem is important, especially for children who are not able to read whole stories or books independently. He feels that his attitude toward reading aloud will be reflected in the attitude of the students. He wants them to know that he really enjoys stories and poems and that reading them is important to him. He demonstrates that he is willing to forgo something else in order to have time to communicate with an author who could not be present. He is determined to present the image of a reader rather than of a reading teacher. He wants reading to be a communicating experience first of all, and he provides lessons for those who want to improve their abilities.

Reading aloud to children increases their listening vocabulary. No part of reading instruction can be considered more important than this because children must recognize words by ear before they can recognize them by sight. They must be able to understand the language of other people by listening to it before they can comprehend that language in print.

Dorothy believes that listening to good models of reading by the teacher who works with children on reading skills is so important that she follows a check list of procedures to assure a good situation for oral reading. She considers the following elements.

1. Dorothy rehearses the story or poem on a tape recorder if it is new to her. She listens to improve the tone and rhythm of reading.
2. She and the children put all other work away.
3. Special places are planned for the children to gather to listen. Some special places are a rug so children can sit on the floor, the lawn under a tree in warm weather, and a stage behind the curtain when special lighting effects are needed. She believes that a good story deserves a good arrangement. Children need to sit near the reader in order to see illustrations and hear the subtle qualities of voice that portray mood and characters.
4. Selections that sparkle and have a touch of the dramatic are chosen. She knows that the children are attuned to television and will resent babyish selections.
5. She is prepared to repeat favorites over and over.
6. She selects some books with only pictures—no text—and invites children to say their own story as she shows the pictures. She encourages them to select a setting and names for characters before

they begin to develop the sequence of events suggested by the pictures.

7. As she reads along, she asks questions—not too many but enough to whet interest. She asks more predictive questions than comprehension ones. This tactic enables the listeners to compare their own ideas with those of the author as the story unfolds. She avoids any possibility of asking comprehension questions that can cause children to feel that they fail. Oral reading to children is a happy time and one of language influence more than one of specific skill development.

Telling Stories

Telling stories to children and by children is as important an experience for language development as hearing stories read (Allen, 1974). It is a much more creative experience for the teacher and for children. It develops contact with an audience in a special way that few language experiences can do. Storytelling by the teacher serves as a model for children in their own storytelling and encourages them to:

——engage in a greater output of language than is required for daily sharing
——embellish language with descriptive terms that are not characteristic of ordinary conversation
——make up expressive dialogue
——use sound effects and physical movements to highlight meanings
——use voice inflections and emphasis that most children do not use when reading what someone else has written
——express ideas in thought units rather than word by word which is characteristic of much oral reading by children
——develop ideas in a sequence that reaches a climax and has an ending.

Telling a simple story is a skill essential for moving into dictation and independent writing that is more than labeling with a word or a sentence. Children who cannot compose a story to tell prior to dictating or writing seldom develop that ability during dictating and writing experiences.

Carmen introduces storytelling to children in different ways:
——telling stories, real and imaginary, herself

——telling the beginning of a story and letting children add to it as
    they have ideas
——letting children who are reminded of something as she reads tell
    what happened to them
——helping children to see stories in the things that happen around
    them
——encouraging children to tell stories about their paintings rather
    than to make mere statements such as "See my ———," "Look
    at my ———," or "This is a ———."

Donald uses storytelling as a major activity to help poor readers in
his sixth grade to understand "how stories go." He finds that most of
the poor readers have never experienced a whole story because they
always lose ideas as they try to figure out the pronunciation of words.
He tries to remember the following points as he sets an example for
the students.

——Tell the story simply and directly.
——Make use of body movements to add meaning.
——Speak in a voice that is appropriate to the characters or the
    mood of the story.
——Change tempo and use pauses to fit the situation.
——Know the story so well that it seems to demand being told.
——Trust words to tell the stories—no props such as flannel boards,
    pictures, and costumes.
——Tell a story the students will read later.
——Take an idea from a story that is read, and make it into a new,
    personal story.

Donald's example encourages students to try telling stories. As
they listen to each other, they get ideas for characters, settings,
sounds, movement, and plots. They are helped by their teacher to see
that these same elements are in the stories they are reading.

Stories told from memory are usually more dramatic than those
read aloud because of the freedom afforded the storyteller. Yet it is
important to retain the way certain authors use words and phrases.
When the beauty and uniqueness of the original language must be retained, a combination of telling and reading can be employed.

Variety should be the guide in selecting stories for telling and reading. Every teacher's repertoire should include nonfiction, fiction,
legends, fairy tales, and every other kind of story from all over the
world. They should be selected to please and entertain, to stimulate

curiosity, to inform, to illustrate the power of the spoken and the written word, and to reveal beauty and truth.

Children must hear stories and poems from many authors if they are expected to understand the language of hundreds of authors as they move into silent reading experiences. They seldom understand what they see in print if they have not heard something like it prior to the silent reading.

Summary of Skills and Abilities for Listening to and Reading the Language of Others

DEVELOPING LISTENING HABITS

—Makes use of past experiences and information in conversation
—Uses imagination in the formulation of original stories
—Recalls content and sequence of stories heard
—Follows simple instructions after hearing them
—Accepts worth of other's remarks
—Speaks in turn
—Realizes that different people speak in different ways and for different purposes
—Catches added meaning by noting gestures and intonations
—Thinks ahead while listening; anticipates what is coming next

LISTENING TO GET INFORMATION

—Understands, remembers, and responds to directions of increasing complexity
—Gets answers to questions from what is heard
—Relays messages accurately
—Can summarize an oral report
—Takes notes from interviews and discussions
—Can follow reading models heard in instructional conferences
—Can organize a sequence and assume the role of a character to dramatize a story
—Is conscious of similarities and differences in word sounds

LISTENING TO EXCHANGE IDEAS AND FORM JUDGMENTS

—Participates in group discussions
—Reads own compositions to an audience
—Grasps the central idea from listening to others read

——Recognizes subordinate ideas in stories heard
——Distinguishes between fact and opinion, fact and fantasy
——Asks proof for facts stated
——Realizes that one's feelings affect one's reaction to what is heard
——Seeks clarification of vague and ambiguous ideas

LISTENING TO ENJOY AND APPRECIATE

——Becomes aware of beauty in the rhythm and sound of language
——Appreciates poetry, stories, music, and dramatization enough to choose listening and reading in learning centers
——Develops an understanding of the role and responsibilities of the listener in different situations—face to face, audience to speaker, speaker to audience, radio, television, recordings, school programs
——Realizes how readers and storytellers achieve various effects
——Realizes the power of language to communicate

Selected References

Allen, Roach Van. *Teacher's Resource Guide, Language Experiences in Reading, Level I.* Encyclopaedia Britannica Educational Corp., Chicago, 1974.

Bracken, Dorothy K. "The Teacher's Function in Developing Listening Skills." In *The Quest for Competency in Teaching Reading,* edited by Howard A. Klein. International Reading Association, Newark, Del., 1972.

Burrows, Alvina T., Dianne L. Monson, and Russell G. Stauffer. *New Horizons in the Language Arts.* Harper & Row, New York, 1972.

Durkin, Dolores. *Teaching Children to Read.* Allyn & Bacon, Boston, 1970.

Elkind, David. "Piaget's Theory of Perceptual Development: Its Application to Reading and Special Education," *Journal of Special Education*, 1 (1967), 357–361.

Fern, Leif. "The Oral Model as a Strategy in Developmental Reading Instruction." In *The Quest for Competency in Teaching Reading,* edited by Howard A. Klein. International Reading Association, Newark, Del., 1972.

Furth, Hans G. *Piaget for Teachers.* Prentice-Hall, Englewood Cliffs, N.J., 1970.

Goodman, Kenneth S. "Reading: A Psycholinguistic Guessing Game." In *Theoretical Models and Process in Reading,* edited by H. Singer and R. B. Ruddell. International Reading Association, Newark, Del., 1970.

Hall, MaryAnne. *Teaching Reading as a Language Experience.* Charles E. Merrill, Columbus, Ohio, 1970.

Hodges, Richard E., and E. Hugh Rudorf. *Language and Learning to Read.* Houghton Mifflin Co., Boston, 1972.

Hollingsworth, Paul M. "Can Training in Listening Improve Reading?" In *Reading Instruction: Dimensions and Issues,* edited by William E. Durr. Houghton Mifflin Co., Boston, 1967.

Newman, Harold. *Effective Language Practices in the Elementary School.* John Wiley & Sons, New York, 1972.

Purkey, William W. *Self-Concept and School Achievement.* Prentice-Hall, Englewood Cliffs, N.J., 1970.

Ruddell, Robert B. *Reading-Language Instruction: Innovative Practices.* Prentice-Hall, Englewood Cliffs, N.J., 1974.

Smith, James A. *Adventures in Communication.* Allyn & Bacon, Boston, 1972.

Strickland, Ruth. *The Language of Elementary School Children: Its Relation to Language of Reading Textbooks and the Quality of Reading Selected by Children.* Indiana University, Bloomington, Bulletin of the School of Education, No. 38 (July, 1962).

Zuck, Lois V., and Yetta M. Goodman. *Social Class and Regional Dialect: Their Relationship to Reading.* International Reading Association, Newark, Del., 1971.

FROM THE RATIONALE

Comprehending what is read—understanding what is heard or read; following directions; reproducing the thought of a passage; reading for detail; reading for general significance; and understanding words and their meaning in context.

Comprehension of what one hears or reads remains something of a mystery despite the voluminous research on the subject in recent years. Herbert D. Simon in a research report, "Linguistic Skills and Reading Comprehension" (1972), says that after his extensive investigations he believes that when children today are taught reading comprehension, the instructional procedures used are based more on the intuitions and accumulated experiences of the teachers than on research evidence. He points to the recent developments in transformational grammar by Noam Chomsky (1965) and others. It is clear, Simon says, that an understanding of language structure is as important in comprehension processes as is information about the meanings of words, word order, and form-class words. The theory generated by linguists suggests that comprehension cannot take place without an understanding of the underlying or deep structure of sentences.

In Dr. Simon's study of the ability of readers to recover the meaning of sentences with deep structure that makes their meaning different from other sentences using essentially the same words, he found that there was a substantial difference in comprehension scores (as measured by several standardized instruments) between those students who recovered the meanings in the deep structure and those who did not.

Examples from the Simon study:
a. He painted the house red.
b. He painted the red house.
c. He painted the house that was red.

a. What the boy would like is for the girl to leave.
b. For the boy to leave is what the girl would like.
c. What the girl would like is for the boy to leave.

The response of students to a series of statements like those above—one statement carrying a meaning different from the others as in the *a* examples—clearly separated those who made high scores from those who made low scores on standardized measures of comprehension.

Recent studies by Carol Chomsky (1969), *The Acquisition of Syntax in Children 5 to 10,* and Patricia Van Metre (1972), "Syntactic Characteristics of Selected Bilingual Children," support the major premise of the

Simon studies. Carol Chomsky identified some syntactical structures in English that are closely related to development levels. These structures indicate a normal move from simple stages to more complex stages in something of a sequence regardless of the age at which the clarification of meanings occurs. Patricia Van Metre used the Chomsky techniques to determine if there were differences in an understanding of the distinguishing syntactical structures between high-scoring and low-scoring bilinguals in third grades. She found a very close relationship between levels of performance on oral language tests of syntactical structure and standardized tests of reading comprehension. She investigated a matched group of monolingual children and found that there was almost no difference between the matched groups of monolingual (English) and bilingual (Spanish-English) groups in knowledge of the test structures. She recommends, as a result of her study, that teacher education for speech and reading take into account the natural language patterns of the students and the structure of language along with continued emphasis on meanings of words, word order, and form classes of words.

The affective domain in reading comprehension is receiving attention also. William Eller reported in a lecture, "Personality Traits as Factors in Reading Comprehension" (1973), at a Claremont Reading Conference, that "we have now established that reader personality is a significant factor in reading comprehension." In elaborating on the statement he pointed out that

1. Conventional approaches to comprehension skill development do not touch on the effect of the personality of the reader on understanding.
2. The field of social psychology must be involved in studying the complex problem of the source of meaning in reading.
3. Experimentation in the relationships of the reader's attitudes toward and motives for understanding what is read should be fostered in reading research.

In a language experience approach it has long been realized that the affective life of a listener or a reader has tremendous influence on comprehension of what is heard or what is read in printed materials. Most of the concern comes from informal sources such as observation and experience and from limited research in the area of the affective domain.

What has been learned is summarized in the following.

—Word meaning can never be separated from phrase meaning.

—Phrase meaning can never be separated from sentence meaning.

——Sentence meaning can never be separated from paragraph meaning.

——Paragraph meaning can never be separated from book meaning.

——Attempts to separate communication into listening, speaking, reading, and writing may be harmful in language development.

——The way the learner feels about self in the process of gaining meanings from hearing and reading determines much of what is comprehended.

Comprehension in Beginning Reading

Language experience approaches rely heavily on pupil-produced reading material for early reading instruction. Words and phrases familiar to the learner are recorded. Charts and books that reflect the real language of learners are prepared and used to develop a sense of what reading really is. Teachers and children study characteristics of the printed language that occur in dictated stories. Children develop a sight vocabulary of words of highest frequency and learn the beginnings of word-study techniques (Allen, Venezky, and Hahn, 1974).

During the beginning weeks (or months, if necessary) children deal with language they already comprehend when they study the details of sound-symbol relationships. For most children the comprehension load is reduced to *zero* through the use of personal language. The vocabulary and the structure are so familiar that there is little need for teachers to probe for evidence that meanings are understood. They do not find a place for asking simple comprehension questions on the materials used for direct word-recognition instruction.

Comprehension emphases during the beginning periods are placed on oral reading to the children, viewing films and talking about what was seen and heard, and listening to recordings of stories with opportunities for retelling. Pupil responses are open and creative. They permit each child to relate the ideas of others to self. There is little emphasis on the rightness of answers. Rather, teachers seek alternative suggestions as children examine their experiences and repeat words and phrases used by authors. These indicators of understanding furnish needed information for teachers. They do not attempt to tie meaning to the little bits of word recognition available to most children. Children are free to explore meaning rather than restricted to predetermined meanings of beginning reading materials.

Douglas is a first-grade teacher who has eliminated completely the use of preprimer readers. His examination of them revealed that the deep structure of sentences such as "Run, run," "Oh, look," and "Come to me" requires a level of interpretation not possible for many children. The distance between the subject and the verb is too great for children to connect them in a meaningful statement. In fact, sentences with the subject implied may be among the most difficult to understand, regardless of how simple the printed words appear to be.

Douglas collects brand names that children recognize and mounts them on cards. As children select cards they can read, he attaches the cards to the chalkboard with a loop of masking tape. Children make simple statements that include the word or words on the card, and a sentence is composed with the card in the proper place. Children repeat the sentences and begin to recognize a familiar word in a printed sentence. Some of the sentences and the cards are copied and bound into beginning reading books.

Theresa has a print set in the Writing/Publishing Center. Children copy statements they have dictated into blank books which become their reading texts. She finds that children can begin reading sentences they have composed faster than they can read the concocted sentences of preprimers.

Marjorie uses one wall to display the dictated stories of children that accompany other stories. They study words on the displayed stories, but they also read each other's stories and talk about them along the lines of: "Could this have happened to anyone else?" "Can you think of another way?" "If you had told the story, how would you have said it?"

Marjorie asks children to choose paintings and stories they wish they had written, ones that make them feel happy, ones that make them feel sad, ones that say exactly what happened. She strives to introduce some mature comprehension skills with materials that are easy and personal for each group. She knows that she cannot order "real experiences" and "real language" from a publishing company.

Developing Comprehension Abilities

Comprehension skills in reading are affected by factors such as:

    —cultural level of the home and the home-rooted language that reflects the culture

  ——level of word knowledge and the attitude of the student toward increasing language power

  ——accuracy and fluency of oral reading of passages written by a variety of authors

  ——level of short-term memory of what is seen and heard in real-life experiences

  ——feelings of self-worth and success during the process of developing abilities to comprehend during reading.

Comprehension abilities are promoted through a variety of classroom activities that emphasize topics such as:

  ——understanding words

  ——comprehending language structure

  ——reconstructing the writer's meaning

Others are added from time to time for special emphasis, but these abilities are continuous in the program and are promoted in several learning centers at all times.

Understanding Words

The size of a student's reading vocabulary is a matter that cannot be pinpointed. It is associated with the idea that certain words make sense to a reader *in context*. A particular meaning is selected in a split second from among the many available to those students with large vocabularies. As simple a word as *run* can be recognized in print, but which of its more than one hundred meanings does the reader apply in any given context?

  There is no simple way to teach reading vocabulary. Two basic ingredients are needed, and they are woven together in an infinite number of designs: (1) nonverbal experience, and (2) verbal experience. A language experience approach makes no attempt to separate the two. Rather, they are orchestrated into the learning environment in ways that keep known vocabulary functioning in multiple ways at the same time that children are being influenced by new words from authors and by new meanings for known words. These influences come from sensory experiences as well as from reading print. They come also from talking and writing as the means of trying out what they may have learned from listening and reading.

CLUES FOR INSTRUCTION

Collect pronouns from writing and reading passages. Find the antecedents expressed or implied so that children are aware that pronouns are always associated with common nouns and proper names. Use lists for games to assure sight recognition of nouns since most of the pronouns are words of high frequency. Lack of proper association of pronouns with their antecedents is a common cause of poor comprehension when reading (Chomsky, 1969; Van Metre, 1972).

Interpret meanings of prepositions as they appear in phrases. Use pantomime and other active demonstrations with objects to illustrate meanings. Contrast prepositions of opposite meanings, such as: *up* with *down, inside* with *outside, over* with *under.* Collect lists of prepositions for use in games and prepositional phrases for use in writing. Use the lists to assure sight recognition since most of the commonly used prepositions are on lists of words of highest frequency.

Watch for figures of speech in what is heard and read. Talk about and illustrate literal as well as figurative meanings. Make lists of figures of speech available in the Writing/Publishing Center.

Interpret meanings of common words in the context in which they are found—*can, bear, run, black, cook.* Use unabridged dictionaries to observe the many meanings of some words. Say sentences with many meanings for the same word.

Select root words and extend them with affixes to see how many variations can be developed.

Collect words that are pronounced alike but have different spellings and different meanings—*red, read; led, lead; two, to, too* (homonyms).

Associate word meanings with objects in word walks and word talks which permit children to identify known objects with known words, and then add one or more words that mean essentially the same thing.

Follow the listening to reading with opportunities for children to identify and repeat words that they have never heard before. Say in chorus the phrases or sentences that include the new word.

Comprehending Language Structures

A sizable reading vocabulary is necessary to reading comprehension, but a mature reader relies on more than vocabulary to understand the message of authors. A reader may know all the words of a sentence and not be able to understand it. The pattern of words may not make sense. The minimal distance principle (this principle involves the distance between the noun that is the subject of the sentence and the verb) may be adjusted so that the subject and the verb are too far apart for the reader to connect them immediately. The heart of meaning may be imbedded in a common word that changes the subject of a complement verb (Chomsky, 1969; Van Metre, 1972). Sentences using the words *ask* and *tell* illustrate this problem in comprehension:

Ask John the color of the book.

Tell John the color of the book.

Sentences that look almost alike can require entirely different responses. To pronounce the words in the sentences does not necessarily yield meaning. The first sentence requires a question as a reply. The second one does not.

Most pronouns are on lists of words of highest frequency. They become a part of the sight vocabulary very early for most children. Yet, understanding the antecedents of pronouns is seldom considered a critical point in comprehending reading. Children who do not understand who *they* is in a passage or who cannot remember the antecedent of *those* can miss the intended meaning—not because the words are not recognized in oral reading, but because the syntactical structure of the sentences is vague, ambiguous, or too sophisticated for the reader.

Another difficulty derived from structure rather than vocabulary is one that was formerly ignored in preprimer readers. Sentences with implied subjects such as "Run, run" and "Oh, look" were used to initiate reading experiences. They required the reader to furnish the subject of the sentence from some source outside the printed material. Children who were fluent in language production could do this, but those with limited language were left to call words in a meaningless context. Fortunately, the work of linguists in recent years has called attention to this problem to the extent that new reading series seldom use sentences with implied subjects as the first sentences in reading. Most recently published series initiate reading from some kind of experience background. Children acquire an inventory of names, words of action, and descriptions in many categories and begin to recognize some of the words of highest frequency from their own dictation and writing. Textbook publishers are careful to use sentence patterns that repeat over and over in conversations and in writing. Teachers can depend on the best published material to include at least four sentence patterns that children use frequently in their own writing and that authors use repeatedly.

1. (Determiner) [1] + noun + verb
   The boys whistled.

---

[1] The word forms in parentheses are not necessary to make the sentence pattern complete.

2. (D) + noun + *be* verb + adjective
   The man is tall.
3. (D) + noun + *be* verb + (D) + noun
   Horses are animals.
4. (D) + noun + verb + (D) + noun
   The children ate some cookies.

Most children use the four sentence patterns when they come to school, but some speak in abbreviated forms and nonstandard versions. These children need direct help in listening to and repeating sentences and poems that illustrate the patterns. They need to work with patterns that lend themselves to substitution of known words to change meanings within the same pattern.

Rabbits run in the sun.
Rabbits jump over the hump.
Dogs run just for fun.
Cats creep when I sleep.

Basic sentence patterns can be expanded by adding adjectives, prepositional phrases, adverbs, relative clauses, compound subjects, compound predicates, and dependent clauses and by linking sentences together to form compound sentences. These expansions do not change the basic patterns. They may add to the word recognition difficulty without changing the basic meaning.

The following sentences illustrate one basic idea expanded in a variety of ways:

The man fed the birds.
The man with the seed fed the birds.
The man fed the birds regularly.
The man and woman fed the birds.
The man and woman fed and watered the birds.
The man who had the seed fed the birds.
Because the man had some seed, he fed the birds.
The man fed the birds and the woman watered them.

Even slight alterations in words change the meaning of sentences. Change of tense is one example.

The man feeds the birds.   (present)
The man fed the birds.   (past)
The man will feed the birds.   (future)
The man has fed the birds.   (present perfect)
The man had fed the birds.   (past perfect)
The man will have fed the birds.   (future perfect)

Alterations may be made by changing positive to negative, by changing nouns to pronouns, and by changing statements to questions.

The expansion and alteration of sentences can be an ongoing effort in learning centers. Most language experience materials provide model sentences that can be altered and expanded. They also encourage children to write their own sentences using a predetermined structure (Tiedt and Tiedt, 1967). Understanding structure as a force in meaning is not left to chance. Teachers do not rely solely on word recognition and word meaning to develop comprehension abilities.

Reconstructing the Writer's Meaning

Reconstructing the meanings of authors serves as a balance in a language experience approach to the constructing of reading material in Strand One. Reconstructing is an ability required for success in and out of school. In most school situations it is the heart of comprehension. Unless readers are able to recover the basic meaning from printed material, it is difficult to imagine that they can engage in higher levels of comprehension requiring interpretation, critical thinking, and evaluation. Reconstructing the writer's meaning might include the following emphases: reproducing the thought of a passage, following directions, skimming to get the general significance of a passage, and reading to get detail.

1. Reproducing the thought of a passage is:
   —following a story sequence without filling in details
   —interpreting a story or poem with a series of drawings
   —interpreting a story or poem through drama
   —finding answers to questions in social studies and science studies
   —retelling a story in one's own words.
   Children who reproduce the thoughts of a passage can be helped by an understanding of the use of topic sentences in paragraphs, introductory statements, and summary statements. They can learn to focus on proper names which will be identified by capital letters. If a story has a repeating pattern of language, such as that found in classic stories like "The Three Little Pigs" and "The Three Bears," children can be encouraged to recover the exact language of the author in order to reproduce the story. They can learn to watch for words of enumeration such as *first, second,* and *third* as clues for the next important idea in a passage. Boldface and italic type are also useful in identifying key words and ideas in a passage.

2. Following directions is:
    —recalling orally the steps in a set of directions before carrying them out
    —working from printed directions
    —producing something that was made from a set of directions
    —participating in games that have specific directions.

Classrooms that are organized around learning centers have abundant opportunities for students to read to follow directions. Most of the centers have the information necessary to conduct independent and small group activities on cards or in folders for students to follow. Success in school requires that printed and oral directions be followed.

3. Skimming to get the general significance of a passage is:
    —finding answers to questions in a large mass of material by moving rapidly to the right place and then reading for detail
    —getting the sense of a passage by reading only portions of it
    —focusing on key words such as subjects of sentences and verbs rather than reading all the words in a passage.

Skimming is an essential skill for success in school. Yet much of reading instruction is centered on the oral reproduction of every word in printed material. Students are handicapped in study if they do not know how to move rapidly through printed material to pick up a general idea. Skimming is a technique requiring knowledge of language structure. The nouns carry the heaviest load of meaning. If children mark out all the nouns, the meaning is destroyed. Conversely, they can read just nouns and get the gist of meaning. If they restore the verbs in the passage with the nouns, they can get enough meaning to be fairly certain of main ideas.

From their earliest reading of stories children should be helped to develop skimming abilities. They can be told to read orally only the words that name things and people. Clues for these words can be found by looking for determiners such as *the, that,* and *those,* for capital letters for proper names, and for possessives such as *his* and *her.* Children who learn to focus on the names in language soon pick up surrounding words in their peripheral vision and get the general idea of a story without the laborious word-by-word reading that has been taught them in many reading instructional programs.

Children who have mastered a sight vocabulary of 300 to 500 words of highest frequency can get ideas for skimming by taking a newspaper or magazine story and marking through all the high-frequency words. They can see that the meaning of the author is still present without most of those words that only serve to structure sentences rather than to carry the major meaning of a passage. The reading of *only* high-frequency words results in meaningless sounds. This type of activity releases children to *assume* the words they know and use frequently and to skim rapidly to find words that harbor ideas and facts that may be useful in reconstructing the writer's meaning.

4. Reading to get detail is:
   ——choosing correct answers to questions
   ——solving problems that require specific information
   ——remembering descriptive categories such as color, size, shape, number, and amount
   ——restating portions of passages in language that matches that of the author
   ——using vocabulary typical of the writer when reporting on reading rather than always putting it in one's own words
   ——choosing correct answers on objective tests.

Ongoing classroom activities require attention to details. Mathematics reading is mostly reading to get details. Science reading requires attention to details if problems are to be solved and generalizations are to be formed. Much social studies information is derived from understanding details when reading.

Learning centers for a language experience approach environment usually include activities that require reading for detail in order to complete tasks. The making of games, the study of language that requires the use of dictionaries and a thesaurus, and making and answering questions to selections in the Reading/Research Center provide continuous opportunity for developing abilities to read for detail. Some teachers develop activities with operations like those on standardized tests to help children read typical test items. They recognize that the language of taking a test is a language experience that continues throughout school life. Abilities in taking standardized tests can be improved through instruction and practice in reading for detail.

Summary of Skills and Abilities for Comprehending What Is Read

BEGINNING READING

——Uses own dictated stories to begin to understand sound-symbol relationships
——Reproduces the main idea of films

——Listens to stories on records and reproduces main ideas
——Listens to oral reading of stories and poems to repeat ideas in author's words, retell stories in sequence, and relate personal meanings with experiences

UNDERSTANDING WORDS

——Associates pronouns such as *he, she, them, it,* and *I* with common nouns and proper names
——Interprets meanings of prepositions such as *down, over, under, into,* and *out of* as they appear in phrases
——Interprets meaning of words in the context in which they are found
——Identifies and interprets figures of speech
——Interprets the meaning of two or more words that are pronounced alike but have different spellings and different meanings, such as *red, read; two, too, to*
——Repeats words never heard before after hearing them in oral reading

COMPREHENDING LANGUAGE STRUCTURE

——Uses basic sentence patterns in speaking and writing
——Distinguishes a noun used as the subject of a sentence from one used as the complement of the verb
——Furnishes a subject to sentences with one implied rather than stated
——Expands a basic sentence
——Alters the tense of sentences

RECONSTRUCTING THE WRITER'S MEANING

——Follows a story sequence
——Interprets basic meanings of stories with art and drama
——Finds answers to questions
——Retells stories in own words
——Listens to directions on tape and follows them
——Plays games that have written instructions
——Skims to get general significance of passages
——Locates topic sentences, introductory paragraphs, and summary sections
——Answers questions of specific detail
——Solves problems that require specific information

——Restates portions of a passage with language of the author
——Understands how to take standardized tests

Selected References

Allen, Roach Van, Richard Venezky, and Harry T. Hahn. *Language Experiences in Reading, Level I.* Encyclopaedia Britannica Educational Corp., Chicago, 1974.

Brown, Eric. "The Bases of Reading Acquisition," *Reading Research Quarterly,* 4, 1 (1970), 56–67.

Chomsky, Carol. *The Acquisition of Syntax in Children 5 to 10.* The M.I.T. Press, Cambridge, Mass., 1969.

Chomsky, Noam. *Syntactic Structure.* Houton and Co., The Hague, 1957.

——. *Aspects of the Theory of Syntax.* The M.I.T. Press, Cambridge, Mass., 1965.

Davis, Frederick B. "Psychometric Research on Comprehension in Reading." In *The Literature of Research in Reading with Emphasis on Models,* edited by Frederick B. Davis. Graduate School of Education, Rutgers–The State University, New Brunswick, N.J., 1971.

——. "Research in Comprehension in Reading," *Reading Research Quarterly,* 4 (1968), 499–545.

Durkin, Dolores. *Teaching Them to Read.* Allyn & Bacon, Boston, 1970.

Eller, William "Personality Traits as Factors in Reading Comprehension." In *Reading in Education, A Broader View,* edited by Malcolm P. Douglass. Charles E. Merrill, Columbus, Ohio, 1973.

Goodman, Kenneth S. "Reading: A Psycholinguistic Guessing Game." In *Theoretical Models and Process of Reading,* edited by H. Singer and R. B. Ruddell. International Reading Association, Newark, Del., 1970.

Goodman, Yetta, and Kenneth S. Goodman. *Linguistics, Psycholinguistics, and the Teaching of Reading.* (An annotated bibliography.) International Reading Association, Newark, Del., 1971.

Hall, MaryAnne. *Teaching Reading as a Language Experience.* Charles E. Merrill, Columbus, Ohio, 1970.

May, Frank B. *To Help Children Read: Mastery Performance Modules for Teacher Training.* Charles E. Merrill, Columbus, Ohio, 1973.

Moore, W. J. "The Skimming Process in Silent Reading." In *Challenge and Experiment in Reading,* edited by A. J. Figurel. Proceedings of the International Reading Association, No. 7, 203–205. Scholastic Magazines, New York, 1962.

Quaintance, William. "Developing Comprehension Through Word Recognition Skills." In *The Quest for Competency in Reading,* edited by Howard A. Klein. International Reading Association, Newark, Del., 1972.

Simon, Herbert D. "Linguistic Skills and Reading Comprehension." In *The*

Quest for Competency in Reading, edited by Howard A. Klein. International Reading Association, Newark, Del., 1972.

Smith, Frank, and George A. Miller (eds.). *The Genesis of Language: A Psycholinguistic Approach.* The M.I.T. Press, Cambridge, Mass., 1971.

Tiedt, Iris M., and Sidney W. Tiedt. *Contemporary English in the Elementary School.* Prentice-Hall, Englewood Cliffs, N.J., 1967.

Van Metre, Patricia D. "Syntactic Characteristics of Selected Bilingual Children." (Ed.D. dissertation.) University of Arizona, Tucson, 1972.

FROM THE RATIONALE   Organizing ideas and information—using various methods of putting ideas from multiple sources into an overall concept that can be reported such as painting a picture, making a collage and montage, sculpturing, making games, composing music, and constructing; planning and producing stories with a sequence of ideas, characters, and settings; planning and producing poetry in predetermined patterns; and classifying briefly the stated ideas of others.

The process of organization—of ordering, relating, and interpreting experiences—is inseparable from the ability to think clearly and to use meaningful symbols. Most authors whose work is published have organized their thinking prior to writing. Artists and composers have organized thoughts in their work. Scientists must organize their thoughts for experimentation and for reporting their observations and discoveries.

An aim of a language experience approach is to develop the abilities of each child to organize the verbal expression of experience for original thinking. To do this there must be continuing influence from the well-organized work of others. Abilities in reading for comprehension are important, but they are no more important than the ability to recognize the strategies other authors use to achieve their goals. As children read and listen to reading, they become increasingly aware of how authors

——stick to the subject under discussion

——relate events in time and sequence

——order ideas in relation to a problem or purpose

——interpret experiences, generalize concerning them, and draw inferences from them.

Studies by Delva Daines, Arthur V. Olson, and Jean E. Robertson, reported in *The Quest for Competency in Teaching Reading* (1972), indicate that the greatest lack of proficiency in reading is in the study skills that require abilities in locating information, reading for different purposes, selecting and evaluating ideas, following directions, using visual aids, and organizing ideas for personal use. Some of this lack may be attributed to past materials and procedures in teaching reading that used the story format almost exclusively. Recognition and comprehension skills in traditional reading programs were practiced daily with material that was too much alike for students to need to analyze the author's strategy and style. So much of the program was bound in hard-case books that teachers and students felt no need to explore beyond the reading textbook for evidence of validity and reliability. Because the planned exercises for each story seemed so sufficient and were so time consuming, there was no inclination nor time left for study skills that promoted the abilities to organize ideas and information from multiple sources.

The appeal of activities that promote those abilities is that they are practical and tangible. They draw on multiple resources in and out of school. They can be reported in many ways that include:

——outlining

——summarizing

——making records and reports of events and achievements in useful forms

——making games and collections for others.

These abilities are not only practical, but they are important factors in the development of the creative person. They provide repeated opportunities for the development of abilities to rearrange ideas, to synthesize information from a variety of sources, and to practice consistency in the presentation of ideas.

In the process of developing the ability to organize ideas and information, children are provided with self-testing activities. As they read and think about something, they realize that they must use skills of organization in order to communicate with others. If they are to communicate, there must be some type of organization that permits others to understand their purpose and meaning.

Outlining

Outlining should not be treated as a skill important in itself. It should be used as a means by which children observe how other authors organize their ideas, how they can collect information for a meaningful presentation, and how they can communicate their own ideas in meaningful ways.

A sense of order develops very early in children. They have a special place to sit, places to put certain things, and routines for daily activities. They listen to stories and learn to repeat portions of them in a sequence of main ideas. They view television programs and tell what happened. They look at their world and select ideas of major importance for crayon drawings and paintings.

Children who work in a language experience approach environment begin the first day of school with outlining ideas for painting and dictating their ideas. Often they talk about a painting as if they were collecting information. Then the teacher asks them to repeat two or three of the important things that are to be written down. The process of selecting and sequencing is a procedure for teaching organizational abilities related to outlining.

After a walk around the building or into the neighborhood, children find it easier to remember what they have observed if they collect their information under headings such as people, animals, plants, and buildings. In such activities they apply outlining principles to information gleaned primarily from firsthand experience. More mature abilities in outlining are developed as children learn to recover the main ideas from what they read and hear read to them.

Arthur begins his work in helping children to understand outlines by putting an outline of a story or chapter on the chalkboard prior to reading. At first he writes the main topics and the supporting ideas. As soon as children give evidence of being able to find and follow an outline when reading or listening to reading, he puts only main topics on the chalkboard and leaves space for filling in supporting ideas that the children suggest. When some of them can participate at that level, he puts *only a blank outline* on the chalkboard. Children read and fill in the outline. They learn the value of skimming first to get a general notion of major ideas before they begin a careful reading to fill in the details. They become critical of reading material that lacks organization and cannot be outlined. The experience helps them to value organization in their own productions.

Dolores uses a lot of cooking as a basic experience for language acquisition. This activity also builds a need for accurate organization of information.

Recipes are treated as outlines for work. The children "talk a recipe" to elaborate on the outline that is printed. They move from the cooking recipes to the use of recipes for writing. Cinquains, haiku, and other simple patterned poems described in Chapter 15 are learned as guides for writing and for the evaluation of writing.

Carlos introduces outlining through music compositions. He shares a collection of classical music. First, he shows and plays the simple melody. Then he adds the harmony to the melody. From there, depending on the original, he adds flourishes to the harmony. Finally, he plays for the class a recording of an orchestra performing the composition. In this way he helps them see that one must have major topics before the supporting details can be meaningful.

Children who write books need a form of outlining as they develop beyond a simple sequence of events to chapters. Those who become involved as authors of long books have need to read other books to study the structure—the design—as much as the content.

Poetry writing places demands on children to outline their ideas and then create the language for them within a design. To write a sijo like those described in Chapter 15, the author must think of six things to say about one thing. Possibilities include naming, color, shape, size, use, sound, taste, smell, motion, and other categories that invite descriptive statements. The tanka, haiku, diamante, quatrain, and other poetry patterns require organizational abilities for outlining that are simple and indirect.

Summarizing

Children who develop the ability to outline also develop the ability to summarize, for it too involves
> —collecting ideas
> —selecting those that are pertinent
> —organizing them for various purposes.

Summarizing what one hears or reads is an ongoing language experience. It is basic to planning a school day and in recording the plans on the chalkboard. It is required for the evaluation of a work period and a school day. Most reading experiences also are summarized in some way through oral summaries, art responses, dramatic interpretations, or written summaries. In fact, the skill of summarizing is such an integral part of communication that it may be overlooked as a set of abilities that needs to be developed.

For reading activities that promote abilities in summarizing, children need selections that they can hear or read in their entirety. Round-robin reading of bits of stories cannot yield this ability. Stories that have a definite sequence should be used for the beginning work in summarizing. Words of enumeration give clues for summarizing what happened first, second, and third. Number words in the titles of stories usually indicate those that are easy to summarize.

The language used in summaries is often more like the language of the authors than it is like the natural, home-rooted language of the student. It reflects a growing ability to adjust one's language to include the influence of new ways of saying things without memorizing the original wording.

Clara works with children who need very much to learn to say things in new ways before they can engage in the silent reading of stories and books. She reads to them and then helps them summarize the stories. As she mediates the language, she asks, "And what did he say?" She may read a portion and let children chorus it back in the language of the author. She may often ask for an individual response, "Can you say the words you hear when I read?" If not, she rereads, and they repeat phrases and sentences together. She knows that many of the children in her class can never read silently with success until they can hear and say things in new ways that are like those used by authors.

Michael uses a lot of projected material to encourage children to summarize ideas. They make slide shows on all kinds of topics. From home they bring sets of slides of trips, organize them into a sequence, and develop a commentary. They learn to summarize in fifteen or twenty minutes an experience that lasted several days. Michael knows that this is exactly what happens when an author writes. Experiences are compressed, and the reader must fill in the time and space mentally.

When Michael and the class go on walks or trips, they always have cameras to help record the experience. The slides or prints are used to help the students recall, organize, and summarize the experiences. He finds that students who had been identified as reluctant, disabled readers when they arrived in his fifth grade are eager and able to work with photographic material. They search their experiences, collect ideas from many sources, organize them, and summarize them in ways that are interesting and useful to others.

Michael then leads the students to see that many good stories and much reading material in social studies and science are like the summaries without the set of slides. The pictures are there in words. For many of the children this experience is the first that makes them aware of the responsibility of the reader during silent reading to furnish mental pictures. They had been so involved in the past in trying to recognize words and sound them out that they missed the pictures that authors painted with words.

Painting following reading is a form of summary available to children. Ability to read a story and reflect its main idea in one painting shows real understanding as well as a talent for summarizing. A series of paintings or a group mural can be developed to summarize long and involved selections.

Dramatization is a summarizing ability when it is related to stories heard or read. The sound and action of drama permit children to recover main events in language which may be new to them. They have the opportunity in drama to practice saying new things over and over as they rehearse and as they present the finished plays several times.

Rewriting stories is another summarizing experience available in language experience approach classrooms. Children hear a story read to them or see a filmed version of one that can then be summarized with a series of illustrations and summary statements. These can be organized into a sequence, bound into a book, and used for reading. Children who would not possibly read the original story silently or orally can read the class-produced summary and participate in follow-up activities without any stigma of "not being ready for that story."

Making Records and Reports

Keeping records, making reports on reading, and organizing presentations based on experiences are common school activities. They require that students condense information into manageable form, make plans for presentation, and evaluate bulk information in terms of main ideas and supporting details.

Children who keep records and report on the records begin to recognize how these abilities are like those of historians, scientists, authors, and teachers who contribute to social and scientific advancement. They find that they must use skills such as:

—keeping ideas and materials in a simple time sequence
—listing ideas in outline form
—listing a variety of materials under a single topic
—keeping a diary of observations of personal events, science experiments, and school happenings
—selecting pertinent ideas from wide reading.

David always keeps a Discovery Center in operation in his classroom. In it he and the class place interesting objects and books. Along with them are a magnifying glass, microscope, measuring instruments, and blank forms for recording discoveries. Growing things might be accompanied by forms with space to record the date, time of observation, and what was observed. Books of information about the plant or animal observed are usually available in the center.

Another type of blank form will accompany an object such as a rock, a leaf, or a twig. When reports are made on the discoveries, children are expected to have the scientific information and vocabulary appropriate for the report.

Adrienne wants the children in her class to develop a sense of history through understanding the people involved. Rather than drilling children on historical information, she helps each one to project self into a period of history and to keep a diary. When the diaries are shared, they reflect interests, ideals, and aspirations along with the repetition of major events during the period studied.

Group-shared experiences can be reported in ways that the students help to organize. In the process they come to grips with problems of selecting important details, organizing them into a meaningful presentation, and reporting them clearly to those who did not have the experience. They make decisions about using reporting procedures such as a panel of speakers, a mural, a tableau, an illustrated book, a panel of illustrations, a question-answer session, and one speaker with questions from the audience to follow the presentation. They discuss and choose from the many options open to them as a result of having observed and experienced multiple ways of communicating ideas within an organizational pattern.

Making Games and Collections

The making of games and the preparation of collections, even simple ones, require
- —awareness of detail
- —statement of purpose
- —judgment and decisions that demand careful thought.

There is real satisfaction in having someone else play games that have been made in the classroom and in seeing others enjoy and gain information from viewing collections of interesting objects.

When children are processing information gained from reading, the making of formless lists of facts assures lack of interest. The same facts can be collected and made into games that have real purpose for others.

Games

Games made by children can review word-recognition skills, arithmetic facts, science information, music reading, spelling, and information that needs to be recalled and reviewed.

The playing of games is not as demanding of students as the making of them, but it does afford the opportunity for mutual help and friendship among students of varying reading abilities.

Stanley keeps available supplies for making classification and matching games. Several children in his second grade are reluctant to engage in the language recognition activities required for reading because of their repeated and embarrassing failures during the previous school year.

Stanley provides cardboard, pictures, paints, glue, and boxes. He also keeps a collection of commercially produced games to furnish ideas for rules, format, and special materials.

The children paste pictures of foods, animals, people, or machines on cards. They select boxes on which they label classifications, and ask players to sort the cards into the different classifications. They do the same thing with cards that have only words on them.

Other classification games require concepts of size: large in relation to small; texture: hard to soft; and the senses of hearing, tasting, and smelling.

The children make games that group things that are related—music notes and signatures, arithmetic problems, words and phrases. They pair things that go together such as cup and saucer, shoe and sock. They match words that are the same in several languages.

Cheri likes to make puzzle games with her class of ten- to twelve-year-olds. She is especially interested in taking a topic of current interest or one from social studies or science to help children establish a wide vocabulary of words that they can read and spell.

Cheri brings to class examples of crossword puzzles from newspapers, children's magazines, and puzzle books. The class discusses the requirements for different kinds of puzzles and practices making some on the chalkboard where errors can be adjusted easily.

Children make individual or group puzzles, try them out, and then duplicate them for the Language Study Center. Frequently they are published in the school newspaper. Each year they collect the puzzles and publish them as a class book.

Nedra helps children in her class to make games of sets of cards to give practice in associating information that belongs together. She cuts cardboard into uniform sizes that are easy to shuffle. A print set is available along with pictures cut from old workbooks and magazines. Using commercial games as models, children make rules that require that a player get a set of cards of a designated number in order to have a book, or trick.

Sets of cards are made of words that are the same, rhyme, or begin alike. Arithmetic sets with the same answer make a book. Items that are products from the same raw material make sets for science cards. Music patterns that are the same can be collected into books for music-reading skills.

Louis has several master cards that he has made for racing games. Some have numbered spaces and some are coded in color. Children in his class make games that require players to move from a beginning point to an ending point by answering certain questions.

The questions are developed by the class as a summary of studies in literature, science, social studies, and current events. The children also make the rules about the number of spaces to move forward for correct answers, penalties for wrong answers, and regressive steps for no answer.

Collections

Collections of things that go together give children a sense of order that has both pleasure and purpose in it. To make collections useful they must plan, make decisions, and call on their artistic sense of arrangement for balance and interest. Through collections children can express individual interests and abilities which lead easily to reading from authors who have written on similar topics. Collections can suggest subjects for writing books that include information and illustrations. They can be used to build vocabularies of words of opposite meanings or words marking contrasts.

Joe stimulates interest in collecting things by using one bulletin board or table to invite contributions from anyone. He might make a sign reading "Buttons." The children add to the collection. Then he helps them to classify them according to material—plastic, bone, shell, or metal. He may ask them to classify the buttons according to the number of holes or some other feature that is obvious, such as color, size, or shape. They can make collages of the buttons or study their origin and use and write stories to use the information. This sometimes leads to an interest in other kinds of fasteners that will be collected by individuals or small groups.

Sometime during each school year Joe and his class sponsor a hobby show for collectors. They set the standards, make the arrangements, and sponsor the show for the whole school.

DeAnn usually has a bulletin board, a large blank book, or a table that has a question or label for collections such as things that fly and walk, things that grow above and below ground, domestic and wild animals, heavy and light things, and water and land forms. Children can contribute pictures, stories, and articles to the collections. When the collections are large enough, they can be arranged into subclassifications. Books, filmstrips, and picture sets are made available for study of the topics of the collections. Some collections become organized learning centers developed by students.

Students in the sixth-grade class of Iris collect words that can be used on posters, book jackets, and books for young children to read. They cut words from magazines and keep them in boxes that classify the words for use by any student who needs them. Some of the classifications are space, politics, ecology, diet, war, peace, alphabet books, and rhyming pairs.

The words in bold type can be used for posters. Some children add interest to books they are writing by pasting in some meaningful words in bold type. They use words rather than pictures for illustrations of reports, stories, and poems. They use cutout words for the titles of books.

Iris finds that this collection is popular year after year. Students watch for words as they read. They make decisions about classifications. They focus on main ideas as they organize their thinking.

Children who develop the attributes of creativity must have repeated opportunities to organize their thinking. They must experience ways of
- ——rearranging ideas into new and personal ways of communication
- ——synthesizing information from a number of sources so that the new organization reflects the ideas of the one doing the organizing
- ——presenting their ideas in a variety of forms and media that make them clear and useful to others.

Children who have these experiences identify with authors whose work is organized in creative and artful presentations. To them reading is much more than just gathering information. It involves appreciation for artistic endeavor. It influences them to try to use well-organized materials as models for personal communication.

Summary of Skills and Abilities for Organizing Ideas and Information

OUTLINING

——Develops ability to make simple outlines, based on materials read or heard, such as:
  ——lists of ideas in sequential order
  ——simple main-topic outlines
  ——detailed outlines including subordinate topics
  ——ideas from different sources under a single topic
——Locates lines or paragraphs in reading context that correspond with points in an outline
——Makes arrangements of ideas from various sources to reveal what are the main ones and what are the supporting details
——Outlines ideas for own poems and stories

SUMMARIZING

——Is able to summarize in writing (or in dictation to the teacher) a story told orally
——Can summarize in writing or in telling ideas gained from experience, observation, reading, and listening
——Is able to locate the topic sentence in a paragraph
——Can select from a group of sentences the sentence that best summarizes a story or article
——Can select from a group of words a word that summarizes a main idea

INTEGRATING AND ASSIMILATING IDEAS INTO GAMES AND REPORTS

——Expresses ideas through writing in the form of stories, plays, poems, and songs
——Uses ideas gained from observation, listening, and reading to solve problems in areas such as science, social studies, and literature

——Can report ideas and information in a simple time sequence
——Can keep a diary of events and ideas
——Reports discoveries and ideas from reading in a variety of ways,
  including:
    ——oral sharing
    ——leading discussions
    ——answering questions
    ——painting and other art forms
    ——dramatization
    ——writing in a variety of styles and forms
——Organizes learned facts into games that show relationships

Selected References

Daines, Delva. "Developing Reading Study Skills in the Content Areas." In
The Quest for Competency in Teaching Reading, edited by Howard A.
Klein. International Reading Association, Newark, Del., 1972.

Darrow, Helen F., and Roach Van Allen. *Independent Activities for Creative
Learning.* Teachers College Press, Columbia University, New York,
1961.

Evertts, Eldonna L. *Aspects of Reading.* National Council of Teachers of English, Champaign, Ill., 1970.

May, Frank B. *To Help Children Read: Mastery Performance Modules for
Teachers in Training.* Charles E. Merrill, Columbus, Ohio, 1973.

Olson, Arthur V. "Using Context Clues in Science and Social Studies." In *The
Quest for Competency in Teaching Reading,* edited by Howard A. Klein.
International Reading Association, Newark, Del., 1972.

Robertson, Jean E. "Using Social Studies Content to Develop Reading Skills."
In *The Quest for Competency in Teaching Reading,* edited by Howard A.
Klein. International Reading Association, Newark, Del., 1972.

Ruddell, Robert B. *Reading-Language Instruction: Innovative Practices.* Prentice-Hall, Englewood Cliffs, N.J., 1974.

Sebesta, Sam L., and Carl J. Wallen (eds.). *The First R: Readings on Teaching
Reading.* Science Research Associates, Chicago, 1972.

Smith, James A. *Adventures in Communication.* Allyn & Bacon, Boston, 1972.

Stauffer, Russell G. *The Language-Experience Approach to the Teaching of Reading.* Harper & Row, New York, 1970.

FROM THE RATIONALE   Assimilating and integrating ideas—using listening and reading for specific purposes of a personal nature; extending personal meanings and using new meanings in experiences in self-expression as a result of reading stories, viewing films, and listening to recordings; talking about things *like* and *not like* that which has happened; and seeing and hearing experiences elaborated and extended in many ways.

Communicating for understanding and enjoyment is a worthy objective and one that may satisfy many who read and write. There are others, however, for whom reading and writing are means to other intellectual goals. There are those who must go beyond comprehension in order to understand subject matter and make scientific inferences. Even those who read and write for their own enjoyment must do more than *just understand* in order to make personal responses to the thoughts of others. They must acquire skills in taking off from what they read into flights of thought that are personal in nature. These skills are identified here as assimilation and integration.

Teachers in a language experience approach take advantage of opportunities for students to exercise their thinking abilities beyond simple comprehension. They use the ideas of others to help children come to grips with their own ideas, beliefs, and aspirations. They take advantage of words that authors use with one meaning to explore the variety of meanings available to each student. They select and use materials that stir the imagination quite beyond anything that an author says.

Productive Thinking in Communication

The work of J. P. Guilford (1969), the psychologist, is influential in the selection of materials and the planning of instruction. In his model of the structure of the intellect (1959), he identifies two major types of productive thinking required of educated persons. They are convergent production and divergent production. Both types of thinking are essential to the assimilation and integration of the many facets of communication.

Convergent production in a language experience approach is promoted and developed by materials and activities that focus on *uniform* responses. Although the results are seldom uniform, the purposes are in that direction. The responses include:

1. Conventional spelling of words in writing
2. Imitation of the sounds of words and phrases so that others can understand
3. Recognition and reconstruction of sentence patterns that occur frequently in written communication
4. Repeating sequences of events and information following reading
5. Following directions when listening and reading
6. Memorizing passages for pleasure, for ready reference, or for both

Divergent production in a language experience approach is promoted and developed by materials and activities that focus on *personal* responses. No absolutely right answer exists. Differences are useful and are treated as valuable assets in the learning environment. Although many divergent responses contain some elements of convergent production, the purposes are clearly in the direction of eliciting different responses from each participant. The responses include:

1. Alternatives to stated facts and conditions
2. Challenges to beliefs and facts found in printed material and heard from a variety of sources
3. Location of related ideas from many sources to support personal ideas
4. Acting out roles impossible in real life
5. Arranging ideas in ways that are unique to the producer—creative writing, painting, sculpting, and acting
6. Adaptation of redundant language patterns to express personal thoughts and observations.

Most language experiences reflect a combination of both convergent thinking and divergent thinking. These related thinking abilities are balanced in the assimilation and integration of basic language requirements for:

— recognition through listening and reading
— prediction in listening and in reading because of familiarity with repeating language patterns
— acquisition of new words and new meanings for known words
— production of personal ideas in unique and clever ways and reproduction of the ideas of others in new forms.

Recognition Abilities

Language recognition abilities in instruction emphasize:

— relationships between the learner's own speech and printed materials that represent that speech (divergent)

—decoding skills that permit the reproduction of the language and ideas of other people in ways in which they can be understood and used (convergent).

CLUES FOR INSTRUCTION

1. Children study on any given subject, and each one records a report on tape. Each one makes a chart of key words in the report. As a group listens to the tape, the child who did the report points to the key words on the chart.

2. Stories and poems that individuals write are made into transparencies. A group follows along the projected image as the author reads.

3. Children who need a tactile experience to learn the sound-letter correspondence of words can say words that the teacher or someone else writes with a crayon on newsprint over window screen wire. The child then traces along the word which is raised like Braille.

4. Children can choose a quotation from something they have read— word, phrase, or sentence. The quotations are copied on adding machine tape in printing large enough for a group to see. On the day following, the tapes can be read by the contributors in unison as each tape is unrolled.

5. Recognition of prepositions in context can be practiced by making a collection of directions and having on hand the articles necessary to carry out the directions:
Put the pencil *in* the cup.
Wear the glove *on* your right hand.
Draw a ring *around* the car.
Put the bean *between* the stones.
Pull the needle *through* the paper.
Put the book *under* the table.
Put everything back *in* the box.

6. Collect word cards of common nouns that can be put together to form compound words: *house, dog, bar, yard, chalk, board*. Provide a pattern for writing these words for the Reading/Research Center.
Here is a dog.
Here is a house.
Put them together,
   you have a *doghouse*.

Look, there's a barn.
Look, there's a yard.
Put them together,
    you have a *barnyard*.

Do you see some chalk?
Do you see a board?
If you put them together,
    you have a *chalkboard*.

7. Work for mastery of recognition of high-frequency words. Since many of these words are nonphonetic, they must be recognized at sight through practice.
    ——Write five words on a card. Children tabulate the number of times they find the words in one story, in one column of a newspaper, or on one page of a magazine.
    ——Write words on ladders that can be mounted on the walls. Children read up and down the ladders. A missed word means a fall.
    ——Children collect in word boxes words they can read and spell.
    ——Older children can take a list of 200 to 300 words of highest frequency and cross out all of them that they find in a newspaper story. Then they can figure what percentage of the high-frequency words are used in the story (proper nouns are not counted in word counts).
    ——Older children can edit their story manuscripts for young children to read. One of the things they do in editing is to increase the percentage of words of highest frequency. The use of the list for this purpose leads toward mastery.
8. Make games using nouns of highest frequency. These can be matching games, sets of card games, classification games, and simple recognition games.
9. Sing songs and chants to get the rhythm of language. Count out the measures and notice the number of syllables in words. Accompany singing with rhythm instruments that require keeping time. Call attention to the fact that every syllable has a vowel sound.
10. List syllables that occur frequently in language and let children hunt for them in words they read. Some which they will find at beginnings, middles, and ends of words are:

at	*en*	*in*	*ook*	*un*
an	*ell*	*ill*	*ot*	*ug*

ay	*et*	*ing*	*ow*	*ull*
all	*ed*	*ight*	*old*	*ut*
	eek	*it*	*oy*	*um*

These twenty-four phonograms with contrasting beginning consonants and inflected endings generate hundreds of common words.

Prediction Abilities

Language prediction abilities in instruction emphasize:

—the redundancy of words and language patterns in dependable
places and in dependable lines of language to an extent that the
listener and reader can know what to expect prior to hearing or
seeing the written language (divergent)

—the acquisition of a sight vocabulary, experience with the collocation of words and phrases, and the recognition of dependable
clues from initial consonants and consonant clusters to an extent
that the right words are assumed to be present as meanings
flow through the reading process at a rate much faster than oral
reading permits (convergent).

Children who mature as readers depend less and less on recognition abilities and more and more on prediction abilities. This development permits them to experience reading as a thinking process in
which the decoding of print is only incidental to the interaction of
ideas between authors and the reader (Wilkinson, 1971).

CLUES FOR INSTRUCTION

1. Use a "feely bag" or a "touch box" containing all kinds of items
   for children to feel without seeing. They choose an item, describe
   it, and attempt to name it before looking at it to confirm their
   prediction.
2. Say two or more words that appear together frequently such as
   knife and *fork*. Children say other words that appear together
   frequently in syntactical structure. As the first word is said, a
   pause invites the completion.
   cup and ———
   shoes and ———
   bread and ———
   in and ———
   up and ———
   Prediction abilities for reading are extended as children anticipate

collocation of terms. They anticipate words and phrases in ways that make reading flow with the ease of oral language.

3. List the characters from a story that has been heard or read. Children create new plots for stories using the same characters. The stories can be taped or written. By doing this the children integrate the notion of story sequences that are characteristic of many other sequences. They increase their abilities to predict how a story goes and thereby decrease the comprehension difficulties that arise from the feeling that every story is different.

4. Show films and filmstrips. Stop at appropriate points for children to predict what will come next. When they check out their predictions, they will be combining divergent thinking with convergent thinking. They will be comparing their own meanings from experience with meanings that are locked in to published materials.

5. Show science and social studies films with the sound turned off. Children can talk to a partner or in groups during the showing. After predictions of the content have been collected, show the film with the soundtrack on. Compare the predictions with the soundtrack version.

6. Show filmstrips with no words printed on them. Say something about each frame. Write or tape at least one response or a summary response. Play the record or tape that accompanies the filmstrip in order to compare and contrast predictions.

7. Look at a story title. Skim rapidly to find names of characters and places. List them and predict a story from a brief look at it. Read to check out predictions.
   Children will begin to generalize that clues for meaning reside in a few words of most stories and that in silent reading they can focus on nouns and verbs to pick up the main ideas of authors.

8. Copy the opening paragraphs of stories on cards for the Writing/Publishing Center. These stories without endings can be completed by children. After several endings have been written, the whole story can be placed in the Reading/Research Center where children can check out their predictions. Interest in reading is usually heightened when the reader has made some type of prediction prior to reading.

9. Find lines of large print in magazines and newspapers. Cut strips that show only half of the letters, top or bottom. Paste them on cards for reading. Children will be challenged to recognize the words and sentences with only half of the print showing.

10. Place mystery items in the classroom from time to time. Lead the

children's attention to the items with arrows or mysterious foot-
prints, ears, or lips. Print key words on whatever is used to lead
children to a closet door or other appropriate hiding place. The
words should furnish clues to whatever is hidden. The child who
predicts closest from the word clues gets to use the mystery item
first. This activity can be used to introduce new books, filmstrips,
games, art materials, and records.

11. Use words of enumeration to increase prediction abilities. Begin
    an account such as:
    "This morning I put seeds on the ground for the birds. The first
    bird ate one seed. The second bird ate two seeds."
    The children can predict what will follow. They can make their
    own prediction stories by stating an enumeration pattern. These
    can be illustrated and bound into books for the Reading/Research
    Center. This same pattern of language can be used with the days
    of the week and the months of the year.

12. Print short story selections on cards for the Reading/Research Cen-
    ter. Leave a blank for every fifth word. Children copy the stories
    putting in the words they think belong in the blanks. Provide a
    key to the words the author used.

Shipwrecked

For many days after ——— set sail, the weather ——— clear but
very hot. ——— a terrible storm came ——— of the southeast. I
——— seen many storms but ——— one like that.

13. Write stories on cards for the Reading/Research Center with blanks
    for all the vowels in the words. Children discover that vowel
    sounds are highly predictable. They do not need to be printed for
    reading language that is familiar.

Pinky and Winky

P—nky —nd W—nky w—r— l—ttl— d—gs. Th—y l—v—d
—n — d—g h——s—. —t w—s — g——d h—m— f—r th—m.

14. Write stories on cards for the Reading/Research Center with blanks
    for the structure words. Write only the words that are used in sen-
    tences as nouns, verbs, adjectives, and adverbs. Children read
    the cards, supplying the structure words by predicting what they

would be. An accompanying set of cards can have the total text printed for comparison purposes.

Children come to rely less and less on calling every word in silent reading and understand that they supply the structure words automatically in most cases.

Peter Rabbit

———— ————— — time ———— ———— four little rabbits. ————
———— Flopsy, Mopsy, Cottontail, —— Peter. ———— lived ————
Mrs. Rabbit ———— — hole ———— — big tree.

One morning Mrs. Rabbit said, "Now, —— children, —— —— going
—— ———— baker's. ———— ———— go ———— —— play. ———— do
not go ————— Mr. McGregor's garden."

15. Make story cards for the Reading/Research Center with only the initial consonant or consonant cluster written for common words (not proper nouns) beginning with consonant sounds. Follow the letter or letter cluster with blanks for each of the other letters in the word. Children discover that they can read many words in context with only initial consonant clues.

Harry and Bonnie c— t— our h— t— pl—. W— pl— b— all d—.

Acquisition Abilities

Language acquisition abilities in instruction emphasize:

——the relationships of speech sounds to personal experiences in ways that permit the learner to name things, to tell how they move, to describe them in multiple dimensions, and to communicate new ideas and experiences by talking, writing, visualizing, and acting (divergent)

——influences from language as other people use it in many forms of communication so the learner uses words and sentence structures not typical of home-rooted language which formed the base for beginning writing and reading (convergent).

CLUES FOR INSTRUCTION

1. Say the conventional color of something, such as: "The sky is blue" or "Trees are green." Children recall exceptions to the usual response. They tell or illustrate other colors they know or imag-

ine. They make use of real experiences, reading, and viewing to assimilate meanings beyond the ordinary.

2. Select cartoons and other humorous pictures. Children say or write punch lines for them. These can be collected into a book that illustrates the wide range of meanings individuals bring to the same stimulus.

3. Write a common word such as *big* on the chalkboard or on a Ditto sheet. Children list as many words as they can that mean about the same thing. For use in the Writing/Publishing Center these can then be arranged as one-syllable words, two-syllable words, three-syllable words, and so on. These lists can be useful when writing poetry with syllabic restrictions. Examples:

One Syllable	Two Syllables	Three Syllables
tall	giant	important
wide	older	gigantic
deep	many	tremendous
king	famous	
lots		

4. Tell familiar fairy tales. At first children act out the lines. Then they begin to say them, using words and language patterns new to them but characteristic of the reading material.

5. Make charts or transparencies of songs that are sung over and over. Follow along the words during the singing so that children associate the sounds of the words with the print. In this way poor readers can be included in a successful reading experience.

6. Plan discussions on the world around us. Children bring newspaper clippings or tell of news heard on radio and television. Each day one child can be a meteorologist to give the weather forecast. In this type of activity they use words that they will find frequently in reading.

7. Let children pretend to be something—animals, plants, objects, rain, snow, rivers, mountains, and machines. Encourage them to tell about their pretend selves—name, size, colors, what they see, how they feel, what they like and dislike, where they have been, where they are going, and any other information that is appropriate. Build oral vocabularies of form-class words that are found in reading through the extension of self.

8. Arrange a series of word boxes with labels on them. Include the labels Characters, Places, Problems, Occupations, Traits, among others. Place the row of boxes in the Writing/Publishing Center.

Children choose one word from each box for writing a story or poem. They must use the words at least once. Children add word cards to the boxes as they find them in their reading.

Word box stories and poems can be bound together in books for the Reading/Research Center. They offer some vocabulary that may not be typical of other reading materials.

9. Charts with the headline "What Would You Find?" can be developed on a bulletin board. Children add words during a period of three or four days. What would you find in a: picnic basket? glove compartment? cafeteria? watermelon? haunted house? spaceship? wrist watch? television set?

Children can suggest topics for this type of language acquisition activity. They may want to share some of the sources in which they find information, and reference reading and research can be stimulated. This activity also encourages careful observation and imagination.

10. Cooking experiences increase meaningful vocabularies in areas such as measurement, fractions, and time. They involve following directions very carefully. Contrast vocabulary is needed to describe what happens as a result of cooking: *hard* and *soft*, *liquid* and *solid*, *smooth* and *lumpy*, *limp* and *crisp*. Vocabularies of the senses are brought into play as children observe, taste, smell, and touch.

Popcorn, pancakes, and applesauce are cooking activities that offer a beginning for a rich vocabulary base when language is exercised before, during, and after cooking.

11. Write simple sentences at the top of sheets of paper. Pass them around or leave them in the Writing/Publishing Center. Students copy sentences and add one word or phrase each time.

Birds sing.
The black birds sing.
The cheerful black birds sing.
The cheerful black birds sing in the morning.
All the cheerful black birds sing in the morning.

Almost all the cheerful black birds sing in the morning.
Almost all the cheerful black birds sing in the early morning.

12. Books called "More Than One Meaning" can be written for pleasure reading. Each student can contribute an illustrated page on a word such as:
A river has BANKS, but no money.
A potato has EYES, but can't see.
A table has LEGS, but can't walk.

Encourage students to browse through dictionaries to find the multiple meanings of words.

13. Extend the children's understanding of idiomatic expressions by saying them, collecting them into books, and using them in the Reading/Research Center.
His goose is cooked.
She jumped from the frying pan into the fire.
They are on the ball.
He lost his marbles.

14. Study origins of words to understand meanings and spellings. Children are interested in knowing that the English language borrows from many others as it grows. They can collect words that came from different languages, and begin to understand why the spelling of some words is not phonetic in standard English ways.

French	Greek
bouquet	phone
racquet	phonics
Spanish	Japanese
patio	kimono
junta	kamikaze
German	
wiener	
sauerkraut	

Production Abilities

Language production abilities in instruction emphasize:
——trying out many forms of communication from many points of view and with many characters, experimenting with numerous

literary forms used by authors, editing original manuscripts to include words and phrases that are not characteristic of home-rooted language, and increasing fluency through speaking experiences that offer opportunities to say things in new ways (divergent)

——mastering speaking, spelling, and writing mechanics to the extent that others can understand personal ideas when they hear or read them (convergent).

CLUES FOR INSTRUCTION

1. Describe the common characteristics of an object such as a carrot—hard, orange, edible. Children produce a quantity of words in a limited time. This activity can be an oral or a written one. Scoring can be based on the number of logical responses in the timed period.
2. Name a common object such as a brick. Children name, in a limited time, all the ways they think a brick can be useful. This can be a group activity, or it can be individual with scores.
3. Tell a usual use for something and then ask for responses about unusual uses. An example may be: "A book is usually used for reading. What other uses can you suggest?" Responses may be: "To prop open a door," "To raise the focus of the movie projector," "To weight down paper," "For the baby to sit on when eating," and "To shade the light from my eyes so I can sleep." Each response is unique to the person making it and represents the ability to think freely beyond conventional responses.

4. Pretend to be a news reporter. Show children a press card and be equipped with a tape recorder for individual interviews. Ask several children questions on a topic of interest such as a trip to the moon.

Interviews can be listened to by the whole class and then transcribed from the tape, edited, and published in a class newspaper along with other news.

5. "Movies" with a soundtrack can be produced by:
    ——formulating a story with a clear and sharp sequence
    ——dividing the dialogue into parts for illustrations
    ——illustrating each part of the sequence on
        ——blank acetate rolls for an overhead projector
        ——a series of uniform-sized pages that fit an opaque projector

(these can be mounted on a roll for ease in pulling through the projector)

——painting large illustrations and making colored slides 2 in. by 2 in. of them for projection with an automatic carousel projector

——making a soundtrack that includes appropriate sound effects to accompany the dialogue

——synchronizing the illustrations and the soundtrack for a production for the class and invited guests.

When a Super 8 motion picture camera is available, children can act out their story, shoot the film, and make an accompanying soundtrack. To do this they have to have prior to the shooting of the film a very precise script that can be timed to the second. Every line has to have meaning that can be portrayed; actors must be able to animate the meanings with body clues.

6. Produce "color stories and poems" based on ideas from lists of colored things. The lists can be generated over a period of time and be a part of the classroom environment or a collection in the Writing/Publishing Center.

In a class where many color stories and poems were read and written, Shauna wrote and illustrated the following.

What Is Green?

Green is the grass,
And green is a tree,
And green can be massive like a sea.

Green can be small like a beetle or leaf,
Or green can be tiny like a seed.

Green can be the morning dew,
And a moth in flight,
Or a GRIM tattoo,
Or even a starfish, to name a few.

Green is the young unripened hay.
Green is the emerald for the month of May.
Green is the lettuce and cabbage we eat.
Green is the socks we wear on our feet.

Oh, green is the color all people adore.
Most people use it in their décor . . .
So . . . use green all the more.
GREEN.

To speak, write, and read color vocabulary is essential. Because words of color occur so frequently in printed materials, children who do not include color words in their language production can be expected to have difficulty with independent reading.

7. Make color books and collages by cutting pictures from magazines and grouping everything of one color together. Some of the pictures can be arranged in a book with captions stating the hues of the colors that appear in the pictures.

Brown

chocolate pudding	oak door
beige socks	buff floor
cinnamon blouse	coffee cookies
walnut table	tan trousers
mahogany chair	

Similar activities can be developed around concepts of shape, texture, sound, smell, and taste.

8. Ask questions beginning "what is . . ." and record the many responses of children in books with one answer and one illustration on a page.
What is a mother?
What is a teacher?
What is a principal?
What is food?
What is spring?
A group of first-grade children in Pennsylvania responded to the question "What is spring?" The results were published in a book for the classroom. Some of the statements dictated by the children follow:

Spring in Pennsylvania (*Miss Trexler's First Grade*)

Spring is a time of happiness. The days are longer. The sun is warmer and the air smells cleaner.
Spring is a time of daffodils, violets and pussy willows.
Spring is a time when grass turns green and trees start to bud.
Spring is a time of planting seeds and watching them grow.

Spring is a time of warm breezes and flying kites.
Spring is a time of birds singing to welcome the new baby animals.

9. Make a "poem tree" with a large branch set in a bucket of sand. Children decorate the tree with poems they write on colored paper shaped in interesting ways. They can use short forms such as the cinquain, haiku, tanka, sijo, triangle triplets, quadrangles, and couplets.

10. Use headline stories to stimulate personal responses to meanings of words. Reserve a space on a bulletin board for newspaper headlines. The whole article should be cut from the newspaper, but the story should be folded under the headline so that only the print of the headline shows. Children are invited to write newspaper articles to go with the headline.

The article is unfolded after several news articles have been written. Students read their interpretation of the headline and then read the article. Sometimes the article with the student writings is bound into a book for the Reading/Research Center.

An example of one headline is: "Mossi Out of Bullpen." All the children who responded wrote bullfight or roundup stories with a bull as the main character. The news article was about a baseball player.

This type of activity can lead into discussions of how we use the same words for different purposes. It also stimulates the reading of material that may appear to be too difficult but can be understood if there is a deep desire to know what another author has said.

Ideas for Reading in a Language Experience Approach

Reading is the result of a broadly based language program in a language experience approach. It happens almost automatically when children live and learn in an environment that provides for continuous assimilation and integration of ideas from the three major strands of the curriculum rationale:

Strand One: Experiencing Communication
The child communicates in multiple ways with multiple media using personal ideas and personal language.

Strand Two: Studying Communication
The child studies the components of language that

have most to do with the reading process, and learns how those components work for self and others.

Strand Three: Relating Communication of Others to Self
The child is influenced by the language and ideas of many people so that personal language changes in the direction of language that is likely to be found in reading materials.

As the effects of the three strands are assimilated and integrated, reading occurs naturally and normally in most children. The processes of assimilating and integrating the twenty substrands into reading are accelerated and intensified through certain language emphases described and illustrated here as language recognition, language prediction, language acquisition, and language production.

These emphases force an overlapping of the three strands and an intermingling of the twenty substrands as illustrated in Figure 2 (page 13). When these occur, reading exists in the learner (Allen, Venezky, and Hahn, 1974).

Summary of Skills and Abilities for Assimilating and Integrating Ideas

LANGUAGE RECOGNITION ABILITIES

—Recognizes the words and syntactical patterns in own writing
—Follows along printed passages when listening to oral reading
—Reproduces passages written by others by reading orally with meaningful interpretations
—Recognizes, in and out of context, the words of highest frequency at a 100 percent mastery level
—Combines high-frequency phonograms with beginning consonants and common endings to generate known words
—Combines known words into compound words
—Edits manuscripts to increase the percentage of high-frequency words for ease of reading by younger children
—Makes games and plays games to increase sight vocabulary of high-frequency words

LANGUAGE PREDICTION ABILITIES

—Completes sentences with predictable language without seeing the print
—Anticipates words and phrases that are redundant in language

——rhyming words
——collocation of words
——repeating structure
——enumeration patterns
——Predicts content of films and filmstrips after viewing without sound and before hearing commentary
——Uses clues such as titles, illustrations, and topic sentences to predict the content of stories prior to reading
——Predicts endings of stories prior to reading
——Recognizes printed words when only portions of the print are visible
   ——top or bottom of print missing
   ——every fifth word missing
   ——initial consonants only printed
   ——words without vowels printed
   ——passages with structure words omitted

LANGUAGE ACQUISITION ABILITIES

——Looks at an object, names it, and describes it in several ways—movement, sound, shape, texture, size, color, taste, smell
——Describes objects and conditions in unconventional as well as in conventional ways
——Extends the meaning of a common word by listing a variety of words that mean almost the same
——Tells stories using words and language patterns of the author
——Assumes roles and produces language characteristic of those roles
——Writes stories that include specified words in meaningful ways
——Chooses one word and lists many words (not synonyms) related by association
——Expands simple sentences into complex and compound sentences
——Understands and uses idiomatic expressions
——Identifies some word origins

LANGUAGE PRODUCTION ABILITIES

——Looks at a common object and describes several of its common characteristics
——Names a common object and tells many ways in which it can be useful, including unusual uses

—Produces new commentaries and soundtrack for films and film-strips

—Makes own slide presentation on a topic of interest

—Extends the meaning of one word, such as a color or size word, into a poem or story

—Writes own ideas in many different forms that include patterned poetry

—Responds in personal ways to headlines, topics, and titles

Selected References

Allen, Roach Van, Richard Venezky, and Harry T. Hahn. *Language Experiences in Reading, Level I.* Encyclopaedia Britannica Educational Corp., Chicago, 1974.

Carlson, Ruth Kearny. *Sparkling Words: Two Hundred Practical and Creative Writing Ideas.* Wagner Printing Co., Berkeley, Calif., 1968.

Carroll, John. "Some Neglected Relationships in Reading and Language Learning," *Elementary English,* 42 (October, 1966).

Chomsky, Carol. *The Acquisition of Syntax in Children 5 to 10.* The M.I.T. Press, Cambridge, Mass., 1969.

Dunne, Hope W. *The Art of Teaching Reading: A Language and Self-Concept Approach.* Charles E. Merrill, Columbus, Ohio, 1972.

Goodman, Kenneth S. "Reading: A Psycholinguistic Guessing Game." In *Theoretical Models and Processes of Reading,* edited by Harry Singer and Robert B. Ruddell. International Reading Association, Newark, Del., 1970.

Greet, W. Cabell, William A. Jenkins, and Andrew Schiller. *In Other Words, a Junior Thesaurus.* Scott, Foresman and Co., Glenview, Ill., 1969.

Guilford, J. P. *Personality.* McGraw-Hill Book Co., New York, 1959.

————. "Frontiers of Thinking That Teachers Should Know About." In *Elementary Reading Instruction: Selected Materials,* edited by Althea Berry, Thomas C. Barrett, and William R. Powell. Allyn & Bacon, Boston, 1974.

Hall, MaryAnne. *Teaching Reading as a Language Experience.* Charles E. Merrill, Columbus, Ohio, 1970.

Henning, Dorothy G., and Barbara M. Grant. *Content and Craft: Written Expression in the Elementary School.* Prentice-Hall, Englewood Cliffs, N.J., 1973.

Moffett, James. *A Student-Centered Language Arts Curriculum, Grades K-13: A Handbook for Teachers.* Houghton Mifflin Co., Boston, 1973.

Smith, E. Brooks, Kenneth Goodman, and Robert Meredith. *Language and Thinking in the Elementary School.* Holt, Rinehart and Winston, New York, 1970.

Smith, Frank, and George A. Miller. *The Genesis of Language: A Psycholinguistic Approach.*   The M.I.T. Press, Cambridge, Mass., 1966.

Spiegel, Dixie Lee. "Holistic Approach to Diagnosis and Remediation," *Reading Teacher*, 27, 4 (January, 1974).

Wilkinson, Andrew M. *The Foundations of Language.*   Oxford University Press, London, 1971.

FROM THE RATIONALE   Searching and researching multiple sources—finding information on topics of interest and on assignments by using interviews, reference books, tapes, films, filmstrips, observations, and other ways that are available when information is needed.

Questions of why, what, how, and when which are vital to the language growth of young children do not stop when they enter school. In fact, children should be stimulated in a school learning laboratory which provides resources not typical of most homes. School environments should encourage them to ask questions that have not arisen at home. School resources for finding answers to questions should be much more than books.

Books, as important as they are, are not enough for present-day learning environments. Every learning situation should provide materials so that poor readers as well as good readers can participate in research activities related to real questions. Poor readers must no longer be denied information in school when they can get that information from tapes, records, films, filmstrips, books with accompanying records, photographs, study print sets, and combinations of one or more of these in packages on topics of interest.

A technique of teaching in a language experience approach is to confront children with questions they may not understand—not because there are no answers, but because they have not found them for themselves. Children are helped to understand that problems are not solved once and for all, but that one problem leads to another, and that solving problems is the great adventure of learning.

A searching attitude is required for any degree of independence as a researcher. Also, some reading techniques are indispensable if a search among printed materials and among catalogued nonprint materials is to be profitable. Locational skills must accompany the question "How can I find out?" if this basic question yields enough information to solve a problem.

Promoting a Searching Attitude

Children who search for answers to their questions may not always find those answers, but if they continue to seek, they demonstrate an attitude toward solving problems that is far more valuable than finding answers every time. They acquire power in using a scientific method of thinking that—it is to be hoped—leads to individual, independent searching.

The self-confidence and assurance necessary to launch into the unknown, into creative thinking and creative production, come from power gained from repeated opportunities to search for answers to one's own questions—not from learning someone else's answers to someone else's questions. This means that teachers in a language experience approach place no emphasis and little value on children's ability to fill in blanks of prepared worksheets. Children may use some such aids as models in preparing their own work material which will be used with their peers in learning centers, but the *process* is regarded as a more valuable learning experience than the *product*. To be able to ask questions that reflect the intended meaning of an author may be as valuable a skill for the searching attitude as the ability to answer questions that already have the major ideas identified.

Numerous oral, writing, and reading skills are practiced when an individual is searching for answers. In addition, data can be gathered from personal interviews, telephone conversations, observation, studying pictures, listening to recordings, viewing films and filmstrips, and testing prossibilities and alternatives.

Lee teaches a fifth-grade class that usually has several children who are branded nonreaders. During the early weeks of school he diminishes the emphasis on reading printed matter and helps every child to develop interests around which future reading can be planned. He invites a series of "experts" to visit his class to serve as resource persons for interviews.

Each child is encouraged to formulate questions. Techniques for carrying on interviews are discussed, guides are developed, and children who have special interest in the area of expertise of the visitor are invited to lead the interviews. But all children can participate. Among the people he invites are an automobile mechanic, an architect, a cook, a jet pilot, and a gardener.

After the series of visiting experts, Lee lets students choose to become experts in some field. The student prepares for an interview by the class members. Searching begins. Students use all kinds of resources to get prepared. Poor readers find resources they can use. Many of them find that they have interests about which they know more than anyone else in the class. Their interest in reading in their speciality mounts as their time for an interview approaches.

Vocabularies can be extended as children search for words to fit into categories that have been agreed on.

Edna suggests broad topics for word lists that children can extend as they read. She begins with something like homes around the world. Children add to the list any word they find that tells the kinds of homes people live in. She uses other topics for which the children search for words in their reading. Some of these topics are imaginary characters, roots that are used for food, kinds of weather, machines that have levers, and waste that pollutes.

Reference books are useful when children search for answers to questions. They should be supplemented with picture sets, filmstrips, and books of information that have an index and a table of contents.

Terry has a bulletin board where she usually has a caption that is a question that came up in a class discussion. "Do all insects have six legs?" is an example. Children search for scientific information, find pictures, and make displays in answer to each question. Terry feels that it is much more important to stimulate a positive attitude toward searching than to have her furnish the answers.

Development of Beginning Research Skills

Persons and objects in their environment help preschool children find answers to their many questions. At school they have additional references to provide the information needed to satisfy curiosity and widen their scope of thinking.

The oral interchange of young children with classmates, teachers, and other adults is a prime resource for young children. It continues to contribute as they learn to use books and other material that involve reading symbols. In addition most modern classrooms have a wealth of nonbook material—toys, plants, animals, machines, maps, pictures, microscopes, charts, study prints, films, filmstrips, and recordings. At home most children have access to television and radio. Some schools provide study trips for groups of children to find out firsthand about things they study and discuss. All of these can be used to build abilities in using resources and to stimulate interest in listening and speaking and in learning how to write and read.

Florence begins the first week of school to take dictation from children in first grade. She displays the stories and reads from them when she is ready to introduce new skills. A bulletin board has several captions on sheets of paper with room to list words from the stories. The captions may include first-time words, words that begin alike, rhyming words, sentences with commas, first words in quotations, first words in sentences, and sentences with question marks.

In their own stories children discover characteristics that are found in stories in their books. By simple researching of their own language, they find most of the characteristics that they need to recognize in the language of others.

Experimenting with common materials helps young children to find answers to questions and to ask new ones. Some common questions that children can research through observation are:

——What colors of paint are mixed to form other colors?
——What effect have light and darkness on the growth of plants?
——What materials produce electricity when a balloon is rubbed against them?
——What kind of paper absorbs water?
——What causes evaporation?

Children can record their discoveries by dictating or writing simple statements. Some may be able to find information in simple illustrated books on the subject. Others may reinforce their information by viewing a filmstrip on the topic. A class diary can be kept on observations when changes occur fairly rapidly.

Teachers of young children initiate research techniques naturally as they provide resources that have lead questions, resource cards, and demonstrations. Some easy ones to provide are:

1. A magnifying glass and wood with different grains, rocks, leaves, or flowers. Children discover differences with close examination.
2. Animal life in an aquarium or terrarium. Children talk about their observations, write or dictate some of them, and extend their information by using books placed in the vicinity.
3. Simple balances for comparing weights. Children guess weights by size and then put items on a balance to check their prediction. They seek answers to why some small things weigh more than other much larger ones.
4. Simple measuring devices. Children make approximations and then check them out with accurate measurement.
5. Maps of areas where children live or have traveled. Trips—real and imaginary—can be charted. Children learn to read the grids on maps and other reference techniques for locating places.

Broad experiences in trying things out, of getting into unknown situations, of being curious about how things work, and of wanting to know what it means can launch children into a positive attitude toward research that requires reading and writing. While they are waiting to read and write well enough for mature research activities, they need repeated successes in finding satisfactory solutions to simple, personal questions. By using multiple resources that require minimum skills in reading, they can participate in research during the period when print reading yields no real information.

Learning to Use a Variety of Resources

To give children only one source that contains a satisfying answer is to limit the development of their thinking powers. The goal in a language experience approach is to give them a variety of resources and let them search out the answers that satisfy them and solve their problems.

Even before children learn to read much of printed material, they can be introduced to the idea of searching in many places to find answers. Picture books, picture encyclopedias, filmstrips, and recordings provide information on many topics. Information that children think has been located in a book they cannot read can be read by the teacher to verify its usefulness.

As children's reading ability increases, they are encouraged to seek their own answers in reading material. In so doing, they soon discover that different books have different purposes. Some are fiction and for pleasure reading only; some are full of facts; some give most of their information through pictures; some have an alphabetic arrangement; and some mix fact and fiction.

Older children usually rely on reading as a means of finding some of their information. They have to know how to locate pertinent information and develop abilities in using a table of contents and an index, in skimming, and in using topical headings and other aids for finding information. They find that encyclopedias are the richest source of specific information and that dictionaries contain definitions that may give them clues for further research. As they work, they find need for abilities in reading charts, maps, and other materials that consist primarily of symbols to be interpreted.

History, geography, and science are examples of subject areas that should be taught in such a way that pupils are required to locate information from numerous sources. In doing so, they recognize the need for the development of locational skills. The procedure for teaching content subjects should require the pupil to use the index, the table of contents, topic headings, and all the important parts of books. Pupils develop the ability to identify unknown words, find their pronunciations in the dictionary, and select appropriate meanings for words in terms of use in context. They come to know through many and varied experiences that no one book, film, collection of objects, or field trip will have all the answers they are seeking. When they learn to use the laboratory of varied resources provided them, they come to enjoy thinking out problems that are important to them.

Children who function as researchers in a learning laboratory must develop some locational skills in order to use printed materials. Indispensable reading techniques of independent readers include skill in using tables of content, indexes, headings and subheadings in texts, alphabetically arranged material such as dictionaries and encyclopedias, and other reference material. Researchers must also develop techniques of skimming to locate needed information. These indispensable skills do not need to be developed in an artificial reading situation. They should come naturally as children search and research information to questions that arise in a live learning environment.

Using Table of Contents and Index

Teachers of content subjects are usually supplied with textbooks that have a table of contents and an index. These are of minimum use in teaching locational skills when one book is used day after day as the text. Science and social studies books can be useful, however, in teaching children how to use tables of content and indexes in other books. Children learn very quickly that researchers do not begin at the first of a book and read every page to the end in order to find needed information. Rather, they go as directly as possible to the information they need by using resources that most publishers provide in books.

Patricia uses textbook sets to teach locational skills. A group of children with identical books race to find answers to questions. They select a question from a stack of cards that Patricia prepared. She reads the question which is answered somewhere in the book the children are using. The winner, the one who finds the answer first, tells the class what key word or idea in the question was used in conjunction with the index or table of contents to find the answer to the question.

When the class first starts having these races, all the questions have key words that are in the index. As children learn to use this clue, questions are formulated that do not contain a word that is in the index of the book they are reading. They have to think of synonyms in order to locate information.

After children learn to find answers to questions by using an index, Patricia inserts cards in the stack that have topics from the table of contents printed on them. When they see or hear one of the topics, they skim the table of contents to locate that topic and then turn to it in the book.

These activities assure children some degree of skill in using other books to find information efficiently and rapidly.

Some books have locational aids and some do not. In many ways the titles and physical appearance of the books give clues before the books are opened.

Conrad has many books in the classroom, so each time a topic is being studied in depth, he puts an assortment of books on a table and plays a game with the students. He asks them to pick on the basis of physical appearance and title only a book that they think will have something in it on a topic he names. He may take a topic such as weather and work from that to various subtopics.

Children learn rapidly that most books of information have a table of contents and an index where they can verify their prediction. Storybooks may have a table of contents but no index. Books for pleasure reading seldom have either. If needed information is in them, the reader has to search for it with no locational aids.

Conrad never relies on one source of information on a topic that is studied in depth, so he feels that he must help students know how to recognize and use multiple sources.

Using Alphabetic Arrangements

Understanding alphabetic arrangements is an indispensable reading skill for carrying out research. It is a skill that can be introduced early in school programs with assurances that normal activities will require its use over and over.

Some experiences that offer opportunities for teaching alphabetic arrangement are discussed here.

1. Use picture dictionaries for browsing and for building an awareness of why and how one word follows another in alphabetic arrangement.
2. Make word books that grow from the use of the initial letter to second- and third-letter arrangements. The words can be ones the children collect and write, or they can be words cut from magazines.
3. Keep word files with dividers for each letter of the alphabet.
4. Read and examine a telephone directory to find names of families represented in the classroom.
5. List in dictionary order words that have been collected on the Word Wall in the classroom.
6. List books on a topic by alphabetic arrangement of the authors and the titles.
7. Use encyclopedias to illustrate a major reference source that has alphabetic arrangement. Notice key words for topics and the use of last names of people. Look for cross-references that send the researcher to other volumes.
8. Play games that require children to alphabetize words in order to win.

Dictionaries are a special kind of alphabetically arranged book for researchers. They are useful in the following ways.

1. They have pronunciation keys to aid with new words found during research.
2. Sources of words that might be useful information in research are found in some dictionaries.
3. Multiple definitions are included so that the researcher has a chance to find a meaning that fits the context of her or his reading material. Children doing research may find words that they recognize at sight but do not understand in a particular setting because the words carry new meanings that need to be looked up in a dictionary.

From the beginning of research activities in primary grades, there should be a collection of dictionaries available. Some should be simple enough for good readers to use independently. Others might be difficult to read, but they will likely be the ones the children need when they study topics of interest to them. If they can find in the dictionary words that are new to them in reading material, they can usually find someone to help them with dictionary pronunciation and definitions.

Using Library Reference Skills

Children who are sincere and earnest researchers need to have easy access to a library and be assisted in developing library reference skills. They need to feel secure amid a mass of materials that have nothing to do with the topics being studied.

One way to establish a secure feeling is to teach the use of the card catalogue which is in most libraries. With some knowledge of alphabetic arrangement, key words, and names of authors and titles, a child can find books, films, picture sets, records, kits of material, and magazines on topics of interest. Everything is coded and arranged in an order so that once the code is understood, materials can be located with a minimum of help from librarians.

Skimming is a reading skill that must accompany efficient use of library reference materials. No researcher has time to read everything carefully. Key ideas must be selected and located in materials by the use of a combination of locational skills that includes skimming to the point at which the needed information is found. At that point careful reading for detail may take place.

Craig locates selections with several place names and/or names of people who are prominent enough for information about them to be found in reference materials. He uses these as models for students to follow in writing literary compositions rather than factual reports. Example:

My Magic Carpet (*Claryce Allen*)

What am I weaving?
Oh, can't you tell?
A magic carpet,
But not to sell.

I'm weaving in stripes
Of red, blue, and gold,
A bit of dark purple,
And orange—very bold!

I'm weaving in magic
And old famous tricks.
It will fly even faster
Than witches' broomsticks.

I'm planning to go
On a trip very soon,
Perhaps 'round the world,
Then on to the moon.

I think I shall fly
To Mexico City,
See cathedrals and gardens,
And parks, very pretty.

By Sugar Loaf Mountain
I'll fly in Brazil,
See world's largest river,
And waterfalls that thrill.

I'll fly on to London,
To Trafalgar Square,
See Buckingham Palace,
The crown jewels rare.

I'll fly then to Paris,
The "City of Light"!
See the Arch of Triumph,
Then Eiffel Tower at night.

To Switzerland's Alps
I next want to fly.
Warm clothes I'll put on,
And skiing I'll try.

In Italy I'll visit
The ruins of Pompeii,
See opera at La Scala,
And the old Appian Way.

In Egypt I'll visit
Step Pyramid at Sakkarah,

Take a trip down the Nile,
See Pyramid of Hawara.

Across oceans to India.
Then a stop in Banaras.
Perhaps in Calcutta
I'll buy me some saris.

When I get to Japan
I'll eat sukiyaki,
See kabuki drama,
And visit Nagasaki.

I'll visit Australia
And Great Barrier Reef,
Try corcodile steak,
Crayfish, and beef.

After seeing these places,
I'll take a short rest,
Then ready my carpet
For its very great test.

I'll see that each thread
And stripe look just right,
That it's clean as can be
For my very long flight.

I'll pack up some food
And put on moon gear,
Then wish very hard.
I'll return. Have no fear!

Craig reads and discusses literary selections. Then he makes activity cards for students to choose in learning centers. On the back of each card he reproduces a selection like "My Magic Carpet" so that it is there as a ready reference. Some of the activities for pupils are discussed over the next few pages.

FOR THE READING/RESEARCH CENTER Read some of the quatrains in "My Magic Carpet" and add a second, third, and fourth stanza about what you might find in one country. You may need to refer to an encyclopedia or to travel books to get some ideas and words that will help you. You will need at least one place word for each stanza.

When you write a quatrain, you must have at least two rhyming words, and some of the patterns you choose may have two sets of rhyming words. Some rhyming patterns you can use are: aaaa, aabb, abab, abcb, abba, abca. The lines should be about the same length and have the same beat as the beginning stanza you choose.

FOR THE WRITING/PUBLISHING CENTER   Make notes about places you have visited. Read travel folders, maps, and geography books to get ideas and words that you can use in writing quatrains. You will need at least one set of rhyming words for each quatrain you write.

Bring to class colored slides you have collected on trips. Use them for ideas for writing and then use them again to illustrate your quatrains when you read them to the class.

Use picture postcards and pictures from travel folders to illustrate quatrains which you might make into a book for the Reading/Research Center.

FOR THE GAME CENTER   Make imaginary trips to places that do not exist. Think up names for people, places, and magic forms of transportation. Put each name on a card. Two or more can play a game by drawing cards as a story is told. The name on the card has to be used in the next sentence after it is drawn. The stories can be nonsense ones.

FOR THE ARTS AND CRAFTS CENTER   Weave carpets to illustrate "My Magic Carpet" or the poems you write. Fold newspapers into tight rolls and weave carpets you can sit on. Use strips of construction paper to develop different designs. If looms are available, weave carpets with yarn or strips of cloth.

FOR THE LANGUAGE STUDY CENTER   Make a trip to a carpet store to look at different kinds of carpets. Notice the different designs woven into them, the different textures, the variety of colors, and the different kinds of threads. Most of the sample books will tell you where the carpets were made and whether the threads are natural or synthetic. You can collect different names for carpet threads and use them in writing.

Susan develops activities that extend students' interest in and knowledge of words. She wants every student to realize through repeated experiences that word recognition is not enough. It is only the beginning point of reading. Words have meanings in context, and most words are used in many meaningful ways in language production. An example of the kind of activity she conducts is her use of one of Claryce Allen's language activities, "See How They Run."

People run!

Machines run!

Animals run!

Roads run!

Even ideas run—

Some people run with the grace of a deer.

Other people run heavily as if they were pounding down the ground for a parade.

When cars run *into* each other, it's an accident.

When they run *out of* gas, it's a tragedy.

Dogs run in special ways.

A poodle runs in a showy way, stopping to look back to see if it is being watched.

A dachshund looks as if it is spreading apart when it runs.

Roads run—

    north—

     south—

      east—

       west—

        northeast—

         southwest—

          around curves and corners.

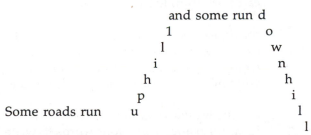

to give you a roller-coaster-like ride.

Ideas can run fast through my head to give me answers to my questions,

                but

computers can run a thousand times faster giving answers to people who are many miles away—
Maybe on the moon.

BUT I CAN
 run slowly,
  run fast,
   run quietly,
    run loudly,
     run easily,
      run heavily,
       run straight,
        run crooked,
         run north,
          run south,
           run east,
            run west,
             run down,
              run up,
               run into,
                run over,
                 run for,
                  run on and on.
                   CAN YOU?

Susan puts selections like "See How They Run" on transparencies. The students read together in many different ways. They bring personal meanings to the words that are the focus of study. Then activity cards are introduced for learning centers.

FOR THE READING/RESEARCH CENTER Browse through a dictionary and make lists of words that have many meanings. You can choose as many words (say, 15, 25, or 50) for your list as you want. Some words you will find are *act, bank, cast, air, block,* and *check.*

FOR THE WRITING/PUBLISHING CENTER Read "See How They Run" to get ideas for using one of your words to write a book to illustrate its many meanings.

FOR THE ARTS AND CRAFTS CENTER Choose one word (or more) for a bulletin board display. Print the word as an art piece. Invite members of the class to contribute illustrated sentences using the word as a noun, as a verb, or as a descriptive word.

FOR THE LANGUAGE STUDY CENTER   Choose one or more words to which you add prefixes, suffixes, plurals, tense endings, and words to form compounds. Examples of words extended in meaning are:

arm	armer	armband	arms
rearm	arming	armory	armchair
armed	firearm	armor	
armpit	unarmed	armament	
disarm			

FOR THE GAME CENTER   Look in a thesaurus. Find other words that mean the same as ones on your list. Make a game with the lists of words. An example is:

break	fracture	smash	rip
	shatter	tear	split

FOR THE DRAMATIZATION CENTER   When reading "See How They Run," write two lists of words:

how	they run	*where*	they run
	slowly		into
	fast		over
	quietly		north
now add more		*now add more*	

Act out the different meanings with a group of friends.

Children who have easy access to a library for reference reading are not limited to one source for reading in a learning center environment recommended for a language experience approach. They are challenged to get involved in the excitement of learning from resources like those that are used by adult researchers who ask new questions about problems and then search in many places and in many ways to find answers to those problems. Teachers deny children a feeling of security, adequacy, and achievement when all of them read the same book and return the one answer in the book as though that answer was sufficient information on many questions. Instead, they should participate with children in ways in which all can be *contributors* to society rather than remain satisfied to be *consumers only*. Together they question, observe, predict, verify, and validate as they search out and research solutions to problems in multiple sources.

Summary of Skills and Abilities for Searching and Researching Multiple Sources

——Can use a variety of resources in the classroom to find answers to his questions
    ——pictures
    ——charts
    ——films and filmstrips
    ——maps
    ——reference books
    ——recordings
——Is aware of numerous resources outside the classroom and can use them
    ——resource people
    ——television
    ——newspapers and magazines
——Uses tables of contents and indexes of books as guides to finding information
    ——searches through tables of contents to locate information on topics and questions
    ——uses indexes to locate information on a given topic
    ——locates in indexes key words of questions
——Searches through reference books to find out if the books contain material relevant to the problem
——Uses dictionaries
    ——to get correct pronunciation and definition of unknown words
    ——to locate items of information that involve more than pronunciation and definition, such as abbreviations, foreign phrases, and dates
——Develops skill in using alphabetic arrangements
    ——can arrange a file of information in dictionary order
    ——can use directories, glossaries, and files that have alphabetic arrangement
——Skims to locate specific information that needs detailed study and analysis
——Summarizes information and ideas
——Keeps record of sources used to collect information
    ——keeps bibliographical information
    ——gives credit for sources used

Selected References

Allen, Roach Van. *Reading Programs: Alternatives for Improvement.* American Association of Elementary-Kindergarten-Nursery Educators, Washington, D.C., 1973.

Cheyney, Arnold B. *Teaching Reading Skills Through the Newspaper.* International Reading Association, Newark, Del., 1971.

Darrow, Helen F., and Roach Van Allen. *Independent Activities for Creative Learning,* 4th ed. Teachers College Press, New York, 1967.

Freidman, Albert B. "The Middle Ages Revisited: Reading in the Electronic Age." In *Reading in Education: A Broader View,* edited by Malcolm P. Douglass. Charles E. Merrill, Columbus, Ohio, 1973.

Hall, MaryAnne. *Teaching Reading as a Language Experience.* Charles E. Merrill, Columbus, Ohio, 1970.

Harris, Albert J. *How to Increase Reading Ability,* 5th ed. David McKay, New York, 1970.

Heilman, Arthur W. *Principles and Practices of Teaching Reading.* Charles E. Merrill, Columbus, Ohio, 1972.

Karlin, Robert. *Teaching Elementary Reading: Principles and Strategies.* Harcourt Brace Jovanovich, New York, 1971.

Moore, W. J. "The Skimming Process in Silent Reading." In *Challenge and Experiment in Reading,* edited by J. Allen Figurel. Scholastic Magazines, New York, 1962.

Robertson, Jean E. "Using Social Studies Content to Develop Reading Skills." In *The Quest for Competency in Teaching Reading,* edited by Howard A. Klein. International Reading Association, Newark, Del., 1972.

FROM THE RATIONALE   Evaluating communication of others—determining the validity and reliability of statements; sorting out assumptions from facts; recognizing an author's purpose and point of view; and recognizing styles that include exaggeration, sarcasm, and humor.

Maturity and competence in reading are evidenced in children who develop abilities to select information and evaluate it. Skillful readers can judge the appropriateness of a word, phrase, paragraph, page, or book to the problem for which reading is being done. They seek out information from many printed sources as well as from other sources. They do not rely solely on textbooks to solve problems or to answer questions that occur to them.

Finding information is not enough, however. Mature readers read critically and in ways that help to determine the validity and the reliability of statements read. After they collect information from several sources, they compare and contrast what they find. When factual differences appear, they check such items as the publication date of a book, the background of the author, the stated purpose of the author, and other data that have bearing on the validity and reliability of statements.

Critical listening and reading are increasingly significant in instructional programs today. Children and adults are surrounded by television, radio, magazines, and newspapers that present such a volume of claims on the listener's or reader's credence that a high level of ability to interpret statements and arguments is a necessity for competent citizenship.

An important aim for reading in a language experience approach is that students develop abilities to interpret what they hear and read in the light of their own experience. They are expected to come to some conclusions about the value and use of reading in their personal lives.

Abilities in evaluating and interpreting the communication of others can be fostered in a learning environment with activities that highlight (1) the evaluation of sources and content, and (2) reading critically.

Efficient readers know where and how to look for the reading materials needed for any given task. They recognize that some reading materials are factual, some are fanciful, and some are a combination of both. In a language experience approach a minimum of four kinds of books is highlighted for children. They are expected to be able to select reading materials for purposes of:

——finding information
——browsing and reading for recreation
——reading skill development
——reading critically
——selecting models and patterns for reading and writing.

Finding Information

The learning center environment recommended for a language experience approach permits children to encounter needs for information to solve problems that they find as assignments or that they select on their own. In some classrooms committees of children develop learning centers for other class members to use.

Marcia works in an open-space environment where children have access to an instructional materials center. During the school year each child is encouraged to join a committee to develop learning center activities. The committee chooses a topic of interest, such as frogs. They find books, filmstrips, records, and songs to go into existing centers or to be used in one large center which they supervise. They study encyclopedias and use dictionaries to find words for games. They make activity cards that require other students to use dictionaries, thesauri, and encyclopedias in order to complete the activity. They prepare tests on information in reading and viewing material.

Marcia is a guide and counselor to the committees. She has goals of helping them to become independent in finding information on any topic of their choice. The pupil-developed learning centers add interest to the learning situation, but the process of putting a center together provides repeated opportunity to focus on the use of:

——tables of contents
——indexes
——glossaries
——alphabetic order
——card catalogues
——key words, including synonyms and other aids for finding information in a variety of sources.

Using reading for personal needs is highlighted instead of procedures that require children to listen while others read orally. In a language experience approach much of oral reading is to share original manuscripts and to bring information or pleasure to a listening audience. Children find information in a variety of places, and frequently there is only one copy of printed material containing particular information. Oral reading from that copy is prepared reading that informs rather than bores the listening audience.

Carlos encourages children to find information on topics of study. He uses some of the individual conference time each week to listen to children read portions of selections they want to read to a group. He helps them with new vocabulary and suggests additional practice when it is needed. This may be practice at home, reading with a buddy, or reading with an older student who is available as a reading tutor.

Carlos knows from personal experience the diminished feeling that results from poor oral reading day after day. He wants children in his class to experience effective oral reading and has found that they will prepare to read orally when they have information to share with class members. He avoids procedures of always testing oral reading in group situations. Rather, he devotes most of his instructional time to individual conferences in which effective oral reading can be modeled and mediated in a private or semiprivate setting. The amount of information shared is not important. One sentence is enough if it is of interest and is read so others understand it.

Some children learn to find information but are not aware of features of books that can help them to evaluate the information. They do not read the preface, the date of publication, and information that might be available about the author.

Roger spends some of the reading time helping students find out about the books of information they use. He helps them to appreciate the different reasons an author would have for writing a book on a particular topic. This information is usually in a preface. Roger wants children to understand that authors with different purposes will say different things about what appears to be the same topic in another book.

Books with a wide range of copyright dates are a part of the reading collection. Roger thinks it important that children know about and use data of this type in making decisions about the information they find. Geography books, science books, and mathematics books are among those that have changed a great deal in recent years. What was a *fact* in 1935 might not be a *fact* in 1975. Research, study, and exploration have changed facts.

Reading activity toward finding information might encourage children to feel that there is still something for them to do to make a contribution to mankind. It lifts reading and reading instruction above levels of simple comprehension and exact replication of language of someone else.

Game Centers can include activities in which active searching for information is the game. They can feature use of the many clues and aids that are printed in books of information.

Language Study Center activities can include those that repeat and review basic abilities such as developing key words to find information on a topic and extending vocabularies to include related words, the same words in other languages, opposites, and the standard spelling of key words. Activities should lead children to use dictionaries, encyclopedias, thesauri, and other materials arranged in alphabetic order.

Activities of the Writing/Publishing Center can involve children in collecting and sharing information in a variety of literary forms. Factual reporting is valuable as a skill for sharing, but children should be able to take the same information and write a story that includes characters and a setting. They should be able to write patterned poems such as cinquains, diamantes, haikus, sijos, and other forms available to them.

The Viewing/Listening Center should be a place where children can find information with a minimum of print reading. Poor readers are not denied full participation in the study of topics of interest as long as records with books, records without books, tapes, filmstrips, study prints, and films are available.

The Arts and Crafts Center provides opportunities for children to share main ideas and topics of interest without having to talk and write. Although much of art does not require children to represent specific information, a part of art can and should do this.

The Dramatization Center synthesizes information gained from multiple sources and puts it together in personal and creative ways.

Reading/Research Center activities related to finding information usually include reference reading, identification of pertinent material, checking out material for authenticity, and organizing it into a meaningful presentation. These activities require the *use* of reading skills that involve tables of contents, topic sentences, introductory paragraphs, indexes, glossaries, and skimming to find specific information. These skills can be introduced in primary grades and repeated for mastery in intermediate grades. They are reading skills that support most studies in secondary and advanced education. They are virtually never developed in programs that feature oral reading of stories and poems almost to the exclusion of other reading skills.

Browsing and Reading for Recreation

Materials for browsing and reading for recreation are essential in the classroom. They may or may not be used for specific instruction. Their value is mainly in furnishing children a continuous opportunity to choose reading when choices are free and open. The collection of materials should be varied to the extent that children can encounter literature in its many forms. Early in their school experience they should have opportunities to begin talking about different approaches, forms, and purposes, such as:

—differences between fact and fantasy

—how to distinguish the real from the imaginary

—when a selection is poetry and when it is prose

—how authors use exaggeration and sarcasm to highlight their ideas

—when an author uses humor to please the reader and an audience.

Printed materials for browsing are necessary only for an environment that promotes communication. Classes with poor readers must have multiple ways for them to come in contact with the ideas and language of other people. They must not be denied contact with the variety in literature just because they are poor readers.

Rita reads something to the class every day. Sometimes she reads a whole story, book, or filmstrip, but often she reads just enough to interest the children in following up in learning centers when they have a chance to do something of their own choice. As she reads, she helps the children deepen their awareness of many forms of writing. She may read the first sentence of a story and let the children predict whether it is going to be real or imaginary. They learn to gather clues from such lines as "Once upon a time . . .," "Long ago, in a far away land . . .," "A strange thing happened . . .," and "Robert was nine years old when . . ."

Rita reads a few lines and lets the children judge whether or not what she is reading is poetry. She wants them to be able to visualize differences in writing before they see the printed forms. She reads comics, riddles, and jokes.

The collection is placed in the learning environment with no requirement that children report to her on their reading. She knows that there will be volunteers begging to tell her about their reading when she schedules individual conferences.

David teaches children who are grouped together because for their age and grade placement they are poor readers of print. He recognizes that most of them have interests and talents that can be extended through browsing and recreational reading. Their failure syndrome relates primarily to word recognition when reading orally.

He makes certain that many stories of interest are on tapes so the ineffective readers can follow along while listening to models of effective reading. When children listen to each other read the models ineffectively, they are not helping each other communicate meaning. He makes some of the tapes and invites students from high school speech classes to do others. He selects filmstrips with a variety of literary styles. Some have printed captions, but most of them have recordings of the text for listening. A few have books to go with the filmstrips and records. Study print sets also are available for browsing. Some have a story sequence, but most of them can be studied individually. Students are encouraged to add pictures to the sets. David wants the students to know that they can learn and participate during the time they are working to improve their reading skills. They do not have to wait until they are good readers to make valuable contributions to the class.

Throwaway materials are useful for browsing and reading. Catalogues, magazines, and newspapers are available and useful.

Don makes a special effort to provide catalogues for browsing. He brings some to the classroom and encourages students to bring others. Often products that are much alike are grouped together. The reading is repetitious. It includes a minimum of structure words and a maximum of form-class words. The same names repeat. Most items are described according to color, size, shape, texture, and price. This vocabulary is useful in general reading, so Don encourages his students to dream of things they would like to have. Sometimes they make their own catalogues of things of special interest. The descriptive material requires the use of the same language and language patterns over and over. In worksheets this repetition is boring; in catalogues it is interesting.

Barbara finds that her students enjoy newspapers for browsing. The general reading level of newspapers is higher than any informal reading inventory would indicate the levels of the students to be, but they seem to get the information in some way. She seldom asks anyone to read from a newspaper verbatim.

Periodically she has a reporter's seminar. Students select an area of specialization and report the latest news. Topics include fashions, sports, entertainment, world events, politics, personalities, want ads, home furnishings, food prices, comics, real estate, and opinion polls.

No student is required to be a reporter; the seminar is a recreational activity. They report on reading of their own choice within a framework arranged by the teacher. Barbara never hints that the activity is to help them be better readers. That is all right, but its purposes are centered on the usefulness of reading for recreation and for information.

Rudolpho is afraid that children in his class will ignore the beautiful bindings that attract him to books. He has made a pegboard display so that the front bindings of twenty to thirty books can be seen. It is known as the Browsing Board. Children can just look at the covers only; they can take a book down, look through it, and put it back; or they can select a book to read from cover to cover.

As an encouragement for reading, A Quiet Place is nearby. This is an area of the classroom where children can choose to go to be quiet. They understand that there is never any talking there. They can read, rest, and even take a nap. Many of them take a book there and stretch out on a big pillow. The cardboard walls give visual privacy. The comfortable furnishings provide relaxation. The nearby Browsing Board invites children to share their time with a good author.

Rudolpho never asks children to report to him on what is read in A Quiet Place. They may do so, but it is not required. Children respond positively to this trust because they value deeply the opportunity for real recreational reading.

Browsing has seldom been emphasized in reading instruction, yet it is a reading activity practiced frequently by children and adults outside of school. Children need to be helped to know how to open a book, scan through it to judge present interest, sample some of it to judge its difficulty, and skim along to find passages that need careful reading. They should know how to use photographs and artwork to aid in understanding the text. They should feel comfortable not reading every word.

Browsing abilities relate closely to predictive abilities in reading. They help readers to guess and then check out the guesses. They minimize the use of recognition skills while making maximum use of other clues used in printed material to help summarize the meanings. How can a person ever enjoy reading as a recreational activity without highly developed abilities to browse?

Reading Skill Development

Many books and kits of material in elementary classrooms are there because they provide material for reading skill development. Children in those classrooms need to understand the purposes of these materials and to develop visual clues that help identify them. They come to realize that many of the materials are collections of stories rather than just one story. Each level in the series is a little more difficult than the preceding one. Their book bindings are usually heavier than those of trade books. There may be follow-up exercises with the story, and sometimes there are lead-in questions. Many of the stories have been written specifically to illustrate a language characteristic or to repeat certain vocabulary. The kits may contain reading cards, exercise books, filmstrips, or records. They usually include test materials and individual records.

In an individualized skill development program such as is required of a language experience approach, children must get to know how to use the reading skill materials. Demonstrations, special lessons, and individual conferences can be used to acquaint children with the materials they will use when they are working on specific skills identified in the reading conference.

No child is expected to read from cover to cover in reading textbooks, but everyone is expected to use them to extend skills and to demonstrate competences in reading and understanding materials at increasingly more mature levels.

Most teachers in a language experience approach have a master list of skills from which they select some for emphasis with each child. In order to have conferences with children about a wide spectrum of skills and abilities, reading materials must be varied and available. There is no place in the program for *one* book used by *every* child. Skill development material should provide opportunities for teacher-pupil conferences on topics such as those listed and developed in *Language Experiences in Reading, Level III* (Allen and Allen, 1967).

1. Oral language skills
   —uses speech to communicate personal ideas
   —speaks distinctly in audience situation
   —uses home-rooted language effectively
   —relates thoughts and events of stories in sequence
   —grows in speaking vocabulary
2. Word-recognition skills
   Phonetic analysis
   —develops auditory discrimination through hearing beginning consonants and rhyming endings
   —develops visual discrimination by identifying words that begin alike and words that end alike
   —learns to substitute beginning sounds and blends
   —uses phonics to discover medial and ending sounds
   —learns and uses the flexibility of vowel sounds
   —identifies redundant sound patterns
   Structural analysis
   —hears and sees common endings such as *s, es, ed, ing, er,* and *est*
   —understands and uses simple contractions
   —recognizes compound words
   Associational analysis
   —draws meaning from familiar background
   —uses verbal context clues
   —learns alphabetic order
   —increases speed in silent reading through predictive abilities
   —responds to collocation of words
3. Oral reading skills
   —reads own sentences and stories with interpretive voice
   —uses punctuation marks effectively
   —is aware of audience situation in reading
   —reads orally with expression and fluency
   —participates in simple dramatization

4. Writing skills
—practices writing letters and numbers
—explores writing independently
—uses simple punctuation and capitalization
—strings sentences together in meaningful paragraphs
—writes stories with sequence and plot
—uses language models to expand writing style
—writes friendly letters and notes
—enlarges expressive vocabulary
—develops proofreading habit

5. Functional grammar
—learns simple rules of punctuation
—learns simple rules of capitalization
—distinguishes name words and action words
—develops awareness of descriptive words
—evaluates language usage with help of teacher
—recognizes common abbreviations
—recognizes modification with adjectives and adverbs
—recognizes modification with phrases and clauses
—changes meaning with voice inflections
—uses variety of sentence patterns

6. Vocabulary skills
—develops background of experience for word meanings through drama, rhythms, and art
—adds to sight vocabulary
—develops, expands, and enriches vocabulary through listening, observing, and writing

7. Comprehension skills
—follows sequence of events in stories heard
—remembers sequence in stories read
—follows directions in learning centers
—reads silently with comprehension
—uses picture clues to identify the setting, characters, and action of a story
—distinguishes fact from fantasy
—asks relevant questions
—draws conclusions from evidence
—relates story to own experiences
—reads to answer questions
—understands main ideas
—integrates meanings into personal communication

8. Study skills
    ——learns to work independently
    ——uses page numbers to locate materials
    ——uses table of contents to locate materials
    ——uses library or Reading/Research Center in classroom
    ——extends information on a topic by finding and using multiple sources:
        ——books, including dictionaries and other reference books
        ——newspapers
        ——magazines
        ——audio-visual sources
    ——organizes topics to present to others
9. Creative activities
    ——participates in creative dramatics
    ——expresses feelings and ideas through painting and other art forms
    ——participates in making story charts and class books
    ——makes individual books to express ideas
    ——tells imaginary stories
    ——writes notes and greeting cards
    ——chooses writing as a recreational activity
10. Literature
    ——develops wider interests through reading experiences
    ——listens to enjoy poems and stories
    ——participates in choral reading
    ——shares reading experiences with others
    ——recognizes humor and imagination in stories and poems
    ——chooses reading for recreation

Many teachers in a language experience approach keep two types of Reading/Research Centers in operation most of the time. One center is for self-selection and personal reading. It contains a wide selection of reading materials and is available to children most of the time. The second center is a place where the teacher confers with individuals and small groups. While most of the children are dispersed to do their work in various learning centers, the teacher schedules conferences to discuss reading progress, reading problems, and future work toward improving reading skills. Usually there is a check list to accompany each conference. The teacher and the student agree on next steps and understand that there will be a report of progress at the next conference. It is at this time that the teacher needs access to a wide variety of reading skill materials to suggest to students.

Reading Critically

Critical readers know why they are reading. They have a purpose. They usually have the why question in mind as they work. The significance of questions in critical reading is deepened to the extent that the reading is related to real problems and real experiences. This is in contrast to shallow activities that give children practice in setting purposes for reading one story after another in a reading textbook. Such practices that disregard the pupils' concerns often lead to frustration, rejection of reading, and a passive submission to literal reading (King, 1972).

There are other questions beyond the why of reading that critical readers deal with. Some are:

What am I reading? Is it fact or fiction?

If it is nonfiction, is it fact or opinion?

If it is fiction, is it realistic or fanciful?

Am I reading a folk tale, a myth, science fiction, or modern fantasy?

The interpretation and evaluation of the major ideas gained from reading can be influenced greatly by knowledge of the literary form. Children who are taught to regard almost everything they read as realism are denied the abilities of interpreting in the light of the author's purpose.

Charles introduces common topics into the learning environment of children in fourth grade. This time he chooses horses.

First, he helps the children to summarize what they think they already know about horses. Their information might then be organized in a bulletin board display. As much as possible the information is restricted to facts.

Next the class goes to the school instructional materials center to look for more information about horses. They collect myths, legends, allegories, and folk tales. They locate music and art prints. They find filmstrips and recordings. They look for information in science books and encyclopedias.

The collection of material on horses is then examined critically. Children read and listen. They view and discuss. They come to grips with information about the purposes of authors, composers, and artists. Did they develop their ideas to record facts or to stimulate imagination? Were they interested in reality or in fantasy?

A critical examination of many materials on horses (or on any other topic) underscores the point that the work of a person must be judged in the light of its purpose.

The culmination of the study of a common topic is in the creative productions by the students. They go back to their original "facts" and add others of interest. Then each student tries to write, paint, or compose two versions of a set of facts. One of the versions is realistic. The other is fanciful. In one there is an effort to keep the information as accurate as possible. In the other the information is used as a base for thinking beyond the facts.

Children who read critically try to understand the author's point of view. They check that view against their own knowledge. They check other sources that appear to be valid. They keep an open mind in order to continue learning.

A child in the intermediate grades in school is not too young to be helped to develop an interest in the documentation of sources and of supports of opinions.

Denise uses adopted texts as sources of fact and opinion in social studies and science. But she does not stop with asking questions that point to the texts. She raises doubts about stated facts and opinions in ways that make students in her sixth grade anxious to prove or disprove statements in the texts. They seek out other sources that support or reject the facts and opinions of the major text. When differences arise, the students try to find out why they exist. They look for copyright dates that might explain the differences. They study the backgrounds of the authors to judge which one might be best qualified to make an acceptable statement. They move on without reaching agreement on all points, but Denise is certain that they do not move on with the notion that all is *right* in every school textbook.

The early years in school are not too soon to involve children in responses to persuasive argument. They hear television and radio commercials and see advertisements all around. Young children need to make critical responses to some of the arguments relating to food, toys, and recreation. Propagandists have clever ways of getting their messages across. Teachers have an obligation to help children respond critically to methods and materials of propaganda.

Carlos has a special section on the Word Wall for propaganda words. His second-graders like the Word Wall and get involved in watching for words in advertisements and listening for them on television. They cut out words from magazines and newspapers and make word cards to add to the list. Some examples of propaganda terms are:

all	none	long lasting	sale
everybody	perfect	complete	½ off
best	cheapest	bargain	save

As words are added, the children recognize that most of them are ones they can read and ones they say all the time. But does the advertisement really tell the truth?

From time to time Carlos will choose an advertisement for an item that is presented as a bargain. The students then try to find out how much the same item costs at other places.

They choose an advertisement that uses the word *all* as a key idea. Then they investigate to see if they can find exceptions. They are quick to question statements that include *everybody* and *best*.

Carlos does not believe that critical reading should be the focal point of a series of well-ordered lessons in a reading textbook. He keeps the idea open and available at all times and is surprised at how often the children question what they read in their texts.

Cathy finds the use of a science text very frustrating in the teaching of problem-solving and critical reading. Answers are too obvious. Solutions are too available. Factual information is too right. In order to relieve her frustrations, she made a collection of science books published years ago. On many topics children read from multiple sources that represent the facts of the topic over a period of fifty years or more.

Children are fascinated to read of the rapid and significant changes that are being made. But Cathy doesn't let them stop there. She asks them to project their ideas into the future. If air transportation was that way fifty years ago and is like this now, what will it be like fifty years hence? What are some of the problems that must be solved in order to arrive at your prediction? Is anyone working on those problems now?

In addition to the focus on dates of publication prior to the making of evaluative judgments, children learn to think ahead of the facts that may be correct for the present.

Critical readers are aware that authors use words to convey meanings that are not found in dictionary definitions. In literary forms such words appear frequently as figurative language that compares and personifies. Literal interpretations deny the intent of an author to convey a meaning that is related to the broad experiences of people.

"He's an old bear" is a simple statement that calls up hints of meaning about the disposition and actions of bears as they have been described and redescribed in folk literature. Seldom does it mean that the person referred to is in any way like the real animal. Critical readers can never be free of the influences that come through cultural heritage, but they can modify their evaluations of the work of others through knowledge of literary forms and strategies.

Selecting Models and Patterns for Reading and Writing

Children who read and write in a language experience approach environment use the work of published authors as models for their own writing. They need some guidance in the selection of authors and some assurance that models are available in the classroom materials. Otherwise, they cannot function with independence in this type of productive activity.

Teachers can stimulate writing with models by choosing appropriate ones for oral reading to students (Appendix B). Following the reading a few examples of how the work selected can be used as a model for other ideas can be expressed by students. When the selection is placed in learning centers for independent work, children will have some notion of what they can do to make the language pattern their own.

There are several language patterns that repeat throughout literature. These can serve as both specific and general models for children to use to express their own ideas. Some of the frequently used ones are enumeration, comparison and contrast, traditional songs, elaboration, and rhythmic and rhyming patterns.

Enumeration Patterns

Enumeration patterns begin with the simplest nursery rhymes and continue throughout literature. Children find that they can adopt their own content to the patterns and make their own verses.

One, Two

Mother Goose	Child's Version
One, two Buckle my shoe.	One, two Kids at the zoo.
Three, four Shut the door.	Three, four Here comes more.
Five, six Pick up sticks.	Five, six Popsicle sticks.
Seven, eight Lay them straight.	Seven, eight Close the gate.
Nine, ten Big fat hen.	Nine, ten Home again.

At the Pond

Claryce Allen	Child's Version
One bag of popcorn. Two ducks to feed.	One bag of seed. Two birds to feed.
Throw three bits of popcorn. Four ducks then plead.	Toss three bits of seed. Four birds then plead.
Throw five bits of popcorn. Six ducks appear.	Five throws to the rear, Six birds appear.
Seven bits of popcorn; Then eight ducks to cheer.	Seven bits quite near, Then eight birds cheer.

Nine bits of corn thrown
  close to the shore,
Then ten ducks appear
  pleading for more.
	Nine bits of seed tossed
	  down on the ground—
	Birds, birds, birds, birds
	  all around!

"Ten Little Indians" is a traditional verse that is useful as a model for children to follow in writing about topics of interest. An example:

Ten Little Climbing Squirrels

One climbing
  Two climbing
    Three climbing squirrels
Four climbing
  Five climbing
    Six climbing squirrels
Seven climbing
  Eight climbing
    Nine climbing squirrels
TEN LITTLE CLIMBING SQUIRRELS!

    Ten climbing
  Nine climbing
Eight climbing squirrels
    Seven climbing
  Six climbing
Five climbing squirrels
    Four climbing
  Three climbing
Two climbing squirrels
ONE LITTLE CLIMBING SQUIRREL!

Children's own compositions can be used as a basic material for activities in learning centers. Some suggestions growing out of "Ten Little Climbing Squirrels" follow.

1. Read the numeral names and change *climbing* to something else that another animal does, such as:

rabbit hopping	worm crawling
bird flying	dog running
frog leaping	fish swimming

Say and sing many other verses like "Ten Little Climbing Squirrels." Write them with one line to a page, illustrate them, and use them in the Reading/Research Center.

2. Make numeral labels, one through ten, big enough that they can be read by everyone in the room. Choose ten children for a game that the other class members can watch. Decide on a motion word and an animal word, such as:

"One hopping toad"	Child number 1 hops out of line.
"Two hopping toads"	Number 2 takes a hop, and number 1 takes another hop.
"Three hopping toads"	Number 3 takes a hop, and numbers 2 and 1 take a hop.

Keep on until all ten have hopped. Then begin to count down until all are back in place.

3. Choose a favorite plant, machine, or insect and make a book on the model of "Ten Little Climbing Squirrels."
   Other ideas for enumeration and counting:
   The days of the week
   The hours of the day
   The doors in the building
   The cars in a parking lot

The vocabulary of enumeration and counting is found in all lists of words of high frequency. Children must deal with the sight recognition of the words as well as with their meanings in order to make progress in reading.

Comparison and Contrast Patterns

Children use words of size, shape, texture, taste, smell, sound, and others that deal with the senses as they respond to observations of the environment. Simple comparisons can be oral responses to a concept such as size.

I am bigger than a turtle.
I am bigger than a dog.
I am bigger than a squirrel.
I am bigger than a frog.

I am smaller than a mountain.
I am smaller than a car.
I am smaller than an elephant.
Am I smaller than a star?

Ideas of comparison can be found in reading selections that can be used as basic materials for learning center activities. "Special Things," by Claryce Allen, is an example.

Special Things

For touching there are special things
  like shells,
    rocks,
    a kitten's fur.
For tasting there are special things
  like watermelon,
    pizza,
    tacos.
For hearing there are special things
  like the telephone,
    the school band,
    the singing of birds.
For seeing there are special things
  like a sunset,
    pictures,
    smiles.
For smelling there are special things
  like the bakery,
    blossoms,
    a pine forest.
For loving there are special things
  like babies,
    mothers and fathers,
    and pets.
For buying there are special things
  like ice-cream cones,
    kites,
    and books.
For trading there are special things
  like stamps,
    leaves,
    cereal box tops.
For keeping there are special things
  like a blanket,
    stuffed toys,
    picture post cards.
For giving away there are special things
  like valentines,

        candy,
        a kiss.
     For laughing at there are special things
        like clowns,
          monkeys,
          and jokes.
     WHAT ARE YOUR SPECIAL THINGS?

Some things to do:

——Read "Special Things" with children, adding three things to each stanza.

——Write poems, using other names for things that are special to each author.

——Make sets of cards of things that go together: Things I like to . . .

eat	play	go to
trade	buy	give away
keep	taste	read

——Put the cards in the Reading/Research Center for groups to choose to read.

"I like to eat peanut butter,
          tomato soup,
           fritos."

"I like to buy bubble gum,
          ice-cream cones,
           records."

"I like to hear motorcycles roar,
          dogs bark,
          our stereo play."

——Pantomime some things that are special and let others guess what they are.

"What is Big?" * was used as a model for Sharon to write.

What Is Tall? *

My name is Sharon.
I am not very tall.

---

* "What Is Big?" by Henry Wing (from *Sounds of Numbers,* Holt, Rinehart and Winston, 1966).

I am not as tall as a door.
A door is taller than I am.
I am not as tall as a house.
A house is taller than I am.
I am not as tall as a tree.
A tree is taller than I am.
I am not as tall as a skyscraper.
A skyscraper is taller than I am.
I am not as tall as a mountain.
A mountain is taller than I am.
A mountain is the TALLEST thing I know.

My name is Sharon.
I am not very tall.
BUT . . .

I am taller than a bike.
A bike is taller than a wagon.
I am taller than a wagon.
A wagon is taller than a skate.
I am taller than a skate.
A skate is taller than a pebble.

I am taller than a pebble.
A pebble is taller than the ground.
The ground is the shortest thing I know.

Ask and *tell* are contrastive words that require much exercise in language situations to clarify their meanings for reading (Van Metre, 1972). The game selection "Inquisitives" is useful as a model for children to practice and then use in their own writing.

Inquisitives

I ask you.
I ask you.
Where are you going today?

I'll tell you.
I'll tell you.
I'm going outside to play.

I ask you.
I ask you.
When are you going today?

I'll tell you.
I'll tell you.
At two o'clock I shall go play.

I ask you.
I ask you.
What are you playing today?

I'll tell you.
I'll tell you.
I'm playing ball today.

I ask you.
I ask you.
Why are you playing ball?

I'll tell you.
I'll tell you.
Playing ball is good for us all.

I ask you.
I ask you.
How are you playing ball?

I'll tell you.
I'll tell you.
I'm playing ball with my right
    hand.
[Pantomime with right hand.]

I ask you.
I ask you.
How else are you playing ball?

I'll tell you.
I'll tell you.
I'm playing ball with my left
    hand.
[Pantomime with both hands.]

I ask you.
I ask you.
How else are you playing ball?

I'll tell you.
I'll tell you.
I'm playing ball with my right
    foot.
[Pantomime with both hands and
    right foot.]

I ask you.
I ask you.
How else are you playing ball?

I'll tell you.
I'll tell you.
I'm playing ball with my left
    foot.
[Pantomime with both hands and
    both feet.]

I ask you.
I ask you.
How else are you playing ball?

I'll tell you.
I'll tell you.
I'm playing ball with my head.
[Close the game with pantomiming
    with both hands, both feet, and
    the head.]

Learning center activities can be developed from the game selection after children have had a chance to hear, say, and play the contrasting ideas.

FOR THE READING/RESEARCH CENTER   Read "Inquisitives" with a friend. One can read the *ask* stanzas and the other can read the *tell* ones. The one who reads the *tell* stanzas acts out the meaning.

FOR THE WRITING/PUBLISHING CENTER Make a book like "Inquisitives." It can be about:

eating	reading
drinking	writing
singing	painting

As you make your book, remember to use the question words: where, when, what, why, and how.

FOR THE LANGUAGE STUDY CENTER Look in storybooks for question marks. When you find one, look to see what word was used to begin the sentence. Make a list of the words authors use to begin questions.

FOR THE ARTS AND CRAFTS CENTER Mold clay figures to show someone playing ball with the right hand, the right foot, left hand, the left foot, and the head.

The language of comparison and contrast requires frequent use of the inflectional endings *-er* and *-est*. It also invites the use of words of the senses that occur often in all of literature. The idea of comparison and contrast is one that helps to clarify meanings and provides natural settings for language acquisition. The patterns are so common in everyday life that authors find that they cannot provide descriptions without using forms of comparison and contrast.

Traditional Songs

Patterns for singing and saying things that have the form but not the content of originals and reflect the interests and observations of children are available for all school groups. They provide a frame of language for saying nonsense things as well as reasonable things.

Original	Child's Version
The Bear Went over the Mountain	The Mouse Crawled into the Haystack

—Traditional

The bear went over the mountain.

The mouse crawled into the haystack.

The bear went over the
  mountain.
The bear went over the
  mountain.
To see what he could
  see.

The other side of the mountain.
The other side of the mountain.
The other side of the mountain.
Was all that he could see.

The mouse crawled into the
  haystack.
The mouse crawled into the
  haystack.

To see what he could see.

The inside of the haystack.
The inside of the haystack.
The inside of the haystack.
Was all that he could see.

Other ideas:
"The bird flew up to the mirror.
. . . .
"She saw herself in the mirror . . ."

"The duck swam over the river.
. . . .
"The other bank of the river . . ."

"The flea crawled out of the dog's hair.
. . . .
"The outside of the dog's hair . . ."

Traditional songs such as "Row, Row, Row Your Boat" can be
memorized and then used as patterns for writing. Some examples:
"Walk, walk, walk your dog."
"Blow, blow, blow you wind."
"Mow, mow, mow your yard."
"Eat, eat, eat your fill."

Elaboration Patterns

Some poems and stories stem from a simple statement and are then
extended and elaborated. An example that is widely used in schools
is "A Maker of Boxes" from *Sounds of Laughter* by Bill Martin, Jr. (Holt,
Rinehart and Winston, 1968). This example lends itself to group composition since there are many ideas needed to fill out the pattern. The
product of a group of children who became familiar with "A Maker of
Boxes" follows.

A Maker of Cookies

Hello! My name is Mr. Chef. I am a maker of cookies.

I make chocolate chip cookies, vanilla cookies, and raisin cookies, and icebox cookies and peanut butter cookies and chocolate cookies and hard cookies and soft cookies.

And all of them are good.

On Monday I make square cookies.

Brownies and date squares and dough cookies.

On Tuesday I make round cookies.

Vanilla wafers, Oreos, and raisin cookies and ginger snaps.

On Wednesday I make crunchy cookies.

I make Rice-Crispy cookies and nutty cookies, and cocoanut cookies and oatmeal cookies.

On Thursday I make pretty cookies.

I make pink-icing cookies and flower-shaped cookies.

On Friday I make holiday cookies.

I make jack-o'-lantern cookies and Santa Claus cookies and rabbit cookies.

On Saturday I don't make cookies. I make books about cookies.

I make fat books and skinny books and narrow books and small books and big books ALL ABOUT COOKIES.

On Sunday I don't make cookies.

I just lay around and EAT THEM!

On my birthday I don't make a birthday cake.

I make a GIANT BIRTHDAY COOKIE!!

On April Fools' Day I make vanishing cookies.

I eat them before anyone sees them.

AND I NEVER BURN MY COOKIES.

> Other ideas for elaborating patterns are:
> painting pictures
> wearing clothes
> driving cars
> planting seeds.

Patterned writing that can serve as models for children's writing can also stimulate them to develop other activities that enhance meanings in language. "A Patch of Green Lace" by Claryce Allen is an example of writing that elaborates a simple idea and then leads to other activities.

A Patch of Green Lace

One day I saw
some tiny winged seeds.

I went back again
and found many weeds.

I went back again
and yellow flowers found.

I went back again
and saw fluffy balls round.

I went back again
on a windy day.

I went back again
and the balls had blown away.

I went back again
and saw leaves dry and brown.

I went back again
Only twigs could be found.

I went back again
on a snowy day.

Nothing could be seen
except snowflakes at play.

In the spring I went back
to the very same place.

What did I see?
A PATCH OF GREEN LACE!

FOR THE DISCOVERY CENTER Think of what happened to the weed seed: first, then next, then next, then next. Now think of something else that grows from seed: beans, carrots, and lettuce.

Make crayon drawings of what happens as the seeds sprout and grow. Label the drawings as you go along. A science book or an encyclopedia might have some help for you.

FOR THE WRITING/PUBLISHING CENTER Plant some seeds and keep a diary of what you see as they sprout and start to grow. If you want to write a book about what you see and what you write in your diary, you can use "A Patch of Green Lace" as a model. Put a stanza on each page and illustrate it.

You may want to change "I went back again . . ." to something like—
"I looked . . ."
"I looked again . . ."

FOR THE LANGUAGE STUDY CENTER   Cut pictures from magazines and arrange them in order to show a baby growing to be a man and a grandfather, or a baby growing to be a woman and a grandmother. Find names for each of the pictures and label them.

Rhythmic and Rhyming Patterns

Pleasing effects can be created by the use of rhymes of sense and nonsense. A traditional verse that children can use is "The Barnyard Song." It begins:

> I had a cat and the cat pleased me.
> I fed my cat under yonder tree.
> And my little cat went fiddle-dee-dee.

Each stanza adds another animal with the sound words of the last line repeated each time so that the succeeding stanza has one more line than the preceding one.

This triplet form can be used to express all kinds of ideas. One example that children have developed is about transportation.

The Travel Song

> I had a car and the car pleased me.
> I started the ignition with a shiny new key.
> And my car went deedle-dum-dee.
>
> I had a ship and the ship pleased me.
> I sailed my ship to the thundering sea.
> And my ship went toodle-too-tee.
> And my car went deedle-dum-dee.
>
> I had a train and the train pleased me.
> I boarded my train on track number three.

And my train went chuggle-choo-chee.
And my ship went toodle-too-tee.
And my car went deedle-dum-dee.

I had a plane and the plane pleased me.
It flew up high and landed in a tree.
And the plane went zingle-zee-zee.
And my train went chuggle-choo-chee.
And my ship went toodle-too-tee.
And my car went deedle-dum-dee.

Another poem that has rhyme and rhythm is the traditional "Whistle, Mary, Whistle." It begins:

Whistle, Mary, whistle.
You want to catch a cow.
I can't whistle, mother.
I don't know how.

An innovation on this well-known poem is about reading.

Read, Lucy, read
And you will have some fun.
I can't read, teacher,
I'd rather skip and run.

Read, Larry, read
Of kings and queens and joy.
I can't read, teacher,
I'm just a stupid boy.

Read, Sarah, read.
The frog just caught a rat.
I can't read, teacher,
This book is just too fat.

Read, Jack, read
Of lions and tigers roaring.
I can't read, teacher,
I find it all quite boring.

Read, Pat, read
Of travels to the zoo.
I can't read, teacher,
I chose this book for you.

Read, Tom, read.
The princess found the pearls.

I can't read, teacher,
This book is for the girls.

Read, Johnny, read.
I've found a book for you.
Oh, boy! Monsters!
I want to read now, too.

Other ideas for additional stanzas:
Write, William, write
Sing, Suzanna, sing
Jump, Jonathan, jump

Repeating language patterns read *with* children can anchor those patterns firmly in the ears. What they hear and say can then be used as a base for writing. The writing gives a personalized experience with the type of sentences and other language sounds that are found in reading materials.

It is imperative in a language experience approach to accept the home-rooted language of children in speech and in writing. It is just as imperative that their language be influenced by models by authors whose work has stood the test of time. Children who move toward self-selection of reading materials must have some prior experience in dealing with language that has characteristics of a predictive sequence such as is found in enumeration patterns. They must recognize the value and artistry of writing in comparing and contrasting patterns to clarify meanings. They must know that many authors take a simple idea and elaborate to extend its meaning. They must appreciate and enjoy the rhythm of language rather than being concerned at all times about recognition and comprehension abilities. *What* they choose to read may be as important as the difficulty level when the choice is one of a model for self-expression.

Summary of Skills and Abilities for Evaluating Communication of Others

FINDING INFORMATION

——Finds multiple materials on one topic
——Uses reference materials to validate information
——Uses features of books such as table of contents and index to locate information

——Uses card catalogue in library
——Identifies key words in a topic of study
——Shares information through effective oral reading
——Reads the preface of a book to find out author's purpose
——Looks at date of publication to validate information
——Knows and uses alphabetic order to locate information in reference materials
——Finds information in materials such as recordings and filmstrips

BROWSING AND READING FOR RECREATION

——Distinguishes between fact and fantasy
——Separates the real from the imaginary
——Identifies poetry as a literary form
——Identifies exaggeration and sarcasm in writing
——Senses the humor of another writer
——Chooses reading for free time
——Skims books to find parts of interest
——Knows the relationships between information in books, records, tapes, study prints, and film
——Listens to records that model good reading while following along the printed material
——Browses and reads many kinds of trade books, reference books, catalogues, newspapers, and magazines
——Reads for pleasure only

READING SKILL DEVELOPMENT

——Uses reading skill materials to improve personal skills
——Discusses skill needs in reading conference
——Uses reading skill materials that are assigned
——Senses improvement in reading skills

MODELS AND PATTERNS FOR WRITING OWN BOOKS

——Repeats in stories and poems language patterns used by other authors
——Identifies repeating patterns by looking at printed language
——Uses own ideas and vocabulary in patterns from other authors, such as patterns of
——enumeration and counting
——comparison and contrast
——story
——elaboration
——rhythm and rhyme

READING CRITICALLY

—Asks questions that can be solved through reading

—Makes a comparison of the treatment of a topic by two or more authors

—Formulates conclusions on the basis of evidence gained through study

—Uses multiple media when searching for answers

—Distinguishes between information gained from direct reporting and that gained from literary forms such as myths, legends, allegories, and folk tales

—Changes opinion on a topic as a result of study

—Understands that an author may write from a slanted point of view on purpose

—Recognizes propaganda techniques, especially those used in advertising

—Checks the date of publication when facts are questioned

—Identifies figurative language such as similes and metaphors

Selected References

Allen, Roach Van, and Claryce Allen. *Language Experiences in Reading, Level III.* Encyclopaedia Britannica Educational Corp., Chicago, 1967.

Cheney, Arnold. *Teaching Reading Skills Through the Newspaper.* International Reading Association, Newark, Del., 1971.

Darrow, Helen Fisher. "Reading, Morality and Individualized Reading." In *Reading in Education: A Broader View,* edited by Malcolm P. Douglass. Charles E. Merrill, Columbus, Ohio, 1973.

Groff, Patrick. "Culture and the Single Textbook." In *Reading in Education: A Broader View,* edited by Malcolm P. Douglass. Charles E. Merrill, Columbus, Ohio, 1973.

Guzak, Frank J. "Teacher Questioning and Reading," *Reading Teacher,* 21, 3 (December, 1967), 227–234.

Heilman, Arthur W. *Principles and Practices of Teaching Reading,* 3rd ed. Charles E. Merrill, Columbus, Ohio, 1972.

Hopkins, Lee Bennett. *Let Them Be Themselves.* Citation Press, New York, 1969.

Karlin, Robert. *Teaching Elementary Reading: Principles and Strategies.* Harcourt Brace Jovanovich, New York, 1971.

King, Martha L. "Critical Reading, What Else?" In *The Quest for Competency in Teaching Reading,* edited by Howard A. Klein. International Reading Association, Newark, Del., 1972.

May, Frank B. *To Help Children Read: Mastery Performance Modules for Teachers in Training.* Charles E. Merrill, Columbus, Ohio, 1973.

Robertson, Jean. "Using Social Studies Content to Develop Reading Skills." In *The Quest for Competency in Teaching Reading,* edited by Howard A. Klein. International Reading Association, Newark, Del., 1972.

Ruddell, Robert B. *Reading-Language Instruction: Innovative Practices.* Prentice-Hall, Englewood Cliffs, N.J., 1974.

Sebesta, Sam L., and Carl J. Waller (eds.). *The First R: Readings on Teaching Reading.* Science Research Associates, Chicago, 1972.

Singer, Harry, and Robert B. Ruddell (eds.). *Theoretical Models and Processes of Reading.* International Reading Association, Newark, Del., 1970.

Van Metre, Patricia. "Syntactic Characteristics of Selected Bilingual Children." (Ed.D. dissertation.) University of Arizona, Tucson, 1972.

Responding in personal ways—performing personally as the result of influences from many sources; and reflecting humanistic qualities of the author, the artist, the teacher, the composer, the architect, the musician, the scientist, and other contributors to society who are dependent on creative self-expression for survival.

In a language experience approach there is no thought that "reading" is initiated at school through a beginning reading program. Reading is a part of life that is as characteristic of human growth as are other vital life processes. Experiences in both the nonsymbolic and the symbolic world are emphasized in instruction when the child enters school. They are assumed, in the majority of cases, to have developed to some extent prior to the school experience. The recognition of primary reading experiences as basic to school progress is required of teachers who propose to individualize, to personalize, to open up, to eliminate failure, to build positive self-concepts, and to achieve other goals that make humane persons out of human beings.

To the present time no reading method has been developed which assures that every child with normal ability in language will achieve success in reading print, or secondary reading. Beyond beginning reading, traditional practices of posing questions to pupils about what is read and how much is comprehended assure frustration and a measure of failure on the part of many pupils. These practices are modified significantly in a language experience approach through emphases on personal responses to primary and to secondary reading experiences. According to Spencer (1970, page 76):

The student's reading of the things of his physical world, and of himself and those who surround him in his social world, will provide the extent and quality of his primary reading experience. It is requisite for the educational development of the student that some time be given in the curriculum structure for the recognition of these experiences as a legitimate part of the reading program.

Most school programs give attention to primary reading abilities in kindergarten and beginning first grade. It is thought that by the time students advance beyond the beginning stages of reading print that the only legitimate function of the school is to keep a focus on the world of printed symbols—to build word-recognition skills, comprehension skills, speed, and concepts. As important as these abilities may be, they do not substitute for or replace the need for continued recognition of abilities to read all aspects of the social environment.

Added to that range of abilities is the reading of mechanical devices and of personal meanings derived from all contacts with people and things. This emphasis in a language experience approach is a recognition of the fact that the achievement of competence with any aspect of reading behavior affects and is affected by the recognition given to all other aspects.

Personal response while reading is the goal of any viable reading program, and it is a required component of a language experience approach. Responding with someone else's answers to questions the reader did not ask—workbook reading materials—is to deny the real purpose of reading.

The three strands of the curriculum rationale for *Language Experiences in Communication* present minimum considerations for a *person reading*. They could be explained forever because they change to some extent with every attempt at application when the application is creative. Every person reads in a different way, and every application of language influence is unique to that person. The major idea is summarized, however, by Peter Lincoln Spencer in an article entitled "Reading Is Creative Living" when he says (1957, page 17):

> There can be little doubt but that what one has experienced is an established part of him, but it may be that we have given too little concern to what one is becoming. The emphasis upon the past gives the impression that life is a process of fleeing or of smug complacency. The future remains to be created. Here is one's opportunity, one's real challenge.

How can we live and learn with children in ways that permit them "to become"—to be a product of the future rather than a duplicate of the past?

One way to begin answering this question is to include *personal response* as a basic ingredient of reading development and to include reading as an essential component of creative living.

Children Respond

Children in a language experience approach environment reflect the influences of their observations, their reading, and their imagination. There is no expectancy that, as a result of reading or hearing a story or a section in a study book, all would respond to the same set of questions and then find out who got the most right and who got the least right. They give oral and written responses to convergent activities when they are appropriate, but the ultimate is the personal response.

Responding to Observations

Who knows which is "best" after reading what seven ten-year-olds said during an observation of springtime? Do the following responses need to be judged, or can they just be enjoyed?

1.   Spring is like a holiday.

—Tom

2.   # Spring

Flowers;
tulips, daisies
fresh blossoms, buds
birds;
robins, doves
moist clouds
baseball
fishing
bicycling
grassy cool winds
blue skies
and
butterflies.

—Jim

3.   # Spring

I walked out of my door, and I knew spring was here. The fluffy clouds and the bright blue skies were as peaceful and as gentle as the beginning of a new world. The birds were singing and the bees were humming. As I walked along I saw a robin sitting in the soft green grass. It was a breezy day and I saw happy children playing baseball. They seemed to be enjoying their spring vacation. I saw fragile flowers. The sunshine was here, and then gone, as it began to get moist and cool and it began to sprinkle light drops of rain.

I turned and began to go back home, thinking how beautiful is the newness of tulips, daisies and even the blossoms of the dandelions, when after a long winter, spring is here.

—Aaron

4.

Spring Time

Spring is the time for flowers
and days to be longer,
For the sun to rise
and the night to fly.

—Jean

5.

Spring Flowers

Ranunculus like a queen's bouquet,
Gorgeous golds and royal purples,
Vibrant reds and brilliant oranges,
The calla lilies a vase to hold them.

Gazania tigers so bold and fierce,
Hide their young till they are grown,
And at night they hide themselves,
But, come daybreak, they unfold.

Calendulas, like brilliant suns,
Send out rays from their centers.
Pansies, like little faces, are
Small and sweet, young and tender.

Iris like a fairy princess' throne,
Deep and rich in color,
Stock like a brilliant feather duster,
Why not give some to your mother?

So ends my tale of the spring flowers.
Oh, dear, I forgot
Daisies. Well, all I can say,
Every plant is a bouquet.

—Elva

6.

Language of Nature

I went to the hills a few days ago
And I heard nature speaking soft and low.
Some folks say you can't hear her speak,

But I heard it all right 'cause I took a peek.
Her language is beautiful indeed
Because she made something grow from every seed;
The humming of bees, the singing of birds,
The pounding of buffalo running in herds,
The rustle of leaves, the spatter of rain,
The moaning of wind when I walk down the lane.
Nature speaks in more than one way
And you can hear her every day.

—Douglas

7.   **Seeds of Freedom in the Breeze**

Growing flowers, red, blue, yellow,
   green, swaying.
New life begins.
Orange, purple—
They're seeds of freedom in the breeze.

Bluish greens roll through the air,
With little round seeds beginning
   millions of lives.
Like veins, the stems carry life to the flowers.

The snow and floods come and kill them,
But new ones begin with the Spring.

—Karin

Which one?

Responding to Teaching Goals

Two teachers can take classes of six-year-olds on the same study trip to a dairy. One teacher can return to the classroom and record the children's responses with a group experience chart. The purpose of the chart is to provide reading material that promotes word recognition. Year after year the chart turns out to be about the same because the teacher has in mind what is needed to achieve her goals. It might be like this:

Our Trip to the Dairy

We went to the dairy.
We rode on the bus.
We saw some cows.
We drank some milk.
We ate some ice cream.
It was fun.

Each year the teacher makes a duplicate copy of the experience chart, cuts it into sentence strips children can match up with the original for a language recognition activity. Children learn the words on the chart.

The other teacher returns with the children to a learning environment in which she has placed books, toys, games, pictures, filmstrips, and records in the learning centers. Children have previewed most of the materials prior to the trip. Now they confirm their ideas as a result of their experience.

While children work in the learning centers, the teacher listens as one child at a time talks about the trip. She records some of what each child says for a special book of personal responses to the dairy trip. This is the kind of response she might hear as a child dictates and she writes:

My Trip to the Dairy (Bret)

We went to the Shamrock dairy and I saw a baby cow be born. The mother cow just stood in her stall and mooed, and was she surprised when she turned around and saw her baby. She didn't even know what happened.

There was the baby, all wrapped up in a plastic sack, and the mother started to lick it off. I didn't know that baby cows came in plastic sacks. It was so cute!

The lady at the dairy didn't know the cow was going to have her baby while we were there. Boy, were we glad she did!

Bret might not have been able to read his story because the fluency of speech produced sophisticated sentences, but the language was his and he knew from the experience that his own speech had made the reading. The experience gave the teacher a clue that Bret would be a fluent reader if his language production could be maintained during the period of time that he was learning recognition skills enough for him to be independent as a reader.

In some classrooms the popping of popcorn is a social experience related to a party. In others it is a language experience that affords interaction with all kinds of descriptive language. It offers visual contrast and comparison instantly.

A teacher of seven-year-olds listened to them talk about a popcorn experience while she mediated the language to encourage the use of descriptive words. This is what she wrote from their dictation following the talking.

Popcorn

Before popcorn pops it is little, hard, and yellow. After it pops it is white, rough, and soft. When it is popping, it sounds like rain on the roof, water dripping from a faucet, fire crackling, and a fire sprinkler. It also sounds like a rotten car.

Popcorn smells like butter and salt. It is delicious and we like it. Popcorn tastes marvelous, salty, and crunchy. It feels like a soft white flower.

Children responded to the popcorn experience in terms of their senses. The quality of their language was raised beyond their home-rooted language through the influence of a teacher who helped them to extend their experiences with words. (The majority of children in the class were from Spanish-speaking homes.) They made this experience and others about popcorn into books for use in the reading program. Because they had invested some of their own talk in the reading material, it did not sound foreign to them.

Responding to Information

Science experiences provide information for children. They research and read. They talk and experiment. Then they make personal responses such as the one published in a book by an eight-year-old:

Sounds (*Mary Ann*)

High sounds.
Low sounds.
There are sounds up in the trees.
There are sounds on the ground.
The world around us is full of sounds.
        BANGS!
          and
        SHOUTS!
                POPS!
               and
               ROARS!
People talking and music playing.
And every sound we hear is made by
  something that is moving.
So that is all I have to say about SOUNDS!

The End

Others in the class may have done straight reporting about the observations and experiments with sounds, but Mary Ann responded in her own way to what she had seen, heard, and read.

Another child in another classroom related sound to music when she wrote:

Music Everywhere (*Elva*)

There's music in the air,
There's music everywhere,
Music in the wind as it blows through the trees,
Music in the chirp of the bird,
Music in the night when the crickets sing.
So listen
And you will hear
Music in the air,
Music everywhere.

Children in a language experience approach classroom have models that permit them to make creative responses to factual material. And they do!

Responses from Personal Observations

Some children fail to respond to instruction in how to read and land in special classes with special reading teachers. Danny had that luck in school. His special reading teacher tried to relieve him of the feeling that he couldn't read anything. She visited with him about the things he could "read" from his personal observations. He grew to the point that he could tell and write stories from real life and from imagination. The first story he wrote and made into a book reveals that he had been reading much nonprint during the time he was failing to read printed material in the school instructional program. One of his stories in his language follows.

My Very Own Dog (*Danny*)

One day my dog he got sick.
He sneezed a lot.
We gave him a lot of milk and he got well.
He played with us.
Then every day he went out looking for a girl friend because he wanted to see some baby dogs.
Then he found one.
Then he was the father of the dogs.
I don't know how many puppies.
Then one day this truck came by and ranned over him.
Then he had a broken leg.
We took him in the house and my father got a ruler and broke it and put it on his leg.
My dog is still alive—but he's tired of looking for girl friends.

Where did a "nonreader" like Danny get the information for his story? How is it that he could read this story but could not read a preprimer in a reading series?

The answers lie in the ability of one special teacher to build an awareness of the many facets of reading and then to release Danny to say what he had to say in his own language patterns and with his own vocabulary. The writing process, though laborious for Danny, helped him to internalize the vocabulary he used in talking so that the printed forms were meaningful. Together, he and the teacher edited the story, paged it, illustrated it, typed it, and then bound it into the first book Danny ever read although he had been in school for three years.

To respond in personal ways to his personal observations was a requirement for him.

Some teachers in a language experience approach want children to respond as authors before instruction begins in language-reading studies. They want to know something of how each child's awareness of the world is related to personal language production. This information precedes any work on language recognition skills, comprehension skills, and fluency in oral reading.

Lisa was in such a classroom when she wrote "When I Won $100,000,000.00." Because Lisa had been in other classes where she had experienced authorship many times, she was able to produce the book during the first week of second grade. Her book told the teacher much about Lisa. She was observant; she was interested in ecology, health, and peace; she gathered information from sources outside the school (especially from television); she had high aspirations and high ability to express herself; and she had made some contact with classical literature. Here is the text of Lisa's first book of the year (without her illustrations and attractive binding).

When I Won $100,000,000.00 (*Lisa*)

When I won $100,000,000.00 I thought I was the president of the United States. Imagine me winning $100,000,000.00

I bought two of the most expensive cars, ten large color television sets, five of the largest mansions, the Grand Canyon, ten bicycles, found a cure for muscular dystrophy, and gave our land freedom.

I stopped pollution and forest fires. I have a chauffeur-driven car.

Wow! It's a great feeling to win $100,000,000.00. I wish I could do more to help my country do the things it needs to do, but I just ran out of money.

The greatest thing I won since winning the $100,000,000.00 was winning a teacher named Miss Allen. I think she's great!

(And just like Shakespeare said, "Money doesn't grow on trees.")

Lisa could not possibly have learned from the first-grade curriculum what she reflected in her story. She had to draw on her out-of-school experiences. They provided her with interests, concerns, vocabulary, and aspirations to express herself in ways not typical of first-grade reading stories. She "read her world" and profited from that reading at the same time that she was learning to read very simple printed materials and learning the mechanics of writing with an alphabetic system.

Responding to Literature

In conventional reading programs the reading of selections from literature is followed frequently by discussions that lead the thinking back into the story. Who? What? When? Why? How? In a language experience approach there may be some looking back into literature, but there is also time and place for children to make personal responses.

A simple type of response is children writing something they know about in the style of an established author. This is illustrated by a group of second-grade students who responded to the work of Margaret Wise Brown. After they had heard, read, and repeated portions of several of her books, they wrote in the style of her *The Important Book* about things not in that book. Some of their responses follow.

Book *(Renee)*

The important thing about books is that you read them.
Some books have pictures.
Some books only have words.
You can use them for paperweights.
But the important thing about books is that you read them.

Roadrunners *(George)*

The important thing about a roadrunner is that it goes fast.
They look skinny.
They have feathery tails.
They act like clowns.
But the important thing about a roadrunner is that it goes fast.

The Earth *(Ben)*

The important thing about the earth is that it turns around the sun.
It is round like a sphere.

People live on the earth.
But the important thing about the earth is that it turns around the sun.

Butterflies (*Veronica*)

The important thing about a butterfly is that it is pretty.
It has four wings.
It has two antennas.
It flies to flowers.
But the important thing about a butterfly is that it is pretty.

In a middle-school classroom where the teacher read aloud something of children's literature each day, a group of students collaborated to produce "Lollypop Land." The story reflects the influence of numerous stories that give children release from the here and now and encourage them to use their minds for flights of fancy.

Lollypop Land (*Brenda, Jennifer, Debbie, Diana, and Suzanne*)

It was a rainy day and Timothy Todd stood staring out the window. He was sad and didn't have anything to do because his baseball game was canceled.

But wait! What was outside his window?

It was a tiny little mouse that was trying to tell him something.

Timothy jumped up and grabbed his coat and put his boots on. He ran out the back door into the rain in search of the mouse. He found it on his porch. The mouse was very friendly and said, "Hi, my name is Millie the Mini Mouse. I have come to invite you to my happy home. Come on!"

Timothy followed her through a field and after a while they came to a river. It was a very bright purple color with pink spots. As soon as they crossed the bridge it stopped raining. They entered a wonderland that Timmy had never seen before. The land was full of lollypops.

Timmy could hardly believe his eyes when he saw all his dreams come true. Then he saw all kinds of funny-looking animals. There was Googles the Gargling Giraffe, Emily the Elephant, Hillary the Hilarious Hippo, Larry Lolly Lion, and Octavius the Jolly-olly Octopus. They were all there in a bunch waiting to meet him.

At first he was afraid of them—especially the lion! But after awhile they were all laughing and playing together. They played about four games of tag, five games of hide-and-go-seek, and six games of hopscotch. Then they all settled down completely out of breath.

After they had rested awhile Timmy said, "I'm hungry."

Hillary (who is always hungry) said, "Let's have a picnic. Follow me."

They all went into the lollypop forest of lollypop trees. They kept going until they came to a small clear spot with one tree. It was a perfect place for a picnic because the yummy food was already there waiting for them. They had lollypop cake, cherry lollypop to drink, and last, but not least, every flavor of lollypop you could imagine. They ate the best meal they had ever eaten in their lives.

After lunch they were all pretty tired so they decided to take a nap in the shade of the lollypop tree.

The first thing Timmy heard when he woke up was "Timmy, what are you doing? You have been staring out the window for an hour!"

His happy day was over but he knew he would remember his friends in Lollypop Land forever.

The End

"Lollypop Land" was edited, illustrated, and made into a book for the classroom library. Its colorful pages and imaginative text brought much pleasure to classmates who read it.

Children in a second-grade class listened to many make-believe stories like those they would find in storybooks and trade books. They told make-believe stories like those they were hearing. The teacher helped them to decide on characters and a plot. After that, they dictated and/or wrote their own stories for a class book. Here is one example of the many that were produced.

The Crazy Chickens (Brenda)

One day a silly boy chicken was trying to sweet-talk a girl chicken. He jumped up and down and all around trying to get her to look at him. She was his chicken girl friend.

He went home and told his chicken mother, "I have a girl friend."

"Cut, cut! I have to tell your rooster father."

"Cock-a-doodle-doo, I think your girl friend is pretty, too," crowed his rooster father.

The crazy chickens married. She layed some eggs and they had some little chickens. They were married. They were so happy that she cackled and he crowed.

Children who respond to life and literature are able to integrate much of what they think and believe into personal productions. For that reason the emphasis on responding in personal ways is not separated from reading in a language experience approach. Personal response is always there in many communicating forms, but it is closely related to reading print when it is in published form.

Beginning attempts at writing on literary levels of communication may involve a single model from an author. As writing experiences mature, there is usually an integration of many stories and poems from many authors. Melinda, in a school district that promoted personal production, was able by age nine to incorporate several well-known story plots into one of her own which she published as "Snowbird." Melinda's book was produced in multiple copies as a contribution to the school district's reading program. Her book, along with many others, was bound in a substantial binding and placed in all the elementary school libraries in the district.

Snowbird (*Melinda*)

It was dusk now. The sun was almost gone behind the horizon. Inside the neighboring house were the parakeets, snug and warm, cuddling. Outside the wind whistled through the trees, making an eerie scream.

There, sitting on an icy branch was the chickadee. It was all puffed out, trying to keep itself warm.

Although there was an extreme difference between the two birds, parakeet and chickadee, not one of them was as different as the snowbird. The snowbird was neither hot nor cold because it couldn't feel. It was neither dead nor alive because it didn't even know it was made of snow. It only knew that it was a bird, a queer looking bird, but a bird all the same.

The little girl that had made her was poor. She had built the bird with love for she hated no one. She loved the little birds and animals.

The little girl lived in a house that was as cold as the chickadee's.

Every day she would look out of her window to see if her snowbird had melted. She wished that it was real, as real as the parakeets next door.

After awhile she got the idea that she ought to paint the bird. So she hunted around the house till she found a bit of paint. She had no paintbrush, so she used her fingers. She had only blue paint so she called it her bluebird.

It seems strange to say, but she felt a new warmth rushing through her in the cold room. The sky brightened and the wind died down. There was a sound of wings and right in front of her was the snowbird.

Was it all a dream? It didn't seem possible, yet when she looked where the snowbird statue had stood, it was gone! Just then her mother called her to supper.

As she turned to say good-by to the little bluebird, it was gone, too. In its place was a spot of blue and right in the center was a red heart.

It had been the real bluebird of happiness who had brought joy to her because of her love.

The combination of exposure to literature and valuing of personal authorship results in a quality of writing by children that is not evident when they always write from their own experiences. As important as that is, it is not enough to foster communication on a literary level.

Responding as Authors

Young Authors' Book Fairs are sponsored by some school groups. They provide an opportunity for children to develop criteria for selecting books representative of their goals for personal writing and to gain the accompanying skills required for publishing. Children who are selected to represent classroom or school groups at areawide fairs usually have opportunities to participate in writing seminars conducted by well-known authors and by college teachers of writing and children's literature. This experience is highly motivating in terms of setting goals for future productions.

Getting ready for a Young Authors' Book Fair involves much more than children writing books. Parents, school administrators, and school board members are involved in planning and decision-making. In the process they come to appreciate the work of teachers and children who are involved. They discover that the children have responsibilities that are very demanding. They learn that selections are made on the basis of criteria that children think are important and that in applying the criteria, the young authors find out much about the mechanics of writing and publishing. A group getting ready for a book fair needs:

—children with the attitudes of scientists to check the validity of facts

—children who have skills in the mechanics of editing and correcting compositions

—children sensitive to language who can consult with authors about style and form

—children talented as artists who can illustrate books when an author does not choose to do so

—children who can type manuscripts

—children who can bind books with sturdy and attractive bindings that withstand much handling

—children who can organize parents into working groups to support the publishing enterprise with scrap materials and needed equipment such as sewing machines and typewriters

—children who can represent the class project to the school principal and the local school board

—children who can share their books with audiences by skillful oral reading

—children who can contribute to writing seminars that will be helpful in setting new goals and raising aspirations for improved publications.

When children are authors in the real sense of having their personal responses published and shared with a large audience, they discover that they need to be able to put themselves in the place of scientists, politicians, homemakers, service persons, ministers, teachers, musicians, artists, soldiers, and others who have ideas and feelings to express. They must assume the attitudes and the conditions of the poor, the lonely, the sick, and disabled as well as those of the happy, successful, and spirited. They extend their thinking into flights of imagination which quite possibly will be into the future; for it is in the minds of youth that the great contributions and events of the future will be born. Children who have had repeated opportunities for personal self-expression are much more likely to think for the future than are children who derive their satisfaction in school from repeating answers to questions they did not ask.

Teachers Respond

Teachers in a language experience approach use multiple methods and multiple materials to stimulate children to discover reading processes that are useful and efficient. They never set out to teach children how to read by a prescribed system. They think of children as having the basic ingredients of reading inside. They interact with children as they help each one to discover nonprint and printed forms of communication. When the ability to read print is achieved, they do not say that they have taught the child how to read. They know that what they did was to release something in the child that had always been there.

Teachers do not attempt to force students' language into uncharacteristic forms. They respond to language that is natural and normal. From natural language they progress continually through influences related to phonology, syntax, and morphology. But teachers always let the child's own language and personal meanings remain in central focus.

Through processes of contrast and comparison each child is encouraged to make choices toward fluency and flexibility in communication. Each child is exposed to artful ways of saying things. Each child learns to use many resources that will continue as influences throughout life. Normative scores are minimized. Personal responses in many forms are maximized.

Teachers who love the language of literature demonstrate that love through the choices they make in their oral reading to children—

But they reflect the feeling that the best books are yet to be written.

They share art objects and art prints that are meaningful and that, to them, demonstrate the great art of the past—

But they imply in their interaction with children that the greatest paintings are yet to be painted.

Inventions of great scientists are shared with enthusiasm and appreciation—

But there is always the real possibility that the greatest inventions for the benefit of mankind are to be made in the future.

Music is a continuing part of the school program, and teachers bring children in contact with the great masters of classical and modern music—

But they reserve the idea that the greatest music will be composed in the future.

Reading in the content fields of the school curriculum is important and is used as a base for understanding places and people and a few of the reasons why they act as they do—

But the teacher who is responsive to children and their potential remains convinced that

——the greatest explorations are in the future

——the greatest governments are yet to be formed

——the greatest structures are yet to be built

——the most important ideas for the benefit of mankind are ahead of us—

And, perhaps, by some chance, some of those who will bring it all about are in our schools today.

Can we offer these potential leaders less than an opportunity to respond in personal ways to reading that

——generates productive thinking?

——allows freedom of expression?

——stimulates individuality with pride?

——values ingenuity?

——satisfies curiosity?

Whatever else might be done in reading programs to achieve the complex skills and knowledge that permit reading processes to be a part of life and living, *Language Experiences in Communication* suggests that there are three major ideas for teachers to hold. These ideas, when implemented, assure a measure of success for each child in reading printed materials.

Idea 1: The natural language a child uses for communication is a basic ingredient in reading. It must remain useful and used throughout the period when the refined skills of reading print are being developed.

Idea 2: Language study is a continuous process that helps each child understand personal language power through comparing and contrasting that language against a grid of studied language characteristics. The basic ingredients of language that are required for reading what others have written are inherent in the language of everyone who produces ideas with a semblance of syntactical structure.

Idea 3:   Growing language is being influenced from many sources and by many people. Each child deserves to try out new forms of communication under the influence of successful practitioners. These influences culminate in personal responses that seek ever higher levels of quality, greater fluency, and increased flexibility in communication.

Selected References

Allen, Roach Van. "Hitching Posts for Reading in the Space Age." In *Reading in Education: A Broader View,* edited by Malcolm P. Douglass. Charles E. Merrill, Columbus, Ohio, 1973.

Biondi, Angelo M. *The Creative Process.* D.O.K. Publishers, Buffalo, 1972.

Fabun, Don. *You and Creativity*. Glencoe Press, Beverly Hills, Calif., 1968.

Fishbein, Justin, and Robert Emans. *A Question of Competence: Intelligence and Learning to Read.* Science Research Associates, Chicago, 1972.

Hopkins, Lee Bennett. "And One Day the World Will Know Me: Poetry for Inner City Youngsters." In *A Forum for Focus,* edited by Martha L. King, Robert Emans, and Patricia J. Cianciolo. National Council of Teachers of English, Urbana, Ill., 1973.

Parnes, Sidney J. *Creativity: Unlocking Human Potential*. D.O.K. Publishers, Buffalo, 1972.

Spencer, Peter Lincoln. "Reading Is Creative Living." In *Twenty-second Yearbook, Claremont College Reading Conference,* edited by Malcolm P. Douglass. Claremont College Press, Claremont, Calif., 1957.

————. *Reading Reading.* Claremont College Press, Claremont, Calif., 1970.

Appendix A

Checklist for Kindergarten Learning Environment

Checklist for Elementary School Learning Environment

CHECK LIST FOR KINDERGARTEN LEARNING ENVIRONMENT

This check list is to be used in rating the extent to which any learning environment has visible evidence that the three strands of a language experience approach are being implemented. It does not deal with the nonvisible aspects of the program.

Tentative conclusions from the use of this rating scale indicate that children who live and learn in an environment with a rating above 3.0 make significant progress toward communication abilities that promote reading and writing.

THE SCORING SCALE

0—*Does not exist* at the time of observation

1—*Present* but on a restricted basis—by permission only or after completion of "regular work"

2—*Present during observation period* but little or no evidence as a continuing part of the program

3—*Present during observation* with visible evidence that the condition is a continuing part of the program

4—*Superior performance of part observed* and/or visible evidence that the condition is an essential part of the program

OBSERVATION TIME

Minimum of 30 minutes recommended for external evaluation. No time limit for self-evaluation

SUMMARY:

Mean score Strand One	
Mean score Strand Two	
Mean score Strand Three	
TOTAL Mean scores divided by 3	

INTERPRETATION

The closer the *total mean score* is to 4.00, the nearer the classroom environment is to satisfying basic requirements for a language experience approach.

Scores below 3.00 reflect a need for improvement in communication opportunities that are required of a language experience approach.

STRAND ONE
*Experiencing com-
munication*

MAJOR IDEA
*This strand emphasizes the
real language of the
learners as basic to com-
munication skill develop-
ment.*

	0	1	2	3	4
Superior performance of part observed. Essential part of program					
Present during observation. Continuing part of program					
Present during observation. Not a continuing part					
Present but on a restricted basis					
Did not exist at time of observation					

ITEMS TO BE CHECKED

1. Is there obvious opportunity for each child to participate comfortably with home-rooted language when talking to "share" with the group?

2. Is the real language of the children used as a part of the room environment through dictated stories and books?

3. Are children free from the fear of using incorrect language?

4. Is space and time provided for children to express their ideas with many media?

5. Is space and time provided for children to participate in puppetry, dramatization, and pantomime?

6. Are there adequate tactile and visual models available for naming, describing, and discussing?

7. Do children have opportunity to listen to their own language recorded on tapes?

8. Is there opportunity for children to respond rhythmically to music?

9. Do children dictate, observe the writing, and illustrate books that are useful in the classroom?

10. Do children have opportunities to respond to meanings in their environment not represented by symbol systems—weather, color, shape, size, texture, emotion, sound, motion?

Raw score totals
TOTAL RAW SCORE
Mean score (raw score divided by 10)

STRAND TWO
Studying communication

MAJOR IDEA
This strand emphasizes an understanding of how language works for individuals.

	0	1	2	3	4
Superior performance of part observed. Essential part of program					
Present during observation. Continuing part of program					
Present during observation. Not a continuing part					
Present but on a restricted basis					
Did not exist at time of observation					

ITEMS TO BE CHECKED

1. Are children encouraged to "read" and respond to their environment through their senses—hearing, touching, smelling, tasting, and seeing?

2. Are children given the opportunity to learn to respond to nonalphabetic symbols in clocks, maps, numerals, graphs, and calendars?

3. Do children engage in conversations to discuss topics such as names of letters, words, and sentences?

4. Are children acquiring vocabularies of names of things, words of action, and words in many descriptive categories?

5. Is vocabulary being extended through teacher modeling, mediating, and offering alternatives?

6. Is there obvious emphasis on developing an awareness of words of highest frequency?

7. Are alternatives offered to children whose natural speech is characterized by gross errors?

8. Do children respond to language structures such as rhyming, beginning sounds, and predictive sentence patterns?

9. Do children have opportunities to identify labels and other words in printed form?

10. Do children have time and place to explore writing by tracing, copying, and writing independently?

Raw score totals
TOTAL RAW SCORE
Mean score (raw score divided by 10)

STRAND THREE
*Relating communication of
others to self*

MAJOR IDEA
*This strand emphasizes the
influence of the language
and ideas of many people
on the personal language of
children.*

	0	1	2	3	4
Superior performance of part observed. Essential part of program					
Present during observation. Continuing part of program					
Present during observation. Not a continuing part					
Present but on a restricted basis					
Does not exist at time of observation					

ITEMS TO BE CHECKED

1. Are many types of books available for browsing and reading together?

2. Are stories and poems read *to* and *with* children every day?

3. Are films and filmstrips used to bring children in contact with the language and ideas of others?

4. Do children have access to records and tapes that accompany books?

5. Do children have opportunity to repeat words, phrases, and sentences of other authors as they listen to reading of language that is different from their home-rooted language?

6. Do children have opportunity to add to the ideas of others as they listen to stories and poems?

7. Are art prints, musical compositions, photographs, and other creative materials available for personal interpretation with personal language?

8. Are choral readings, finger plays, songs, and rhymes a part of the language program to bring children in contact with other's language?

9. Do children have the opportunity to look in a variety of places for information on the same topic?

10. Do children have opportunity to evaluate communication of others—real from imaginary, fact from fantasy, poetry from prose?

Raw score totals
TOTAL RAW SCORE
Mean score (raw score divided by 10)

CHECK LIST FOR ELEMENTARY LEARNING ENVIRONMENT

This check list is to be used in rating the extent to which any learning environment has visible evidence that the three strands of a language experience approach are being implemented. It does not deal with the nonvisible aspects of a program.

Tentative conclusions from the use of this rating scale indicate that children who live and learn in an environment with a rating above 3.0 score higher on reading achievement tests than those in classrooms with lower scores.

THE SCORING SCALE

        0—*Does not exist* at the time of the observation

        1—*Present* but on a restricted bases—by permission only or after completion of "regular work"

        2—*Present during observation period* but little or no evidence as a continuing part of the program

        3—*Present during observation* with visible evidence that the condition is a continuing part of the program

        4—*Superior performance of part observed* and/or visible evidence that the condition is an essential part of the program

OBSERVATION TIME
Minimum of 30 minutes recommended for external evaluation. No time limit for self-evaluation

SUMMARY

Mean score Strand One	
Mean score Strand Two	
Mean score Strand Three	
TOTAL Mean scores divided by 3	

INTERPRETATION

The closer the total mean score is to 4.00, the nearer the classroom environment is to satisfying basic requirements for a language experience approach.

Scores below 3.00 reflect a need for improvement in communication opportunities that are required of a language experience approach.

STRAND ONE
*Experiencing com-
munication*

MAJOR IDEA
*This strand emphasizes the
real language of the
learners as basic to com-
munication skill develop-
ment.*

	0	1	2	3	4
Superior performance of part observed. Essential part of program					
Present during observation. Continuing part of program					
Present during observation. Not a continuing part					
Present but on a restricted basis					
Does not exist at time of observation					

ITEMS TO BE CHECKED

1. Is there obvious opportunity for each child to participate comfortably with home-rooted language in both talking and writing?

2. Is the real language of the children used as a part of the room environment?

3. Are children free from the fear of using incorrect language?

4. Is space and time provided for children to express their ideas with many media?

5. Do children have opportunity to listen to their own language on tapes and/or through oral reading of their own stories and poems?

6. Is space and time provided for children to participate in puppetry, pantomime, and dramatization?

7. Is there opportunity for children to respond rhythmically to music?

8. Do children produce original manuscripts of poems and stories that are useful in the reading program of the classroom?

Raw score totals
TOTAL RAW SCORE
Mean score (raw score divided by 8)

STRAND TWO
Studying communication

MAJOR IDEA
This strand emphasizes an understanding of how language works for individuals.

	0	1	2	3	4
Superior performance of part observed. Essential part of program					
Present during observation. Continuing part of program					
Present during observation. Not a continuing part					
Present but on a restricted basis					
Does not exist at time of observation					

ITEMS TO BE CHECKED

1. Do children have opportunities to see their speech sounds written by adults through processes of dictation?

2. Does the adult (teacher) visit with the children to help them understand sound-symbol relationships from personal speech?

3. Do children have conversational abilities to discuss topics such as names of letters, words, sentences, and spelling?

4. Is there evidence that children are using vocabularies of the form-class words (nouns, verbs, adjectives, and adverbs) as a part of the planned program for extending language?

5. Is there obvious emphasis on the development of a sight vocabulary of high-frequency words?

6. Are alternatives offered to children whose natural speech is characterized by gross errors?

7. Do children participate in editing manuscripts for publication?

8. Do children have opportunities to respond to meanings in their environment not represented by symbol systems—weather, color, shape, emotions, motion, sound, size, texture, etc?

Raw score totals
TOTAL RAW SCORE
Mean score (raw score divided by 8)

STRAND THREE
Relating communication of others to self

MAJOR IDEA
This strand emphasizes the influence of the language and ideas of many people on the personal language of children.

	0	1	2	3	4
Superior performance of part observed. Essential part of program					
Present during observation. Continuing part of program					
Present during observation. Not a continuing part					
Present but on a restricted basis					
Does not exist at time of observation					

ITEMS TO BE CHECKED

1. Are many types of books available for browsing and reading—recreation, information, reading skill development, own publications?

2. Are films and filmstrips used to bring children in contact with the language and ideas of others?

3. Do children have access to records and tapes that accompany books?

4. Do children have opportunities to repeat words, phrases, and sentences of other authors as they listen to reading of stories and poems that are different from home-rooted language?

5. Do children have opportunities to add to the ideas of others as they listen to and read stories and poems?

6. Are art prints, musical compositions, photographs, and other creative materials available for personal interpretation?

7. Is choral reading a part of the reading program that brings children in contact with language and ideas of others without requiring excellent reading skills?

8. Do children have the opportunity to research on topics of interest and relate findings to their personal questions and observations?

Raw score totals

TOTAL RAW SCORE

Mean score (raw score divided by 8)

Appendix B

Books with Patterned Language Useful as Models
for Children's Writing

Aliki. *Three Gold Pieces*. Pantheon Books, New York, 1967.

Anglund, Joan Walsh. *Spring Is a New Beginning.* Harcourt, Brace & World, New York, 1963.

———. *What Color Is Love?* Harcourt, Brace & World, New York, 1966.

Baum, Arlene and Joseph. *One Bright Monday Morning*. Random House, New York, 1962.

Block, Marie H. *Ivanka and the Dragon.* Atheneum Publishers, New York, 1969.

Brandenburg, Franz. *I Once Knew a Man.* The Macmillan Company, New York, 1970.

Brown, Marcia. *Peter Piper's Alphabet.* Charles Scribner's Sons, New York, 1955.

Brown, Margaret Wise. *The Important Book.* Harper & Brothers, New York, 1949.

———. *The Inside Noisy Book.* Harper & Brothers, New York, 1942.

———. *The Runaway Bunny.* Harper & Brothers, New York, 1942.

———. *The Wonderful House.* Golden Press, New York, 1960.

Browner, Richard. *Look Again.* Atheneum Publishers, New York, 1962.

Chapman, Gaynor. *The Luck Child.* Atheneum Publishers, New York, 1968.

Charlip, Remy. *Fortunately.* Parents Magazine Press, New York, 1964.

Chase, Richard. *Billy Boy.* Golden Gate Junior Books, San Francisco, 1966.

de Angeli, Marguerite. *The Goose Girl.* Doubleday and Company, Garden City, N.Y., 1964.

De Bois, William. *Lion.* Viking Press, New York, 1965.

de Regniers, Beatrice Schenk. *The Giant Story.* Illustrated by Maurice Sendak. Harper & Brothers, New York, 1953.

———. *How Joe the Bear and Sam the Mouse Got Together.* Parents Magazine Press, New York, 1965.

Donamska, Janina. *If All the Seas Were One Sea.* The Macmillan Company, New York, 1971.

Elgin, Benjamin. *Six Foolish Fishermen.* Children's Press, New York, 1957.

Emberley, Edward. *London Bridge Is Falling Down.* Little, Brown and Company, Boston, 1957.

———. *The Wing of a Flea.* Little, Brown and Company, Boston, 1961.

Francoise. *Jean Marie Counts Her Sheep.* Charles Scribner's Sons, New York, 1952.

Frasconi, Antonio. *The Snow and the Sun.* Harcourt, Brace & World, New York, 1955.

Geisel, Theodore Seuss. *If I Ran the Zoo.* Random House, New York, 1950.

Grifalsoni, Ann. *City Rhythm.* The Bobbs-Merrill Company, Indianapolis, 1965.

Grimm Brothers. *The Fisherman and His Wife.* Follett Publishing Company, Chicago, 1969.

———. *The Shoemaker and the Elves.* Charles Scribner's Sons, New York, 1960.

Hample, Stoe. *The Silly Book.* Harper & Brothers, New York, 1961.

Heller, Aaron, and Robert Deschamp. *Let's Take a Walk.* Holt, Rinehart and Winston, New York, 1963.

Hoffman, Felix. *The Wolf and the Seven Little Kids.* Harcourt, Brace & World, New York, 1957.

Holdsworth, William Curtis. *The Gingerbread Boy.* Farrar, Strauss and Giroux, New York, 1970.

Jacobs, Leland B. *Poetry for Chuckles and Grins.* Garrard Publishing Company, Champaign, Ill., 1968.

Johnson, Crocket. *Harold and the Purple Cow.* Harper & Row, New York, 1969.

Kahl, Virginia. *The Duchess Bakes a Cake.* Charles Scribner's Sons, New York, 1955.

Kraus, Robert. *Whose Mouse Are You?* The Macmillan Company, New York, 1970.

Kredensen, Gail, and Stanley Mack. *One Dancing Drum.* S. G. Phillips, New York, 1971.

Langstaff, John. *Ol' Dan Tucker.* Harcourt, Brace & World, New York, 1963.

———. *Soldier, Soldier, Won't You Marry Me?* Doubleday and Company, Garden City, N.Y., 1972.

Lionni, Leo. *The Biggest House in the World.* Pantheon Books (Random House), New York, 1968.

McLeoud, Emilie W. *One Snail and Me.* Atlantic-Little, Brown, Boston, 1961.

Myller, Rolf. *Rolling Round.* Atheneum Publishers, New York, 1963.

Oppenheim, Joan. *Have You Seen Trees?* Young Scott Books, New York, 1967.

Potter, Charles Francis. *Tongue Tanglers.* World Publishing Company, New York, 1962.

Rand, Ann. *Umbrellas, Hats and Wheels.* Harcourt, Brace & World, New York, 1961.

Roberts, Cliff. *The Dot.* Franklin Watts, New York, 1964.

Scheer, Julian, and Marvin Bileck. *Rain Makes Applesauce.* Holiday House, New York, 1964.

Schulenitz, Uri. *One Monday Morning.* Charles Scribner's Sons, New York, 1967.

Sendak, Maurice. *Where the Wild Things Are.* Harper & Brothers, New York, 1965.

Slobodkin, Louis. *Millions and Millions and Millions.* The Vanguard Press, New York, 1955.

Spier, Peter. *The Fox Went Out on a Chilly Night.* Doubleday and Company, Garden City, N.Y., 1961.

Sullivan, Joan. *Round Is a Pancake.* Holt, Rinehart and Winston, New York, 1963.

Turner, Nancy Byrd, and Tibor Gergely. *When It Rained Cats and Dogs.* J. P. Lippincott Company, Philadelphia, 1946.

Wellesley, Howard. *All Kinds of Neighbors.* Holt, Rinehart and Winston, New York, 1963.

Wing, Henry Ritchet. *Ten Pennies for Candy.* Holt, Rinehart and Winston, New York, 1963.

———. *What Is Big?* Holt, Rinehart and Winston, New York, 1963.

Zemach, Harve. *Mommy, Buy Me a China Doll.* Follett Publishing Company, Chicago, 1966.

Index